THE AMA GUIDE

FOR MEETING AND EVENT PLANNERS

THE AMA GUIDE

FOR MEETING AND EVENT PLANNERS

Catherine H. Price

amacom

AMERICAN MANAGEMENT ASSOCIATION

Library of Congress Cataloging-in-Publication Data

Price, Catherine H.
    The AMA guide for meeting and event planners / Catherine H. Price.
        p.   cm.
    Bibliography: p.
    Includes index.
    ISBN 0-8144-5928-5
    1. Meetings—Planning.   2. Business communication.   I. Title.
HF5718.P73   1989
658.4'56—dc20   88-48028
                                                                              CIP

Printing number

10   9   8   7   6   5   4   3   2   1

CONTENTS

Acknowledgments   *ix*
Foreword by Donald E. Diorio   *xi*
Introduction   *xv*

PART ONE

THE BASICS OF MEETING MANAGEMENT   1

1.	Overall Planning Structure	3
2.	Program Design	11
3.	Speakers and Other Program Participants	19
4.	Site Selection	26
5.	Agreements and Contracts	36
6.	Data Collection, Evaluation, and Reporting	45
7.	Marketing and Promotion	52
8.	Graphic Design and Printing	62
9.	Registration	70
10.	Attendees' Services	80
11.	Special Events	90
12.	Food and Beverages	98
13.	Audiovisual and Other Media	111
14.	Budgeting and Financial Management	120
15.	Math for Meeting Planners	128
16.	Liability and Insurance	136
17.	People Management	142
18.	On-Site Management	148
19.	Exhibits	163
20.	Selecting a Meeting Management Firm	172
21.	Establishing Your Own Meeting Management Firm	179

PART TWO

QUICK REFERENCE GUIDE   189

Guide 1.   Overall Planning Structure   191
                Exhibit 1-1:   Planning Schedule Example   195
                Exhibit 1-2:   Preplanning Questionnaire   205

Guide 2.   Program Design   209

Guide 3.   Speakers and Other Program Participants   214
                Exhibit 3-1:   Speaker Requirement Form   217
                Exhibit 3-2:   Program Moderator
                                 Worksheet Example   222
                Exhibit 3-3:   Panel Information Worksheet
                                 Example   223
                Exhibit 3-4:   Workshop Information
                                 Worksheet Example   225
                Exhibit 3-5:   Speaker Confirmation Letter   228
                Exhibit 3-6:   Speaker Information Memo   229

Guide 4.   Site Selection   230
                Exhibit 4-1:   Meeting Prospectus Example   245
                Exhibit 4-2:   Site Selection Checklist   254

Guide 5.   Agreements and Contracts   260
                Exhibit 5-1:   Negotiation Form   264
                Exhibit 5-2:   Hotel Contract Example   265

Guide 6.   Data Collection, Evaluation, and Reporting   274
                Exhibit 6-1:   Function Data Collection
                                 Form   276
                Exhibit 6-2:   Registration Data Collection
                                 Form   277
                Exhibit 6-3:   Conference Evaluation Form   278
                Exhibit 6-4:   Program/Session Evaluation
                                 Form   280
                Exhibit 6-5:   Data Collection Report
                                 Format   281

Guide 7.   Marketing and Promotion   285
                Exhibit 7-1:   Advertising Contract
                                 Example   292

Guide 8.   Graphic Design and Printing   293

Guide 9.   Registration   301
                Exhibit 9-1:   Daily Check-Out Sheet   307
                Exhibit 9-2:   Registration Personnel
                                 Check-In/Check-Out Sheet   308
                Exhibit 9-3:   Registration Form Example   309

Guide 10. Attendees' Services   310
    Exhibit 10-1: Attendee Needs
                  Questionnaire   318
    Exhibit 10-2: Attendee Needs Chart   320
    Exhibit 10-3: Child-Care Information and
                  Release Form   326

Guide 11. Special Events   328

Guide 12. Food and Beverages   336
    Exhibit 12-1: Meeting Report—Food-and-
                  Beverage Form   342
    Exhibit 12-2: Bar Readings   343

Guide 13. Audiovisual and Other Media   344
    Exhibit 13-1: Audiovisual Supplier Request
                  Form   351

Guide 14. Budgeting and Financial Management   353

Guide 15. Math for Meeting Planners   361

Guide 16. Liability and Insurance   366

Guide 17. People Management   371

Guide 18. On-Site Management   378
    Exhibit 18-1: Facility Personnel   383
    Exhibit 18-2: Function Attendance Form   384
    Exhibit 18-3: Function Attendance
                  Summary Form   385
    Exhibit 18-4: Hotel Reservations Pickup
                  Report   386

Guide 19. Exhibits   387
    Exhibit 19-1: Exhibitor Schedule Example   400
    Exhibit 19-2: Program Book Listing
                  Example   401
    Exhibit 19-3: Exhibitor Registration Form
                  Example   402
    Exhibit 19-4: Exhibitor Housing Request
                  Example   404

Guide 20. Selecting a Meeting Management Firm   405

Guide 21. Establishing Your Own Meeting Management Firm   413
    Exhibit 21-1: Daily Timesheet Form   427
    Exhibit 21-2: Postage Usage Form   428
    Exhibit 21-3: Copying Summary Form   429

Exhibit 21-4:   Client Expense Summary
Form   430
Exhibit 21-5:   Independent Meeting Planner
Contract Example   431

APPENDIX

A QUICK REFERENCE GUIDE FOR INTERNATIONAL AND
FOREIGN MEETINGS   435

Guide 22.   International and Foreign Meetings   437

Glossary   *451*
Resources   *459*
Index   *463*

ACKNOWLEDGMENTS

They say you are what you eat! I say you are whom you work for and with. I have been fortunate in the past nineteen years to work with those who have encouraged freedom and allowed creativity. They believed in me more than I believed in myself. They gave me assignments filled with challenges. They shared their knowledge and experience freely.

I gained government experience in Washington, D.C., with the White House Conference on Children and Youth; I gained association experience with the National Conference of State Legislatures, National Professional Management Corporation, and the American Society for Surgery of the Hand; and as owner of Price & Associates and its two divisions, The Meeting Company and Events Extraordinaire, I gained corporate experience with my corporate clients and many colleagues—suppliers and planners alike—who took the time to teach me, usually one on one, about their areas of expertise. To those organizations and to those people, I thank you.

With all the experiences and shared knowledge, I could not have written this book without the daily support of two individuals: Sally Hossock and Ruth Ann Zook. Sally took my propensity for wordiness and cut and cut and cut to make my Quick Reference Guide truly a *quick* reference. Ruth Ann checked my numbers for accuracy, conducted searches to ensure a balanced and complete manuscript, and pushed me to hold out for the right publisher: AMACOM.

A final thanks to my editors, Adrienne Hickey and Karen Sirabian, whose patience, perspective, and polish contributed to my manuscript.

I am very proud of what this wonderful and varied combination of people have given to the book that I have written for you! Enjoy!

FOREWORD

In 1987, total worldwide spending for domestic and international tourism exceeded $2 trillion and represented 12 percent of the world's economy.[1] And in the United States, 25 percent of all trips taken by Americans in 1987 were business trips. This is up 13 percent from 1982.[2]

Tourism can now be considered the world's largest industry. In fact, spending for world tourism exceeds the GNP of any country except that of the United States.[3]

The meeting and hospitality business, as part of world tourism, is greatly responsible for this phenomenal growth. And why not? People are traveling more often and farther from home base than ever before. Also, more meetings are being conducted today than ever before. As Cathie Price points out in *The AMA Guide for Meeting and Event Planners*, echoing *Megatrends*' John Naisbett, "There is no end to meetings."

The exciting and ever-growing business of meeting management constantly challenges both novice and veteran meeting planners to stay current. Since the early 1980s, new meeting concepts and business practices and the increase in overall meeting activity have forced new and experienced planners alike to redefine their positions and to learn anew. What was once a matter to be handled by assistants and administrative staff is now managed by professionals.

New ways of writing contracts, more intense and diversified programs, contract negotiations with new legal twists, new hotel (site) concepts, airline deregulation, more and greater events, new tax laws, and a greater demand for unique food-and-beverage presentations have all contributed to the professionalization of meeting planning.

What does all this new activity mean? Well, for one thing, it means that billions of dollars—or yen or marks or lire—are being pumped into our and

1. World Tourism Organization
2. *Travel Tips*, Business Travel Division, Westport Travel
3. World Tourism Organization

our neighbors' economies via our industry, a trend that is obviously positive for many reasons. It also means that more skilled and experienced meeting planners are needed to effect all of this business—to conduct, orchestrate, lead, and manage meetings and related support services all over the world.

Well, where do these people come from? How do they become skilled and experienced? Certainly a good question! Often I receive calls from prospective planners who want advice about where to begin. I usually take the time to meet with them because I believe in continuing education and in helping people get started. (Remember, this is a business made up of people, people who may someday become your sources.) When we meet, I always begin by saying, "Get involved through professional organizations such as Meeting Planners International (MPI), The National Association of Exposition Managers, the American Society of Association Executives (ASAE), and other like organizations." As a member of the Greater New York Chapter of MPI for eight years, I have learned this lesson well. I began my involvement at the committee level, worked on many chapter projects and events, and was soon elected to MPI's board of directors. I now serve as the chapter's treasurer, and I co-chair our annual auction and social. My experiences have been invaluable. The contacts I've made, the friends I've met, and—most of all—what I've learned have combined to play a major role in my own successes.

Then I tell the newcomer, "Acquire the 'attitude.'" Our business usually requires a lot of hard work and long hours. It's not as glamorous as one might think; without the right attitude—the desire to do whatever it takes to get the job done—you're destined to fail because you can only delegate so much. You've got to get your hands dirty to make it work right. Remember: "Commitment = Excellence."

I doubt that even one person whom I've counseled has left my office without knowing deep down inside whether or not meeting management was for him or her. I may sometimes sound harsh, but the reality is, it's a tough business. To be successful, a meeting planner must be committed, always demand excellence, and always *follow through*: "Inspect ⇄ Expect."

Knowledge, experience, leadership—keys to success in any field, but doubly important in the business of managing meetings—are attributes without which you cannot be successful and without which you cannot take the first step.

In *The AMA Guide for Meeting and Event Planners*, Cathie Price presents a logical, systematic approach to our profession, embellishing the whole concept of programs, systems, and checklists. The book serves as one of the more comprehensive and thorough meeting management guides written to date. It will help refresh us veterans and serve as a guide for novices.

Part One, "The Basics of Meeting Management," is designed to help the novice planner walk through the process of planning a successful meeting step-by-step; each chapter's broad overview of the subject at hand is followed by real-life examples and practical advice on problem solving. This first section gives the newcomer a condensed and balanced overview of meeting planning, covering all the bases from program design to food and beverages to on-site management.

The very comprehensive and easy-to-follow Quick Reference Guide in Part Two is chock full of diagrams, charts, and formulas designed to help you with those hard-to-solve problems. Cathie Price feels that this section may be preferred by the more experienced planner, but I recommend it for all. Both the novice and experienced planner will find it a helpful resource in answering those knotty questions that we all face now and then, and its ease of use will put you on the right track and save you a great deal of time.

In fact, I had the opportunity to use Part Two just recently. One of our own planners was having problems scheduling (time) and ordering (quantity) bus transportation. An easy flip to Guide 10, "Attendees' Services," in Part Two gave her the information and formulas she needed, and she was able to make the right decision. Her group was moved successfully.

Whether you're a first-time planner, an experienced corporate or association professional, or a private consultant, you'll find the time-saving Quick Reference Guide to be an excellent planning resource. Each Guide corresponds by subject matter and in order to a chapter in Part One and includes the various forms, checklists, and formulas we have all grown to identify as indispensable tools of our trade.

While this book is not the end-all to meeting management, it will certainly provide you with a unique, two-fisted approach. I enjoyed having the opportunity to read it, and preparing this Foreword has helped me to refresh my own skills and learn some new applications as well! I trust you will find it as helpful and inspiring as I did.

Always remember:

$$\text{COMMITMENT} = \text{EXCELLENCE}$$
$$\text{INSPECT} \rightleftarrows \text{EXPECT}$$

Enjoy!

DONALD E. DIORIO
National Director, Hotel Operations
American Management Association

INTRODUCTION

This work is the result of nearly twenty years of experience planning large conventions, conferences, workshops, fundraising events, and committee and board meetings. It is also the result of an extensive review of the literature and collaboration with meeting and hospitality industry experts—a continuing process that intensified during the preparation of this book.

I wrote this book in an attempt to end the frustrating search for bits of information hidden in long paragraphs of technical books and past issues of professional publications. But the book is not only for the full-time meeting manager; it is also for those in corporations, associations, government agencies, and academia who are charged with planning a meeting as one of many responsibilities, and for those who are just starting out in the field.

As you will note throughout the book, there are significant differences between corporate and association meetings. Corporate meetings usually do not involve registration fees and are marketed using an invitation format targeting a carefully selected group of people. Associations generally charge registration fees for their meetings, and conduct mass promotional efforts to attract attendees. Corporate meetings generally involve smaller numbers of attendees and spend more per person than associations. Corporations tend to book meetings in resort locations, while associations more often hold meetings in large convention hotels and convention centers. Despite these differences a planner must go through the same basic steps outlined in this book for both types of meetings.

Some meeting planners are responsible for the program, the facilities, and the exhibits; others are in charge of the program and facilities only; still others arrange only the program. This book assumes that the meeting planner is in charge of all aspects of the meeting, from program to budget. In this way, readers can benefit from those areas that concern them particularly but still be aware of the other elements involved in order to do the best job.

HOW TO USE THIS BOOK

Part One of this book, "The Basics of Meeting Management," is designed for the less-experienced planner. Each chapter contains a broad and candid discussion of various topics related to meeting and event planning, such as program design, marketing, printing, and budgeting, specifically designed to stimulate the thinking of those new to the field.

Each chapter begins with an outline of the steps involved in that particular area ("Getting It All Together"), followed by practical advice on ideas that have worked well, pitfalls to avoid, checklists and forms that can be used ("Overall Planning Tips"). The last section of each chapter ("Problems and Strategies") supplies, in a question-and-answer format, solutions to potential problems that might occur. The Quick Reference Guides and Exhibits referred to in these chapters can be found in Part Two.

The experienced planner may want to turn directly to the Quick Reference Guides in Part Two. This section contains quick references of guidelines, formulas, definitions, measurements, and other pieces of information that are difficult to find when you need them. The section is organized by subjects that correspond to the chapters in Part One. Each subject area begins with a Quick Reference Guide that outlines the major areas involved; if appropriate, it is followed by a variety of checklists, forms, examples, formulas, and other key information.

Each day brings new ideas that could have been included. This book is only a beginning. As John Naisbitt says in *Megatrends*, "There is no end to meetings." We join the rest of our high-tech society in experiencing information overload and in facing the need to formalize basic skills to prepare for new and continuing technological developments. But the ultimate product will not change the personal touch of a meeting, where people talk to people—not to machines.

PART ONE

THE BASICS OF
MEETING MANAGEMENT

1

OVERALL PLANNING STRUCTURE

GETTING IT ALL TOGETHER

Nothing is more basic to meeting planning than establishing a reliable system for managing the myriad details, people, and, unfortunately, problems that inevitably arise. The unorganized person just won't survive!

ANALYZING THE MEETING

The planning process begins with an analysis of the meeting itself. The questions that begin this process are: Why are we having this meeting? What do we hope to accomplish? Who will attend? Why will they attend? What will they hope to accomplish? How will the event be financed?

Numerous questions can follow, depending on your organization. Don't be put off by what you feel may be too many questions when you are eager to begin work: That is how a strong foundation is established. If too few questions are asked, a meeting can suffer from a lack of focus and direction.

Keep in mind that during the planning stage there are many options and hurdles to anticipate. Some things increase complexity tenfold and others simplify by an equal amount. A party in the hotel, for example, is always simpler to arrange than a party in a warehouse or distant field with no power, no restrooms, and no kitchen. That is not to say that you shouldn't have an off-site party, but the details should be considered in the planning stage. In the same vein, the site is often selected before the program has been set, and you may have to anticipate a problem fitting the program into the available space.

ASSEMBLING YOUR TEAM

The next important stage of the planning process is assembling your team. Broadly speaking, the team should consist of decisionmakers and implementers. Decisionmakers are the people who define the parameters and are ultimately responsible for the success or failure of the event. Implementers are those who do everything from negotiating contracts to inviting speakers to making sure that the right speaker is in the right room and that the microphone works.

More specifically, the planning team will probably include people or committees with the following functions and responsibilities (the meeting planner may do all or any combination of these, depending on the organizational structure).

Meeting Planner

The planner is the central coordinator or events manager and does the following: negotiates and recommends contracts for signature; solicits bids from suppliers and hires and supervises suppliers; prepares and recommends budgets and monitors expenses throughout the planning process; establishes the planning schedule, sets deadlines, and monitors progress; recommends policies and procedures, supervises registration, maintains communications; sets up filing systems for controlling documents and reports; prepares personnel schedules for on-site activities.

Decisionmakers

Decisionmakers may include the organization's president, CEO, executive director, chairman of the board, corporate officer, and certain department heads. They approve the concept of conducting the meeting, the budget, and all policies; they sign all contracts, accept legal and statutory liability, supervise the meeting planner, and approve promotional materials for consistency with the organization's public image; they are legally responsible for payment of all bills, fees, deposits—essentially all policy, legal, and financial issues.

Technical Staff

Various tasks requiring technical expertise may be assigned to in-house personnel or to subcontractors. The following list identifies key specialists and briefly describes their responsibilities.

- *Issue, program, and product specialists:* Recommend program topics and speakers.
- *Marketing and graphics specialists:* Design graphics and write copy for promotional pieces; coordinate printing; identify and generate customer and other industry-related functions; provide mailing lists.
- *Accounting department specialists:* Develop accounting systems.
- *Public relations and media department specialists:* Coordinate high-tech presentations; handle press relations; prepare and distribute press releases.
- *Data processing department specialists:* Assist with selection of computer equipment and meeting software packages or programming.
- *Legal department specialists:* Review contracts, agreements, liability risks.
- *Training and personnel department specialists:* Prepare training materials for on-site personnel (paid and voluntary) and conduct training sessions.
- *Administrative department specialists:* Evaluate and recommend insurance coverage and risk-management procedures.

Support Personnel (Clerical)

Members of the clerical support staff handle typing and computer data entry, make copies, maintain files, process incoming and outgoing mail, and stuff attendee packets; they may keep daily activity logs for registration, expenses, and income; they direct incoming calls; they follow up on requests for brochures and answer routine questions such as dates and costs.

Among the many things your team must concern itself with are:

- The program content and format
- Speaker selection and allowable fees and expenses
- The meeting site
- The budget and establishing financial controls
- Marketing of the event, including mailing lists and mail processing
- Press relations, if required
- Printing marketing pieces and choosing their number, format, theme, logo, and colors
- The option of exhibits, sponsorships, and other revenue and program enhancement opportunities
- Transportation to your meeting or event
- Registration and housing and the accompanying policies and support items, such as name badges and materials to be given to attendees

DEVELOPING RECORD-KEEPING SYSTEMS

Often, the meeting planner becomes the central coordinator of all information. Therefore, record-keeping systems are essential to organize, control, and monitor activities. The organizational system you set up must include a planning schedule, deadlines, forms, and checklists to expedite the process and capture the details in a structured, usable, quickly retrieved manner. The system's documents become the files and records you will need for reporting, evaluating and planning for future events. For example, you will need financial record-keeping systems; invitation and registration record-keeping systems; systems for tracking the confirmation of speakers, their place on the agenda, the meeting room where they are speaking, and the costs of their participation.

The list given under "Record Keeping" in the Quick Reference Guide for this chapter (see Part Two) will give you some idea of the scope of the forms needed. Many examples of these appear throughout Part Two of this book, and should be used as tools for developing your own.

ESTABLISHING POLICIES AND PROCEDURES

Another important planning issue has to do with establishing policies and procedures in the early stages. (Again, see the list in the Quick Reference Guide.) The key to effective management is deciding the rules up front and advising the people they affect. Simple things—such as registration cutoff dates, administrative penalties for cancellation, payment and reimbursement procedures for speakers, to name a few—need to be established and communicated or meeting planners will find themselves continually answering the same questions and mediating disputes.

You may also have to live with existing policies and procedures: Some suppliers require deposits and some organizations don't pay deposits; some company presidents want to make all decisions, and some want only to be told where they should be and when; in some companies, printed materials may have to be reviewed three times by five people; in some, contracts must be reviewed by the legal department; some companies require a purchase order for a pencil.

Internal accounting and decisionmaking procedures can slow the meeting planning process to a snail's pace. It may not be realistic to expect to plan a meeting in three months if existing internal administrative procedures are extensive. Staff meeting and reporting requirements can be a help or a hindrance, and you must keep those factors in mind if you want to stay on schedule.

PREPARING A PLANNING SCHEDULE

A successful meeting planner must have many attributes, but two important characteristics are good organizational skills and attention to detail. A key tool that will help in this regard is the planning schedule (see Exhibit 1-1 in Part Two).

The planning schedule is a detailed list of all required tasks and steps, the required completion dates, and the person, department, or committee responsible for each. It should be prepared by the meeting planner.

Organizing Tasks

The first step in preparing the schedule is to outline and organize all of the tasks into three categories: those to be done before the event, those to be done on-site, and those to be done after the event.

An important aspect of this step is to determine deadlines or completion dates. Deadlines are a critical management tool that are established to give staff, speakers, and registrants time to plan and make decisions. Keep in mind that the real deadline is the day the meeting or event begins; every deadline missed in the interim backs up against that unmovable date.

Deadlines should be realistically set and then taken seriously. After nineteen years of planning meetings, I am a pretty good estimator of the time it takes to do various tasks, but unfortunately I still make mistakes, so I automatically increase my estimates by 10 percent. Presuming changes and adjustments, I add another 5 percent. Then I hope that my convention services manager doesn't decide to get a divorce in the middle of my project, or that there isn't a flu epidemic. You may encounter the inevitable effects of Murphy's Law, but plan and persevere.

You can write up the planning schedule either chronologically or by task category. In the chronological list shown in Exhibit 1-1, tasks are arranged in the order they must be done. To arrange a schedule by category, first write down every category (promotion, program, speakers, finances, registration) and then list the tasks that fall under each. If you are working on a computer, you can code your master list by category, by stages (pre-, on-site, post-), or by date. That allows you to look at your list from various perspectives by keying in an additional code or two.

Assigning Responsibility

Once you have your master list of tasks, you need to add completion dates and the name of the person or organization responsible. (I prefer names because they are specific.) If possible, program your computer to print tasks by person responsible as well as by completion date and general category. It is important to let everyone know about responsibilities and deadlines as early as possible.

Communicating

It is critical that members of the planning team communicate effectively with one another. Nothing is worse than working on a project and never quite understanding the logic of the process. Communication means listening, asking questions, and exchanging information, and the first form of information exchanged should be the planning schedule. The completed schedule should be submitted to all individuals who have planning responsibilities and to their supervisors for review and approval.

Using the Schedule Properly

The value of the planning schedule is minimized if you do not use it on a daily basis. Keep a record of your progress by noting the date when each task is completed. You may find, for instance, that one person is behind on a daily basis but meets the ultimate deadline, or that your deadlines are unrealistic. A detailed history will either reduce your worries or be the basis for more realistic planning in the future.

Be conscientious about using the planning schedule on a daily basis. Add those tasks that you did not include and delete those that are found unnecessary. If you haven't been through this exercise before, you will learn from your omissions or miscalculated estimates. As a student of the adult learning process, I remind you that you learn more from your errors than from your successes. Using a system that points out your misjudgments can be painful, but don't despair—the rewards are well worth it. However, don't reinvent the wheel. Learn from others' experiences, too, by reading professional publications and by talking to those around you.

THE BUDGET

You cannot have a successful planning structure without a budget and priorities for how the money will be spent (discussed more fully in Chapter 14). Financial decisions affect every area of the meeting and must be established early in the process and monitored on a regular basis.

The importance of having all the planning issues covered is that, by anticipating problems, special needs, and hidden costs, you can be calm during the storm of the meeting. If you always ask yourself, "What the worst is that can happen?" and then have a solution ready, you will have a reservoir of strategies to be used at a moment's notice, no matter how serious the crisis.

OVERALL PLANNING TIPS

CHECKLISTS

Meeting planners have checklists for everything imaginable. In fact, the Convention Liaison Council has published an entire book of checklists. (See Resources.) There are site selection checklists, food-and-beverage checklists, budget preparation checklists, exhibits checklists, and registration checklists—many examples of which are included in Part Two of this book. Reviewing these lists will help you think through the details of your meeting. While I have never found one I didn't have to adapt to the unique requirements of my particular event, a quick review will spark your thinking in areas you may have forgotten. The questionnaire in Exhibit 1-2 is a useful think-through list of general planning issues.

EXPERT RESOURCES

Throughout this book, I emphasize the importance of talking to other people. It is a quick way to learn because it allows you to focus on your issue or problem and ask follow-up questions.

Look first at your company or organization. If you don't already know what expertise exists, find out. And don't always assume a person's current job title indicates his or her only area of experience. You may discover that the receptionist once ran the front desk at a hotel or that the personnel manager has won creative writing awards, skills that are useful in many areas of meeting planning. Fortunately, most people think planning an event is fun and therefore will welcome the invitation to be a part of the team.

Outside your organization, there are professional companies like mine that, for a fee, will assist you in a consulting capacity or take full responsibility for selected or all areas of your meeting. (See Chapter 20.) Also look to suppliers of services. Call the post office, printers, or a mailing house to plan the time frames and tasks for promoting your meeting.

Identify the people who will become your team on the project, whether in-house or outside, paid or volunteer. Just remember that, ultimately, everyone gets paid, whether in "comps" (complimentary passes and tickets) and favors or in dollars.

COMPUTER SOFTWARE PROGRAMS

Software programs exist to help you in planning and executing your meeting. As mentioned earlier, if you lay out your planning schedule with your computer in mind, you can sit back and relax while it sorts the data in any order you want.

There are also programs that will reduce the time you need to allow for certain tasks, such as registration and reporting. (Chapter 9 discusses computerized registration packages.) The most current information is available in professional publications. The key is to explore all your options during the planning stage. It will save you time and money, while keeping you sane and organized in meeting your deadlines.

PROBLEMS AND STRATEGIES

PROBLEM: We have trouble meeting our deadlines.

Strategy 1:   Go back to the planning schedule. If you are planning carefully, you should be able to identify the bottlenecks. You may be planning time according to what it should take, not what it does take.

Strategy 2:   You may need more people, people with better skills or incentives to motivate others.

Strategy 3:   If deadlines are imposed on you "from above," try to increase your control of the process. If you are constantly working on "I need it yesterday" projects, advise the decisionmakers of what they can expect in three months, six months, twelve months. Let them choose the areas to be compromised.

Strategy 3:   Most new meeting planners have no idea how much time it takes to prepare for a polished event. As you educate yourself, send relevant articles with key points highlighted to your team members.

Strategy 4:   Look at your own effectiveness. If you are not confident, professional, and knowledgeable, you are not operating from a strong position. You need the respect and support of both management and your team. You can be the world's hardest worker and still be ineffective; it is not always someone else's fault.

Strategy 5:   Delegate! Don't try to do it all yourself or look over people's shoulders when you do give them a small task. As you need the trust and confidence of others, you have to extend the same to them. Responsibility is a great motivator.

Strategy 6:   Keep other people's schedules in mind when deadlines are set. Orders from the top also influence your team members' priorities. Be sure management supports, not conflicts with, your schedule.

PROBLEM: How can we juggle simultaneous projects without short-changing any of them?

Strategy 1:   Lucky is the meeting planner who doesn't have this problem. Set up your projects so that each individual meeting's schedule can be merged into a master schedule. Your computer can do this for you, but you need to design the final product first. And don't forget to add the project name or code. Otherwise, your master schedule may tell you to do a budget in January without indicating which meeting's budget is due.

Strategy 2:   Set up a tickler filing system by month, week, or day, if necessary. It's easy to get immersed in one project and let the others fall behind. Just remember, it's easier to keep up than to catch up.

Strategy 3:   Speak up when you find the work load is unrealistic, especially if you are getting more than your fair share of projects. While it may be that people are complimenting you by trusting you with assignments, they may also simply be taking advantage of you. You may have even asked for it. Whatever, don't risk your reputation or health attempting to do the impossible.

PROBLEM: There are always so many additions, deletions, and changes.

Strategy 1:   Don't let the "change monster" wreck your carefully made plans. Know your group well enough to translate, in the planning stage, what they say they want into what they really want.

Strategy 2:   If the problem is coming from upper managers, ask a lot of questions and give them your opinions. Too many planners say, after the fact, that they knew something wouldn't work but did what they were told anyway. Speak up, but be sure your opinions are well founded; education and experience will back you up, as will facts (see next strategy).

Strategy 3:   Facts are your best ally. The more you document about your meeting, the better the decisions will be. Chapter 6, on data collection, will help you think through what you need to know.

Strategy 4:   Try bringing in a consultant if your team or its management is unfocused. This person may say the same things that you have been harping on for years, but with the "expert" status that an outsider brings, people may finally take heed. Remember, at home you are a local planner, when you leave town you are a national authority.

2

PROGRAM DESIGN

Let's be honest: The program is, without question, *the* vital ingredient of any meeting. Oddly, it's the area planners most willingly relinquish control of to others. We leave it in the hands of technical experts, chief executive officers, committees, and whoever else happens to be around and willing to tackle the task.

I don't understand why. Program design is the most challenging part of meeting planning, and it is a golden opportunity for meeting planners to move out of support roles into management. High-salary professional meeting planners spend their time on the program and the finances, hiring assistants to handle the details. I can hear some of you saying that you *are* a part of the planning team for the program. Well, do you help to make the decisions or do you only implement them?

GETTING IT ALL TOGETHER

What is the program? It encompasses all of the activities planned for the attendees, from the moment they arrive until they depart. It includes the content, recreation, meal functions, receptions and parties, tours, exhibits, *and* informal and unscheduled (free) time. What is program design? It is the structuring, balancing, and pacing of the program by combining major topics and sub-topics, passive and active sessions, serious and fun presentations, and formal and informal times to provide professional and personal growth and networking opportunities for participants. The program is like a jigsaw puzzle. When you start the puzzle, all the pieces are there—but what a mess! The design is putting the pieces in order. This is more difficult than it sounds because of the many needs and expectations coming from bosses, association or committee members, attendees, speakers, and suppliers.

While you may not be an expert on the subjects covered in the program, you should know more about the design of the program than anyone else. To help put it all together, use the Quick Reference Guide for this chapter in conjunction with the planning steps described below.

PURPOSE OF THE MEETING

The first step is to prepare a statement on the purpose of the meeting. Identify whether your objective is to educate, to inform, to solve problems, to introduce new products or services, to generate revenue, or whatever. Explain why the meeting is being held and what the organization hopes to accomplish.

THE AUDIENCE

Next, you need to know something about the attendees. Will the audience be primarily male, female, or mixed? Are spouses and children invited? If so, should special activities be planned? Have the primary attendees met together? Will they know each other? What is their knowledge or skill level in relation to the subject of the program? What is the group's personality? Is it fun, serious, verbal, formal? This may not seem like a major issue, but it can make a huge difference in the success of your program. There is a big difference between state legislators and hand surgeons. I have organized well-attended, successful conferences for both of these groups, and neither would have liked the other's meeting.

That brings us to why the attendees will sign up in the first place. Their needs and expectations should not be overlooked. The sponsoring group is often so concerned about the organization's needs being met that it forgets about the attendees. The meeting planner should play a strong role in monitoring the program plans to see that the attendees are not forgotten.

SELECTING TOPICS, FORMATS, AND SPEAKERS OR PARTICIPANTS

Prepare a master list of topics or activities that are required for your particular meeting and list educational topics important to your group. Once your list of topics is complete, you can begin the task of assigning a format to each topic. Some may be debates, others may be group discussions, still others, lectures. Finally, there is the challenging task of finding the right person to successfully implement the selected format.

TIME ALLOTMENT

In addition to determining what time of year the meeting will be held and how many days it will run, time allotment means establishing time allowances for each topic and presenter. To do this, you must rough out a program agenda showing the activity, the format, the amount of time allotted, the sequence (daily), and the topic.

BUDGET

Prepare a budget listing all program costs, such as: meeting-room rental, attendees' materials, speakers' fees and expenses. (There is more on budgeting in Chapter 14.)

PROGRAM DESIGN TIPS

In designing a successful program, the planner must consider the environment, mood, tone, and atmosphere of the meeting; format of the sessions; the time allotted to each topic and segment; and the sequence of events.

ATMOSPHERE

The mood or atmosphere of a meeting directly affects how information is imparted and how well attendees will process that information, i.e., how they learn.

Adult Learning Styles

When planning the program for a meeting, most people don't stop and think about how adults learn. There are three basic types of learning:

1. *Intellectual learning.* Involves remembering, understanding, evaluating, and analyzing.
2. *Learning of physical skills.* Involves speed, accuracy, consistency, and reliability—for example, surgery, typing, or calligraphy.
3. *Psychological learning.* Involves emotions, feelings, values, attitudes, and beliefs.

If you are a Republican, your political beliefs will probably make you hear the same speech differently depending on whether it is delivered by a Republican or a Democrat. A group of CEOs will react differently according to whether the speaker is a professor who has never run a corporation or "one of them." An improperly dressed speaker may lose the respect of the audience before the first word is uttered. Personal values affect the psychological side of learning just as much as content affects the intellectual side.

If you stop to think about how and when you learn, you can gain insight into the same process for your program's attendees. To help you along, consider the following learning modes:

Most Common Learning Mode	*Preferred Learning Mode*
Listening	Talking
Answers	Questions
Watching	Doing
Tense	Relaxed
Bored	Interested
Sitting far away	Closeness to speaker
Uncomfortable	Comfortable
Old information	New information
Technical	Practical

You can add to this list and then look at your own programs. Attendees need a balance between receiving information and processing that information or relating it to their own situations.

If you are attending a seminar on employee relations, many times during the presentations you will automatically think of your boss, your secretary, and your organization's style of dealing with employees. You discard what doesn't apply and, if the seminar is good, you'll adopt some new ideas. During the breaks, lunches, and receptions (informal time), when you are talking to other people in small groups or one-to-one, you talk about specific real-life problems. This is the glue that binds the speaker's concepts to real life. If your breaks are too short or your speakers too theoretically oriented, you block learning.

The meeting planner's role is to work with the content experts, think through these ideas, and build a valuable experience for the attendees. The bottom line is that if nobody has listened, it really doesn't matter what has been covered.

Attention Spans

Most people do not stay "tuned in" for more than twenty minutes. Your attendees mentally check in and out regularly, and if you don't have a varied, fast-paced program, they will probably check out for good.

Most programs have a parade of speakers, each for thirty, forty-five, or even sixty minutes. You had better have a dynamic speaker and a fascinating topic if you allow that. Sitting from 9:00 A.M. to 5:00 P.M. with fifteen-minute breaks and a luncheon speaker is deadly. Most television news programs don't let the same person talk for more than one minute at a time, and the in-depth shows switch from one expert to the next so fast that you can hardly match the faces with the philosophy. Television producers keep things moving because they know people's attention spans are short and they don't want to risk losing their audience.

Meeting planners are show producers, and while they may not be competing with television, they can learn a lot from what TV programs do to maintain attention.

Retention Levels

Just as the attention span has to do with concentration, the retention level has to do with memory. People remember only 10 percent of what they hear. As low as that sounds, I doubt if we really remember even that much. How well would you do on a test covering a seminar you attended a week ago, a month ago, or a year ago? Of course, not much information is new, and our needs for information change. Retention increases when information is focused on current problems or new projects.

When only written words, figures, or illustrations (such as in a book or handouts) are utilized, retention increases to 20 percent. But by combining what is heard with what is seen, you can double the retention rate. For program design, that means adding audiovisuals, dramatizations, or some other visual reinforcement. Remember, the more senses you utilize, the higher the level of retention. The studies have already been done; we just need to read them and incorporate the information into our body of knowledge about meeting planning.

MATERIALS

There is no way attendees can absorb all the information presented at a meeting, nor should they have to. The materials prepared by your organization or presenters should be the referral source for referencing ideas and facts. You may be sure the company introducing a new product is going to "sell" the product in the presentation and provide the technical specs in a handout. As a meeting planner, you should develop materials supportive of the overall communication goal of the sponsor—whether it's a corporation, an association, or a government agency—measured against the audience's need to know or interest in the subject. Materials range from sales brochures to technical papers to long and detailed proceedings. In addition to the presentation-related materials, general conference materials must be prepared, such as the on-site program book, a guidebook to the exhibits, and promotional materials on your organization or products.

Evaluate your materials for visual appeal; don't just fill a packet with volumes of copied paper. Consistent or complementary colors, a border, an attractive typeface, and an easy-to-read format all encourage the reader to use the materials. In one situation, the conference coincided with the organization's tenth anniversary. To tie that theme to the handouts used, I asked all speakers to prepare a list of the ten most important points and limit them to one side of one sheet of paper. Those handouts were in great demand, especially among people who were unable to attend certain sessions. Be creative. Materials don't have to be boring!

FORMATS

Formats refer to the types of presentations your program includes: panels, debates, workshops, lectures, and so on. Let's say you are offering a session at your convention on new legislation affecting your industry. There are several ways this information can be presented, with the first and most common being the lecture. Either your lobbyist, legislator, or other experts can give a speech, or you can have a panel of several experts (which usually results in three speeches instead of one). You can make the panel more interesting and fast paced if you hire a professional interviewer and use a talk-show format. You might also consider using several small groups; such a format would allow the attendees to talk directly to the expert(s). Those are four ways to present the information, and many others are equally worthy of consideration. Just remember, offering too many sessions in the same format is boring and ineffective.

Be creative. Arrange tables and chairs in a circle or semi-circle and have the presenter in the center. This is very effective if the audience is to be interviewed. Get rid of head tables and set the stage as a living room. Better yet, if your budget permits, order sofas and living-room chairs for the audience, or set up counters with bar stools, or get bean-bag chairs and serve beer!

I could go on and on with formats, but the point is: Break the mold. Don't simply rely on lectures and panels, with classroom and theater setups using head tables and lecterns. I am not advocating never using these, but vary what you do and make format decisions based on what you want to accomplish. The format has as much to do with the success of a meeting as the content does.

Effective formats take time and a lot of work with speakers and other program participants—even for the lecture format, speakers need guidance—but it's well worth the effort.

TIME ALLOWANCES

There are countless opportunities for a program to get off schedule, and it's almost impossible to catch up. The primary reason for time overruns are inaccurate estimates on how long it takes to do certain things. Can 100 people get coffee, go to the restroom, and call their offices in fifteen minutes? Because most attendees feel that the exchange of ideas and information is one of the most valuable aspects of conventions, will they have time for such an exchange in fifteen minutes? Just moving 100 people out a room takes several minutes, and getting them back in takes even longer.

Whether for breaks, luncheons, movement from general session to breakouts, or resetting of rooms, schedule a realistic amount of time. If the program begins at 9:00 A.M., allow a few "hidden" minutes on your agenda if you anticipate starting a little late. Enforce speakers' time limits. Nothing frustrates the attendees more than a program running late and eating into their breaks and other informal time.

Generally, I think programs are overscheduled and leave the attendee tired and frustrated rather than receptive and stimulated. Again, I caution you to keep the attendee in mind and to remember that a well-run meeting includes maintaining the program schedule.

PROBLEMS AND STRATEGIES

PROBLEM: There's too much information and too little time.

Strategy 1:   Focus the speakers' topics so they can get to the point quickly. For example, don't have a presentation on "The Impact of the Tax Reform Law on the Meeting Industry." Instead, narrow the scope to "The Three Most Important Changes in the Federal Tax Law for the Meeting Industry."

Strategy 2:   Provide speakers with a definite presentation time limit and enforce it. For example, advise the speakers that they have fifteen minutes for the presentation or approximately 5 minutes per tax law change, plus a ten-minute question-and-answer period. Ask them to have three questions prepared to use if there are no questions from the floor. Dead time is no good either.

Strategy 3:   Establish priorities for all agenda topics and eliminate those that are of limited interest or that can be touched on in other presentations. For example, eliminate the presentation on state tax changes and have the moderator mention critical state tax points when summarizing the presentation on federal tax changes.

Strategy 4:   Change the format to allow divergent views to be presented more quickly. For example, instead of a panel with three fifteen-minute presentations, use a talk-show format (with an interviewer or host) and allow a total of thirty minutes, thereby cutting fifteen minutes.

PROBLEM: Sometimes our meeting rooms can be uncomfortable, noisy, and cramped.

Strategy 1: Set room temperatures at a level comfortable to the majority of attendees and inform attendees prior to their arrival what the temperature range will be. For example, in your early meetings with the hotel, talk to the engineer about the thermostat setting for your meeting. I recommend a range of 67°–70°, based on the number of people and the size of the room (a large room should be cooler than a small one). In written materials sent to attendees before the event, advise registrants of the setting and encourage them to plan their wardrobes accordingly.

Strategy 2: Check movable walls, if they're used during your meeting, for sound bleeds. For example, if a large room has been divided into smaller rooms and groups meet simultaneously, noise may carry (bleed) through the walls, especially if PA systems are in use. Ask for an empty room in between to use as a buffer zone. If you control all of the rooms, avoid using PA systems if at all possible, even if you have to come up with a creative room setup that places all attendees closer to the speaker. If another group is using adjacent facilities, find out what type of program will be conducted. If it's the Mormon Tabernacle Choir, you will want to change rooms or schedule your break at the performance time.

Strategy 3: Don't allow smoking in the meeting room. Ask the hotel not to place ashtrays in the meeting rooms and to add additional ones to the pre-function areas. You may also want to allow smoking at meal functions or have a designated smoking area.

Strategy 4: Encourage attendees to stand and stretch between presentations. With a little encouragement, they might stand when they applaud a speaker. You might also have the moderator announce a one-minute stretch break. Longer exercise breaks led by an instructor can also be incorporated into the program.

PROBLEM: Attendees are reticent about participating actively in a session.

Strategy 1: Prepare a series of questions to stimulate attendees' thinking. For example, ask each speaker or your technical staff to prepare questions related to the subject that they feel are most important. Use these as a handout for the session.

Strategy 2: Set up the room so that attendees are sitting as close to the speaker as possible and are in view of other attendees. Tables arranged in hollow-square, conference, or large semi-circle formats are more informal and conducive to participation.

Strategy 3: Select your moderators for their skill in group dynamics rather than their position in the organization or industry. The best moderators are good summarizers, have a sense of humor, and either already know or make it a point to meet some members of the audience to call on if the session is dragging. Moderators should be familiar with the subject under discussion and should be prepared to ask questions to clarify and direct the discussion. They should be authoritative enough to control the time schedule (and excessive talkers). Moderators can make or break your program.

Strategy 4:   Let attendees know in advance what part they will play in the program. On the list of program topics, describe or mention the format of each session. Ask attendees to bring examples of work they have done relating to the program topics. If they will be asked questions about what they do or procedures they follow, provide those questions in advance. Prepare detailed agendas and let attendees help decide what the order of discussion will be.

3

SPEAKERS AND OTHER
PROGRAM PARTICIPANTS

Program design and speaker management are two of the most difficult areas for the meeting planner because they are normally handled by upper management or within a specialized department of the organization. This chapter assumes that you, as the meeting planner, are responsible for selecting speakers. Even if this is not the case, you still will have a role to play: You may have to offer suggestions, help upper managers write and communicate their ideas to program participants, recommend policies and procedures, or follow up after invitations have been extended or accepted. Whatever your role, you will find suggestions in this chapter that will help to make for a more successful and varied meeting.

GETTING IT ALL TOGETHER

WHO ARE THE PEOPLE ON THE PROGRAM?

A program requires a variety of types of people—speakers, moderators, interviewers, workshop leaders, trainers, discussion leaders, panelists, expert witnesses, summarizers. I could go on, but the point is, a good program will have, if not all of these, several. I advocate junking use of the word "speaker" for every warm body on the program. If we must have a generic term, let's use "program participants." But don't confuse that term with attendees, who are also often called participants. By using the word "speakers," we lead people to believe that they need only come prepared to speak, when they should be leading, training, interviewing.

Scrapping the term "speakers" is a fairly easy way to make a dramatic difference in the quality of programs offered. The challenge is to see how many different types of people you can use to communicate the required information without having them read speeches.

Successful professional speakers learn very quickly that reading a speech is not good for business. They talk to their audience; they usually move off the stage, walk around, and look the audience squarely in the eye, their lavaliere mikes hanging loosely around their necks. These speakers are often looked upon as entertainers, and there is nothing wrong with speakers being entertainers. In fact, the problem arises when a speaker is not entertaining.

I am experienced enough to realize that there is more potential for entertainment and therefore entertaining speakers in some subjects than in others, but I do believe that more often than not, that is a cop out. Meeting planners must be more selective, more demanding, and more detailed with speakers. We have got to learn how to bring out the best in poor speakers who may happen to be the recognized expert in a field. I cannot imagine that most speakers would not welcome guidance on the subject's desired focus as well as the type of attendees and the level of their knowledge.

As the competition to attract meeting attendees grows, attendees are becoming more selective about where they spend their budgeted meeting dollars. Programs with high-quality, knowledgeable speakers, a variety of types of program participants, and focused and varied presentations will capture the market.

Just as the design of the program is one of the most creative aspects of planning a meeting, the management of program participants is one of the most challenging. Your program's participants are the transmitters of all that you hope to communicate. Both the planner and the presenters need to reevaluate the importance of the participants' role.

LOCATING PEOPLE

Thinking about program participants actually begins in the program design phase, because this is where you decide what you plan to communicate and how you will do it. As you select a topic and a format, you must ask if you can locate or recruit qualified people at a price you can afford.

Once you know the boundaries of who you need and what you have to offer, you can begin researching, brainstorming, asking knowledgeable people in the field or your colleagues with related and respected experience. Don't automatically use your staff, board of directors, congressperson, and friends as key presenters. Not only may they not be the best, it may be harder to keep them focused on your goals and the audience's interest in the subject. Besides, how do you tell your congressperson or the chairman of the board that the fifteen minutes are up?

CLARIFYING ROLES

While you are researching your resources, begin to define—in writing—what you want each person to do. What role does this person play in the conference? What does that role mean to you? Will the participant automatically understand what you expect? Probably not, so I suggest you write a description—a short paragraph—explaining exactly what is expected of each program participant.

DEVELOPING CONTENT GUIDELINES

The next step is to develop a written list of points or questions you would like to have included in the speech, discussion, or workshop. Then communicate these points to your program participants in writing, through briefing meetings, or in reviews of their plans. This is also a good time to go over the schedule and the importance of adhering to it on-site—a key aspect of managing program participants.

Some topics are so broad it would be pure luck if the speaker/leader touched on them without some guidance. The question you may ask is, Why tell the expert? The answer is that the experts usually have no way of knowing what has been covered in past meetings, and they may not know the level of the audience's knowledge or its current interest in the subject. All speakers have favorite aspects of a subject, areas in which they are most comfortable and require the least preparation. Without guidance, speakers head straight in that direction, and you will have given them a license to do what they want rather than what you or the audience wants. They aren't wrong—you are, for abdicating your responsibility.

The meeting planners who think through these program issues to the same extent they think through the logistics will succeed. It is not hard, it's logical. What would you want to know if you were asked to speak to or lead a group? Ask speakers whom you respect what would be helpful to them. Call potential attendees and ask them what their interest in a particular subject is.

Research takes time and requires you to become a three-minute expert in a variety of subject areas. That's one of the things I like best about meeting planning: It offers the opportunity to learn about so many different subjects. But it is also an area where you may delegate if the resources are available to you. If you do delegate, don't give the job away without explaining what you want, indicating why you want it, and supervising the product to keep it on target.

PROGRAM PARTICIPANT TIPS

REFERENCE CHECKS

Throughout this book you will be reminded to check references—and don't stop with one, check several. Be sure to check with people who have had recent experience with the participant. A good speakers' bureau will help you in identifying groups that have utilized an individual's services. People at the bureau will be honest because they don't want you to be dissatisfied with their service. But if you're on your toes, you will also check the bureau's references. Ideally, you will have heard the speakers yourself and can evaluate their performance by your own standards, but that isn't always possible.

If you are getting references on an industry expert, be aware that colleagues may be hesitant to give their honest opinion. If you have the names of three people, ask their colleagues whether they have heard all three speak. Then ask which one stands out significantly over the others. It's always easier to sing the praises of one person than to blast another. When checking references, don't forget to keep the audience's knowledge and values in mind. In addition to performance abilities, consider the person's technical background, political orientation, or religious philosophy if those would be important to the group. Your reference checks should address the broader scope of issues appropriate to your group.

SPEAKER REQUIREMENT FORMS

Good forms do two things for the meeting planner: (1) They act as checklists or reminders so you won't forget critical information, and (2) they provide an organized system for collecting and easily retrieving that information. Forms are also a quick and easy way to put things in writing.

Use the sample speaker requirement form (Exhibit 3-1) as is, or modify it to meet your specific needs. For example, if you want information from speakers about their audiovisual needs, send them a form four to six weeks prior to the event; you may wish to include a brief cover letter with the form you send. But even I don't use the speaker requirement form exactly as it appears in this book. Mine is stored in our computer so that I can easily adjust it to the differences of each meeting; I don't have to reinvent the wheel and begin from zero. Maintain one master form that has every possible item and edit it to suit your current needs.

There is no limit to what you can or cannot ask, depending on the value of the information to what you are trying to accomplish. Normally, I wouldn't ask the number of children a speaker or program participant has unless the program is on children and families and the parenting experience is relevant.

SPEAKER INTRODUCTIONS

There are numerous ways to obtain speaker bios, and the worst is to ask for a résumé. That document is often three to five pages long and covers the dogs, children, and club memberships—little of which may have anything to do with a person's credentials in the presentation area. The most organized way to handle bios is to establish a written format that includes the required information for each presenter. (See Exhibit 3-1 for a sample format.) This may include the prospective speaker's years of experience in the field; educational, licensing, or certification credentials, if important to your group; accomplishments in areas directly related to the presentation; and related employment. I usually throw in a ringer, such as, "in twenty-five words or less, explain why you feel you were asked to speak on this topic." Or, I ask how the presentation relates to plumbing contractors or whoever the audience might be. If certain speakers don't have good answers, I know I'll have background work to do with them prior to the meeting.

Regarding format, I like to have the information on each individual speaker typed double-spaced on three-by-five index cards that easily fit into a moderator's pocket. Each speaker's cards should be grouped separately, bound together by a rubberband, and organized by session time. The top card (cover) includes the day, time, room, moderator's and speaker's names, as well as the session topic. One bio card per speaker allows the moderator to quickly make the introduction. If you can arrange to have the speaker and introducer meet prior to the introduction, the process will run even more smoothly.

For a high-tech meeting, you can add a photo on a big screen and a professional reader can prerecord the introductory information. In any case, the introduction should be short and to the point, with the more detailed information in the program book, if required.

FEES AND HONORARIUMS

Fees are what are usually charged by a speaker or participant, and vary from a token amount to $25,000 and up for top speakers with immediate name recognition. Honorariums, which are offered by the sponsoring organization, are usually of smaller amounts, particularly in the corporate setting. In some cases, particularly associations, participants may be offered complimentary registration instead of payment.

Because I like to have everything spelled out and in one place, I send out a financial agreement even if the agreement is to pay nothing. Although many planners don't like to mention fees or reimbursements if none are provided, it really is best to clarify the arrangement in writing.

EXPENSE REIMBURSEMENT

To avoid embarrassment and confusion, have your controls prepared and clearly communicate your policies and procedures to participants in advance (see Exhibit 3-1). If you don't say that you reimburse coach class and a speaker flies first class, you may have to pay the first class fare or risk offending a valued program participant. Areas to think about in addition to transportation and lodging are:

- Shuttles versus taxis
- Meal allocations
- Local versus long-distance telephone calls
- Laundry and dry cleaning
- Personal items
- Conference versus nonconference meals

I'm sure you can think of others; the point is to consider each item *before*, not after, the fact.

Next, decide how you will reimburse participants. Program participants may be placed on the master account. While this is a nice gesture, it is much harder to collect for non-reimbursable expenses than to simply deduct them when the expense report comes in. If you do place speakers on the master account, put the room only, not incidentals.

Because airline fares can be a sizable out-of-pocket expense for the program participant, you may want to prepay airline tickets and wire them to attendees, or have your travel agent handle ticketing and bill your organization's travel account. (Be sure to get copies for your financial records.)

Credit cards have minimized the need for cash advances, though there are still occasional requests. Set up procedures for cash advances and decide on what the ceilings will be.

There is no right or wrong if you have guidelines, and your guidelines may vary depending on the value of the individual to your program. A keynote speaker may be allowed to travel first class, have a suite, and incur unrestricted expenses; a workshop speaker may not receive VIP allowances. You can have policies for different types of speakers, but keep your agreements clear and minimize your exceptions.

Your policy should include a reasonable time for submission and payment of expenses. People like to get paid within thirty days, and I like to receive invoices in thirty days. The meeting's books should be closed and balanced in 90 to 120 days at the most. If you fail to inform your speakers of the deadline, your books may be open for a year. There are worse problems, but this is an irritant that can be avoided.

TRAVEL ARRANGEMENTS

It is useful to have a speaker request form on which participants can indicate when they will arrive and depart, whether they need transportation to and from the airport, and what their hotel reservations preferences are.

However, don't make speakers' travel arrangements. Experience has taught me that this is an area to avoid if at all possible. Flights change and so do speaker's schedules, and you will spend far too much time making arrangements if you're a middleman. It's easier if each individual works directly with a ticketing agent. If you must be involved, be sure you ask for seating preferences, find out whether specialty meals are required, and arrange for advance boarding passes. If you make mistakes in this area, your best speaker may arrive enraged and convinced that you are incompetent. You are a meeting planner, not a travel agent. If your speakers need assistance, refer them to your organization's agent or have your agent contact speakers directly. Travel is one of the few areas where the use of a professional will not add to your costs.

WORKSHEETS

In addition to speaker request forms (which the speaker fills out), it is helpful to have a variety of information sheets, which you prepare, containing guidelines and an outline of what you expect from each program moderator, panel member, or workshop leader (see Exhibits 3-2, 3-3, and 3-4). These may also contain policies and procedures on financial arrangements, audiovisual usage, and other data that can be picked up from the basic speaker requirement form (see Exhibit 3-1).

THINK THOUGHTFUL

It takes only a moment more to be thoughtful and is well worth the time to have your program participants feel appreciated. Thoughtfulness begins with your communications prior to the meeting; make sure participants have the required information to be effective and comfortable. A confirmation letter and general information sheet are two basics (see Exhibits 3-5 and 3-6). Other touches include airport pickup; a welcome note; wine, fruit, candy, cookies, or flowers in their room when they arrive. Preregister speakers and have their badges and materials waiting in their rooms. You will think of other things you can do depending on your own style and that of your organization, but the key is to be thoughtful and appreciative. Certainly a speedy thank-you note and prompt reimbursement of expenses is the final consideration in this area. Speakers deserve the same courtesies suggested for attendees in Chapter 10. Review those ideas when preparing for speakers.

PROBLEMS AND STRATEGIES

PROBLEM: What can we do about speakers who come late or don't show up at all?

Strategy 1: The solution will vary depending on how much time you have to develop your strategy. Always have a back-up speaker in mind, such as a knowledgeable, well-spoken staff person, corporate officer, or respected attendee. You may ask each moderator to come prepared to "cover" for a late or absent speaker by inserting a few jokes or by leading a question-and-answer session with the audience. Another tactic is to reorganize the sequence of speakers and add a few minutes to each person's time.

Strategy 2: Require all speakers to "check in" a minimum of one hour prior to their scheduled time. If there are any no-shows at that point, go to the telephone and try to find out why they aren't there.

Strategy 3: Always get the speaker's home phone number and airline flight number, as well as the scheduling secretary's name and phone number. You may not be able to get in touch with a speaker who is circling the city at 10,000 feet. The more resources you have for emergency follow-up, the quicker the problem will be defined and a solution identified.

Strategy 4: Don't panic! And don't lose control of the program schedule by adding a break or announcing an extended lunch period. As soon as you do that the speaker will appear and you will have a real mess on your hands. Find a quiet corner where you can think clearly about your alternatives, discuss your plans with key conference officials, and make the required adjustments.

PROBLEM: Sometimes the audience has trouble hearing a soft-spoken speaker.

Strategy 1: On the speaker request form, ask speakers to rate their voice quality ranging from soft to very strong. Discuss the information with the person who will be handling your microphones on-site. Special equipment or adjustments can be made with advance notice. You may also pay attention to voice quality in your telephone follow-up.

Strategy 2: Always do a final check of microphones and inform speakers and moderators about how to use them to their best advantage.

Strategy 3: If the soft-spoken person is someone from the audience who is participating in a question-and-answer period, have the moderator to repeat the question. Also, for this format have audience microphones conveniently placed around the room or have staff members assigned to move about the room with hand-held microphones. After you've spent time and effort planning the program, don't spoil it by failing to think through your sound system.

4

SITE SELECTION

Site selection is one of the most important, most challenging, and most misunderstood areas of meeting planning. It is important because the space and flow of a meeting can greatly enhance the program's objectives and interactions among people. It is challenging in that you have a puzzle, usually one without all the pieces, that you have to anticipate and visualize in a variety of different structures. And it is misunderstood because all too many people see it as a glorious opportunity to be wined, dined, and given free "vacations" as a perk to their job.

Well, there are a few perks, but the site selection process is a time-consuming, serious, and often physically and mentally exhausting process. It requires thoughtful advance preparation, in-depth "discovery" interview skills, a keen eye for details, and an exceptional memory, especially if you are visiting several facilities in one day. It is these skills that are necessary, with the addition of appropriate follow-up to verify the facilities' ability to meet the commitments of space and service that they have been freely promising in the pre-contract discussions.

In this book, site selection and contracts each have their own chapter, but I encourage you to read them together. The reason is that once the contract has been signed, all promises not spelled out in the agreement are potentially lost. Most hotel contracts only confirm rates, dates, a specified number of guest rooms, and a very general reference to meeting-room requirements. I assume that your decision of one site over another was based on more than that; otherwise you could have limited your search to the Yellow Pages.

In short, the issues in this chapter are moot if you do not wrap up your "deal" with a good contract, and the details in this chapter are critical to arriving at a good agreement. Both are necessary.

In some ways it is a game, but no one has to be the loser. The planner wants a successful event, and the hotel wants to make a profit. I prefer to work with hotel personnel who will honestly discuss their need for a profit. People at a profit-oriented hotel usually see to it that their facility provides the best service to meetings, because they realize that service means repeat business, and repeat business means profits. Second, there are no- or low-cost ways a facility can help my budget, which leaves more dollars to spend in areas that help its budget. That concept of "working together" makes the process successful.

Clearly, this chapter is written from the planner's perspective, as is Chapter 5, on agreements and contracts, but I caution you to deal fairly and honestly. You must know not only your market but the facility's market as well. You must know your needs and its needs. You must know your group's strengths and weaknesses as well as those of the facilities. It is the informed planner who is perceived as a professional and is dealt with as such.

For the hoteliers reading this book, you must know the limits of your authority to make decisions and promises and your facility's specifications. When I tour a hotel and the salesperson doesn't know room capacities and can't answer routine questions, my professional respect for that person—and the property represented—is diminished.

GETTING IT ALL TOGETHER

THE HOTEL MARKET

The beginning point, as noted above, is to know the hotel market and your group. You must first understand that hotels make a profit from guest room sales, not from sales of food and beverages. Once you realize that, a series of questions must be explored. You need to know the high, low, and average rates for each property. You should know occupancy levels at various times of the year and week. You should know the general economic situation in the city and within the hotel.

Look internally for stable ratios of staff to guests and at staff turnover. (See Exhibit 4-2.) How long has your salesperson been there? The general manager? Request a copy of the staffing roster and ask for lengths of employment.

Along the same lines, look at the hotel's ownership structure. A hotel that is part of a chain may be owned and operated by the chain, or may be franchised, and thus carry the chain's name but be owned by a separate entity. In either situation, management of the hotel may be performed by a management company, whose reputation you should check.

Each of the foregoing arrangements is not of itself good or bad; you simply need to be aware of the structure. For example, there are hotels operated by management companies whose standards are higher than the corporate franchise name implies and vice versa. This is just the tip of the iceberg for your market research, but it's enough to stimulate your thinking if you have not been attentive in this area.

THE PROSPECTUS

Next, to use a tired but true phrase, is to *know your group*. Roughly, "your group" includes the company or organization you are working for, the program's goals and requirements, the budget, and the attendees' needs or preferences.

The formal document that profiles your group is called a "prospectus." (See the guidelines given in the Quick Reference Section.) The first section should introduce your organization and the specific meeting in a general way. While the introduction should be factual, it may also be considered a promotional description emphasizing your organization's purpose.

Section II should relate to your site requirements for this specific meeting, to include the number and type of guest rooms, preferred rates, dates and pattern (for example, Monday arrival, Thursday departure), and your moment-by-moment needs for meeting rooms. This breakdown should include room setup, anticipated attendance per room, and any special space eaters, such as projection equipment, screens, or head tables. In such cases you may indicate your total square-footage requirements as a total number, or per person if higher than normal allowances are required. This is also the time to specify ceiling heights, freight access, or any other required features. Be sure to advise the hotel if commissions are to be paid to you or to any third parties other than the direct booking agent. A simple statement that says rates are either commissionable or noncommissionable will do.

A facility should be able to determine from this section whether it can accommodate your group. If you have ever repeated the same requirements over the phone to 15 different properties, you will quickly realize the benefit of including site requirements in your written prospectus. Not only will you ensure that everyone receives the same information as part of a well thought out plan, you will ultimately save time and gain well-deserved respect for a professional approach.

In Section III, describe your group's history, either regarding this specific meeting or a similar one. This is the place to demonstrate that your assessment of your group's needs is accurate, that the facility must deliver what you are asking for. Include past cities, properties, and numbers broken down in every way possible.

Especially as related to numbers, your group history plays an important role. You can be sure the hotel will check your past history; prospective hoteliers will want to find out about your guest/sleeping room rates and pick-up, your meal counts, your total master account charges and credit record—and all too often they'll elicit a few choice editorial comments from the prior facilities managers, which may be to your benefit or disadvantage. The inexperienced planner probably has no knowledge of this underground grapevine. The experienced planner not only knows it exists but controls the information released. How? By requiring in the contract that any report or data about the meeting must be approved prior to release by the hotel, thereby giving the planner an opportunity to adjust any incorrect or misleading information.

One of the most difficult problems for the hotels, especially when you consider their profit is generated from guest room sales, is when, say, 300 rooms are requested and no basis for arriving at that number is given. Hotels either need a history or a rationale for the requested number of rooms. If you want it all with no guarantees and no history, you can and should expect to pay heavy penalties if you fail to meet your confirmed requirements.

Section IV is a detailed day-by-day time-and-event specification. The hours, event (or use), and location should be itemized for each day of the meeting.

Once your prospectus is complete, you should review potential hotels, select those that meet your criteria, and send them a copy. You might even enclose an RSVP card and ask the hotel to return it indicating its intent to submit a bid. A three-to-four-week response deadline should be established. You don't want to wait on bids from hotels that are not interested or do not have dates available.

SITE INSPECTIONS

After careful review of the proposals, you are ready for your site inspections. The tendency for most planners is to overschedule their site-inspection appointments and to respond to the invitations of all hotels that want to see them rather than only those appropriate to their meeting. Three to four hours per facility is the minimum needed for a thorough inspection. The "interview" portion should take one to two hours and the walk-through, depending on the facility size, one to two hours. Then give yourself one hour—alone—for notetaking, measuring, and revisiting areas you're having trouble remembering. It's best to do this on-site, so you can go back to the room or ask the salesperson to fill in the gaps.

There are numerous site selection checklists (including the one in Exhibit 4-2) that are useful in devising your own form. You don't even have to have a form, but a system for capturing comparable data is going to be valuable when you make your final decision.

REFERENCE CHECKS

Finally, I suggest you check references of the final properties under consideration. Ask for the names of three companies that have held meetings similar to yours in the hotel in the past month. That ensures a response based on the current level of service and limits the ability of the hotel to give you their best references. We have all had "star" performances—you want to find out about the typical ones. Even a bad reference can be good if it helps you anticipate problems and prepare solutions in advance. At one time or another, we have all been in the position of having only one site option, but that is no reason to be less thorough. If this is the case for you, think in terms of site evaluation rather than site selection. Regardless of the number of choices, you must know the capabilities and limitations of the facility and the staff—the building and the people.

And don't forget about the hotel's general manager (GM). I usually ask the bell or housekeeping staff who the GM is and see what comments are volunteered. There are various approaches to finding out more about the facility. Some planners visit the hotel unannounced, others take a secret tour of the service areas, and some have private conversations with guests and in-house groups. The key is not so much how you approach site selection, but that you are thoughtful and thorough.

NEGOTIATION

Negotiation is the thread that should have been woven throughout the entire process. Actually, negotiation is an important-sounding word for the give-and-take discussion between the hotel salesperson and the planner. The key to success in this area is not only to know what you want in relation to what you must have, but to know the other business as well as or better than the "other side's" representative. Unfortunately, the reverse is usually true: The hoteliers know more about planners than planners know about themselves or their meeting.

Negotiations ultimately form the basis for the contract, which is the focus of the next chapter. But it is important to remember that the contract is the written version of all that has been discussed and agreed to in this stage. There should not be any surprises or glitches if you have been open and honest in your pre-contract discussions.

SITE SELECTION TIPS

CONVENTION BUREAUS

A convention bureau exists to expedite the process of booking meetings into its city. A bureau usually produces guidebooks summarizing the specifications of the various meeting facilities and services, including contact names and telephone numbers. Staff members will make preliminary hotel contacts for you and set up inspection tours of the city or facility.

Convention bureaus also are an excellent resource for local service contractors. My primary objection is that they are usually required to send "leads" to all member facilities, which can result in a flood of calls from hotels inappropriate for your group. The key is to discuss their procedures up front and then determine the usefulness of their service to you. Often a simple request to limit the lead distribution only to the hotels that meet your criteria will suffice.

Bureaus also publish a monthly or quarterly listing of all meetings and events booked into the city, although they are limited to those either booked through them or reported to them by their members. Because of their broad knowledge, they can often assist you in identifying conflicts that might affect attendance or facilities availability.

HOLIDAYS

One cannot be reminded too often to check the holiday calendar before confirming dates, specifically religious and international holidays. For example, September is a heavy month for religious holidays. It is also helpful to know the significance of the holiday to measure the impact it will have on your attendance. Not all holidays are equally important; Presidents' Day will not have as much of an impact on meeting plans as Labor Day will. And don't forget about election days, graduations, or other significant happenings that could create a conflict for attendees. You may not be able to plan around every holiday, but the "must" ones are those important to your group.

UNIONS AND OTHER HIDDEN COSTS

In the site selection process, costs beyond guest room and meeting room rates should always be discussed. Taxes and gratuities are variable, as are the complimentary items such as microphones in the meeting rooms. Labor can be a real factor, especially in a union facility. Some union policies are so restrictive that you must pay workers each time you turn the lights on or off, change a light bulb, or move a table from one side of the room to another.

With regard to union facilities or cities, you should also know the dates for contract negotiations and renewals. Strikes or bad feelings can greatly affect the success of your event. Obtain a list of every union organization that contributes to your meeting and find out what the terms of each organization's contract are.

GUEST/SLEEPING ROOMS

Guest/sleeping rooms are the rooms with beds occupied by your attendees. They may be called singles, double/doubles, king, parlors, suites, condos, or a host of other names. Rates are based on an equally extensive number of factors. Rates begin with the term *rack*, which is the highest rate (usually quoted to the person who walks in off the street). There is a corporate rate, group rate, government rate, travel agency rate, and so forth. Meetings usually qualify for the group rate, which is negotiable based on the size of the group, the length of stay, the time of year or week, the availability or market conditions, the total dollar value of your business, and opportunities for repeat booking. If you call a hotel and simply ask for its rates, you will have shown your hand as a novice.

The rates issue grows in complexity when you inquire about which rooms you get at that rate. The simplest and most common structure is *run of the house*, which means an attendee will get any room in a category (single, double, and so on) available at the time of check-in, with the exception of rooms on special floors such as the concierge or other VIP floors. If you are given three different rates for one type of room, ask the hotel to specify how many rooms are in each category and what the differences are in room quality, location, and so on. All too often, only 5 percent exist at the low rate, 10 percent at the mid-rate, and 85 percent at the highest rate. Also, always ask to see the worst room in the hotel, write the number down, and make the hotel sign a guarantee that none of your attendees will be assigned a *worse* room. You may have to specify what "worse" means—in terms of size, location, or decor.

When you tour the guest room area of hotels, look at the halls, carpets, walls, lighting, fire exits, elevator locations, locations of ice and soda machines, signage, general cleanliness, and maintenance. Also, if it's 2:00 P.M. and room service trays in the hallways haven't been picked up, this could indicate a staffing or service problem.

Once inside the room, check everything you checked in the hall, then turn on the shower for hot and cold temperatures and water pressure, turn on all the lights and TV, call the operator to see how long it takes your ring to be answered, open the drapes—generally see what works and how well it works. The advantage of staying overnight in the hotel is to experience all hotel services at peak times of usage.

MEETING ROOMS

Basic to evaluating meeting rooms is to know your room setup and other items, such as audiovisual equipment, to be placed in the room. The four major setups are conference, banquet (or rounds), schoolroom (or classroom), and theater. When you talk or write to a hotel, you need to request meeting rooms by telling them either the setup and number of attendees per room or by the square feet needed per person and the number of people. For example, you could say either, "I need a theater setup for 200 people," or "I need 24 square feet per person for 200 people."

Staging, audiovisual equipment, dance floors, and decorations are space-eaters, so you will need to advise the hotel of other items or special setups that will increase your overall need for space.

In selecting meeting rooms, note ceiling heights, posts, unusually shaped rooms, and lighting. Look for the location of switches and outlets, and watch for low-hanging chandeliers that may interfere with projection.

Noise considerations should take into account air space, movable walls, and service corridors. Remember, there is no such thing as a soundproof air wall unless corridor-width air space is designed between the two walls; even then you wouldn't want a dance recital going on next door.

As with the rest of the hotel, you should observe colors, ambiance, cleanliness, quality of furniture, and proper functioning of equipment.

FOOD AND BEVERAGES

Food and beverages usually constitute a high-cost item for the planner, and a hotel's prices should be evaluated as a part of the site selection process. (For an in-depth discussion of food-and-beverage issues, see Chapter 12.) Over the years, I have developed a few key questions that give me a reading on the general price structure. First, I ask the price of a gallon of coffee, knowing the range is from $15 to $30, and make a quick judgment of the hotel's prices based on where their price falls within the range. Then I ask for the mid-range price of a lunch or dinner and for the number choices available above and below that range. This rough test gives me a general sense of the hotel's costs in relation to my budget.

Hotels are usually less flexible in their food prices than their room rates, especially if you wait until after the contract is signed to negotiate food and beverage. Hotels are often reluctant to guarantee prices more than three months prior to the event because of the fluctuations in the costs of food items. This is not generally acceptable to planners because they need to prepare a budget one to three years ahead of time. One option is to have current menus signed and dated and insert a contractual clause that limits price increases by tying them to cost-of-living increase or to some other predetermined percentage. Even with this option, prices should be finally confirmed one year out.

Don't select a site on the basis of prices alone. If cost seems to be your only criterion, the hotel may try to lower its price by reducing the number of services, the quality or freshness of the food products (lesser cuts of beef, canned versus fresh vegetables), and possibly the size of the portion. A loss of service and quality can eventually be more damaging than a few added dollars. There is more about this in Chapter 12, but consideration must begin in the site selection process.

PROBLEMS AND STRATEGIES

PROBLEM: Often after we receive a contract or proposal from a hotel, we're called and told we must sign the contract within twenty-four hours or lose the space.

Strategy 1: Read your proposal, specifically looking for the date by which you must make a decision. This obligates the hotel to you only until that date; if another group wants the space, you do have to sign the contract or release the space.

Strategy 2: Establish the length of time allowed for a tentative hold in the early discussions. Tell the hotel when a decision can be expected and work around that date. You can be sure the hotel won't continue to hold uncertain space while watching other good business walk away.

Strategy 3: Be honest with the hotel. Don't hold tentative space too long, especially if you are only marginally interested. If you are 99 percent sure you will use the hotel, say so and ask for an extension until a decision can be finalized. The real strategy here—as in all other areas—is to be fair and honest.

PROBLEM: More than one meeting has been ruined because of another group in the hotel during our meeting.

Strategy 1: Ask the hotel who else is booked during your meeting. To ensure that you get the information, add a line to your contract requiring the hotel to provide it.

Strategy 2: While you cannot prevent a hotel from booking other business, you can include in your contract a description of the types of groups or activities that would be an inappropriate mix. You may state that an incompatible booking will constitute reason for a no-penalty cancellation. In such case, the hotel will ultimately have to make a decision between its ethical obligation and the value of the opposing pieces of business.

Strategy 3: If it is simply a matter of noise, such as a peppy sales program, meet with the other group's representatives and try to coordinate your program around their loud times.

Strategy 4: Require the hotel to leave air space (of at least one corridor width or ballroom section) between you and any other group. (This should be a hotel's standard practice.)

PROBLEM: Despite its promises, a facility is not always able to comfortably accommodate our disabled attendees.

Strategy 1: Read the handicapped requirements in the Quick Reference Guide and any other articles that will help you anticipate the variety of needs. One excellent resource is *The Planner's Guide to Barrier Free Meetings* (available from Harold Russell Associates, 235 Bear Hill Rd., Waltham, Mass. 02154). The publication was prepared in 1980 in collaboration with the New England Chapter of Meeting Planners International.

Strategy 2:   Define what you mean by "handicapped equipped" and ask the hotel to back up its statement with specifics.

Strategy 3:   Ask your attendees with handicaps (visual, auditory, dietary, ambulatory) to discuss unique needs with you or the hotel before arriving. Most problems can be resolved with advance notice.

Strategy 4:   If specific guest/sleeping rooms are equipped for the handicapped, be sure they are set aside for your group several days in advance of arrival. A non-handicapped person may be occupying the room and may not be scheduled to check out before you need the room.

PROBLEM: Hotels frequently oversell their rooms, and my attendees have to stay elsewhere.

Strategy 1:   Negotiate an agreement in advance with the hotel regarding the penalties if this occurs. The usual practice is that the hotel will pay the room charge and transportation between the two facilities until the person can be moved into their reserved facility.

Strategy 2:   Stay in close contact with the reservations department so that you know when you are entering the high-risk zone of oversell.

Strategy 3:   Advise the hotel to contact you before they "walk" anyone from your group. You can then assist with the solution by personally explaining the situation to the attendee or, if necessary, giving that person your room or moving a staff member.

Strategy 4:   Be sure your attendees understand the hotel's guarantee policy. If the attendee declines to guarantee a room with a credit card or advance payment, usually the hotel will hold the room only until 6:00 P.M. on the scheduled arrival date. That person will be the first to be "walked" if the hotel is oversold. Encourage attendees to guarantee their rooms.

Strategy 5:   At 6:00 P.M., if the facility is full, review the hotel's "no-show" printout and establish the order in which members of your group will be moved. You might also indicate where you want them moved, if there is a choice.

PROBLEM: The hotel's cutoff date is so early that many of our attendees are unable to get rooms.

Strategy 1:   If you can use your past history to prove to the hotel that the rooms blocked will be sold, the hotel will be more flexible in negotiating a two- to three-week cutoff date.

Strategy 2:   If the hotel is inflexible and you know you will pick up the rooms, you can guarantee the remainder of the block. (Interestingly, planners who won't take that risk themselves are usually the first to complain about hotels that refuse to do so.)

Strategy 3:   In your negotiations, be sure you have agreed that the room reservations made after the cutoff date will remain at the group rate, on a space-available basis.

Strategy 4:   Communicate all these policies to your attendees. While you cannot ensure that they will read the information, you can protect yourself and your organization by providing it.

PROBLEM: Members of our group like to share rooms, and the hotels are less than helpful in matching people.

Strategy 1:   Personally, I don't believe that matching up roommates is the hotel's responsibility, although many try to be helpful. But if members of your group want to find a way to be matched up with roommates, discuss this up front with the hotel and develop a mutually workable plan.

Strategy 2:   Revise your hotel reservation card to allow attendees to indicate if they would like to be matched with a roommate. Have them indicate male or female (because names alone can be confusing), and encourage them to list any preferences, such as smoking or nonsmoking. You might also indicate that roommate changes on-site will be allowed only if space is available.

Strategy 3:   Require any people you or the hotel match to sign a waiver of responsibility. You don't want to find yourself in a lawsuit because of stolen items, damages, or other unfortunate occurrences.

5

AGREEMENTS AND CONTRACTS

The contract is the legal agreement that binds your organization to the facility or other service provider. Legal is the key word, and it can be an expensive word if you take this responsibility too lightly. While hotels and planners' organizations have not jumped on the lawsuit bandwagon with the same frequency as some other professional groups, cases do exist. The facility usually initiates the suit when cancellation of a confirmed booking occurs. It is more difficult for planners to initiate suits, especially when they have casually signed the hotel's contract. The standard hotel contract binds the planners to meet certain criteria and binds the hotel to very few beyond a certain number of sleeping and meeting rooms at a specified rate.

But times are changing, and the industry as a whole—planners and suppliers—are becoming more sophisticated. Even attorneys are finding the hospitality industry is a profitable ground for specialization. Rest assured that the frequency of lawsuits will increase in direct relation to the attorneys' interest in this industry. That is one red flag; the other is the state of the economy. In a bad economy, facilities have a more difficult time replacing cancelled business. From the planners' perspective, maintenance of the facility and service level are likely to be cut back in a bad economy. So don't isolate yourself from these outside forces.

GETTING IT ALL TOGETHER

NEGOTIATION

The time and money you may spend in a lawsuit are far better spent up front negotiating your "deal" and preparing a contract reflective of the agreements reached in the negotiation stage. Look closely at the negotiation guidelines given

Portions of this chapter are drawn from articles by the author previously published in *Convention World*, a Bayard publication.

in the Quick Reference Guide, and remember that many of these issues should be kept in mind during the site selection process. As was stated in Chapter 4, site selection, negotiation, and contracts are all closely tied together.

It may sound repetitious, but you must know your organization, your meeting, your attendees, your budget, and your history in order to negotiate or establish the terms of the agreement:

- If your organization has a policy against paying deposits, you must negotiate this as a part of the contract.
- If your attendees register late, negotiate a later cutoff date for holding the room block.
- If you require more than the average number of square feet per person in your meeting room, include this in your contract.
- If your selection of a facility was based on certain meeting rooms, don't allow the hotel to move you to other rooms without your approval.
- If your attendees are big spenders who tip well, run up large bar bills, and order gourmet dinners, negotiate based on total revenue to the hotel rather than just your meeting budget.

It's impossible to mention all the variables that influence negotiations and, ultimately, the terms of the contract. The point is to know where you want to end up—before you begin.

It is all too common for the inexperienced planner to get caught up in the myriad of details, forgetting the broader implications of what is being signed—both stated and unstated. Ask yourself the "what if" questions.

- What if a union strike occurs?
- What if the hotel fails to pay its liability insurance?
- What if renovation occurs during your meeting?
- What if the property is sold?
- What if the property deteriorates?
- What if the staffing level drops?
- What if the service level declines?
- What if your attendance or exhibits outgrow the facility or city?

The "what ifs" are different for each group, each property, each city, and the length of time prior to the meeting that the contract is signed. But they must be addressed in the contract.

As the planner you clearly have the advantage in the negotiation and contracting stage. Once the agreement is signed, especially if you have a substantial cancellation penalty, the facility gains the advantage. While this isn't a chess game, there are strategies that can benefit you down the road. The key is to think about all your needs and list them according to what you want, what you must have, and what you will give up. (See Exhibit 5-1 for a worksheet.) Then either put them in the contract or in an attached, signed addendum to the contract.

An important part of the negotiation process is to openly discuss all issues with the individuals you will be contracting with. Keep in mind that the contract is a protective device for both parties. You want to be sure that the verbal discussions are in fact confirmed agreements.

Omissions are just as important as stated terms. I've often heard planners boast that the contract was signed without a cancellation clause. I can assure you that any signed contract carries penalties for violation of the terms whether stated or not. The unknown is what the penalties will be, at what point they go into effect, and how disagreements will be settled. It is not only naive but irresponsible for a planner to avoid these issues during negotiations.

Finally, negotiate a fair agreement. We will lose when a hotel "gives away the store" for a confirmed booking. If a hotel doesn't make a profit, it's unlikely to provide quality service or facility maintenance; the result is an unhappy client—and no return bookings. Ultimately, we are all after the same thing—a successful meeting—and are very dependent on each other in achieving it.

ELEMENTS OF A CONTRACT

If you have not already prepared a draft of your contract for the facility, you should do so now. You should also request a copy of their contract. It is the merging of these two documents that results in a successful agreement.

The elements you should consider fall into the following categories:

- Dates
- Guest/sleeping rooms
- Meeting rooms
- Food-and-beverage functions
- Audiovisual and other equipment
- Renovations and construction
- Service level
- Safety
- Handicapped accessibility
- Labor charges
- Parking
- Airport pickup and other guest services
- Insurance, both liability and indemnity
- Contingencies, especially if your agreement is based on factors unknown at the time the agreement is signed
- Allowances and restrictions, which can be anything from what you are allowed to put on the walls to booking groups that may be in conflict with your organization or activities
- Deposits, payments, and interest rates
- Union and auxiliary contractors
- Assurances pertaining to licenses, permits, or certificates necessary to the performance of the facility's obligation to you
- Insurance
- Cancellation
- A statement of the conditions that constitute breach of contract

These categories will help you outline the contract. Then you have to specifically address the terms with each category. It is prudent to meet with an attorney, particularly to discuss the legal verbiage that most of us don't readily understand. Incidentally, these are usually standard, generic statements that once incorporated into your agreement do not vary with each contract. But you must understand what they say and mean.

Finally, you must be sure the contract names the legally responsible parties and then have the agreement signed by the person(s) with the legal authority to enter into such an agreement. If you sign on behalf of your organization, be very sure you are protected from any personal liability.

Original, signed contracts should be filed safely away with each of the parties involved.

AGREEMENTS AND CONTRACTS TIPS

DATES

Carefully check your dates to be sure you are covered beyond your *major* arrival and departure days. If your staff, committees, or exhibitors need to arrive early or stay later, provisions should be specified. It also never hurts to pull out a calendar and double check the dates, days of week, and year. Sometimes the smallest details can cause the greatest problems.

GUEST/SLEEPING ROOMS

Early in the contract, the number and type of rooms blocked are listed along with the rates. If your meeting is more than one year away rates may increase during that period; therefore, current rates should be stated along with an agreement on when the rates will be confirmed and a structure for setting the rates at that time. The structure can be either a maximum percentage per year based on past increases, adjusted according to the cost-of-living increases per some official source, comparable rates at competitive hotels, or whatever measure works for both parties. The key is to spell out the index in advance.

You may also want the hotel to specify when and how individual reservations of attendees will be confirmed. Surprisingly, not all hotels send confirmation notices, so be sure to specify confirmations if they are important to you. You also need to spell out the hotel's procedures for guaranteeing reservations, its deposit requirements and policy on refunding of deposits, and what methods of payment are acceptable. Hotels traditionally have a cutoff date after which your room block is lost. This date is negotiable, but it is normally four to six weeks prior, which allows the hotel time to resell rooms not being used by your group. Tied to this date should be a statement ensuring that your attendees will be charged the group rate if space in the hotel is available.

If adjustments are needed regarding check-in and check-out times, specify your requirements. Hotels are usually less flexible in this area because of laws in some states that prohibit the removal of a person from an occupied room if payment is made or promised. The greater frustration is when a hotel has oversold rooms and your attendees arrive to find that, despite a guaranteed reservation, no rooms are available. Address this in your contract, requiring the hotel to pay for the attendees' rooms and transportation until they can be accommodated in the hotel holding the reservation.

The guest/sleeping-room block usually includes a complimentary policy that allows the contracting organization one complimentary unit for every 50–

100 rooms occupied. Some considerations are whether the policy applies to each night individually or to the total rooms occupied throughout the meeting. The "units" policy, similar to a point system, allows you to earn according to the type of rooms occupied (for example, a single or double room equals one unit per night; a one-bedroom suite equals two units per night) and to then apply these units to the type of room you need (for example, fifty units are required for a complimentary single or double room; one-hundred units for a complimentary one-bedroom suite). Allowances are most often based on one complimentary room per fifty rooms occupied, although the trend is moving to one per hundred. This is very negotiable, and often you can request one or two suites over and above the policy and special, lower-than-group rates for your staff.

Attendee considerations also include matching of roommates, phone, and pay-TV charges, especially if you have a student group. That brings us right back to the importance of knowing your group's needs and structuring the agreement with those issues in mind.

FUNCTION SPACE

This section of the contract specifically outlines the date, time, setup, or square-footage requirement of each function room. (See Addendum I to Exhibit 5-2.) Hotels prefer not to specify the meeting room(s) by name, which allows them the flexibility of moving groups around; from the planner's perspective, that is unacceptable. Most planners select a site based on the availability of certain rooms, and these rooms should be listed in the contract. A provision should also be included that requires a written request and signed release for any changes in function space. If I can accommodate a hotel's request to release or change a meeting room, I will happily work with them, but I will not jeopardize the success of my event.

Depending on the number of sleeping rooms and the size of your food and beverage functions, a fee may be charged for the rental of meeting rooms. Again, this is a highly negotiable area. The deciding factor is often the ratio of sleeping rooms to meeting rooms. Remember, a hotel's profit is in sleeping rooms, and meeting rooms sell sleeping rooms. If you are using only a small percentage of their available sleeping rooms and want all of their meeting space, the price will be high for space rental, if they will hold it for you at all. (Many hotels will not reserve meeting space alone more than three to six months in advance, in the hope that another group will want both meeting and sleeping rooms.) If you are dealing with a convention center, remember that all of its revenue comes from function space, so rental fees are higher and less negotiable.

In summary, the key factors are the date, hours, room (by name), type of setup, and rental costs. Beyond that, you should consider move-in and move-out hours; cost items such as chairs, podium, stage, or dance floor; draping, setup charges, and cleanup; security and labor charges; heating, lighting, outlets, and phone jacks; food service; and any other requirements or costs that are attached to your ability to use the function space.

SAFETY, SECURITY, AND ACCESSIBILITY

Assume nothing! Make sure your contract guarantees the existence of key safety and security factors and spells out the extent to which they exist. Certificates of inspection may be required as attachments to the contract for elevators, alarm systems, and other areas involving public safety. Meeting and sleeping rooms may require additional security systems, such as re-keying of all locks, limiting access to certain floors or wings, or requiring that guards be on duty. Certainly, handicapped accessibility should be confirmed. If your requirements are not standard, include the cost of upgrades in your contract.

FOOD AND BEVERAGES

Your contract should address food-and-beverage costs—usually a menu confirming prices can be attached to the contract. If prices will increase, the terms, much like those for sleeping-room rates, should be stated. Food prices are highly volatile based on availability, preparation time, and labor costs, and are usually less negotiable than other areas. The contract objective should be to obtain a protective ceiling; save your real negotiations for the chef.

But you should contract for a certain level of service by specifying the number of servers and busboys for your events. Since labor is the most expensive item in your food costs, many hotels cut corners here, and the speed and quality of service suffer.

Specify details regarding the color or type of linens required, centerpieces, plants and other decorations, bar costs, and corkage fees. It is not likely that all these items are necessary for every event, but don't overlook those of importance to your group.

RENOVATIONS AND CONSTRUCTION

If you have ever arrived at the meeting site in the midst of construction or renovation, you will agree that is not an acceptable meeting environment. To protect your organization, a clause should be included in the contract that specifies dates that a facility will be under renovation, area(s) of the facility affected, an agreement regarding stop-work during your event, and a non-recourse option to move the meeting if any of the above change, in addition to paying any costs that are incurred by your organization, plus a penalty for the inconvenience. If renovation is planned in the facility you are contracting with, it is advisable that you watch it very closely.

If you are contracting with a not-yet-built facility, be equally specific about the completion date, and add a hefty penalty if you cannot hold your meeting because of a contractor's failure to meet an overly ambitious construction schedule. You may even want to require that a copy of the construction schedule to be attached to the contract and that a monthly progress report be submitted.

CONTINGENCIES

Contingencies cover promises that may be affected by future uncertainties. Your entire agreement may be contingent on the addition of 3,000 square feet of meeting space, or a new convention center being built and operational, or twenty-three flights a day arriving in the city. One planner put a contingency clause in the convention center's contract, but not in the hotel's. When the center wasn't ready, the meeting had to be moved to another city, creating a flood of lawsuits from the hotels.

RESTRICTIONS

Restrictions are a two-way street. The hotel may not allow pets in the room, signs taped on walls, or liquor served on Sunday. These may be internal policies or state laws. In some cases, restrictions apply to a group's nonprofit status, which can be expensive if you thought you were tax-exempt and discover that certain cities or states do not accept that status. Restrictions can also be initiated by your organization. If you are hosting a meeting for recovering alcoholics, you don't want a free cocktail hour for guests or in-room bars. If hospitality rooms are not permitted except by prior approval of your organization, you may want to restrict the sale of suites or on-site distribution of invitations to only those approved by your organization. If you are hosting a right-to-life convention, you may not want a pro-abortion group next door. A restriction may be as simple as not allowing a band on the same floor as your function during your sessions, or allowing only members of your group to use the pool during certain hours.

Beyond state laws—and even those can be bent—there is no limit to what you can ask for and what the facility can approve or deny. If certain restrictions are critical to your selection of a site, include them in the contract.

CANCELLATION

We have already established that a contract is a legal, binding agreement and carries penalties when broken. The contract should state very specifically what the penalties will be, otherwise only the courts can determine what dollar amount will be assigned as a penalty. While this has never been enforced in real dollars lost, the risk is too great to take. The cautious route is to estimate the total dollar value of business to the facility versus the lead time necessary for the hotel to replace the business. Then openly discuss with the hotel staff a series of dates and monetary penalties. An average-size meeting of 100 to 500 people may not carry any cancellation penalty until three to six months prior to the event. As the time gets closer, the penalty increases. I have had contracts that carried penalties based on the sleeping-room rate times the number of sleeping rooms blocked on the peak night, on total food-and-beverage estimated revenue, and on meeting-room charges. Each was unique because of the contracted event(s). Some are unique because of the size and others because of the long- or short-term nature of the booking. An easy answer does not exist, but the fact is you are protected only if you either set a penalty or state that there is no penalty. An expert attorney may even find a loophole in a stated clause, but your risks are minimized.

STRATEGIES

PROBLEM: Cancellation penalties are so high that our organization's board of directors will not want to sign it.

Strategy 1:   Show board members the dollar figures that the facility stands to lose and explain the risks on both parts.

Strategy 2:   Add an additional clause that negates the penalty if you book a similar meeting with the property within one year.

Strategy 3:   Add a clause that negates the penalty in proportion to the income the hotel is able to recover. It is difficult to document unless information about all bookings (meetings, guest rooms, and food-and-beverage revenues) is supplied to you at the time of cancellation and within one week following the dates your meeting would have been held.

Strategy 4:   Send a signed and dated memo to your board indicating the potential penalties when unstated versus stated.

Strategy 5:   Realize that many properties will not agree to a contract without stated penalties.

PROBLEM: We cannot get a facility to sign our contract.

Strategy 1:   Be sure your contract covers the same key items in their facility's contract.

Strategy 2:   If you can, add addendums to the facility's contract. Some chains have strict policies requiring clients to sign their contracts, but most allow addendums to be attached. As long as the hotel's contract and your addendums cover all the issues, it doesn't matter who wrote it.

PROBLEM: What can we do to ensure that the level of service at the time of the contract doesn't drastically change by the time of our meeting?

Strategy 1:   Add a "level of service" clause to your contract that defines poor or unacceptable service. Then add a specific dollar penalty for each such incident.

Strategy 2:   Require the hotel to provide five references, groups that held similar meetings one to three months prior to yours. Hearing their experiences may not solve your problems, but will help you prepare for them.

Strategy 3:   Add a statement that releases you from the contract if three of the five references state that under present management they would not return to that facility.

Strategy 4:   Don't negotiate all the profit out of the hotel, or you may find it can't afford to maintain the service level you require. Granted, the hotel should be able to deliver on its promises, but sometimes it gets caught short—just as planners often fall short of filling their room block 100 percent.

Strategy 5:   Realize that the contract can't solve all your problems. Double check your people skills.

PROBLEM: What are the best things to do to avoid legal problems?

Strategy 1:   Have an attorney review your contracts before they are signed, not after.

Strategy 2:   Be very sure the person who signs the contract for the facility not only has the authority to sign, but the support of management in meeting the terms of the agreement.

Strategy 3:   Verbally review the contract with the facility staff to ensure that they understand each clause in the contract.

Strategy 4:   Be sure you can deliver on your part of the agreement.

Strategy 5:   Document all conversations and recap the key points in a memo to the facility. Courts love the written word.

6

DATA COLLECTION, EVALUATION AND REPORTING

GETTING IT ALL TOGETHER

Through every stage of planning, you will focus on numbers. Your first call to a hotel involves numbers—number of people, number of guest/sleeping rooms, number of functions, number of days, number of dollars in your budget, how much income, how many expenses. As the planning progresses, you have to know the number of items to be printed and the number printed of each piece; the number of microphones, meals, signs, flowers, gifts, and on and on.

All of these numbers form a data base and must be collected, analyzed, interpreted, and finally documented in a useful format for future planning. This process completes the circle from concept to evaluation. It is your measuring stick for past meetings and your most important guide for the next event.

The key areas are financial, attendance, food and beverages, program, and facility. Also document Personnel, marketing and mailing, and any other areas that give you information for future planning, decision making, or improving your next event.

The best test of the value of data collection and reporting is the impact the data has on the people who receive the report. Sometimes you'll see the lights go on. One client was recently shocked to learn that 40 percent of its attendance came from fifteen companies. That client is now adjusting its marketing efforts to encourage corporate groups by offering special rates. Another group was overbooking meeting space because it expected *all* registrants to participate. The data showed that "all registrants" included staff, volunteers, and speakers—people who did not routinely attend functions. Thus, the group was able to reduce meeting space by 25 percent. For one group, the lunch guarantees (the minimum it must pay for) were reduced by 300 people per function because the data showed that 20 percent of registrants did not participate in scheduled luncheons, but 105 percent (attendees and guests) attended evening awards functions. The luncheon savings alone was worth the money it took to prepare the report.

The possibilities are limitless. The key is to determine the data needed up front so your end result is consistent and accurate. If you want to know the average age of your attendees, you have to devise a method for collecting that data. If you want to know attendees' positions within a company, instead of just asking for titles, you might also ask how many people report to them. If you anticipate the answers and plan how to organize your report first, you will likely ask better questions.

Data collection is valuable only if you take the time to analyze the results. For the most part, meeting planners are not numbers people, and they avoid dealing with statistics beyond the most basic requirements. Don't succumb to that tendency. Tear apart everything you do, count actual numbers, and compute percentages for each category. Percentages allow you to compare categories and show you the pattern for your group. Don't forget to document the variables that affect each year. A poor economy, high air fares, or high hotel rates can affect attendance. Once the meeting has started, bad weather may increase the number of people attending functions, good weather may reduce the number. A great city versus a city without pizzazz may have an impact. A meeting in your headquarters city may be more profitable; you reduce travel and shipping costs and increase attendance because of your local credibility. In your analysis of the data, try to explain fluctuations due to variables and make notes for future planning.

HISTORICAL DATA REPORT

First go to past files and see what already exists. This is called your "group history." While the information may be sketchy if the data haven't been seriously collected, you will at least know what does and does not exist.

If the meeting or event has occurred for ten years, go back to find dates, location, and headquarters hotel; then see if you can locate attendance figures, and hotel room block, pick-up, and rates (the "room block" is the number of rooms reserved each night of your event; the "pick-up" is the number of rooms actually utilized each night.) Then you might begin to look for past budgets, financial reports, lists of attendees, evaluations by attendees, and program books. The more you find, obviously, the more detailed your historical report will be.

Next, look at alternative sources of information. Hotels and other suppliers often keep group records or histories that they are happy to share. In fact, it is a source of irritation to me that many suppliers have more data about a group than the planner. Committees, past officers, and your in-house records are also valuable sources of information.

But look for facts, not opinions. I once asked members of a group how many people had attended past meetings. They said 300 to 400. When I asked how they knew, they explained that the room was full and it was a big room. When the facts were researched, it turned out that this group had never even achieved an attendance of 200 people! We all know that a room can appear full if you stand at the back and look at the heads, but an actual count will reflect the inconspicuous empty seats. People often see what they want to see, not the reality.

Begin to evaluate requirements for data with respect to your organization, the federal government (for tax information), legal requirements, and such other areas as continuing education credit for attendees. (Continuing-education transcripts are treated, for the most part, like college transcripts, and kept indefinitely, unless otherwise determined by the designating body.) You'll soon find yourself accumulating file after file. The next step is to summarize the important information from each file into an organized historical report. Then set up your filing system so you can reference the master documents' data easily. If this hasn't been done before, you do have a big job ahead of you—but I happen to think it's an interesting one.

Once you have the past well documented, you can creatively approach the data, records, and information you will want in the future. Among my most useful records are detailed breakdowns of expenses and revenues. I have special food-and-beverage forms that, at a glance, tell me all I need to know for future planning. I also have expenditure reports with consistent categories that compare expenditures over the past years and express percentages so that I can eventually identify trends (such as 20 percent of the budget consistently allocated to marketing).

I have forms for attendance, registration types, date of registration, date of payment, amount paid, company affiliation, and whatever else I might want to know. For example, I have session attendance forms that, when counts are taken and recorded on-site, will tell me how to plan meeting rooms in the future. (See Exhibit 6-1.) These are only a few examples, but they should spark your thinking.

DATA COLLECTION TIPS

DATA COLLECTION FORMS

Meeting planners certainly have more than their share of forms, but too few are for data collection. So don't limit your search to that field only. Talk to the "numbers" people in your organization and take advantage of their systematic minds. If all else fails, adapt a form you are already using. It doesn't even have to be a form—you may simply need to reorganize your notes. However, the advantage of a form is that all you have to do is fill in the blanks; you don't have to remember what all the categories are every time. Two examples of data collection forms are given in Exhibits 6-1 and 6-2.

COMPUTERIZED DATA COLLECTION

Computers are valuable to the meeting planner for processing registrations, collecting data, and reporting results. To select the right software, review current articles in the monthly professional publications for meeting managers (trade and professional magazines are listed in the Resources section at the end of this book), and follow up by making direct contact with the companies of interest. Last, but probably most important, get in touch with users of the various software programs. If you haven't purchased your hardware, wait until you have selected the software so that you will have maximum options.

Service is also an important consideration. The package I use limits us to thirty-to-sixty free consultation days after the first telephone call. Often, different problems occur in the reporting stage, which may be from three to six months after the first meeting was set up. Service contracts are expensive for the infrequent user, and it seems unfair to pay a premium for a few answers, especially if the user's manual is vague or unhelpful. I suggest you negotiate hard on service and consultation extensions, especially for the first year of ownership.

Different software programs generate different types of reports, among them:

- *Attendance reports*—by date registered, by method of payment, by sessions preregistered for
- *Hotel reports*—by hotel, by arrival date, by room type
- *Financial reports*—by method of payment, by amount paid, by date received

In addition to reports, most systems can produce mailing labels, confirmation letters, registration lists, receipts for payments, and tickets, and other items.

Meeting software packages are already very user friendly, but scrutinize them carefully *before you buy* to identify "missing elements," such as vague instructions in the manual, the lack of a section of "what if's" for problem solving, or the omission of reports you want. Unfortunately, you can't always think of everything during the selection process, and you may not "miss" a report or other feature until it's too late; just try your best to thoroughly research the software in the pre-purchase stage.

EVALUATION FORMS

There are people who do nothing but devise testing and evaluation methods, so look for a good book that discusses the techniques in layman's terms. Combine the techniques with your need for information, and you will be ahead of your colleagues. (Be sure your evaluation form isn't so long that you will have to pay the attendees an hourly wage to fill it out!) Exhibits 6-3 and 6-4 are examples of some types of evaluation forms.

I also suggest that you limit the questions to information you will truly use. Don't ask attendees what they thought of the hotel if you don't plan on going back anyway. Ask which services within the hotel they used or liked; that will help you choose the next hotel. For example, if 40 percent of the attendees used the car rental desk, look for that service at your next site. If you don't plan to ask the keynote speaker back, don't bother to evaluate him or her. Ask what attendees liked or disliked about the speaker or presentation. If respondents consistently answer that the speaker had a good sense of humor and make little mention of technical information, you are one step closer to your program decisions for the next year.

If your organization either discounts attendees' opinions or never reviews their evaluations, don't waste your time gathering data. Information that's collecting dust on a shelf is the same as no information—except for the time you lost gathering it!

OBSERVATION AND INTERVIEWING

Evaluation of the program by attendees is only one aspect of evaluating a conference. All too often, we base our assessment of success on the evaluations of the program and facility. Both of those being "good" or "excellent" can dilute a multitude of "could have been betters" on the planning end. For this reason, in addition to the items listed in the Quick Reference Guide for this chapter, list your own observations, and even interview attendees on a range of issues that *you* consider important.

PERCENTAGES

Percentages allow you to consistently compare categories. I fell in love with percentages when I finally pulled together a spreadsheet of a client's meeting expenditures over the years and translated everything into percentages. Once translated, what had been just a page full of numbers turned into an unbelievably clear picture. The client's manager had not realized that each year they had spent 25 percent of their conference budget on marketing, 25 percent on food and beverages, 20 percent on the program, and 4 percent on miscellaneous. Their budget had increased consistently by 10 percent, but they always spent the same percentage of their budget in the respective categories.

Many hours were spent getting to this point, but the budget process then became pretty simple. Ultimately, the managers made changes in the percentage allowances based on their goals. They reduced their marketing costs by changing their four-color brochure to two-color and added a well-known keynote speaker to their program, which in turn helped market the program and significantly improve its content.

This is only one example, and the same results may have come about without translating numbers into percentages, but I believe that the final picture made the difference in how the organization perceived what it was doing.

REPORTS

Why not make reports pretty and easy to read? Help the users quickly get to the meat; if you don't, they may not look past the first paragraph. My reports meet at least two needs: "theirs" and mine. They (the clients) usually want to see only a summary of totals with percentages (for example, of 422 attendees, 42—or 10 percent—were first-timers). I, however, want the back-up data so that I can quickly check hard facts. If I spent 25 percent on food and beverages, later I'll need a breakdown of that expense (for example, four breaks, two lunches, one dinner).

After the summary and back-up details comes the third part: a narrative analysis that explains everything. You can also provide a per-person cost for expenses. Your company may open its eyes when a report shows expenditures of $25 per person on marketing and $8 per person on program. (An example of how to structure a data collection final report is given in Exhibit 6-5.) There are various ways of presenting the data: charts, graphs, forms, paragraphs, spreadsheets. Use whatever is appropriate to your organization.

Finally, put the report together nicely. Give it a sturdy typeset cover, add the logo, and have it bound (staples will do). This is an important document—treat it as such. Be prepared with extra copies because everyone will want one. And don't forget to put your name on it: "Prepared by _____." You deserve the credit and recognition.

PROBLEMS AND STRATEGIES

PROBLEM: Not enough evaluation forms are returned to make the information useful.

Strategy 1:   Stop each session a minute or two early and ask attendees to evaluate the just-completed session before they leave the room. This allows attendees time to complete the form throughout the program and lets them know you think it is important.

Strategy 2:   Have someone at the last session assigned to collect the forms.

Strategy 3:   Use a different form for each day or session so you will not miss those who leave early.

Strategy 4:   As an incentive to turn in evaluations, use completed forms to conduct a drawing for a desirable prize. If you want the evaluations to be anonymous, give a ticket to each person when the form is turned in.

Strategy 5:   Don't make the forms too long or too complex.

Strategy 6:   Don't put the full responsibility on the attendee. Develop an alternative evaluation system that you, the volunteers, or the hotel staff fill out. Find out what questions attendees asked. If a lot of them wanted to know, "When is the next flight out?" that gives you a clue about their interest level. If there are more people outside the session than in, you have another clue. If the coffee breaks are humming, the speaker was probably pretty exciting. Take off your staff badge and ask attendees how it's going. If the people who make up your support system pay attention and report their observations, in writing, you will have a truckload of good information.

Strategy 7:   Send attendees a follow-up memo thanking them for the information they provided and announcing changes based on their suggestions. Play up the positive responses, but don't misrepresent people's responses or your credibility may be forever lost.

PROBLEM: We don't have the time to collect the data.

Strategy 1:   Make time! If you believe something is important, or if you enjoy doing it, it will get done.

Strategy 2:   Delegate; assign responsibilities. Often, the "busiest" people are inefficient and refuse to delegate. Take a good look at yourself. If your company has an accounting office, ask it to complete the revenues and expenditures report. Ask your secretary to tally past evaluations. Does your company use college business or marketing students as interns? If so, put them to work on your project tallying data sheet results. Then take the helpers to lunch as a thank-you, offer to put a letter in their personnel files commending them for the extra effort, or offer to list their names in your report. Be creative, appreciative, and give appropriate recognition. That's how teams are built.

Strategy 3:   Design forms that make the process easy. And prepare the data collection forms so they can be included in the report without retyping or writing.

Strategy 4: Set up your system in the beginning, not *after* the meeting or event.

Strategy 5: Don't try to do it all at once. Begin with key areas of importance to you and your organization and add more detail and new areas each year.

PROBLEM: We handle only a small part of the meeting; therefore, the data is not available and would not help our group.

Strategy 1: No matter what your part is, there is information that will help you next year. Organize what you do have access to, and share it with your colleagues. It will help you and may be an incentive for others, especially if you offer to organize all the reports into one major report.

Strategy 2: Prepare a proposal for your supervisor outlining the possible reports, their value, and how the process can be implemented into your current planning and evaluation structure.

PROBLEM: This is a first-time event, and there is no way to anticipate what will happen.

Strategy 1: Set your system up now so you will have a history of this meeting for planning the next one.

Strategy 2: Talk to other planners with similar meetings and review professional publications for national averages.

Strategy 3: Make conservative planning judgments. It is always easier to upgrade than to reduce.

7

MARKETING AND PROMOTION

Meeting planners are often responsible for marketing and promotion—for delivering x attendees—and your success as a planner is often measured by the effectiveness of your marketing efforts. Promotional materials, such as letters, brochures, advertising, and news releases, are used to get the word out.

In this chapter, I emphasize the thinking through of marketing and promotion more than I do the mechanics. The mechanical things must be done, but the risk of failure is significant if you don't think about what you are doing, why you are doing it, and for whom you are doing it. Many of the procedures in this book work as well for one group as for another. They are mechanical, routine procedures and practices, but only you and your organization can determine what is the best marketing approach for your attendees. There is no "wrong" way; if something works for your group and appropriately communicates your organization's image, then it's right for you.

To successfully promote a meeting, you first need to be sure that you have a meeting people will want to attend. Second, you need to encourage the sponsor, maybe your boss, to be realistic about the attendance goal. Try to set a number that's a little lower than what you think you can deliver. Third, evaluate your obstacles. Is there enough time to properly market the program? Are there scheduling conflicts, such as college graduations, April 15 tax filing, or annual events or conventions that your potential attendees routinely attend?

The point is, if attendees are really the most critical ingredient, then consider them in the beginning. It's dangerous to promote a meeting based on your organization's needs rather than on the attendees' needs.

There is a lot of competition for attendees—just look at the opportunities that cross your own desk each day. Which ones do you toss, which ones do you read? Do you ever follow up to see how many attendees your competitors drew, or try to figure out what role their promotional pieces played in their success?

I think that all too often we just follow, copy, assume. We don't look at the market from the perspective of need versus saturation, the sponsor's credibility versus the competition's, the costs and incentives versus the value of the conference. Planners must also consider the drawing power of past successful events and potential attendees' word-of-mouth recommendations.

The last point may not seem very important, but it caused a major fundraising event I was working on to be canceled. Three key community leaders felt the sponsor had not treated them with the attention they deserved, and when asked by other invitees if they were attending, they quietly and simply said no. Without further questions or explanations, word quickly got around, and the event was essentially blackballed. The petty reasons may never be known, but a lot of time and money were lost because the sponsors were more focused on the event than the attendees.

When you consider promotional materials, don't simply include ten key items in your brochure or invitation and feel you've done your job. Look broadly at the entire process of marketing your meeting.

GETTING IT ALL TOGETHER

TYPES OF MEETINGS

Compulsory Events

The type of meeting or event you are planning will affect how you proceed. For example, there are corporate meetings that "advise" attendees of where to be and when to be there. All expenses are usually paid by the sponsor. The attendees' choice is, though subtly presented, to attend or resign from the company. The attendees' motivation is obvious, but the meeting can have a negative impact, especially if it requires cancelling the family vacation. It is necessary to communicate to such people the importance of the events, explain why they were selected, and describe the benefits and value of their participation to each of them personally and to the organization. While the company clearly expects total commitment from employees, it is good psychology to recognize workers' sacrifices and loyal support.

Incentive Meetings

Such a meeting is held as the corporate reward or for outstanding performance. Some meeting planners get involved in the total conceptual design of incentive programs, setting the sales and production goals as well as planning the reward, which is often a meeting in a highly desirable resort location. The recognition that accompanies the invitation is usually sufficient motivation to attend, and spouses are often invited. Who wouldn't want to go? Because you don't have to motivate those invited to attend, planners often use a dramatic invitation to stimulate those who failed to earn the reward this year to work harder so they will be invited next year.

"Conglomerate" Meetings

The most difficult of corporate meetings are the ones that bring together a company's distributors, franchisers, sales reps, and other loosely tied field people. The planner's job is especially hard if attendees are expected to pay their own way. Such a group is comparable to association meeting attendees; a relationship and credibility exist among those invited, but the costs versus the value to participants has to be the marketing focus.

Annual Meetings

Associations are membership-based organizations providing education, legislative monitoring or lobbying, certification, and other services to special-interest or professional groups. They are run by and for their members. They are usually nonprofit, tax-exempt organizations that rely on dues, meeting fees, service fees, and, to a varying extent, contributions and grants.

Whatever they choose to call the yearly gathering—annual meeting, convention, conference, or incentive—one is almost always held. The purpose for attendees is education, networking, recognition, and conducting official association business. The purpose for the association is to promote the organization and to raise operating capital.

The key to marketing the association's annual meeting is to offer a quality educational program. That may not be the real reason people want to attend, but participants need a strong educational program to justify their attendance and expenses to the company or the IRS. Remember, you have to get the potential attendees' interest or the request to attend will not even be submitted to the company for approval. So there are some dual, albeit subtle, considerations in your marketing. I don't have statistics, but I can assure you that most meeting fees and expenses are paid out of business accounts, not personal accounts.

"Public" Meetings and Seminars

These are sponsored by individuals, corporations, associations, or entrepreneurs and are marketed to anyone who is likely to come up with the fee. Such meetings are usually held to make a profit, to promote an organization, service, or cause, or to offer continuing education courses. They require large promotion budgets and carefully developed marketing strategies. You will probably need to use professional services and sophisticated techniques that are beyond the scope of this book if that's the type of meeting you are responsible for marketing. You should recognize, however, that the basic promotional considerations are the same; the difference is in targeting (locating) your market.

The deciding factors in determining where you fit in the above categories are (1) the extent to which you have to create a market and (2) the recognition, credibility, and power of you or your group to achieve success based on the invitation alone. If there isn't an existing credible structure, you are probably in the "public" arena.

MARKETING CONSIDERATIONS

There are three parts to your marketing strategy:

1. *Penetrating.* You must get the right people to read your promotional pieces and sell them on the value of their participation.

2. *Timing.* You must reach your targets when they have the need, problem, interest, or time. That's tough, but you can try to anticipate the timeliness of your program. An investments program will likely be more successful in a strong economy. Tax subjects are most popular from December through April or May, and issue programs draw best when the legislature is in session. Most are not so obvious, but a hard look and a few telephone calls may be a good investment of your time.

3. *Selling.* Keep in mind the real influencers and decision makers, who may range from the attendees' boss and board of directors to a spouse, if the benefits of participation extend to them. And don't discount the children, who can be most persuasive in getting their parents to attend your meeting at Disneyland—as a family of course!

TYPES OF PROMOTIONAL MATERIALS

With all these considerations, you ultimately have to prepare the announcement of your event. The most common methods—and the things people most often respond to—are brochures, invitations, and personal letters. The supportive methods include promotional advertising in trade or general interest publications, posters, flyers, mailing inserts, features, human interest stories, public service or paid announcements, public endorsements, and word of mouth.

Gimmicks include fabulous giveaways or door prizes, or sand, confetti, or some other ridiculous attention-getter that falls out of the envelope or mailing tube when it's opened. There are odd-size mailing pieces, videotapes, pop-up letters, and, most recently, one accompanied by 3-D glasses for "putting the invitation in perspective." (I admit it worked, if all you wanted recipients to do was read the invitation. If you wanted them to attend, it didn't.)

Your budget will certainly be a deciding factor in what type of materials you will prepare, but a lot can be done on a lean budget. My favorite brochures for meetings are the well-organized, easy-to-read ones, not the four-color fancy pieces where the design controls the copy.

Other budget considerations are the number of mailings, how much each piece will cost to mail, how much time you have to prepare the mailing, and when you need to receive the response. Depending on your budget and priorities, you may even decide to send each invitation by overnight mail.

In choosing your promotional materials, you have to weigh a variety of factors: your organization's budget, values, image, and credibility; your attendees' loyalty, interest, ability to pay, and other commitments; your lead time for planning, availability of materials, and personnel support; and your skills in selecting qualified suppliers and supervising the implementation of your plan.

PROGRAM BOOK ADS

The program book is the official printed program for the entire event, listing meeting locations and times and a variety of other pertinent information. While the program book itself is not strictly a promotion piece—it is usually distributed at registration—it merits some discussion here. Many organizations sell ads for this book, and such ads are often solicited in preliminary promotional pieces, like the exhibitors' brochure or the general conference announcement.

Therefore, when planning your copy and layout, you must include this information if it is appropriate to your meeting.

If information about ads is not properly communicated, you can end up with a real mess on your hands when the ads begin to come in. Advertisers need to know the actual size of the printed ad, whether your program book will have margins, borders, or other graphic influences and what you will accept as camera-ready copy. Discuss this last point with your printer in advance; you don't want to end up paying to clean up someone else's copy. Be aware that photos can be an expense to you if they're not already cut in and laid out.

The best strategy is to send a contract to all program advertisers outlining your specifications and notifying them which charges will be billed to them. (See Exhibit 7-1 for a sample.) When setting deadlines, allow ample time for returning items or correcting mistakes. Advertisers can be a valuable revenue source, so you want to keep the process as painless as possible.

MARKETING AND PROMOTION TIPS

PROMOTIONAL INFORMATION

Regardless of the type of piece you select to promote your meeting or event, there is certain basic information you need to include. The most obvious are the program's title, sponsor(s), date(s), and location. Incidentally, errors and omissions often occur here, especially in the proofing process, so double-check everything for typos. Be sure to verify all dates and to specify the day of the week as well as the date. Also include names, addresses, and phone numbers of various people: the sponsor, special events coordinator, registration coordinator, program coordinator, facility manager, and so on. It may seem like a lot of names to list, but it will ultimately save time in call handling by minimizing referrals.

You should include an agenda that provides the program topics, speakers, and content description by day, time, and location. If you know who your keynote speakers are, be sure to highlight them. Providing titles and affiliations is a necessity, and bios—however brief—will enhance your marketing effort.

Information that encourages attendance includes:

- Availability of continuing education credit(s)
- Tax deductibility
- Promotion of the conference site
- Special group activities and events
- Organized trips for before or after the event
- Good weather
- Guidelines for appropriate attire
- Items included in the conference fee
- Transportation options (air and ground)
- Special program for guests and children
- Hotel rates and policies
- Your conference rates and policies

All may not be needed for your group, but try to second-guess what they will want to know, even down to such amenities as beauty parlors and barber shops, babysitting, shoeshine, and secretarial services, and facilities such as a health club, golf course, tennis courts, racquetball courts, running track, swimming pool (heated for winter?), jacuzzi, and so on. If the facility has a gourmet restaurant that requires advance reservations, listing that information is also helpful.

You will also need to include with the brochure a response form for making reservations, usually a registration form for the conference, and a housing or hotel reservation card for the facility or the housing coordinator. Other forms may be added for special events, CEC credits, etc.

The registration form needs the attendee's name, address, and telephone number. Don't forget to ask for titles and affiliations if you want that for badges or your records. The form also needs a registration category if you have more than one type, such as member, nonmember, guest, speaker. Be sure to list the accompanying fees and method of payment. If charge cards are an option, request the card type, account number, signature, and expiration date. Some organizations charge a processing fee for credit cards; if yours does, say so.

If attendees are required or allowed to preregister for specific sessions or special events, provide a section for doing so on the form. If attendance is limited to a certain number, instruct registrants to indicate their first, second, or third choices.

It is also considerate to inquire about attendee's specific needs, especially as related to health problems and handicapped requirements.

Be sure you don't include information on the return form that attendees will need later, such as important names, addresses, and phone numbers. If you must, put such information both on the registration form and in the brochure.

You can include a hotel reservation card or, as I do, use the hotel's card as a guide but have it printed in the brochure. Don't forget about the hotel's cutoff date for reservations or you will have a real disaster on your hands.

Finally, you need to think about how the forms will be returned. If payment is required and your budget allows, include a preprinted envelope. If payment isn't required, you can preprint the reverse side of the return card.

POSTAGE REQUIREMENTS

The post office is very specific about its size, shape, and weight requirements and the accompanying costs. Some sizes are not acceptable at any cost. The smart planner checks before printing. You can ask your printer, but if in doubt take your mock-up to the post office and have it approved and signed. Check international requirements if you will be sending mail outside the United States.

PACKAGING

Packaging encompasses the copy, layout, and folding or binding, as well as the envelope or self-mailer format. Be consistent and clear, use descriptive headlines, and organize information logically. How it looks says a lot about you and especially your organization.

PROOFREADING

The person who prepares the brochure should never be the primary proofer. Have several people review it with an eye to spelling, grammar, clarity, and typos.

BLUELINES

When you go to print, always request a "blueline" (or "blues") which is the negative copy (usually printed in blue ink) made after the plates. If typeset copy falls off the page after the last proof is approved, that omission will show up in the "blues." This is your final chance to make corrections before printing unless you require a press proof. (Chapter 8 discusses this in more detail.)

MULTIPLE MAILINGS

Multiple mailings are attendance builders. You can reuse the same piece or send updates as details and speakers are confirmed. The idea is to keep your organization's name and meeting in front of your target market.

MAILING LISTS

There are companies that develop, maintain, and sell mailing lists. They have catalogues you can peruse to find exactly what you want. Mailing-list catalogues are great resources if you realize they usually guarantee an accuracy rate of only 80–90 percent. If you order and mail to 3,000 names, you can expect to get back more than 300 pieces marked "undeliverable," and that doesn't count the ones delivered and then tossed because the addressee is no longer there. In addition, this type of list usually generates only a 1 percent return. If you buy 3,000 names, you can expect about thirty attendees from that mailing. This is not necessarily a negative, just a fact to incorporate into your planning and your budget.

PROBLEMS AND STRATEGIES

PROBLEM: It takes so long to get the program portion of the brochure together that we have time for only one mailing, and that scarely gives attendees time to respond.

Strategy 1:   Market your meeting throughout the year. Include articles in your newsletter; add a tag line to your letterhead announcing the dates, location, and theme; send a "save the dates" mailing focused on the preliminary details.

Strategy 2:   Prepare the brochure as best you can, leaving conspicuous "holes" in the program, and pass it around to in-house people. Maybe you can shame the delinquent people into action.

Strategy 3:   Set your deadlines back several weeks or months.

Strategy 4:   Call weekly meetings for progress reports.

Strategy 5:   Talk to your boss about the problems and try to get a memo or stronger commitment. Unfortunately, the culprits are often top managers, people who typically have other priorities beside your brochure.

Strategy 6:   Within reason, let the delinquent individuals set their own deadlines, then ask them about their progress every day.

PROBLEM: Editing of the brochure is minimal until the final typeset version comes back; then the changes are so major it's like starting over, and it wrecks our budget.

Strategy 1:   To many people, the printed word looks different, even reads different, from the typed draft. If you have this problem, typeset your copy and have people edit that instead of typed drafts. That will add dollars to that budget area, but it may save time. Also, if you keep good records, you can show the costs of copy changes *after* typesetting.

Strategy 2:   Ask your best writer to clean up the copy before you take it to the typesetter.

Strategy 3:   Don't let your program people write copy. It usually isn't sales copy anyway, which is what your promotional materials should be. If you have a highly technical audience that may be acceptable, but think of your audience first, then assign the writing.

PROBLEM: My brochure always looks homemade. What can I do?

Strategy 1:   Spend some money on a graphic design. A good designer can create a professional-looking promotion piece that is not necessarily expensive to print. You may increase your design costs, but you'll reduce your printing costs.

Strategy 2:   Use a "quick-printer." Such photocopy shops are inexpensive, and most can do two-color offset printing with borders and headlines. Many can professionally machine-fold the brochure, too.

Strategy 3:   Explore other options, such as do-it-yourself typesetting companies and proven desktop publishing software systems.

Strategy 4:   Take a look at other brochures and incorporate the elements you like.

PROBLEM: Our mailing lists are never up-to-date; by the time we get the undeliverable pieces back, it's too late to mail a new one.

Strategy 1:   If you are marketing more than once a year, your undeliverables should be corrected immediately. Don't wait for your major conference mailing.

Strategy 2:   Send a postcard asking individuals if they want to continue to be on your mailing list, especially if they have not participated in several years.

Strategy 3:   Tie your computer system to your mailing lists so registration information is used to automatically update old files.

Strategy 4:   Hire a service. This is too important to let fall by the wayside.

PROBLEM: We never get press coverage for our meeting, despite our efforts to get the word out.

Strategy 1:   Invite a reporter to sit in on one of your panels or moderate one of your sessions. That will get the press involved and interested.

Strategy 2:   Carefully review newspapers for at least a week, evaluating their general announcement areas. Most papers have a section devoted to meetings, usually a simple listing with the phone numbers of contact people. Call the paper and ask what you have to do to have your meeting listed and when your announcement must be in.

Strategy 3:   Take a critical look at your topics and speakers. If you can't find anything "newsworthy," your press release will probably be tossed. Politics, the economy, famous people, and the downtrodden (such as homeless people) are areas likely to capture the interest of the press.

Strategy 4:   Call newspapers and try to set up an appointment to discuss each one's criteria, decisionmaking process, deadlines, slow news days, and so on. There are generic deadlines for writing an effective press release, but the best advice is to develop a personal contact within a paper's structure.

Strategy 5:   For nonprofit organizations, explore radio and TV public service announcements. Regulations require that a certain amount of air time be given in these areas. Public service announcements are rarely aired during prime time, but they are free. Give local cable talk shows a call and ask the same questions you asked the newspapers.

Strategy 6:   Talk to the local convention and visitors bureau—it exists to help you. Bureau staff members are usually active in the community, and they should know the people to contact and the type of coverage given to meetings.

PROBLEM: We are on a tight budget. How can we inexpensively produce a good-quality, professional brochure?

Strategy 1:   You can save on mailing costs by utilizing the less expensive bulk mail. This requires a permit fee and you must adhere to very specific regulations imposed by the U.S. Postal Service. The real cost of bulk mail is that it takes up to three weeks for delivery.

Strategy 2:   If you need faster delivery and will be sending brochures out by first-class mail, be sure each piece can be mailed for 25 cents, or within your budget allocation. Even a few cents more can play havoc with your budget, especially if you have a large mailing list.

Strategy 3:   Use free or low-cost items from the local convention and visitors bureau. Those organizations usually have quality promotional pieces on the local area that you can include in your mailing.

Strategy 4:   If you typeset your brochure, save money by reducing changes *after* typesetting. Changes can end up costing more than the original typeset charges.

Strategy 5:   Check paper costs, not only in actual price but for "hidden" costs; some paper types must be scored before folding, which is an additional cost.

Strategy 6: Use standard ink colors. A black-and-white piece can be very dramatic if you spend a little extra on design.

Strategy 7: Send only what you must to promote the meeting. Save information regarding weather, dress, and so on for registrants only.

PROBLEM: From year to year, our attendance is either stable or dropping. What can we do to build attendance?

Strategy 1: Promote the event all year long in regular mailings, newsletters.

Strategy 2: Exploit the special aspects of your meeting, such as spouse and child programs, themes, speakers.

Strategy 3: The best tactic is to evaluate your registration list over the past four to five years and survey the dropouts. A simple but well-worded and well-designed questionnaire should give you some information. You might even do a telephone survey to increase the response rate and to learn more. People will often tell you more in a personal conversation than on a sheet of paper.

Strategy 4: Look at your competition and possible date conflicts. Also look at the economy generally and in your industry and compare against the costs of attending your meeting. Sometimes the answers are obvious with a little research and a little critical thinking.

Strategy 5: You may be in a rut with your program and speakers. If your program isn't current, interesting, and fun, freshen it up and promote your "new look" in your mailings.

Strategy 6: Have you cut the cost of your promotional materials so much that they are ineffective? Reevaluate your budget priorities and your promotional pieces and activities.

8

GRAPHIC DESIGN AND PRINTING

Meetings require a great number and variety of types of printed pieces: promotional pieces, program books, tickets, handouts, invitations, menus, bulletins, registration forms, packets, and badges. Each organization has its own printing requirements and value system in relation to quality and budget. While some printed pieces may use more complicated techniques, such as four-color printing, foil-stamping, or embossing, the basics of printing apply to every item. Remember, such pieces are your primary method of communication and make a statement about your organization. You are projecting an image. You are also trying to interest attendees, exhibitors, and advertisers in participating in your program. The printed materials must be consistent with your organization's image, the audience you are attempting to reach, and the tone of the event. Packaging and use of a theme can enhance the overall marketing process.

If you haven't thought through these issues and the many other design and printing decisions facing you, you are probably falling short of your goals. Even those planners who place a great emphasis on printing must continually evaluate their product against new trends, market changes, and overall effectiveness.

GETTING IT ALL TOGETHER

TYPES OF PIECES

The first step is to make a list of all the pieces you will print. The logical place to start is with your promotional materials. Will there be one, two, or three pieces? What is the purpose of each? Some groups begin with a "save the dates" type of announcement, possibly in a postcard format. The second piece may be to promote the site with general program information. The third might be your detailed program with meeting registration and hotel reservation information. Simultaneously, you must think about your budget and key dates and deadlines.

GRAPHIC DESIGN

Once you know the what, when, and how much, you are ready to sit down with a designer and begin the creative process of design and packaging. To be fully prepared for this meeting, you should know the purpose of each piece, the type of people you are trying to reach, the tone of the event (fun, upbeat, serious, or classy), the theme, logos, and colors you must use, the amount of copy, and your budget. It is also helpful if you have examples for guidance on what you do or do not like.

The decisions you make at this point are going to determine what your final costs will be. Special effects such as embossing, die-cutting, and foil-stamping are expensive. The number of colors increases your costs, especially if you go to a full four-color piece. Other cost factors are paper quality, photographs, finishing techniques (folded, bound, or stapled), and envelopes, if necessary. The printing world is filled with many more opportunities for spending your money than are listed here; these are some of the most common.

Regardless of your budget, the concept-development and design stage is fun. A minimal budget can make the process more challenging and the final product even more interesting. One of my favorite brochures, on brown grocery-sack-type paper, was printed in black ink, using a child's handwriting instead of typesetting, and had a corrugated cardboard cover. This piece won a national award. Other memorable pieces have been done on stark white paper with black ink. If you don't have a big budget, don't be intimidated when you discuss design. Be creative.

You may be asking yourself if you even need a graphic designer. Well, you may not need an expert with the title, but you do need input from someone experienced with printing and with a keen eye for design, whether it is in selecting colors, typestyles, or paper. Many printers offer this service, will work with you, and will do a very good job. But generally I feel that design is critical, and your money is well spent in this area.

THE PRINTING PROCESS

The printing cycle basically begins with rough copy and a rough layout. Once approved, the layout is completed, and after another approval, you move to final art, photography, graphics, and copy. Typesetting and other mechanical tasks should also go through a cycle of proofing, corrections, another proofing, and another approval. This is your last chance for changes before negatives and plates are made.

Next you will translate your print specifications into a bid request from several qualified printers. (This process can actually be started well in advance of final art.) Qualified printers are usually selected based on the type of press they have. A printer that is accustomed to high-volume, four-color work is best for you only if those skills match your requirements. You should request copies of a printer's work on jobs similar to yours. Check references on the quality of work, the service level, dependability, and response time. Find out whether deadlines were met.

It is wise to remember that a printer's bid is based solely on the information you have provided. Any change will change the price. The greatest variable is usually the amount of copy and changes required during typesetting. I've seen people turn down $200 special effects that would have greatly enhanced a piece and then throw away $500 on sloppily prepared copy requiring multiple changes. The more finished the information you give the printer, the more cost- and time-effective the project will be.

The cycle ultimately comes back to you for final proofing and a signature and approval date. The safest route is to check bluelines (or "blues"). This is a copy of the piece after it has been shot (filmed) prior to going to press. If you only proof from the art boards, copy can literally fall off between your office and the studio where plates are shot. The only way to catch that type of error is to proof the blues. But any other changes at that point are expensive, because the plates must be re-shot. The only remaining responsibility for you may be a press check—proofing the piece pulled before the final run. Changes at this stage are considerably more expensive than at the blueline stage, but it is important to check four-color brochures, especially fine-art–quality reproductions where color accuracy is critical.

After materials have been printed and the ink has dried, the finishing begins: trimming, scoring, folding, binding, and special effects. The time frame will vary from one to eight weeks, possible more, depending on the complexity of your project, paper availability, the delays caused by editorial changes and slow approval, and other jobs ahead of yours at the printer's, embosser's, and bindery.

Now you must be prepared for distribution. Will the pieces be individually mailed or shipped to the meeting site? Many large printers and mailing houses offer distribution services, but if cost is a consideration, you may handle the processing internally. Either way, you should have ten file copies pulled and delivered to you. Review the ten pieces for accuracy and consistent quality before you release the order for distribution. Some things to look for are:

- Evenness in ink coverage
- Straightness on the page
- Smudges
- Reproduction quality of photographs
- Straight folds
- Even cuttings
- Secure bindings
- Overall quality of the printer's work and attention to your specifications

DESIGN AND PRINTING TIPS

STYLES OF TYPE

If you have ever looked at a book of type styles, you know the choices are mind boggling. Each type style has a regular, medium, and bold variation, and often each is available in italics. The most common categories of styles are serif, in which letters have flourishes or straight lines at the end of each stroke, and sans serif, in which letters are unembellished. **Serif** provides a more traditional, conservative look; sans serif is more modern, in vogue. In selecting a type style, you should look at a full page printed in that typeface to judge the ease of reading.

PREPARATION OF COPY

Clean copy reduces typesetting errors and costly reset charges. For the best results, copy should be typed on one side of 8½-inch-by-11-inch white paper. Pica or elite typewriter sizes are easiest for the typesetter to read. Allow generous margins, and double space all copy. You should keep handwritten changes to a minimum; when you must make them, write clearly. Most dictionaries have a chart of accepted editing symbols that easily communicate inserts, deletions, transpositions, upper case, lower case, and so on. Consistent use of these marks will help the typesetter understand what you want and will avoid the confusion of using too many arrows, lengthy instructions, and so on. Typesetters will set exactly what you provide, even the typos, so be sure your copy is precisely as you want it. Keep in mind that it is expensive to change copy once it is set in type—changes can add as much as 50 percent to the cost of the job.

PAPER AND ENVELOPES

Paper and envelopes are available in standard sizes and colors, which are more cost-effective than special-order envelopes. Standard paper sizes are:

- Letter (8½ inches by 11 inches)
- Legal (8½ inches by 14 inches)
- Pocket (4 inches, 6 inches, or 12 inches by 9 inches)
- Any multiples of 5½ inches by 8½ inches

Envelope sizes offer more options, especially if a perfect fit is not required, but make sure that the size is one accepted by the post office. Paper is most often selected according to weight, texture, and color. Printers have their own standards for determining paper weight; in themselves they are unimportant, but you will need to use the weight terminology to communicate clearly with your supplier. Cover stock is a stiff, heavier paper often used for postcards, covers, or brochures. If this stock is to be folded, you will have to add a minimal cost for scoring (creasing), which allows the piece to be folded smoothly. Text stock is a medium-weight paper used for the inner pages of a book—usually 50 to 60 pounds, or 70 pounds if two-sided printing is used. Good paper can make an average brochure look wonderful, but select wisely. Does the paper pick up fingerprints easily? Tear easily? Print photographs nicely? Will it survive the mail?

POSTAL REGULATIONS

Before finalizing a design, be sure that the piece can be mailed easily and without additional costs. At the time you are selecting the envelope or designing the self-mailer, check with the post office about mailing costs and about any regulations that would limit the size, shape, or weight of your piece. If you are using bulk mail or enclosing response cards or envelopes with prepaid postage, you will have even more regulations to consider. Correcting oversights in this area can be expensive and time-consuming. Large mailings must be sorted and bunched by ZIP code prior to mailing. A "little" error ordering labels arranged some way other than by ZIP code can take hours for you to sort. Mailing requires a lot of attention in the early planning stage.

MAILING SERVICES

A reliable mailing service is well worth the cost. A good service is experienced in postal regulations and can provide valuable advice if you contact it early in the planning stage. A mailing house prefers to use cheshire labels because they are cut, glued, and applied to the mailing piece by machines. Pressure-sensitive labels will likely be your choice if they are to be applied by hand. Your decision will probably be based on the size of your mailing and the number of pieces that must be inserted.

COLOR SELECTION

Your design can call for anywhere from one-color to four-color process printing. Four-color is used whenever colored artwork, such as a photograph or painting, must be reproduced. The process involved is separation of the artwork into the four basic colors: magenta (red), cyan (blue), black, and yellow. Millions of hues can be created by mixing these basic colors. Cool colors are blues, greens, purples; warm colors are reds, oranges, yellows.

The standard printer's reference to color is by the PMS number, a universally accepted color-identification system. When planning colors, keep in mind that each color doubles the press time and plate charges, which may not be significant unless you are going from one color to four. Certain colors—for example, orange or yellow—can make copy difficult to read and can distort photographs.

SPECIAL EFFECTS

Many special printing effects are available, with prices and time considerations ranging broadly. Screens that reduce the ink coverage in certain areas of copy, creating the illusion of a second color, can be quite inexpensive. A screen of black, for example, would produce gray. Reverses, in which the area around the copy is inked and the copy is left the same color as the paper, are often used in headlines that are boxed or in borders and tabs.

The term "bleed" refers to a more expensive technique that prints ink to the edge of the page. The process requires that the paper be trimmed after printing, which is costly. Another expensive effect is embossing, which raises or recesses the copy. The end result is usually subtle and elegant, especially on textured paper, where the embossed area provides a smooth contrast. Die-cutting is necessary to achieve any unusual cut in the paper or angle, such as when a portion of the cover is cut out to reveal a logo or photograph on the next page. Foil-stamping is an effect similar to embossing in which a metallic look results. In choosing any of these special effects, be guided by your budget and by whether the effect is a necessary design element.

FINISHING

The finishing work is the trimming, scoring, folding, and binding that occurs after printing and before delivery to you. Heavy paper stocks have to be scored for a clean fold. Folds can in fact be a special effect. There are French folds, jaw folds, corner-to-corner folds, short folds, barrel folds, accordion folds, and unbalanced folds. Decisions about folds should be made at the design stage and coordinated with copy placement.

In lieu of folding, you may bind the brochure into a book format. Your options are:

- Loose-leaf binding (as in the traditional three-ring binders)
- Spiral or coil binding (like calendars)
- Saddle-wire bindings (machine-inserted staples in the folded crease)
- Perfect binding (using glue, like a paperback book)
- Sewn binding (the most expensive and least-used type, reserved for high-quality hardback books)

In selecting a binding, consider durability, flexibility in inserting additional pages, the ability to open the piece to a completely flat position, and costs. Other finishing processes include varnishing, plastic coating, laminating, die-cutting, and embossing. (These are also considered special effects, but here the process occurs after printing.)

TYPES OF PRINTING COMPANIES

There are two basic types of printing companies: commercial printers and quick-print companies. Commercial printers offer large-format presswork (from newspapers to posters to brochures), multi-color work, and extensive services—typesetting, graphics, binding—in addition to printing. The capabilities of commercial printers vary depending on their skills and market. Quick-print companies, which are often photo-offset storefront shops, rarely offer more than one or two colors, print small quantities only, and offer limited services. They may do some typesetting, simple layouts, and minimal binding or folding. Either type of company is likely to subcontract parts of your job to specialists, especially for binding, embossing, and foil-stamping.

THE PRINTING BUDGET

Your budget is generally a compromise between your needs and the dollars you have to spend. As a rule, the more complex the design, the higher the price. For example, two-color printing is about 30 percent more expensive than one-color, and four-color can be as much as three to four times the cost of one-color. The fewer different types of pieces you have to print, the lower the costs will be; therefore, combine as much information into one piece as possible. When multiple pieces that are the same size and stock are required, group (gang) them to run together. You'll save on inking and press setup charges as well as optimizing your use of paper. Tickets and badges are ideal gang items. Using standard paper sizes and using the same paper for different jobs can reduce costs.

Instead of perforating the paper, print dotted lines as a cutting guide. The major savings have to do with your own effectiveness: provide clean copy, make minimal changes, plan in advance to avoid rush charges, limit your use of special effects, and obtain firm bids. Mailing costs can be saved by using self-mailers, keeping the total weight per piece within the minimum postal allowance, using bulk rate rather than First Class, and by pre-sorting First Class mail. Your goal should be to save in areas that do not affect the quality and will not risk the potential for a positive response from your market.

PROBLEMS AND STRATEGIES

PROBLEM: Our brochures always have errors, which we don't see until after the brochures are printed.

Strategy 1:   Face it: You (along with many others) are not a good proofreader. Always have a person unfamiliar with the copy proofread for you, and pick someone who is skilled in that area.

Strategy 2:   Recruit a reader to read the original against the final copy. A person looking for typos may miss a dropped sentence or other errors that change the content.

Strategy 3:   Begin with clean copy, and keep the changes to a minimum.

Strategy 4:   Double-check *everything.* Often the worst errors occur on the cover, in headlines, or in other easily overlooked or very familiar places. While typos are bad, printing the wrong dates or misspelling the host organization's name is disastrous.

Strategy 5:   Prepare a proofing checklist. Omission of simple information such as your telephone number or return address can easily go unnoticed, especially if the information was there and later fell off the art board.

PROBLEM: We really have no money, but we want a more professional look than we'll get by typing and photocopying our material.

Strategy 1:   Spend a little more on your paper. A heavier weight and nice texture will upgrade the overall appearance, as will using white or a neutral color.

Strategy 2:   If your order is for 100 or more, ask your quick printer to use an offset printing press rather than photocopying. The cost may even be less.

Strategy 3:   Keep your design and copy simple. Typesetters or quick printers can usually add a simple bold line as a border to create a finished but clean look.

Strategy 4:   Check the price of using colored ink, possibly a color the printer already has scheduled for the press. Smart planning and good negotiations can avoid additional charges.

PROBLEM: We always run out of brochures before the meeting and have to pay for reprinting.

Strategy 1:   The general rule is that the first piece off the press is the expensive one; the rest are yours for just the cost of the paper. Compare the cost of an additional thousand to the reprint costs. More is always better when printing.

Strategy 2:   Be sure your printer is delivering the right amount. Most printers overprint to compensate for errors and test runs. If your printer doesn't, have your bill adjusted or require the cost of reprint to be borne by the printer.

Strategy 3:   Before ordering your printing, update your mailing lists to purge them of duplicates and incorrect addresses. Also, get actual counts on the lists you plan to purchase and include any new target markets.

PROBLEM: Our brochures are never sharp and clean.

Strategy 1:   If your logo is the problem, ask your printer for veloxes of the original in a variety of sizes. These are high-contrast black-and-white proofs, also called PMTs. (Keep in mind too that each time you copy something, you lose some resolution.)

Strategy 2:   Always lay out your art on clean, heavy art boards. The final product will not be better than what you begin with.

Strategy 3:   If you are using a copy machine, be sure the surface under your paper is clean.

PROBLEM: We always have a few items that must be rush jobs. Is there any way to avoid these charges?

Strategy 1:   Negotiate all your printing needs up front, not item by item. The volume may be an incentive for the printer to waive these charges.

Strategy 2:   Carefully plan and coordinate with the printer, especially if rush jobs can be scheduled during normal business hours rather than during overtime hours.

Strategy 3:   Investigate the possibility of using a printer in the meeting city. Often that gives you an extra two or three days and avoids rush charges.

9

REGISTRATION

The bottom-line purpose of registration is to find out how many people are attending. You need to know how many meals to guarantee, how many chairs to put in a room, how many programs and badges to print, how many buses to order, and every other "how many" related to your meeting or event. The goal is, or should be, to get as many attendees as possible to register in advance. If you are charging a fee, you want prepayment as well, to provide operating capital or, if you are in a sound financial condition, investment or interest-earning capital.

In addition to providing an accurate head count, registration serves a variety of other purposes, not the least of which is indicating who was there. Your registration list can generate lists of names, professional affiliations, geographical breakdowns, or types of registrants (guests, students, members, nonmembers). You may also want to know what attendees plan to do during your conference, such as which sessions and special events they plan to attend. You may even want arrival and departure information if you are planning an airport shuttle service.

You must decide well in advance what is related to your event and what your *needs* for the various types of registration information are. This becomes the checklist for preparing your registration form. Because I am a data-oriented person, I consider both what I really need to know now *and* the statistical or historical information I will want for future years. Remember that once your registration forms begin to come in, your major marketing effort is either over or almost over, although the event itself may be many months away.

The registration process is one of your most valuable planning tools and can get your meeting off to a smooth professional start. Just how smooth and professional depends greatly on the value you and your organization place on the process. As a consultant, I've handled registration for a great variety of groups with a wide range of value systems. The biggest messes occur either when there are no policies and procedures or when they are not followed. The result is only as good as the system. You need to schedule cutoff dates for preregistration early enough to let you get your system organized and in place for the transfer to on-site registration. You need to minimize exceptions (I don't like *any* exceptions, but we must be flexible).

One of my recent disasters had to do with the meaning of preregistration. The confusion was the use of the term for both attendees who had registered and paid, as well as those who had registered and *not* paid. The client has now been convinced to use the terms "prepaid" and "nonpaid." One of the problems created by nonpaid preregistrations is that they often don't show up, which throws your numbers off. They also slow up the preregistration line because of the time it takes to process payments, and the procedure becomes confusing to the registrar, resulting in an increase in the error rate. If the number of attendees is small, that may not be a problem, but as the number increases, you have to streamline the system and adhere to the rules.

Finally, but certainly not least important, consider the attendee. If you have never done so, you should try registering sometime. Chapter 10 focuses specifically on attendees' services, but you can't be reminded too often to look closely at attendees' needs and the experiences you create for them. Registration is their first personal contact with the host for this specific event. A negative experience at that point can set the tone for all to follow.

GETTING IT ALL TOGETHER

FEES AND POLICIES

You really need to begin with the previous year. All the data you collected will now be useful. Start with the number of people who registered, and make a chart showing the date mailed or the first day a registration form was received, going day by day up to the last day people registered on-site. For each day on the chart, compute and write down the total dollar amount received and the percentage of total receipts. (Obviously, if you had no fees, skip that section.) Now look at your policies and procedures for registration, such things as cutoff dates, and with a red pen draw heavy lines. You are trying to figure out what impact these rules had on the process. Did it work? Only you can be the judge of whether your organization's goals were met.

As you work through this evaluation you can expand the information, if you have it, to include such things as cancellations, refunds, changes, and walk-ins versus preregistrations. You should also compare interest earned on all early-bird or preregistration money with the higher rates for on-site or late registration.

Incidentally, if your records allow it, don't mix different sources of money. Make a separate chart for money from exhibitors, another for sponsors, and so on. One registration system may work perfectly while the others are a mess. Because you don't want to fix what isn't broken, you have to keep each revenue source separate.

Another impressive exercise is to list every registration exception, if your organization is excessively guilty of those, and next to it indicate the amount that should have been collected. Subtract one from the other and—*Voila!*—you have the total lost revenue for exceptions. You can do the same with your comps. Comps are like credit card charges. You don't think about paying until the bill comes in, and then you can't figure out why it is so high. You, the planner, are as responsible for advising and educating your organization in these areas as the accountant is on tax issues.

You should also figure out the costs per paid registrant—for example, if you have $30,000 in total expenses and 100 paid attendees, then the cost per paid registrant is $300. Then perform this same exercise using total registrations including comps, staff, speakers, everyone. Compare these figures to your fees. This is another way of demonstrating the profit-to-loss ratio. Your boss or board may take a harder look when they realize how much each nonpaid registrant increases the burden of those paying. The ultimate purpose is to make adjustments in your registration fees and process before you market next year's event.

Based on a similar presentation to one of my clients, I recommended a 50 percent increase in fees and a tightening of and adherence to the policies and procedures. Money was tight for their attendees, who weren't wealthy to begin with, but we tried it. My clients had a record attendance and did not receive a single complaint. The fact is, most attendees don't remember what the fee was last year. They look at the current fees, see how much they can save by paying early, and check at what point they can cancel and still get their money back.

Being optimistic, people usually feel in April that by August life will be under control and they can attend a conference. In July, to register for a conference in August may seem impossible. So get to them early with a significant savings incentive, and use their money for five months. Once most people pay and put the dates on their calendars, they attend.

Now that you have your general fees and policies and procedures ready, you can add to your revenue by charging extra for special events, tours, sessions, and so on. Some groups charge a $10 fee for registration processing and an extra $3 to $5 fee for using a credit card. You can add whatever you want to. Rarely does a person see a $10 administration fee (plugged in just above the total line) and decide not to attend. I am not suggesting you gouge your attendees, but be realistic about what your costs are.

PREPARING THE REGISTRATION FORM

In preparing your registration form (and marketing brochure), you need to be especially clear about cut-off dates, cancellation penalties, and refunds. State it clearly both on the form and in the brochure copy that attendees keep. You will have fewer problems down the road if you make the form easy to fill out. If the spouse must complete a separate form, say so directly. Each time you review a form, make a list of what would have made the process clearer to registrants. Look at other forms, evaluate them, and incorporate what you like into yours.

Computers have changed the way many organizations register their attendees. If you have worked on computers, you know it is much easier to coordinate your needs with the computer's capabilities *before* you finalize your system. Even the layout of the form can be organized to help the data entry person.

The time-eaters in registration are the problems that could have been avoided with a well-thought-out system.

PROCESSING RETURNS

Once your mailing is out, you are in the next phase, which is processing the returns. Be sure to keep good records on a daily or weekly basis to measure the success against the past year and to evaluate the effectiveness of new policies and procedures.

Included in registration processing is usually a confirmation letter, receipt, badge, labels, and tickets as appropriate for sessions or special events. You can either mail these to the attendee, distribute them on-site, or use some combination of the two. My preference is to mail the confirmation and have badges and tickets distributed on-site in the conference packet. The number of people being processed may influence your decision. If a preregistered attendee only has to pick up an agenda and badge, you will save yourself time on-site. If you mail all the items, however, you will have to increase your mailing costs, so financially there may not be an advantage.

Also, if you mail tickets and badges you will have to devise a system for handling changes either on-site or in your office. (Whatever you do, you can be sure there will be changes and cancellations.)

The best-planned systems can become disasters on-site, often over what appear to be minor issues. Something as "simple" as whether a purchase order (PO) should be considered paid or nonpaid can cause major problems. Let's assume the PO arrives during the early-bird rate period, but payment isn't received until on-site or after the conference. What rate is in effect? In some ways the situation is similar to a credit card transaction, because you show payment prior to its actual placement in your account. The difference comes in processing. Once the credit card charge has been approved, processing is complete. With the PO, a check will still have to be accounted to the attendee when it comes in. This is the type of issue that confuses the process if you haven't predetermined your procedures.

During registration, be sure you register *everyone:* speakers, VIPs, board members, and staff. This poses another preregistered-versus-prepaid dilemma. Some groups ask speakers and board members to pay the appropriate fees. You will want such people to have professional-looking badges (which are printed prior to registration), but if they haven't prepaid you will have to decide if they are considered prepaid or on-site registrants.

BADGES

There are companies that specialize in badge preparation if you are not computerized. Badges are an important part of a meeting, both as a registration control system and as a way to assist attendees in meeting each other. Attendees appreciate nice, large-print badges, and they will thank you for them. The trend is to have the registrants' first name on the first line, extra bold. That's fine if you ask for a badge name on the registration form, but don't try to second-guess what a person wants to be called. I'm Catherine, but I want to be called Cathie— and that's with an "ie." If you put "Kathy" on my badge, it just won't be me.

The plastic badge holder also has come a long way in the past few years from the old hard plastic and pins to soft with bulldog clips, pocket, strings for skiers, and heat-laminated. One group I know keeps a healthy supply of each and lets the attendee pick among the softcover choices. Now that's service!

REGISTRATION PERSONNEL

Not the least of your concerns is personnel for registration. If you use your own staff, be cautious of their other commitments on-site. If your numbers are large and you can afford it, I suggest you hire local personnel. Convention and visitors bureaus usually offer this service at a reasonable rate and provide experienced workers. Whatever your source, you need to prepare very clear instructions in writing and provide a training session. If possible, get the instructions to the workers several days before the training so that they are not starting out cold.

All workers handling money should have their own cash box and be responsible for balancing their accounts at the end of the shift. Preparing a daily check-out form to be used by registrars may be useful. (See Exhibit 9-1.) Have workers sign in and out if you are paying hourly wages. (See Exhibit 9-2.) Scheduling staff members' time can be a major task. Be sure to consider minimum calls (minimum number of hours of guaranteed work) and overtime (to be avoided), and schedule accordingly.

For large amounts of money, hire a security guard, and assign an accountant to be responsible only for setting up cash boxes, checking out balanced cash boxes, and making deposits. You may need to establish a relationship with a local bank for deposits and transfer of funds to your bank. Or you can call hotel security to accompany you to the safe-deposit box.

The important thing to remember about on-site registration is that you will have to reconcile the records when you get back home. If your system isn't well organized on-site with immediate balancing, you may never figure it out. You are lucky if registration fees are not a part of your process. Those of us who depend on fees to pay for the meeting realize that what is addressed in this chapter is only the tip of the iceberg.

REGISTRATION TIPS

REGISTRATION CATEGORIES

Registration categories serve several purposes. They allow different rate structures, they provide ID categories for badges, and they help in defining your market. This area seems more appropriate to associations than corporations, so you might evaluate your needs against the needs of the attendees. Categories may include:

- Members
- Nonmembers
- Board of directors
- Host committee
- Speaker
- Staff
- Guests
- Spouse
- Supplier
- Exhibitor
- Top producer
- One-day-only events
- Special events

REGISTRATION FORMS

Your marketing piece and your budget may influence the format of the registration form, especially its size and whether it is attached to the brochure or is an enclosure. The general marketing rule is to have few if any separate pieces of paper. (Using self-mailers eliminates inserts.) Place the registration form part of the marketing piece so that the piece isn't destroyed when the form is removed, and so information important for the attendee's future reference isn't returned with the form. Don't provide a postage-paid return card if payment is to accompany the registration form; if you want to make it easy, include a return envelope. The form should have clear instructions and should be laid out in an easy-to-read format. (See Exhibit 9-3.)

If registration is computerized, your form should be designed to expedite the data-entry process. Consistency in organization and code assignments will minimize errors and increase efficiency.

REGISTRATION CONFIRMATION

As a courtesy to your attendees, you should send a letter to all preregistrants confirming receipt of their registration and payment and providing details necessary to their plans to attend the conference. This is a chance to inform registrants about everything from transportation options from the airport to suggested attire for the different sessions, activities, and social functions; it's also a good idea to list the credit cards accepted by the hotel and to provide any other information that will assist them in planning for the trip and ensure their comfort once they arrive. (Review Chapter 10 when preparing this correspondence.) Again, your computer is a great time-saver in generating these letters.

BADGES

Gone are the days of using bulletin typewriters to create badges. Once again, the computer has come to our rescue. The key planning factors to consider in the badge preparation process are the size and imprinted information for the badge card stock, the type of plastic holder, and the process that will be used to create badges for registrants, such as continuous-feed paper.

You should decide in advance about the information and format of the copy. The registrants' information should be the priority, with the sponsor, theme, or registration category secondary. Do a mock-up of the badge exactly as it will be—including the registrants' information laid out exactly as it will appear on the card.

- Will it be three lines or four lines?
- Will "Dr.," "Mr.," "Ph.D.," or other professional titles be included?
- Will company's name, city, and state be included?
- Will departments or divisions within a company be noted?

To save yourself some time and trouble, advise attendees of the information included on each line and the number of characters allowed per line. Let them make the decision. Remember, a computer badge line may fit eighty regular-size characters, but with larger fonts (typefaces), only twenty characters may fit. For this and many other reasons, test your program with maximums. Like everything else, problems are easier to solve early on.

REPLACEMENT BADGES

Attendees are often very casual about wearing their badges, leaving them in the room on yesterday's clothes or losing them. If you view badges as a control mechanism, be aware that a "lost" badge can be worn by anyone, and a non-paying attendee is the same as a free registration. Looked at this way, the replacement cost of a badge can be very expensive. To discourage "loaning'" badges to nonpaying participants and to encourage attendees to keep their badges, many organizations charge a badge replacement fee ranging from $3 to $25. Most attendees will go in search of the badge before they pay the replacement cost. It will not prohibit abuse, but it does discourage it.

TICKETS

Many organizations, primarily associations, require attendees to present tickets at meal functions and often at sessions, if space is limited. Registration is the logical place to disseminate tickets, whether they're mailed with the confirmation or handed out at the on-site registration desk.

If you are using tickets, plan carefully; it's a time-consuming task to put each individual's unique combination together. If you wait until you arrive on-site, the registration process will be measurably slower.

The best procedure is to select a computer system that will print tickets for each registrant's requirements, but you should also look for a system that allows you to color-code tickets for easy identification when distributed on-site. Many organizations attach the tickets to the badge, so there is minimal confusion on-site. You should also have a "ticket-exchange desk" for those who need to make changes in their selections. This ticket-exchange desk is different from the ticket exchange for food functions described in Chapter 12.

REGISTRATION MATERIALS

In addition to a badge and tickets, the attendees will need certain information to participate in the meeting, the most important being the agenda or program book. This should clearly list the title, time, and location of each session. As the meeting grows in complexity, a host of other items are included, making the program book in fact an actual book. Speakers' names and biographical background are usually included. Annual meetings of the larger associations print letters of welcome from local government officials and association VIPs, as well as exhibit floor plans and indexes to the various booths, local maps and points of interest, conference policies and procedures regarding badge replacement, and emergency and safety information. In planning your program book, review Chapter 10 to evaluate the services and information that may be useful to attendees.

Attendees also often receive a list of preregistered attendees showing their affiliations and addresses. Listing office addresses and telephone numbers is usually not a problem, but you might consider adding a line on the registration for attendees to indicate if they prefer not to be included on such a list. This list is not only a valuable networking tool on-site, but encourages follow-up communication after the conference. Because exhibitors will pay dearly for these lists, you may want to promote them as part of your package for exhibitors or sell them after the meeting.

Other registration materials include information about your organization and special conference events; order forms for purchasing tapes of sessions; gifts and promotional items; coupons from local restaurants, stores, and service agencies. Each group has its own value system where these optional items are concerned, but I caution you to handle promotional materials tastefully.

Packaging for these materials ranges from imprinted folders with pockets to three-ring binders, from plastic briefcases to plastic sacks, depending on the budget, volume of materials, and image the sponsoring organization wants to communicate. Usefulness throughout the conference should also be a consideration, especially if materials will be handed out throughout the meeting. From the perspective of a meeting planner who has "stuffed" registration packets, I suggest you use a packaging design that does not make the "packing" and "unpacking" unduly cumbersome. And speaking of "stuffing," you will also have to schedule and plan for personnel to assist with this process and have the people and materials well organized.

ON-SITE REGISTRATION

In planning for on-site registration, you should select a highly visible location. Leave space behind the registration booths for handouts, and be sure there is plenty of room in front for lines to form. Organize the various registration booths and tables according to your registration needs. Establish separate tables for preregistered attendees and for those registering on-site. Within these two prepaid categories, arrange names alphabetically if large numbers are expected. Some conferences may require a separate area for guests, speakers, exhibitors, press, and other large or important contingencies.

There may also be a need for special booths—for tickets, messages, information, which, while not necessarily registration activities, most logically fit into this area of planning because of location and personnel. All registration-area furnishings should be ordered from a decorator. If your meeting has exhibits, use the same firm that sets up exhibit booths (in such cases, the registration-area furniture is often complimentary).

Each area will require personnel who are trained specifically for their responsibilities; often, they are fluent in languages spoken by international attendees. Provide written instructions and conduct a practice session. Again, instructions should be clear, concise, and logical. It is also helpful to provide workers with background information on the sponsoring organization, attendees, program, and a list of frequently asked questions. Personnel should also be familiar with the facility's layout—that is, they should know where restrooms, telephones, restaurants, or meeting rooms are located.

Signs are another important consideration. The more you can anticipate attendees' needs, the fewer questions you will have to answer. Large conferences often place people in the registration area to provide directions and answer questions. Keep in mind that signs on easels will not be visible in a crowded area.

A well-managed registration area will set a positive tone for the meeting to follow and frees you to handle the last-minute details for these events. Hire personable people, train them well, and organize your activities for quick processing. To maintain an "efficient" look throughout the conference, prohibit registration personnel from bringing food or beverages into the registration area.

COMPUTER SOFTWARE

Computer software is available to expedite registration, not only in processing the basics but in reporting, sending confirmation letters, creating badges, and controlling attendance of those not registered. Each year more registration software programs hit the market, and each year they are more sophisticated and more competitively priced. Just remember, there is no perfect program, and a key to selection is the ability to adjust a program to fit your needs. You may also need a hard disk, compatible printers, and training, and you may also have to have your system on site. Look at all the costs, research the options carefully, and exercise good judgment. Be assured, a good program will save you time.

PROBLEMS AND STRATEGIES

PROBLEM: Registration lines are always very long. It seems as though everyone waits until the last minute to register.

Strategy 1:   Provide incentives for early on-site check-in. For example, draw from the names of the attendees who register during nonpeak hours and present the winner with a prize.

Strategy 2:   Reevaluate your registration procedures. Determine how long it should take to process one person in each category, and compare this to the actual time. You may see some delay-causing procedures that you didn't anticipate, such as credit card approval. Even if you can't correct it for the current year, you will at least be better prepared next year.

Strategy 3:   Set up writing counters in the registration lines for completing on-site forms and preparing checks.

Strategy 4:   Add jugglers, magicians, mimes, and other quiet but entertaining acts to keep registrants from getting restless. Another option is showing some of the old silent movies on big screens. Serve coffee and snacks to increase the sociability aspect.

Strategy 5:   Rent take-a-number machines or devise a similar system that allows attendees to move around while waiting.

PROBLEM: I can't get attendees to preregister.

Strategy 1:   Look again at your policies and procedures. If the difference in the prepaid and on-site fees are minimal, there may not be sufficient incentive.

Strategy 2:   Check your cancellation fee; if it is too high, your attendees may not feel it is worth the risk of loss, especially if the difference between prepaid and on-site fees is minimal.

Strategy 3:   Your cutoff date for preregistration may be too early. Be sure it's an incentive and not a deterrent.

Strategy 4:   Check the policies of similar groups and find out what response they receive from attendees. You may find you have a last-minute group.

Strategy 5:   Add an additional incentive—gift, prize, airline ticket—for the 500th or 1,000th person to preregister. If you do this, also add an early-bird prize so that they don't all wait until they think 999 are in. Incentives work well if you think them through so they don't backfire or create a negative feeling.

10

ATTENDEES' SERVICES

The poor attendee—without whom we would not have a meeting—is often the most neglected person in the entire process. Attendees are all too often thought of in terms of numbers and dollars only. Unfortunately, I have been as guilty of this kind of neglect as anyone.

As planners, you have been working on every detail for a year or more. You've burned the midnight oil updating impersonal mailing lists, processing faceless registrations, proofing badges against illegibly written names, thinking of every nonregistered VIP who should be registered. You've prepared promotional materials for attendees, selected meals, ordered room setups, audiovisual equipment, and flowers, and lined up entertainment.

You think you have been thinking of attendees. But have you actually thought about what those people are leaving behind to attend the meeting and what their expectations or needs are upon arrival? Often the in-between time (traveling) is your worst enemy: a flat tire, a cancelled flight, a rude taxi driver, or a long wait to get in a hotel room. This chapter takes a hard look at attendees' needs and other areas that can make their meeting experience a pleasant one or a nightmare. From housing and transportation to simpler services, there are many things a planner can do to make attendees feel more comfortable and at home.

GETTING IT ALL TOGETHER

DETERMINING ATTENDEES' NEEDS

The list of attendees' needs is limitless: Where can a parent find soy milk for a child? Where is the briefcase that someone left in a session yesterday? Why wasn't a reservation form or check received? You hear about all the problems: The room is too hot; the room is too cold; the room next door is too noisy; the room needs more chairs; the room needs more coffee. You want to throw your hands up and scream, but you can't. You also can't fix everything, and you can't please everyone.

What's really necessary is that you try in advance to plan for what attendees will need. You must try to make every attendee feel important, and you must try to be helpful when unexpected crises come to your attention. With the vast array of conferences, services, and products for an attendee to choose from, you may find that you need your attendees more than they need you.

The place to start is with a familiarization (or fam) exercise for attendees. Its object is to prepare a group profile by listing everything you know about your actual or potential attendees.

A questionnaire (see Exhibit 10-1) is useful in this respect and can be sent to attendees prior to the meeting. Provide some incentive for recipients to complete the questionnaire and return it with their registration forms, such as gift subscriptions to trade magazines, tickets for a free drink, or a discount on the registration fee. The questionnaire can cover such things as where they are from; religion; nationality; values; levels of sophistication; level of knowledge or expertise regarding the conference subject; if children or spouses will accompany them; if special diets, handicapped or interpretive services will be needed; if they are used to luxury; and a litany of other things.

But be sure you understand the answers. A hotel once spent a lot of time and money building wheelchair ramps for a conference with handicapped attendees, only to find, upon the attendees' arrival, that they were visually handicapped and couldn't operate the elevators until Braille numbers were installed. Small details can make for big problems.

The next step is to make a list of all possible attendees' needs and expectations. (See the "Attendees' Needs" tickler list in the Quick Reference Guide.) Head Start mothers will likely need child-care services, press will need telephones and typewriters, students may need a quiet study area, doctors might need light boards for comparing x-rays, and your VIP or incentive group will need the "TLC" that goes with their hard-earned reward.

After you explore the unique needs of your group, look at the basics regarding the city, the facility, and the event itself—from the attendee's perspective. These issues may range from the amount of cash or the type of clothing the attendee should bring, to signage to assist in directing attendees to conference sessions.

If you are really thorough, you will make a chart and put a solution beside each of the attendees' needs, expectations, or problems. (See Exhibit 10-2.) The solution may be as simple as providing an information center staffed by a knowledgeable local person, or hiring registration personnel who are fluent in key languages, or instructing door monitors to check the rooms at the end of each session and bring all items to the information center.

Once you have all this information about your attendees, you need to communicate it to those who need to know. In some cases the hotel needs to know. The handicapped-equipped rooms (often limited in number) may not be available to your group if you don't let the hotel know in advance that you need them. If you are counting on the shoeshine service the hotel offers, be sure it isn't closed for renovation during your meeting. If 500 people with second-sight dogs are arriving at the airport on December 8, advise the airport and ground transportation services. If such dogs are charged as a second "person," let the attendees know. Incidentally, if you are inviting visually handicapped attendees, you might consider providing an audiotape in lieu of the traditional printed brochure.

As a conference attendee I've often wished the planner had organized the brochure according to when I needed to read the information: Section 1 would be what I need to read when I'm deciding whether I will attend; Section 2 would present what I need to know to register for the conference; Section 3 would be what I need to know when making my airline reservations; I'd read Section 4 just before packing; I'd read Section 5 as my plane is landing; and so on.

We send attendees a multi-page brochure organized according to some graphic artist's need and wonder why attendees don't use it. We do the same thing with on-site program books. We are all guilty of getting so caught up in the mechanics that we forget the purpose—the attendees. If you think I'm wrong, start asking meeting planners and conference sponsors what the most important part of their meeting is. Most will probably answer camaraderie, and no one really plans for that. If they did, breaks would be longer, speeches shorter, and parties would not be interrupted for awards.

Even when we ask attendees to evaluate the meeting or event, we are asking based on our need to know, not their need to tell. Maybe we can afford this luxury if the return and growth rates are high. But as the competition gets tougher and the attendee gets smarter, our market—attendees—will force adjustments.

HOUSING

Housing is an important aspect of an attendee's needs. Housing arrangements can be handled by your staff, within the hotel, as a service of the convention and visitors bureau, or through an independent meeting management company. Each type has its own policies, systems, and fees. You will have to do some investigating to determine if your budget allows for this service and which system fits your attendees' and organization's needs best.

Encourage your group to make guest/sleeping room reservations early so that they are assigned their preferred room and so that you can evaluate how the system is working. You will need regular reports on the number and types of rooms assigned and to whom they are assigned. You want to be sure that your guest room assignment policy is being carried out.

The larger the group, the more complicated the process, because there may be two or more hotels involved, with different rates and of varying quality as well as different policies for cancellations and changes. You also have to be concerned with guest rooms for speakers, exhibitors, and staff.

Guest/sleeping rooms can be reserved for the attendee in several ways:

- The attendee reserves a sleeping room by mailing to the hotel the completed hotel room reservation card (furnished by the hotel) or form (furnished by the meeting sponsor). The hotel's housing bureau processes reservations from your group and provides you with a housing report.
- A room list is prepared in advance by the planner for staff, VIPs, speakers, and others not responsible for their own reservations.
- The attendee completes a hotel room reservation form at the same time and on the same form used for conference registration and sends it to your office or to an address designated by you. The housing room reservation can be

processed by someone on your staff or by a professional housing bureau whose services you have contracted. A room list is then sent to the hotel.

- The attendee completes a hotel room reservation form and sends it to the housing bureau, which may be a part of the convention and visitors bureau in the host city or a contracted housing firm. The bureau may or may not charge a fee for this service.

TRANSPORTATION

Ground Transportation

There are three commonly used types of ground transportation: buses, vans, and limousines. On special occasions, horse-drawn carriages, antique or classic cars, dealer-sponsored cars with volunteer drivers, ferries, gondolas, or other unique conveyances may be used. Because this is not a book on transportation, the focus will be on buses. Limousines and vans carry fewer passengers and may cost more, but otherwise require the same considerations as buses.

Clearly, transportation becomes more complex as numbers increase and pickup and drop-off locations vary. For meeting planners, transportation may be required to shuttle attendees between hotels and the headquarters or convention center, to special events, on tours, to and from the airport, or for small VIP groups such as a private board of directors party.

Evaluate all your transportation needs by date, departure and arrival times, and staging time. (For purposes of transportation, "staging" or "spotting" refers to the time empty buses arrive at the site to be loaded until pullout time.) If you aren't experienced in this area, take all the information you have and sit down with tour operators or bus companies. As with everything else, talk to several of the best and then use your own judgment.

At some point, you will need to drive each route, stopping and starting exactly as your buses will and at the time of day they will be traveling. Also consider the day of the week; there are big differences between weekdays, weekends, and holidays. Keep in mind local holidays, festivals, and other factors that have an impact on traffic. The day after a local election or Super Bowl, if you're in the winner's home town, can be reason enough for a spontaneous parade.

Bad weather, parades, faulty equipment, and road construction are your worst enemies. With the risk of accident and equipment failure, inspection certificates and insurance should not be forgotten. You also want to be sure a company isn't sandwiching you around their "bread and butter" service contracts. City buses will finish their city routes before they come to your event. I well remember my first busing experience: There were 5,000 people standing on the curb and not a bus in sight. We were waiting for city buses that were casually finishing their rush-hour routes!

Buses are one problem; people movement is another. City streets were not built for loading even 1,000 people at the same time. So carefully think through waiting areas for buses and for people. If numbers are high, you will need a lot of your own personnel, armed with walkie-talkies, for "staging" assistance.

Drivers and guides, if required, can make or ruin a trip. When checking references, ask about personnel, demand the best drivers, and, if at all possible, keep the same drivers throughout your meeting. They get to know your group, and you receive a very personalized service.

Official Airline Services

A number of years ago, the airlines added meetings and conventions to their marketing program. The purpose was to provide an incentive for conventioneers to travel via a particular airline. Thus, meeting planners can offer the added service of a special discounted rate on the airline selected to be the "official carrier" for the meeting. While few meeting planners receive the national attention given to the Olympics and national political conventions, we have the responsibility in many cases for negotiating with the carriers and selecting one and, occasionally, two carriers.

Often the chief criterion is the frequency of flights out of major cities heavily populated by your attendees and into your convention city. The special rate packages are less important when an abundance of discounted fares are in effect. In fact, if attendees can get comparable or lower rates without using your service, you suffer the loss of any complimentary tickets that may otherwise have been earned.

Airline services usually include:

- A percentage off coach fare (may be negotiated to a percentage off the lowest fare available at the time of booking).
- Complimentary site inspection tickets to the association for every 50 tickets sold, also negotiable.
- Usually, one or two complimentary site inspection tickets for the meeting planner to the meeting site (check the restrictions carefully).
- A central 800 reservations number for travel reservations. If you provide the necessary information, operators will provide specialized travel plans according to your program schedule.
- A manifest listing all travelers that booked through the 800 number.

If enough attendees use the 800 number, the airline's report showing arrival and departure times can be the greatest service in alerting you to heavy registration times, peak ground transportation service needs, and necessary meal adjustments for those arriving late or leaving early. However, an official airline service is time-consuming to negotiate, and information about it must be listed in the program announcement, which may be a problem if you are tight on space.

Most association planners use the "official airline" concept if the numbers are sufficient to mutually benefit all involved. Evaluate the benefits to your organization and your attendees, especially if your numbers are in the 400–500 range of expected attendees. The greatest benefit begins at 1,000+ in my opinion. You will know how the people at the airlines rate your potential by the number of telephone calls they return and by their willingness to negotiate.

While an official airline may not be necessary for corporate groups, especially if all attendees are departing from the same city, an airline will usually work with you on a group rate (often lower than the official airline rate) because you can guarantee a certain number of tickets.

ATTENDEES' SERVICES TIPS

HOST COMMITTEES

Particularly for association meetings, host committees are usually very eager to welcome attendees to their city and to assure that they have a wonderful time. Give committee members ribbons or buttons, to make them easily identifiable to attendees. Point out members of the host committee in your preconference materials and at the opening session. Let them help with crowd control and movement, local information, airport greetings—all areas that are hospitality related.

It is to your benefit to get to know committee members prior to making assignments. One person may be very comfortable walking over to a stranger standing alone, someone else may prefer the security of the information booth, and one of your less friendly members may be ideal for enforcing the wear-your-badge rule among attendees.

Once you have made your assignments, discuss them with the respective individuals. Be sure they clearly understand what your needs are and the importance of their task, and ask if that is a comfortable assignment and schedule for them. Volunteers are a precious commodity—but don't just leave them to their own devices.

MESSAGE AND INFORMATION CENTERS

An information booth can provide the answer to a multitude of attendees' questions and problems, especially if you place it in a location easily accessible to the attendee and staff it with helpful, knowledgeable people and useful materials. In addition, the booth can serve as a message center and lost-and-found area. Expanded services might include car rental and airline reservations. It should be equipped with a telephone, message pads, pens, local maps, restaurant guides, general tourist information, and general conference information.

This is an ideal responsibility for a local host committee, if you have one. Otherwise, the convention and visitors bureau will often provide personnel. This cost is minimal, even complimentary in some cities. Prepare written instructions for booth personnel, but ask for advice. You may benefit from their past experiences.

PUBLICATIONS CENTERS

A publications center, also offering souvenirs of sponsor-imprinted items, is a service many attendees appreciate. It can also be a revenue producer for the organization. If you do get into the retail business, you must fulfill state and local requirements for the collection and payment of sales tax.

If you don't want to get into the sales issues, but want to enhance the educational value of the conference, set up a resource area or center for displaying appropriate publications related to your industry. Items in the center may be provided by your organization or attendees may be invited to contribute outstanding examples of their work.

SIGNS

When planning your signs, take a walk around and evaluate the need, placement, format, and safety issues. If you have large crowds, you may need to place signs up very high—even hang them from the ceiling! It is not inappropriate to consider signs on sticks held high above the crowds. The point is, if you need signs, be sure they are useful to those for whom they are meant. Hotels and convention centers are more frequently adding small signs outside meeting rooms to identify the group or session. They serve small groups well and eliminate the hazard and unsightliness of easels. TV monitors recessed into the walls will ultimately provide electronic signage for our meetings. I welcome the demise of cardboard signs on unsightly easels.

It is also important to consider the size of lettering on signs. The Quick Reference Guide for this chapter provides guidelines.

INFORMATION FOR ATTENDEES

Attendees are significantly less experienced with the conference agenda, facility, policies, and procedures than you are. It is important to have informative, well-designed materials. This information can be in one major piece or in several mailings timed to meet the attendees' need to have the information. It is appropriate to repeat the information in on-site materials as well. If you review the attention spans and retention levels discussed in Chapter 2, you may find it useful in developing your materials.

Be creative in your organization and format. People are much more likely to read a section titled "The Ten Most Frequently Asked Questions about This Meeting" than one called "General Information."

Many planners provide first-day orientation sessions and, more frequently, first-timer sessions for attendees. This level of consideration to attendees is notable. But even here you don't want two or three boring speeches. Have small groups at round table with a "host" to discuss the conference and identify its goals, the agenda, registration procedures (if they haven't yet registered), attire, transportation, hotel floor plan, location of sessions, or local (nearby) activities. This is also a great opportunity for newcomers to meet others in the same situation.

The goal is to make attendees feel so comfortable and secure that they will come back next year.

TAPING OF SESSIONS

Technology has added a great service—audiotapes of sessions. Soon, videotapes of presentations will be available. This is one of the few services that can also become a profit center with little effort on your part. If this interests you, contact a professional taping service (the hotel or the audiovisual company may be able to refer you). If you can show the company a good potential for sales, they will tape the sessions at no cost to you and impose minimal requirements—such as a comp room for staff and a table prominently placed for sales—and then give you a percentage of the sales. It can be mutually beneficial to the attendees, sponsors, and company producing the tapes.

SPECIAL SERVICES FOR SPECIAL PEOPLE

Every meeting has a variety of special attendees—the officers, board of directors, speakers, special guests, honorees, award recipients, high government officials, press, and, don't forget, the staff. Each of these deserve some special considerations and each organization should decide how to treat them personally or as a group. But of critical importance is this group's need for more detailed briefings on the meeting functions, the location of rooms, restrooms, time of appearance, and introductions to other very important people. Put a special ribbon on their badge so everyone knows they are a very important part of the event.

A personal welcoming note is an inexpensive, but appreciated, touch. If your budget allows, have refreshments, flowers, or a small gift put in their rooms. Be particularly attentive to VIPs' personal preferences; for example, don't serve wine to a person who objects to alcoholic beverages.

If complimentary rooms are available, provide them to special guests, or upgrade their rooms to suites. Certainly, meals should be provided if they are your guests. Also, tactfully let them know whether there are restrictions on what they may spend or how they may travel. If possible, provide airport pickup, greeting them at the gate and assisting with luggage and hotel check-in. It is wise to "advance" the entire trip from pickup to actual delivery to their room, so that you do not lead them down a wrong corridor or find their room dirty or, worse, occupied.

For groups like the press, individual treatment may not be appropriate, but amenities such as additional typewriters, telephones, and coffee will make them feel welcome. An extra touch might be small press-size notepads with your logo imprinted on the cover. Members of the press attend conferences hoping to conduct interviews with VIPs and get an edge on newsworthy stories. Their goal is rarely to promote your organization, so don't expect the unreasonable. Supplement their press kits with newsworthy information that is correct and easy-to-use information should it be needed.

Staff are special people, too, and often the last considered. A few extra perks, such as nice rooms, coffee and snacks in the staff office, and a little personal time will keep them refreshed without guilt—and they won't have to fight attendees for a cup of coffee during the breaks.

HANDICAPPED SERVICES

Always give your attendees an opportunity to indicate their handicapped requirements, and respond to them on a personal, direct basis. There are excellent articles that will guide you in anticipating their needs. Especially in the site-selection process, your handicapped attendees should be considered. (Refer to Chapter 4 for more details and for specific resources.)

CHILDREN'S PROGRAMS

You may know little about children—why they cry, when they sleep, what goo-goo-ga-ga means, how to change diapers, how to get little arms through miniature sleeves, what they eat, or why parents want to bring them to meetings. But some parents do, and help should be provided.

If your program includes child care, consider insurance requirements; facility requirements; personnel licensing (sitters and nurses); laws (local, state, national); equipment (with a sharp eye to safety); food and beverages; children's allergies, health problems, and medications; releases and waivers; and a host of other issues. Properly done, this is an expensive program and one from which you are not likely to recover your costs.

Child care is somewhat like liquor service—the liabilities are great. Be sure you have every parent sign a release and permission form for you to approve medical treatment if needed. (See Exhibit 10-3.) And have your attorney review the wording of both. There is nothing more precious to parents than their child.

Aside from child care, special programs for children will be appreciated. Children love activity, so the best children's programs are filled with recreation and play. Sports such as tennis, golf, bicycle rides, and other noncontact sports are good for girls and boys. Tournaments are excellent and ensure everyone has a chance to get involved. Tournaments also have prizes and children will definitely like that. Children also love to eat, and an inexpensive trip to the pizza parlor will keep them entertained for hours. Pizza parlors and other youth-oriented restaurants are often filled with video games, so beware of the potential for the quick disappearance of money if this is available. (I recommend avoiding video games unless they're in a tightly controlled environment.) There are also excellent museums of particular interest to children and specialists in dealing with children are usually available to keep the experience interesting.

For the younger child, such activities as puppet shows, an art or coloring contest, or easy craft activities are appropriate. Remember, little ones tire easily and will need a nap and some snacks.

PROBLEMS AND STRATEGIES

PROBLEM: Before we even see our attendees, they are frustrated because they can't check into their rooms for several hours.

Strategy 1:   Provide a hospitality room for early check-ins. Set up refreshments and perhaps a video on the city or a first-run movie.

Strategy 2:   Post the hotel's check-in and check-out hours next to the travel information section of your brochure. If early arrivals can't be avoided, at least people will be aware of the potential wait.

Strategy 3:   Offer an early-bird shuttle to major attractions and shopping or a tour of the area for early arrivals.

Strategy 4:   Negotiate with the hotel, prior to signing the contract, to add extra housekeeping personnel on your major arrival day, especially if it is another group's major departure day.

PROBLEM: Some attendees have unrealistic expectations.

Strategy 1:   When you list the services you do provide, include a list of those you don't provide.

Strategy 2:   Suggest that attendees with special needs consult the hotel concierge to see whether the facility provides that service.

Strategy 3:   If you have a lot of certain types of request, set up a VIP service desk and charge attendees for special personal arrangements such as child care, limousines, dinner reservations, theater tickets, hair or nail appointments.

Strategy 4:   If it isn't legal, don't do it!

PROBLEM: Emergency calls for attendees are delivered to the conference officials and we are unable to locate the attendee.

Strategy 1:   Always advise the hotel switchboard to leave messages in the attendee's room.

Strategy 2:   Conference materials and on-site announcements should clearly advise attendees that emergency messages are treated the same as any other messages. They must check the message board!

Strategy 3:   Have the message center ask if it is a death or life-threatening situation. If so, advise conference officials to watch for the attendee.

Strategy 4:   Use good judgment and don't overreact. An emergency to one person is a daily crisis to another.

PROBLEM: Attendees make their plans late and then want exceptions to the rules.

Strategy 1:   For VIPs, plan for exceptions, especially as requested by your boss or corporate officials.

Strategy 2:   For the masses, stick to your rules. Word spreads, and if you aren't careful, exceptions will become the rule.

Strategy 3:   Evaluate exceptions on a case-by-case basis. Some are easier to handle than others.

PROBLEM: Are there special touches that can make our meeting more memorable to attendees?

Strategy 1:   Gifts and mementos for attendees provide a lasting memory. There are companies that specialize in gifts with personalized logo and themes.

Strategy 2:   Hotels will happily deliver gifts to attendees' rooms—for a price. Logo cookies, fortune cookies with conference-related fortunes, or any such item will put a smile on your attendees' faces.

Strategy 3:   Certainly, special theme parties and unusual events, if you truly allow your group to have fun, are great opportunities for memories.

Strategy 4:   One group opened with a game—a scavenger hunt—to help attendees get to know the hotel. Participants were divided into teams, so new friends and a competitive spirit were fostered. A comfortable feeling about the hotel and cocktails brought everyone back together.

Strategy 5:   Good food, good friends, and a good program can be all you need, especially if you create a warm, sincere environment.

Strategy 6:   Think about your past memorable experiences and ask others about theirs. What was your most memorable event or conference? What made it memorable?

11

SPECIAL EVENTS

Everyone loves to have fun, and special events can and should be fun both for the attendee and the event planner. Not all meetings have a special event and not all special events, like fundraisers or company parties, are tied to a meeting. However, whether they are together or separate, they require the same skills.

What are special events? They are gala dinners or receptions, theme parties, sporting events, creative breaks, dances, tours, special programs, performances. They take the ordinary and make it extraordinary. They may have decorations, unusual locations, entertainment, unusual menus, creative themes, special transportation, gifts or prizes, surprise appearances of celebrities or robots. The sky is the limit. (Actually, the budget is the limit, but you can still be creative.)

The fact is, much of the planning for meetings and special events is routine and tedious. You are dealing with a myriad of details that you plan, follow up, check, and check again—and you'll still wake up in the middle of the night thinking of one tiny but critical detail that you will check on again in the morning. Creativity is the ingredient that keeps projects exciting and fresh and will definitely help you avoid burnout.

Now that we've established the importance of this area for the planner, let's think about the attendee. Regardless of what other experts may tell you, the attendee comes to your meeting for "people interactions." After people attend meetings, they remember the western party at a local dude ranch, the surprise of dragging out of the last session to find a Mexican theme break, complete with margaritas, the opening session's multimedia extravaganza. Those are special events in my book, just as much as tours, spouse or companion programs, tennis and golf tournaments.

Special events are necessary to loosen up and lighten up attendees so they can interact on a real person-to-person level.

GETTING IT ALL TOGETHER

First you begin with an idea or several ideas, and then, unfortunately, most of us have to look at the budget. Is it affordable? If not, how can we adjust the idea to make it affordable? Then you look at the attendee and the organization: You probably don't want a margarita break for teetotalers or a three-hour bus trip for five-year-olds. But don't try to second guess your audience either. In years past, for instance, I would have said not to have a dance for sufferers of *spina bifida*. But recently I was in a hotel hosting their international convention and the hotel lounge was filled with attendees in wheelchairs; so was the dance floor, from the youngest to the oldest. They were having a great time.

Once you have matched the idea, budget, and people, you are ready to develop the idea into a structured plan. What will it take to pull this off? You are back to the basics of meeting planning: site selection, catering, transportation, decorations, entertainment, insurance, repeal of city ordinances, themes, costumes, lighting, sound, security, licenses.

From a management perspective, you also have to evaluate the reality of the lead time available to plan the event and the actual planning hours needed versus the time your staff can commit. It is the thoughtfulness of these early plans that will determine the ultimate success.

And remember, you are not alone. In this age of specialization, you have a wealth of "experts" in every area. Professional meeting and special events companies, because they plan these events routinely, can oversee all or a part of your event and will advise you of opportunities and pitfalls. You will also find suppliers of services expert in their individual areas. A bus company will help you in routing and scheduling, a decorator can help you with space requirements and setup times, and a golf pro can help you structure a tournament. (See also the extensive transportation guidelines given in the Quick Reference Guide for this chapter.)

You also must do your own homework by talking to other planners who have conducted similar events, by reading related articles in professional publications (see the Resources at the end of this book), and by checking the references of all suppliers.

Finally, in getting it all together, don't rush or make hasty decisions. The highly creative people you will be working with are all too often high strung and demanding. Hold on tightly to your money, put everything in writing, and give yourself time to carefully think through *your* needs; don't be trapped by *their* needs.

SPECIAL EVENTS TIPS

THEME DEVELOPMENT

Themes have been developed for almost every imaginable area. Here are just a few:

- Ethnic themes
- Movie themes
- Negative themes (such as a very successful annual dull party theme)

- TV themes
- Storybook themes
- Historical themes
- Motivational themes
- Geographical themes
- Sports themes
- Seasonal themes
- Holiday themes
- Way-of-life themes
- Animal themes

- Mystery themes
- Transportation themes
- Futurist and space themes
- War themes
- Political themes
- Color themes
- Costume or dress themes
- Personality themes
- Food themes
- Current events themes
- Hollywood themes

Themes can be a very powerful and a memorable experience, or they can be a disaster. If a theme involves attendees' participation with either costumes or games, the risks are higher. In such cases (more than ever) you need to know your attendees, and often it's best to have attendees sign up in advance. Most people are willing to accommodate requests such as "black tie," "casual," or "western wear," but they might draw the line at dressing up as Queen Victoria or a favorite rock star. (Incidentally, waitpersons in costume are quite acceptable.) If you insist on having attendees in costume, hire a local costume company to set up a rental room at the hotel.

On the other hand, everyone appreciates creativity, especially new ideas or a new twist to old ideas. The interaction that takes place among attendees at well-planned, well-executed theme events makes them worth the time, effort, and expense.

SITE SELECTION

Meetings are primarily held in hotels and convention centers. For special events, site possibilities, in addition to the meeting facility, are the world at large. Sites can be in open fields, at public buildings, parks, zoos, museums, on trains or planes, on city streets or waterfront docks, at glamorous stores, and any other place you can think of.

Hotels offer the fewest problems because of their full-service orientation, but attendees often enjoy a change of scenery. Off-premise locations usually require transportation, rental fees, security or off-duty policemen, insurance certificates, and special liquor licenses. For outside locations, generators or other electrical power sources may be required, as well as a tent or back-up rain location, portable toilets, and additional laborers for cleanup. In public buildings, there are often ordinances that do not allow the sale of liquor; therefore expenses may increase for host bars.

Convention bureaus, special events companies, decorators, caterers, and bus companies have broad knowledge of the local area and its accompanying requirements. Local committees are helpful but are not normally as familiar with the less obvious options.

Themes often influence the site selected for a special event, so have your idea in mind first if the theme is most important. Otherwise, you may select the theme based on local opportunities. Either way, some guidance is important, such as formal versus informal; budget; dancing, entertainment, or foods as the focal point; time of year; size of group; male/female mix; age mix; time schedules.

There is always the chance that you will be the first to use a particular site for a party, but if others have gone before you, call them. It's always good to know what's ahead of you.

CATERING

You will make a big mistake if you presume that an outside caterer is similar to a hotel food-and-beverage department. Caterers' kitchens are set up at the event site; the food has been pre-cooked and transported in warming ovens. In some cases, running water is not even available. This requires different skills, different equipment, and different food-ordering on your part. If the event requires delicate handling of food, have a test meal at the site with food preparation exactly as it will be for your event, including transporting it in the truck or warming oven. (This can take place anywhere from three to twelve months before the event.)

From city to city there is also a great variance in equipment owned by a caterer. In some cities, a caterer's bid includes everything down to the napkins and silverware; in others, you will be charged one price for the meal and an additional price of almost equal value for rentals. There may also be an additional charge for personnel, including the chef. You must have the caterer itemize everything in the bid; take nothing for granted.

With caterers it is important to visit the kitchen. Some excellent caterers work out of their homes. I have seen beautiful, spotless kitchens, and I have also seen kitchens with cats perched on the cutting counters. (Actually, the one with the cats had been given the highest recommendations, so sometimes you need to do reference checks on the references—be sure your references have the same standards you do!)

Personnel training and cleanup procedures should also be discussed. You can learn a lot from an honest discussion with a respected hotel food-and-beverage director, and from a meeting with the best caterers in your city. They will all try to sell you on their own uniqueness, often highlighting the flaws of their competitors. Experience is the best teacher, so learn from the experiences of others tempered with your own good judgment.

Don't forget the legal and insurance issues. A caterer should be licensed as a business and have a health department certificate. It should also carry a general liability policy. (See Chapter 16 for more on liability.) If mention of these items brings questioning looks, move on. One exception to caterers' liability coverage is the trend toward requiring the party host to carry liquor liability. Most service companies require the host to purchase the liquor, although they will handle ordering, delivery, and bar service.

SPORTING EVENTS

Knowing a sport does not qualify you to set up a tournament. You are the expert on your group, especially as it relates to number of participants, time scheduled for the event, and general skill level of players. But a professional in the planned sport, with experience in setting up tournaments, is a critical ingredient. The pro will assign handicaps, pair players, set up start times and scoring procedures, arrange for judges, ball chasers, caddies, equipment, etc. Of course, you should be involved in setting the tone (serious or fun), selecting prizes and giveaways, preparing a budget, arranging transportation, ordering food and beverages, registering attendees, and providing final court and player information. You should require that players sign disclaimers if health problems exist or safety is at risk. The pro and/or the resort should be certified and insured. But remember, any official event of your meeting places you, at a minimum, in a third-party liability position. As the risk increases, so should your insurance.

COMPANIONS' PROGRAM

The part of your program that has gone from being called a wives' program to a spouses' program, and now to either a guests' or companions' program, has evolved from consisting of primarily women-oriented activities (shopping, luncheons, teas, fashion shows, cooking classes) to gender-neutral events with more emphasis on enrichment. Actually, we should forget the companion's relationship to the attendee and just provide an open track of activities labeled the "enrichment program." This would allow attendees and guests both to switch from professionally related topics to personal growth and "see-the-city" topics and tours.

Women still outnumber men as guests at conferences, and there are still women who like to cook and shop. Even men registrants sometimes cook and shop. My point is, don't take all presumed women-only activities out of your program; just add variety and balance.

Conference planners should consider whether they want to encourage guests (both adults and children) to attend. If their attendance is desirable, keep this group in mind during site consideration (city, meeting space, room rates), and as you develop and prepare promotional materials, plan your budget, compute total numbers, conduct registration processing, and establish a fee structure—essentially, as you make all your plans.

A local committee or professional company can be a great asset, but the planner should not abdicate control. This is as much a part of your meeting as anything else. An unhappy guest can cause more trouble than fifty attendees, especially if that guest is the president's spouse! Take a fresh look at the whole program. The best tactic may be to involve your attendees with guests, balancing genders, ages, and years of attendance to recommend an alternative agenda. Whatever you do, ask a lot of questions of a lot of people and evaluate your end product.

PHOTOGRAPHY

You will definitely want a photographer for special events. Photographs are wonderful additions to a newsletter and scrapbooks, and often are treasured gifts for attendees. The type of photographs range from formal posed studio-type pictures, to candid action shots. For gifts, theme photos can be taken, such as the old tintype with guests in western costumes or against theme-oriented backdrops representative of the event site.

Associations often sell the photographs, posting ordering time and information on a bulletin board for attendees. Corporate functions more often use the photos for gifts. In either case, you should have file copies of the best photos for your organization's own internal use.

Regardless of the purpose, you need to carefully select photographers to be sure of their ability and experience as related to your needs. You should check prices, development time, and the product you will receive. If pictures are taken throughout the entire meeting, it's a good idea to request contact sheets so you can pay only for developing those prints you want. The Quick Reference Guide for this chapter sets forth guidelines for selecting a photographer.

PROBLEMS AND STRATEGIES

PROBLEM: How can we guard against excessive alcohol consumption?

Strategy 1:   The trend today is to have a cash bar at all functions, even if the proceeds are designated to a charity. At dinners, complimentary wine is limited to two to three bottles per table; after that, payment is requested. It is also possible to offer mineral water or no- or low-alcohol-content beer and wine.

Strategy 2:   Legally, you are in a greatly reduced liability situation with a cash bar or limited number of drink tickets issued per person. Facilities and caterers reduce their liability by using 1-oz. pours (something you should require if it is not already their practice). It is not inappropriate to designate nonalcoholic bars when traditional cocktails are served *sans* alcohol.

Strategy 3:   Activity and food reduce the impact of alcohol on the system, so plan activities such as dancing, and don't skimp on the food.

Strategy 4:   The final caution is to be observant, even to the extent of placing monitors at the doors to assist attendees or find alternative transportation if they are driving. Fortunately, there is an increased awareness about the dangers of alcohol, but a good party is a ripe environment for slipping into old habits. Thoughtful planning and keen observation are your best weapons.

PROBLEM: But it never rains this time of year. . . .

Strategy 1:   Never think that it won't rain, sleet, or snow. If weather can ruin your event, always have a backup location.

Strategy 2:   Don't rely on the weather forecaster. Use your own judgment and make a decision early enough to set up the new location and to advise attendees.

Strategy 3:   Check the seasonal and historical weather patterns. Morning rain in Portland may sock you in for three days, while on a coast you may have frequent but light showers. It rarely snows in June or September in Colorado, but it can and has. Weather patterns change quickly in the mountains, near water, and on islands. It's wise to also know a little about hurricane, tornado, and monsoon seasons and movement patterns. While you are facing an issue that falls into the "act of God" category, a little research can provide a likely/ unlikely guide in the preplanning stage. Don't forget about wind (which can be more miserable than rain), excessive heat, or evening chills.

Strategy 4:   Dressing properly can minimize the excessive heat effects and evening chills, but only if your attendees are advised and come prepared. Suggested attire is always a courteous inclusion in promotional materials, even down to the shoes if the flooring or terrain is unusual.

PROBLEM: The music was great, but no one danced.

Strategy 1:   Try to match the music to the taste and experience of your group. If the group is slow starting, hire professional dancers for the first few numbers and then have them select partners from the audience to join them. Be sure to preselect and ask audience participants so they are not embarrassed and are willing.

Strategy 2:   If you want to deliberately mismatch the music (e.g., country and western) and the audience, you had better have an adventurous group. Then hire dance instructors to teach them the basics.

Strategy 3:   Hire a music group or orchestra that plays music you can dance to and one with a leader that relates to the audience. Again, check references. Here, as with any entertainment, you have to personally preview the performance, oversee flow of the show, and approve the exact music planned for your event.

PROBLEM: How can we find entertainment to please everyone?

Strategy 1:   Avoid the obvious ethnic, sexual, political, or religious offenses.

Strategy 2:   Preview all entertainment and require a moment-by-moment, word-for-word script. Most entertainers operate from a script, so this shouldn't be difficult. Have the script reviewed by several key people in your company or organization.

Strategy 3:   Do not let the local arrangement committee select the entertainment. They may make recommendations, but it is much harder to reject their selection than to maintain control. The danger is that you will have a messy political problem and a bad show.

Strategy 4:   You often get what you pay for. If you have a limited budget, don't spend it on a comedian—that's too risky. Instead, use a professional or semi-professional dance group or musicians, possibly even from local schools or colleges.

PROBLEM: We can't offer special events, but is there anything we can do to add zip to our meeting?

Strategy 1:   Theme breaks or even different foods at breaks can add a special touch. In the morning, you can offer an egg-based entrée, sausage biscuits, pigs in a pancake, fruit kabobs, yoghurt, or whatever can be picked up easily. Look at the hors d'oeuvres menu for ideas such as mini-quiche. These items usually cost no more than danishes, but they add a little flair. In the afternoons, you might have a chili break, ice cream sandwiches, hot dogs, popcorn, or granola bars. Save the dessert from lunch and have a dessert bar. Add a few carts for food and you have a mini-special event.

Strategy 2: If you keep your eyes open, you will find inexpensive novelty items to incorporate, such as robots that can be "set loose" during the break. Or, you can add an aerobics session just before the break. If your audience is fashion conscious, have a local department store host a male/female fashion show. Think of your group and plan a surprise!

Strategy 3: One group with no money held the "First Annual Dull Party," which was great fun and had a big turnout. Despite the cash bar, cheap hors d'oeuvres, and only an inexpensive DJ to liven things up, the evening was a huge success.

PROBLEM: Special events lose their momentum when the speeches and awards begin.

Strategy 1: If you must have speeches and awards, keep them to no more than five minutes each and thirty minutes total. Have all presentations and acceptances scripted.

Strategy 2: Hire an expert moderator, possibly a local TV personality, who is accustomed to keeping a program moving along and will interrupt when necessary.

Strategy 3: Tie the speeches and award presentations to your theme and make it a legitimate part of the evening.

12

FOOD AND BEVERAGES

If meetings exist that do not have some food and beverages, they are rare. Meal functions provide the opportunity for networking, social interaction, general recognitions, awards, and a badly needed mental break from the intensity of the formal program. If you have read Chapter 2 on program design, you already know these breaks are an integral part of the program and enhance the learning process. Also keep in mind that your attendees do have to eat, and if your programs are scheduled as tightly as most, there isn't time for them to eat in public restaurants.

Creativity in this area can add greatly to the meeting experience and is usually a boost to the attendees' attitudes. Chefs and planners keep a watchful eye on food and eating trends. And, I'm happy to report, creativity in this area doesn't have to break the bank: granola bars, fresh fruit, and herbal teas are no more expensive than danish, juice, and coffee. Today, breaks tend to be healthier, lunches are lighter, and seated dinners are fewer, with activity-oriented special events increasingly popular.

As you read through this chapter, try to visualize your meeting without food and beverages, with the traditional functions, and then with some of the fresh new food ideas and themes. You can almost feel the ambiance of the meeting change. With that in mind, be assured that these food-and-beverage events are very necessary to a successful meeting.

GETTING IT ALL TOGETHER

NUMBER AND TYPE OF EVENTS

The cost of food-and-beverage functions is usually included in the meeting budget and often can be recovered when registration fees are collected. The number and type of events included vary, as do the costs. Among your first decisions is identifying those functions that will be included as an official part of the conference. The most common for each conference day are lunch, two breaks, and a continental-type breakfast. Over the entire period of the conference, many groups have a reception and a dinner. There is no right or wrong scenario. One should also consider the social interaction that occurs during meals, theme opportunities, keynote presentations, recognitions, awards, and other features that enhance the broader meeting objectives. An additional key consideration is whether there is time or space for attendees to use nearby public restaurants.

Simultaneously, you must think in terms of your budget. Corporate budgets are usually more lavish than associations', which must recover costs in fees from attendees. This is the only boring part of this chapter, because once you have made these basic decisions, you are on the road to creative implementation.

Whether you are a planner with a limited budget or one who cares little for value for the dollar spent, you must be very cautious and realistic in making your decisions. You must carefully review menu prices, consider increases if prices are not guaranteed, and add an automatic 20–25 percent for tax and gratuity. While taxes and gratuity vary from state to state and property to property, you may be assured they are going up, not down. If you are tax-exempt, you may only have to add 15–18 percent for gratuities, but, again, be sure your tax status is accepted in the city or state of your meeting.

TYPE OF FOOD

Food is another of those areas where you really need to know your group. While the trend is toward lighter meals, there are still meat-and-potato lovers, ethnic and religious considerations, and age and diet factors. Because food is culturally and socially so important, consideration given to group preferences is well worth the research.

Along with food comes the mood issue. Chicken Breast Chaucer seems so right for the basic seated lunch, while a lunch pail filled with sandwich, fruit, and a cookie is perfect for a stroll through the exhibit hall or a walk to a nearby park. Vary breaks from the traditional coffee, soda, and cookies by setting up a place to make your own ice cream sundae. A tray of hot biscuits with wonderful jellies is more creative than a tray of danish (and it's fresher!). Chefs are clearly becoming more interested in personalizing their menus, but it's the responsibility of the planner to initiate the discussions. Hotels still have "bingo menus," where you order B-4 (breakfast number 4), L-23, or D-18. It is your choice whether you call a number or create.

The best approach is to let the catering coordinator know what your budget is, either for each event or the total amount for the conference, along with the number and type of events you want to have. Discuss the preferences of your attendees, your ideas, and ask the chef to propose options that would be possible within your budget.

Timing can also be an important consideration. Often for breaks I want foods that can be quickly picked up. For example, fruit kabobs are quicker and easier than sliced fruit on a tray, which requires attendees to fix their plate before moving on. Similarly, making an ice cream sundae takes longer than picking up an ice cream sandwich (but if you have time and space the sundae is more fun).

GUARANTEES

Once you have decided on your menus and confirmed your prices, you will begin to think seriously about guarantees. For those unfamiliar with the term, the guarantee is the minimum number of meals you want served and will have to pay for. Once you have set your final guarantee, usually twenty-four to forty-eight hours in advance of the function, you cannot lower the number. But you can increase it as long as there is food to serve and space to seat people. The chef will advise you of the outside limit if you ask. In addition to your guaranteed number, most hotels have an "overset" policy of 3–10 percent (usually 5 percent). This means that if your guarantee is for 100 people or meals, the hotel is prepared to serve 105. You are only obligated to pay the guaranteed number, unless the actual number served is higher.

Because meals are expensive, the professional planner takes the process of guaranteeing very seriously. Records are kept of the total attendance versus the average number of attendees attending food events. If only 90 percent of your attendees traditionally attend meal functions, you can save 10 percent by adjusting your guarantee to more closely reflect your group's participation level. Some planners additionally reduce their guarantee by the percentage of the hotel's overset. In the example above, it would be by a total of 15 percent. As you are playing the number game, you should also consider the weather (more people may stay if the weather is bad or may leave if the weather is good), placement in the program (early check-outs on last day), and the availability of other restaurants, shopping, and diversions.

I hate to call it a game, but it is a numbers game. As in any other game, experience pays, and knowing your group's history is critical. The prize is a considerable savings in your budget, minimal waste, and few empty seats, which is good for your organization's image.

As you move around the function, you should take a count for your own records and to compare to the hotel's count. With regard to the bill, many hotels will present the check at the end of the function. Not only is this in poor taste, but it places a difficult burden on you to review the bill when you may be preoccupied with more pressing responsibilities. You should arrange to have all checks held until later in the day when you can focus your attention on the review of numbers, prices, and total charges.

Once you sign the check, it goes to accounting and is next seen when you receive the master bill. Disputes are difficult to settle then, but simple if they're corrected before they go to accounting. In addition, you should require that each event's charges be prepared on a separate check so that the amounts correspond to your spec book or their event orders. Also require the hotel to put the amount (12 dozen) or the number (305 people) served and the guarantee on each check. This seems like a minor detail, but hours are saved later both when you review the bill and when you prepare your financial reports.

For those new to meeting planning, the "spec book" consists of the written specifications of your meeting—usually for a large meeting—bound into book format (also called a staging guide or, more colloquially, "the bible"). It is the major written document outlining all your needs, requirements, and preferences to the hotel and other suppliers.

RECORD KEEPING

While there is a chapter specifically on data collection, some information, especially where hotel billing is concerned, must not only be recorded immediately but must be in agreement with hotel records. I am referring to the food-and-beverage report and the bar-reading reports. Once a room has been cleared, there is no way to recapture the facts, and overcharges in these two areas are expensive.

The purpose of the food-and-beverage report is to allow you to systematically document your final guarantee and your actual count of meals served during the function. The hotel will be taking its count at the same time, and you can compare notes before the attendees adjourn. A calculator allows you to immediately figure tax, gratuity, and any other charges so that you know what the bill should be before you receive it. Obviously, if attendance is less than or the same as your guarantee, you will be charged based on the guaranteed (GTD) number; if attendance is higher, you will be charged based on the actual number.

Exhibit 12-1 (the meeting report for food and beverages) should be completed on-site beginning with the first food-and-beverage service, which may be in the staff office. Incidentally, it's a good idea to bind the forms in the back of your spec book because you will be using them together. Always check your spec book to mentally reconfirm the quantity and items ordered. That is also a good place to write down the guarantees, along with the date and time they're given. There is so much to remember, and having the date and time help you recall what you did last. Also write the hotel's banquet event order (BEO) number in your spec book next to its listing, and staple a copy of the BEO to the back of the prior page. While this takes a little extra time before the meeting starts, it saves time during the meeting because everything you need is at your finger tips.

Some hotels refer to an EO (event order) or CO (catering order), rather than a BEO (banquet event order). Regardless of what it is called, that form is the basis of the hotel's internal system for communication, record keeping, and accounting. To expedite communication with the hotel on-site, you will need to reference the order number for changes, guarantees, and dispute resolution. Some planners rely solely on their copies of these forms and do not prepare a spec book. That has never worked for me because, in addition to hotel data, I need information about other areas, such as flowers, personnel, audiovisual equipment, and so on.

Now back to the food-and-beverages meeting report (Exhibit 12-1). It has been designed for one event per line. First the date, time, room, and function name should be entered. That information can be typed in before you leave the office for the meeting. If you use one form per day, you will have room to write in any events added on-site (and there are always a couple, such as committee and other small-business or spontaneous social functions). Once you receive your BEOs, you can add those numbers in the appropriate column. (I like to receive BEOs from the hotel two weeks prior to my arrival, but all too often they arrive the day I get there.) Compare them with your spec book, mark any changes, additions, or clarifications in red, staple them in your book, and write the BEO number in your spec book and on the food-and-beverage report, along with the last guarantee. That basically sets up your system, and from that point on, everything is entered in pencil on the report during each event. Keep in mind the fact that the hotel goes exclusively by its BEOs, so changes or corrections not made on its form may be missed by staff responsible for implementing your requirements.

TICKET EXCHANGES

Ticket exchanges are particularly useful in monitoring attendance for guarantees, and they certainly enhance an orderly movement into the dinner room. The ticket-exchange procedures can become complex, especially for large dinners, so each detail should be carefully thought out.

The most common practice is to give each attendee a coupon in the registration packet that must be exchanged for a valid dinner ticket. In the general registration area, but out of the main crowd area, set up and identify a ticket-exchange booth. Provide the personnel staffing the booth with a floor plan of the table placement and place a number on each table to assist attendees in identifying the table of their choice. The floor plan should reflect the stage area, multimedia presentation areas, dance floor, and any other information that will assist attendees in table selection. Obviously, the best tables go first, which encourages early exchange.

Tables should be crossed off the floor plan when they are filled. Usually, marking an overlay made of heavy plastic wrap with a grease pencil or colored dots will do the job and allow for changes—and there will be changes. This is where the process gets confusing, so explore all the possibilities in the beginning, prepare solutions, and write them up as "procedures" for ticket-exchange personnel.

Next, you have two options: (1) You may distribute the tickets without taking names or (2) you may require attendees to sign a sheet or card corresponding to the table number, if you think they will want to know who else is seated at the table. In either case, the tickets should be filed or banded together, with the table number both on each set (groups of eight or ten depending on the number of people at each table) and on each ticket for easy distribution (and as a reminder to ticket holders of their table number).

The key to this process is to limit ticket exchange to those with tickets in hand. Often, groups will try to reserve spaces for friends who have not yet arrived or not picked up their packets. If you allow them to save space for these people, the process will be a miserable failure. You may have two or three people reserving places for the same person, good seats left empty, and an inaccurate count for your meal guarantee. I recently heard about a group that used random seating the first evening, thereby successfully discouraging "clique" seating and encouraging interaction among people who had not known one another before. This process was handled by having a single person or a couple draw a table number out of a bowl.

If you have reserved seating for VIPs, advise them of their table prior to the opening of the convention and eliminate them from this entire process. But do be sure that VIP tables are marked "full" on the floor plan before the first ticket is exchanged.

Here are some helpful hints:

1. Print coupons and actual dinner tickets in different colors to avoid confusion.
2. Write names, if required, in pencil so you can easily make changes.
3. Have attendees write their names and final table numbers across the top of the coupon, and file them alphabetically so that attendees can be easily located.

FOOD-AND-BEVERAGE TIPS

HOST VS. CASH BARS

Organizations that offer host-bar (free liquor) service to their attendees are quite often subject to the same liability risk as bars who overserve patrons. The trend is to set up cash bars, which puts a greater burden of liability on the hotel or caterer. Some organizations provide a limited number of tickets for free drinks; others require payment for drinks but indicate that revenues will be donated to a charity. Whatever your choice, be on the lookout for heavy drinkers. Ask bartenders to notify the sponsoring organization about offenders.

With a cash bar, you may require the hotel to give you a report on the types and amounts of drinks sold, although you do not have to be concerned about lost or stolen liquor, which is a problem in hotels, especially in hotels that tempt their employees by leaving liquor bottles in the service corridors.

In a host-bar situation this is your concern until the liquor has been counted. Host bars are high-ticket items and should be monitored very carefully. The bar-tending form (Exhibit 12-2) is useful in this respect. To minimize problems, I require the first count to be done in the room where the function will be held before the event begins. You must know the brands, number of bottles in each brand, and size of each bottle, down to the last bottle of beer and carafe of wine. If the bars arrive prestocked, you will have to fill out a sheet for each bar, and number the sheet and the bar correspondingly. If bars are not prestocked, all liquor can be placed on a central table and counted prior to placement on the individual bars.

It is critical to conduct the final count the same way you conduct the opening count and before the liquor is removed from the room. You also must review these requirements very specifically and clearly with the beverage manager. While the bar-reading form has a column for price, this does not have to be recorded during the count as long as your spec book or the BEO lists the agreed-upon price for comparison against the final charges.

In the column titled "Name," you should list the brand (such as Jack Daniel's); in the "Size" column you should list the bottle size (such as liter); if you have the price, enter this in the "Price" column; and under "Start Number," enter the total number of bottles—liters of Jack Daniel's, for example. This sounds simple; somehow it never is—primarily because you are usually in a hurry and beverage managers seem to take great joy in making the process as confusing as possible.

Hold on to your sheets until the last drink is poured and prepare for the final count—before the bars leave the room. At this point, the bartenders or beverage manager will line up all bottles, including every empty, and with a quick eye will judge the number of drinks used. Have a scratch pad handy, because the judgment call will be per bottle and you will add up the total for the brand (for example, Jack Daniel's), for entry on the bar-reading report. If the hotel accepts opened bottles back and credits you with the unused portion, your job is done. If you must pay for any opened bottles, you will have to count these bottles, have them boxed and taped for delivery to a secure area accessible only to your organization, until needed again.

Some points to remember: If you must pay for all partials (opened bottles) you can reduce the number left over by having fewer bars, as each bar is likely to have one of each brand open. Be sure the seals are not broken on the bottles when the first count is taken. The hotel will consider those partials, and, additionally, you cannot be sure a lesser brand was not poured into a more expensive empty or that the bottle was not watered down.

This last point leads to the phrase "marrying" the bottles. This means that all Jack Daniel's partials will be poured together to make up full bottles. You may allow this process during the final count (it does make the count easier), but you do not have to. If the hotel keeps the partials, the choice is their's; just be sure the bottles don't come back to you that way at the next reception. When you begin the process again, you will want the seals unbroken for the same obvious reasons.

You should also require that a 1-ounce jigger be used to pour. If you consider that a 1-ounce drink is $4 and the bartender pours $1\frac{1}{2}$ ounces, each drink will be $6, and a double will cost $12 by their pouring standards. Unless you require a per-bartender drink talley, you will be charged based on consumption. For example, a fifth is counted as twenty-three drinks; if a $1\frac{1}{2}$-ounce pour is used, you are paying for twenty-three drinks but receiving only 18 actual drinks poured.

The hotel's goal may be to sell more drinks, which automatically happens with a heavy pour. Your goal is to control costs and consumption, thereby requiring a measured pour. If you watch, you will always find a control measure on a cash bar, because the hotel is the loser with heavy pours. Rarely are they found on host bars, because you are paying the bill. Tips should not be allowed at host bars. You, as the host, will be charged an automatic gratuity—your guests should not have to pay.

Clearly, cash bars are simpler and safer. Your costs are limited to a bartender's fee (imposed if you do not reach a minimum level of sales), and you significantly reduce your liability. However, there are times when only a host bar is appropriate, and in such cases you must be prepared to monitor your costs and liability.

CORKAGE

If you bring your own or donated liquor into a hotel, presuming management will let you, you will be charged a corkage fee, which is a service fee for handling and serving the liquor. Negotiate this fee in advance (ideally, per bottle or keg rather than per person or per drink). You will probably also have gratuity added, but not tax. Check your charges carefully. These bottles should be inventoried much like a host bar, before and after. You can ask that empties be returned to you to assure a control on loss. I cannot remind you too often that theft of liquor by the staff is a major problem, especially when liquor is left unattended in the service hallways. That is why your inventories must be conducted in the room where service is to occur.

HOSPITALITY SUITES

Hospitality suites are an important part of some meetings and are prohibited by others. They can be sponsored by the organization, exhibitors, or friends of the organization or industry. While the tendency is to think of wild parties, liquor, and entertainment, they can be as simple as coffee and danish for speakers, spouses, or other special groups.

The rules for parties in suites are often more flexible than in banquet rooms, specifically with regard to unattended, self-service bars. Suites should be reserved well in advance and control of who receives the suites carefully coordinated with the hotel. In addition to the usage of suites, other controls include the amount of liquor delivered to a suite, the hours it is open or closed, the type of entertainment allowed, and the type of telephone calls permitted (usually local only if you are paying). Suite parties should not conflict with official conference activities.

Many conventions prohibit not only private suite parties but any private entertaining for selected groups of attendees. This is hard to control, other than by imposing penalties (such as loss of suite privileges or priority exhibit space in future years) if such activities are discovered. The competition for attendees' time and attention can be disruptive to the broader goals and create a negative attitude among excluded guests. Be thoughtful in your planning and controls. Activities should be prohibited if they do not enhance the overall program.

ORDERING HORS D'OEUVRES

Hotels have a tendency to try to oversell the number of hors d'oeuvres per person. Five to eight per person for one hour is average. You can go with fewer by adding cheese and fruit trays, nuts, and chips and dip as filler items. They are less costly, last longer, and add to the appearance of your table.

Hors d'oeuvres are usually priced by the piece, pound, or tray. The cost includes labor, linens, room rental, napkins, serving dishes, tables, chairs, and so on, but it is important to remember that if the food is purchased frozen, you may not be getting the best value for your dollar. Ask which items are freshly prepared and order from that selection.

One of my pet peeves is "cubed" cheese. I'm not sure why hotel caterers serve it, unless it's because they buy in bulk at less expensive prices. I prefer to put out whole pieces of imported cheese that the guests can cut themselves. Over the years, though, I've fought the cubed-cheese battle—and lost.

When thinking through your ordering, don't just look at prices, look at the value for your dollar. Often a $400 to $600 baron of beef is a better value than 400 chicken wings. The key is to evaluate a variety of options. Order more of fewer items. Consider that each person will try one of everything and will go back only to favorite items. Play the numbers game—give them three choices instead of six and have lots of the three rather than a few of the six. If you event is several hours long, ask the chef to bring out one-third of the food each hour, so the late arrivals don't find an empty table.

Most of what I have learned over the years has resulted from candid discussions with the catering manager, chef, and sales staff. You can be sure they know the ins and outs of ordering. Your ability to establish an honest relationship with those people will enhance your event and save your organization dollars.

ORDERING LUNCH AND DINNER

The major difference between lunch and dinner is about 2 ounces. The lunch portion is traditionally 6 ounces and dinner 8 ounces. Those 2 ounces can cost you $20 to $40. In evaluating the two menus and accompanying prices, be prepared to ask some hard questions about the differences. Evenings may include candles and sauces, but not a significant difference. Ask for more. A fresh-flower centerpiece for a table of ten people may cost $25.00, but that is only $2.50 per person. The issue in all food-and-beverage considerations is to explore the costs.

I often negotiate food-and-beverage costs during contract negotiations, but—unlike other areas—these are negotiable at any time, based on your flexibility and the chef's. As always, I respect an organization's (hotel's) profit motivation, but I also believe in fairness, honesty, and smart shopping. Your organization's expectations should be your guiding light.

SERVICE LEVEL

Unfortunately, the average number of waiters is one per twenty-five covers, or place settings (people). If you have tables of ten people, there will be one waiter per two-and-a-half to three tables. Generally, I feel this is inadequate, although I am more flexible if there is one busperson per table to pour beverages and to respond to special requests (for more coffee, rolls, or water). While I realize labor is the most expensive cost of a meal, if I'm planning a gala I want service to match quality.

My suggestion to you is to require one waiter per ten people unless extensive bus service is guaranteed. If your budget is limited, ask waiters to preset salad, beverages, extra rolls and butter, and place a pot of coffee on each table—but remember, preset of anything is not as elegant as white-glove service. Counter as many problems as possible with advance planning.

You should also ask how plates are served. There are some systems, such as the "wave" or "snake," that expedite getting plates on the table, thus allowing waiters more time for service—here again, not as elegant as the station method, which allows one waiter to handle all needs at an assigned table. Other systems are time consuming, resulting in some patrons who have finished eating before others have started. Even walking distance from the kitchen to tables can be time consuming.

TAX AND GRATUITY

Some states allow taxes to be added before gratuity is charged. While this seems minor, the dollars add up when you pay an additional 15 percent on the tax rate. You should ask the caterer or food-and-beverage department how the procedure is handled. A study by the National Association of Exposition Managers (NAEM) states when hotels and convention centers must levy tax on gratuities and service charges. The Association's guide (available from the NAEM—see Resources at the end of this book for the address) also advises how planners can avoid paying the tax.

DECORATIONS

Decorations include everything from the color of linens (tablecloths and napkins) to candles, centerpieces, lighting, plants, and theme props. In planning your food-and-beverage events, be sure to ask what is available, in which colors, and what the costs of each are. Those items available within the hotel are usually offered at a low cost or free of charge. A first for me recently was encountering a hotel that had no centerpieces. (Normally, standard bud vases or silk flower arrangements are available at no charge, with a special or fresh-flower arrangements offered for a fee.) However, much to my surprise, the hotel with no centerpieces went out of its way to cleverly decorate food tables specifically for a Halloween party, even dressing the waiters in costume.

Some food-and-beverage departments will have five or six different colors of linens, others will have more in room decorations or theme props. The personality of key staff members is reflected—they have their own tastes, value systems, and budgets. Some are more creative with ambiance, others more creative in the kitchen. If you understand and work with the personality you are dealing with, you can have a great event.

A word about candles. They are beautiful—and dangerous. The only fire I ever directly experienced in a hotel was caused by a waiter who stuffed paper in the candleholder to make the candle stand up straight. Ultimately, the candle burned down to the paper and the table exploded with fire. No one was hurt, but the evening was disrupted.

EMERGENCIES

The incidence of accidents and emergencies increases at food-and-beverage functions. Be prepared to deal with a fire or with people choking or suffering allergic reactions by knowing the location of fire extinguishers and identifying in advance people with emergency medical skills.

THEMES

Themes used to be limited to special dinners and parties. Now the trend is to have theme breaks, theme luncheons, themes in the exhibit hall—essentially throughout the program. Sometimes there are a variety of themes scheduled throughout the meeting; other times, one theme is tied to the entire event. Themes can be seasonal, motivational, geographical, or just a fun idea. There is nothing better than a theme that works and nothing worse than one that falls flat. (Chapter 11 discusses themes in more detail.)

PROBLEMS AND STRATEGIES

PROBLEM: The mealtime program is always interrupted by waiters serving, clearing, or moving in and out of the room.

Strategy 1:   Meet with your banquet captain before the meal to review your program schedule. This can be months to hours before, depending on the complexity of the program. Compare their time needs with yours and jointly schedule the program.

Strategy 2:   Ask that a pot of coffee be placed on each table either with the meal or the dessert. This assures your guests will have coffee and saves waiters' time in pouring.

Strategy 3:   Order a dessert that can be pre-set and have the salad pre-set. While this is not my preference, it does save time when the program is tightly scheduled or mealtime is limited.

Strategy 4:   Advise waiters in advance to leave the room when an activity begins, such as the introduction of the keynote speaker.

Strategy 5:   Serving time can be reduced with an increased number of waiters. Discuss the hotel's policy and request more at functions where time is at a premium.

PROBLEM: We are always operating on a shoestring budget. Are there ways to cut food-and-beverage costs?

Strategy 1:   Select a facility with food prices appropriate to your budget or one that will negotiate prices in the contract.

Strategy 2:   Present an honest budget to the food-and-beverage manager, either one total figure with the events you must include, or a per-event budget. Ask for a proposal with two or three options per each event.

Strategy 3:   Cut corners: Ask for champagne glasses for orange juice (they hold less), save the luncheon dessert for the afternoon break.

Strategy 4:   Check out all the angles to get the best deal. For hosted bars for less than 100 people, the best buy is by the drink; for more than 100 people, by the bottle. Per piece is the most expensive way to order hors d'oeuvres. Also, remember: fewer items and more of each.

Strategy 5:   Be creative; a beer and hot dog reception can be fun and economical. A health break with whole fresh fruit is appealing and reduces coffee consumption. Try hot chocolate on a cold wintry day or iced tea on a hot day; consumption is usually limited to one serving versus continual coffee refills.

Strategy 6:   Don't be afraid to present your ideas to the food-and-beverage managers. They can learn as much from us as we do from them.

PROBLEM: We seem to be locked into the same straight-from-the-menu ideas. Are there new trends or different ideas to pick up our events?

Strategy 1: Review the hors d'oeuvre menu for morning break ideas, looking for such things as mini-quiches, pigs in a blanket, or ham-and-cheese rolls.

Strategy 2: Ethnic foods and lighter foods are increasingly popular, but as their popularity increases, guests' tastes become more refined. Be sure the chef is skilled in the ethnic food you are ordering.

Strategy 3: Look at local restaurants or recipe books to see what new trends are in. Dim sum is a popular weekend brunch idea, fast-food "McMuffins" can be easily adapted in a hotel, salad and sandwich bars are versatile, and even a mug of soup (drinkable, such as consommé) is different and satisfying.

Strategy 4: Think pretty. Serve chocolate-dipped strawberries; set up rolling dessert carts or trays; present flambé desserts in a darkened room; use the color combinations on a plate; and garnishes, such as a slice of lemon in the ice water, add interest and appeal.

Strategy 5: Breaks are a favorite idea for creativity, and I find attendees eager to see what will appear next. While you can add elaborate themes, costumes and music, just adding a little variety is all you usually need. Instead of danish, serve bagels and cream cheese; instead of fruit trays, fruit-and-cheese kabobs. Serve hot-sausage biscuits, ham-and-cheese croissants, mini-quiche, popovers, ice-cream sandwiches, fudgesicles, chili and non-alcoholic beer, granola bars, giant cookies, or even a huge bowl of candy bars, or—for the health minded— bowls of crisp apples.

PROBLEM: We always have a few vegetarians who request a different meal as their plate is being served. Is there an easy way to plan for this?

Strategy 1: Add a special-diet request line on your registration form and advise attendees that requests must be in writing twenty-four hours prior to the first meal function.

Strategy 2: Be aware of the type of vegetarian. There are those who eat only foods from plant sources, others add dairy products, others add eggs, some add both. Some options include pastas, rices, grains, tomato-base soups, raw vegetable salads, fresh fruits, stir-fry vegetables, baked potatoes, yoghurt.

Strategy 3: To assist waiters in locating special requests, especially if there are quite a few, you might designate certain tables as vegetarian. Your other option is to serve everyone a vegetarian meal, salad, and pasta, with appropriate sauces and fruit for dessert, which may not be appealing to all guests.

PROBLEM: Our final budget is always blown on coffee. Are there ways to reduce or control costs?

Strategy 1: If you have based your budget on one-and-a-half to two cups per person per break, translate that to gallons and ask the hotel to stop refilling at that point. Any additions must then be preapproved if payment is expected.

Strategy 2: Limit the time coffee is available. If your break is twenty minutes long, have the coffee removed afterward.

Strategy 3: Add a water table to the break area, and set it up so that attendees have to walk past the water to get to the coffee.

Strategy 4:   Negotiate a per-person price rather than a per-gallon price.

Strategy 5:   If decaf packets and tea bags are made available, be sure to count the number put out and left; the same is true for soda. If the price is on a consumption basis, hotels may still charge for the number put out rather than counting what was actually consumed.

Strategy 6:   Know your group. If members are heavy coffee drinkers, increase your budget.

PROBLEM: Especially for major dinners, seating is always a problem—from getting attendees in the room to determining where and how to seat them.

Strategy 1:   To get people in the room, especially if you have music or a dance floor, have the music begin immediately and have a performance on the dance floor. People will usually move in faster to see what is going on, but they may stop to watch on the way to their seat.

Strategy 2:   Nothing ruins the tone of an elegant evening more than crushing bodies racing to reserve a table for their friends. Thus, many groups have pre-dinner seat selection by ticket exchange.

Strategy 3:   If tables or seats are sold (as in fundraising dinners), signs with the purchaser's name may be sufficient. To expedite seating, a large chart should be prepared for attendees to locate the general placement of their table. Table numbers can either be distributed with the ticket or posted on a list.

Strategy 4:   Often by prearrangement with the hotel, the overset can be higher than normal to avoid having to break up couples at separate tables. Usually, the hotel will place reserved signs on these tables to prevent their use until needed. This type of overset does not increase the amount of food prepared—only the available seating.

PROBLEM: I never know when to have a buffet versus a seated meal function.

Strategy 1:   Buffets should be considered only when time is not a factor.

Strategy 2:   Buffets are ideal if your numbers are uncertain. It is easier to stretch the food in a buffet, especially if you have waiters serving and if you select items such as a baron of beef that can be sliced thinner or thicker based on attendance.

Strategy 3:   If cost is the issue, buffets are not necessarily cost effective. The hotel must prepare more items and in sufficient quantity to serve every item to all guests. The negotiable factor is that fewer waiters are required, thus reducing labor costs.

13

AUDIOVISUAL AND OTHER MEDIA

As noted in Chapter 2, the importance of visual presentation is directly related to the learning process. Retention is at least doubled when a person both sees and hears information. A 3M-sponsored study by the University of Pennsylvania Wharton School, which focused on the overhead projector, found that presenters using the overhead were considered "better prepared, more professional, more persuasive, more highly credible, and more interesting." Additionally, information was absorbed faster, with a more favorable response to those using this equipment. And the meetings were over sooner, allowing more interactive time among attendees.

Unfortunately, as the world has become more accustomed to the visual, from movies to television to video (just look at the dollars spent on a thirty-second commercial!), much of the meeting world has kept its head in the sand. (The notable exception are medical meetings. Doctors rely heavily on slides, x-rays, and pictures to visually support their presentations. And in so doing, they can cover a highly technical subject in ten to fifteen minutes—even less when the pressure is on.)

At the same time, the options for visual presentations are expanding to include sophisticated new technologies. Electronic writing boards, teleconferencing, closed-circuit television—these are just a few of the choices available today. But the bottom line, however, is the *effective* use; equipment alone is not sufficient. Whether you are using traditional audiovisual presentations or new technologics, the room setup, the quality and appropriateness of the visuals, and the accompanying verbal presentation are all keys to success.

GETTING IT ALL TOGETHER

AUDIOVISUAL PRESENTATIONS

Planning Considerations

The beginning process is to communicate with your speakers regarding their needs. Unfortunately, this usually happens after you have selected the site, which may prohibit certain types of presentations in certain rooms. You can either adjust the room assignment to match audiovisual requirements, or you can advise speakers of their options within the designated room. If you know your group, you will likely be able to anticipate their needs during the site selection process.

It is worthwhile to hire an audiovisual specialist (consultant) to work closely with you in the preplanning, on-site, and bill-review stages. Consultants are experienced in bid solicitation, negotiations, room setup, technical safeguards, and problem solving. By utilizing their areas of expertise, they can release you to focus your attention on your best areas. Their cost effectiveness should not be measured by their direct cost to you, but by the costs they save you by skillfully negotiating lower prices, implementing the flow and multi-use of equipment, and by obtaining upgraded equipment for standard prices.

Keep in mind that "audiovisual" also includes the basics:

- Microphones
- Recording equipment
- Spots and other lighting
- Lecterns
- Pointers
- Flip charts
- Projection stands
- Extension cords
- Labor (setup and operators)
- Supplies such as markers and transparencies

Your on-site instructions (spec book) should include setup and tear-down times, rehearsals, taping of loose wires, back-up requirements such as microphones and projector bulbs.

Site Selection

With regard to site selection, among the most important issues are ceiling heights and obstructions such as posts and low-hanging chandeliers. Mirrored walls or windows can be a problem or an expense if they have to be covered. Distances are very important, such as the projection distance, the distance of the audience from the screen, the distance from the screen to the last row of chairs, and the distance behind the screen for rear-screen projection. (Specific guidelines are given in the Quick Reference Guide.) All of these issues are related to space and square-footage and require very specific scale drawings. These seemingly minor details are critical factors. Numbers of attendees must be considered, along with pre-blocking of the room for setup, lighting, electrical, and certainly safety.

Many hotels have an in-house AV (audiovisual) company whose representatives can accompany you on your site-inspection tour. This is most often a private company that has been contracted by the hotel to provide "in-house" services for clients. The AV company's familiarity with the facility and direct experience with a variety of setups can be invaluable for planning and learning. As the specifics become defined, you will have to prepare diagrams for each room and each event. You will also have to prepare your order (equipment, supplies, technical staffing) for each event and confirm all prices.

On-Site Considerations

The key to success on site is to check every room and every piece of equipment and have back-ups available in minutes. "Checking" means someone should: (1) speak into every microphone to assess sound quality and volume; (2) test equipment with slides, transparencies, or film, which should be checked for focus and proper operation; and (3) check taping of wires and cords for safety. If speakers are required to operate their own equipment, be sure they are provided with the operating manuals for their equipment and have been trained in the operating procedures not only for their equipment but for light controls and other room features, such as blackout drapes if there are windows.

Many groups with audiovisual presentations set up a speakers' room or "ready" room. One piece of each type of equipment is set up for rehearsals. This allows slides to be organized, film to be tested, and so on. It is a nice consideration for speakers and reduces the lead time they need in their presentation room.

AUDIOVISUAL TIPS

SCREENS

The screen is the most important equipment consideration in planning for presentations. If you have a choice, choose a square shape rather than a rectangle, because vertical and horizontal slides will fit better. The bottom of the screen should be at least 5 feet off the floor. The size can then roughly be judged by measuring the distance of the room from screen to back row and dividing by 8. For example, if the room is 80 feet long, you would need a 10-foot screen. The screen height plus 5 feet should tell you how high the ceiling needs to be to accommodate the screen. You should then allow the screen height times 1.5 as the distance from the screen to the first row of chairs. (For example, a 10-foot screen $\times$ 1.5 = 15 feet from screen to first row of chairs.)

While this sounds simple, the shape of the room and obstructions complicate the formulas. There are certainly more complicated formulas and more accurate ones, but this will do if you don't have an audiovisual whiz kid at your heels.

The best screens for slides and film are called fast-fold, usually are 12 feet by 12 feet or larger. The screen snaps onto a large frame. Setup is longer than for a simple tripod, but the better image is worth it. Once you get to this size, you will need to use special lenses on the projector, so expect the costs to increase in several different areas.

MICROPHONES

Some of the worst problems with microphones are a result of wiring (patching) them into the house sound system. If your event is important—such as the general session—add your own separate sound sytem to your major room. Sound problems include squeaks, feedback, ringing, hollow, booming, and humming. Most are correctable by lowering the volume or moving the speaker further away from the microphone. The most common problems are solved by turning the microphone on or plugging it in.

There are many types of microphones, the most common being those placed on some type of stand and those hung around the neck for greater mobility of the speaker. The newest type are cordless mikes, often used by performers. Usually, the speaker is given a choice based on the suitability of one over the other for the presentation style. Many hotels offer one complimentary standard microphone per room. (Don't expect it to be the more expensive cordless mike.)

VIDEO

Video players are becoming increasingly popular and are certainly less threatening than other AV equipment from an operational standpoint. The flaw is the limitation concerning the screen size. Monitors larger than 7 feet are still prohibitively expensive, and the 7-foot screen will handle only 100 to 150 people. A 19-inch TV screen handles only 15 to 25 people. The solution is to use multiple screens (as sports bars do), which increases the costs. Video is an excellent option for live transmission to an overflow room, for communications into guest rooms, for message centers, and for general conference updates and announcements.

The standard videotape formats are $\frac{3}{4}$-inch and $\frac{1}{2}$-inch VHS or Beta. Know which you need and don't make assumptions. Paying attention to these details will ensure that you order the right equipment.

SESSION TAPING

Taping decisions should be made on the basis of how the tapes will be used. If the use is internal (for notes and reports), you can simply patch your recorder in to the house sound system, although you have have to use more complicated systems for multiconversation recording. If the purpose is for re-sale, hire a professional company. If the sales potential is high, they will not charge you directly, but will generate their income from a percentage of sales. The usual procedure is a 10 to 30 percent commission back to your organization, plus one complete set free. Other negotiable items include a free tape to each speaker of his or her presentation and one free tape to each attendee.

If you are taping sessions, either you or the taping company must provide very clear guidelines to the speakers. Often, the opening thirty minutes or so are spent in introductions around the room, which can't really be heard. Also, attention must be paid to speaking into the mike or repeating audience questions. A few reminders will result in a better product for everyone.

If you tape, you must have a signed release from each speaker. If they decline, you cannot tape that session without risk of a lawsuit. Often, speakers decline if confidential information is being shared; others prefer to sell their own tapes for personal profit rather than someone else's.

SLIDE PRESENTATIONS

Most frequently for slide presentations, you order the screen and projector, and the speakers bring their slides in their own trays. Variance in tray and slide sizes can cause serious problems, particularly if you have international speakers.

Most U.S. equipment is designed for slides no larger than 3.2 mm (⅛ inch) in thickness and trays limited to eighty slides per tray. Plastic mounts are also most effective for clarity and for easily dropping into the projector. If more than one screen is being used (for groups of 1,000 or more), speakers should be advised of the need to bring multiple sets of slides. Slide projection problems usually occur when slides are poorly mounted or when a bulb (projection lamp) burns out. Keep an extra bulb and tweezers handy to help solve those kinds of problems.

Most speakers using slides require a remote control device to advance slides as they move through their presentation and frequently need tape recorders and synchronizers to coordinate the audio with the visual. A thorough checklist and rehearsal room will minimize, if not eliminate, crises.

Not to be forgotten are the multimedia or multi-image slide presentations. If you have done the rest alone, don't risk your job here. These presentations are usually expensive productions and are a featured segment of a key conference event. They can consist of, for example, twenty different slides being projected on one screen, followed by three the next minute, one the next, all computerized and completely synchronized to sound. Close coordination needs to occur between the production company and the equipment and technical support company. The room should be available many hours before the event for setup and run through. A faulty or upside-down slide can ruin a show. You should be a part of the process, but from a quality-control perspective rather than a technical one.

AUDIOVISUAL COMPANIES

Usually, an AV company has been contracted by the facility to handle the AV requirements for its clients. You are not required to use that company, but there are several advantages to doing so. The first is its knowledge of the facility; equally important, such a company has "emergency" equipment, supplies, and technicians readily available. A possible disadvantage is that you may not get the best person for your requirements.

As with all other contractors, you should check the quality and diversity of its equipment, the technical knowledge of its people, and references in relation to your specific needs. There is no rule that limits you to one company or to a specific person. You may use one for your routine requirements and another for your "productions." Your objective must be the best product!

In order to make sure that all of your requirements are met, it is helpful to fill out an AV supplier request form, ideally one to three months before the meeting. (See Exhibit 13-1.) You should fill out a form per room per session for every piece of equipment or accessory you will need.

Finally, you will have to review the bills on a daily basis. There are often hidden costs with audiovisuals, such as extension cords, light bulbs, special lenses, labor minimums, supplies, and so on. Request that charges be broken down per room or per day, depending on the structure of your bid. The key is that you understand the charges and the bill, and can settle disputes immediately.

TELECONFERENCING

When the term "teleconference" first emerged in the 1960s as a new format for meetings, there was a great deal of excitement, curiosity, and, from some quarters, fear that it would end the need for face-to-face meetings. In reality, the problem has been that it has taken longer than expected to produce a high-quality cost-effective product, as well as an appropriate market for the product.

The Technology

Teleconferences, or electronic meetings, are those that incorporate audio, video, and other electronically transferred information and deliver it from one location to many locations. You may have an audioconference (voice only), which is a telephone conference call on a grand scale; or a videoconference (visual and voice), which is much like having your television station producing a program for audiences in multiple locations. Within videoconferences, there are two subtypes: The ad hoc type is usually a one-time "event" in which everything is set up exclusively for that program. The "fixed" teleconference is permanently set up for the frequent user, especially when the location of the audience is also fixed.

The process for these types of meeting is highly technical and beyond the scope of this book. But, conceptually, the process involves an earth-to-satellite transmission station (up-link) at the point of generation of the meeting. From the receiving station (satellite), the information must be transmitted back to earth (down-link) to each of the locations of your audience. Much like reserving space in a hotel, you call companies (carriers) who reserve and transmit satellite space and time, and who will assist you in preparing for your event. Bonneville, VideoStar and Wold are well-known companies that provide this type of service.

Uses

The primary users of teleconferencing are corporations that have found it cost effective because it eliminates the cost of travel and lodgings for a large number of people. If all or a part of a large group is on staff, the value of "lost" time while they travel to a meeting site can be substantial. Corporate uses include:

- New product or line introductions
- Press conferences
- National, regional, district, and other types of
  internal corporate meetings
- Training programs

J. C. Penny, Chrysler Corporation, General Motors, and Procter & Gamble are but a few of the major corporate users that have installed permanent video-conferencing networks.

Use of this process is more limited among associations because they are not usually responsible for payment of attendee expenses or impacted by their time away from in-house work. Therefore, there is a higher risk to the association because the cost savings primarily benefit the attendee. When an association does teleconference, it usually charges a fee, much like the conference registration fee. Universities are also users, especially for guest lecturers otherwise unavailable because of time and fee demands.

Clearly, there is a role for electronic meetings, but I do not believe they will ever replace traditional meetings, conventions, and conferences because of their impersonal nature and the dubious cost effectiveness for fee-based meetings.

Implications for Meeting Planning

If you are a part of an organization that uses this technology, you will find that there are changes in the way meetings are planned. A much stronger team relationship must be established with the technical producers; timing is critical and programming must be carefully scripted; and television production aspects—such as set design, lighting, makeup, and wardrobes—must be considered.

Logistically, you will have from two to fifty or more sites to select; coffee breaks, lunches, dinners to order; and support personnel (from moderators to greeters to technicians) to hire and coordinate. You will, by necessity, evaluate sites differently, selecting those that can provide fixed receiving equipment (the Holiday Inn chain is one supplier that has publicized this capability). It is most efficient to rely on a hotel's national and regional sales offices to coordinate the booking requirements.

A key ingredient to a successful teleconference is the ability to have interaction between the various sites and the point of program generation. Your programming may also incorporate graphics and other supportive visuals in a way that is technically different from what is done at a traditional meeting. The list could go on, but this should give you some perspective on the technology and its impact on the meeting planner.

OTHER HIGH-TECH OPTIONS

There are other electronic and high-tech options that should be mentioned. Meeting Planners International (MPI) has an excellent reputation for using a variety of media at their annual conference. Its attitude, "to try and fail is better than to do nothing creative at all," is laudable.

Lasers

Lasers add color and energy to your meeting, whether a vibrant logo, your speakers' names in lights, or images projecting key presentation points. Or, you can beam sculptures, place a canopy over your audience, or add animation as the final drama.

If you want to incorporate lasers into your program, contact a specialist or other organization that has successfully used this technology to explore your options, costs, and lead time. Costs are still quite high (from $6,000 to six figures), although the lead time to produce a show can be fairly short—a couple of weeks to a month. Once on site, the producer will need access to water (to cool the lasers) and electrical outlets. Lasers are safe, but you should coordinate closely with the hotel.

Closed-Circuit Television

Closed-circuit TV offers a variety of opportunities especially useful for very large groups. For example, the general session can be projected in overflow rooms or press rooms, or large-screen projections of speakers' faces, as they speak, can be a real enhancement for excessively large audiences. Similarly, products can be displayed as they are referenced in the script. By smart planning, you may receive double benefit from this technology if you videotape the program for future use or to sell to meeting attendees.

Electronic Writing Boards

Electronic writing boards are particularly valuable for small groups, replacing the flip chart and pages of paper hung around the room. The added attraction is that copies may be made on the spot for immediate distribution to attendees, or graphics may be transmitted from a distant speaker or site.

High-Tech Slides

Computer-generated slides enhance the creativity, dimension, and colors of slides. In a high-tech world, meeting planners should reevaluate their budgets to include a few of these unforgettable touches.

PROBLEMS AND STRATEGIES

PROBLEM: Audiovisual equipment can ruin the ambiance in a room. Our problem is blending it so it's not so obvious.

Strategy 1:   Hire a decorator or audiovisual company to drape the area above, below, and on the sides of the screen.

Strategy 2:   Use a slide with your organization's logo, one that is theme-related, or one with scenery for still projection onto the screen.

Strategy 3:   Place plants around the lower part of the screen, so the projection lights off the screen will be less obvious.

Strategy 4:   Combine all of the above, using the screen to enhance the environment.

Strategy 5:   If the projection area is the problem, use the projection booth for your setup.

Strategy 6:   If a projection booth is not available or appropriate to your screen placement, use a remote corner or set up the projection against the back wall.

Strategy 7: The most attractive option is rear-screen projection. A special screen allows the projection to be set up behind the screen. The look is very clean and, while a little more expensive, well worth the cost. The key consideration is space, because this setup requires more room (at a minimum, 15 to 16 feet) from the wall or corner.

PROBLEM: Our overhead setup never works for slides. Is there a way to avoid using two screens?

Strategy 1: While one screen may be technically possible, the overhead requires easy access by the user for placement of transparencies or writing; slide projection does not. The overhead also requires a fairly close projection distance from projector to screen, also not necessary for slides. The best solution is to pre-set a screen for the overhead or opaque projectors and use a separate screen for film and slides.

Strategy 2: If space for additional screens is a problem, you will at a minimum have to move the overhead out of the way so that film or slide projection is not obstructed.

Strategy 3: Organize your overhead presentation and slide presentation so that a short break occurs in between, allowing time for adjustments in the setup.

PROBLEM: Our biggest problem is getting speakers to tell us in advance what, if any, audiovisual equipment they will need.

Strategy 1: Have basic equipment on quick reserve: a slide projector, screen, and overhead projector. For those "questionable" sessions, make sure the audiovisual company is alerted to a possible rush setup.

Strategy 2: If speakers have not returned their audiovisual requirements request forms or have provided incomplete information, follow up with phone calls until you have the individual AV requirements.

Strategy 3: Evaluate your information to ensure that your expectations, deadlines, and requirements are very clear. Don't bury the information in a lengthy letter; prepare a summary of deadlines and accompanying requirements. While I disrespect irresponsible speakers, I like to make sure I've considered their busy schedules and make their participation at my meeting easy.

14

BUDGETING AND FINANCIAL MANAGEMENT

The budget is the real meeting shaper; it puts all the "talk" into perspective. You find out what is really important to your CEOs, members, or clients. It doesn't have to be an extravagant budget; actually, in these economic times, there are very few of those. The interesting point is where the dollars are spent, specifically when compared with the stated goals.

You can't talk about expenditures without an evaluation of potential revenues. Fortunate indeed is the person who has a financial history of the meeting, or better yet, a budget not dependent on the collection of fees to cover costs. If you have ever planned a "first-time" meeting, you will have experienced all the anxieties of trying to predict how many will attend and how much they will pay. Will you have one or ten corporate sponsors? Three or thirty exhibitors? You need some idea of revenues before you tackle the expenditures. This ceiling or range becomes a major management and planning tool for you.

The history is as important to the budget process as staff resources are to the planning schedule. If you don't have a group history, you can, at a minimum, seek out trends for similar programs or evaluate the general economic outlook. Normally, in good times, attendance is higher and supplier costs are less negotiable. Correspondingly, bad times mean fewer attendees and greater flexibility in negotiations. But this is not always true, so check the implications for your own meeting. A meeting that emphasizes selling skills or employment opportunities may be better attended in tough times.

Also in the trends area, meeting publications survey readers and publish results that tell you how dollars from corporate versus association meetings are being spent. There is a lot of good information available if you take the time to seek it out. Our industry's trends, suppliers, respected colleagues, and your files are the most obvious sources. All too often, the budgeting process is seen as purely mathematical, while it is really an intellectual process in a mathematical format.

The budget as a document is an important planning tool, but the true value is in the degree to which you use it and in the accuracy and thoughtfulness of the preparation process. Remember, the budget is a plan that reduces all you know or can find out to figures. The planning schedule reduces all you know to people, task, and deadlines. It is this combination that determines the road you will take. The goals are the foundation; the planning tools are the supporting beams. Add a healthy dose of creativity in the interior design (program, speakers, food, and beverages), readying this empty structure for the energy that only the attendees can provide. Ultimately, it is this combination that determines whether the result will be success, mediocrity, or failure.

The meeting planner's role in establishing the budget varies depending on the organization's structure. In some companies or associations, the budget process is closely guarded, and the planner is involved only in the area of his or her responsibility. In other cases, a budget would never be prepared if the planner didn't force the issue. This chapter assumes you do have input in, if not overall responsibility over, the budgeting process. If, for some reason, you do not, you still can arm yourself by knowing more than anyone else about the financial and economic issues directly or indirectly related to your meeting.

GETTING IT ALL TOGETHER

FORMAT

The beginning point in preparing a budget is research. Research can be in the form of bids, the economy in the host city, past financial reports on the same or a similar meeting, seasonal advantages or disadvantages, or national economic trends, such as the price of gasoline. You don't have to be an economist, but you do need to think, observe, and have written notes.

You must take apart financially the meeting you are planning. There are many ways to divide your meeting into general categories that may or may not relate to your internal accounting system. (Discuss this with your accountant or financial officer.) You will save yourself many hours if your beginning budget has the same format as your final financial report.

If the meeting has only one account code, you will have a lot of flexibility in formatting your budget. If you are required to bill a variety of costs to a variety of accounts, prepare to work closely with your accounting office in the beginning. That aspect of budgeting is most difficult when government contracts are involved or when direct, indirect, overhead, and general and administrative costs must be broken out.

The point is not that you understand the mathematical formulas for your organization's accounting, but that you interface with the system for efficiency and accuracy.

Now that you know what they want, you look at all anticipated expenses and plug them in under the appropriate category. This detailed itemization includes:

- Promotional materials
- Badges
- On-site materials
- Speakers

- Special events
- Signs
- Security
- Labor

- Audiovisual equipment and personnel
- Decorations
- Food and beverage
- Staff travel
- Gifts
- Awards
- Ribbons
- Registration and other on-site personnel
- Room rentals

- Insurance
- Legal
- Gratuities
- Recreation
- Office equipment
- Taxes
- Shipping
- Postage
- Storage
- Photographer

At this point, you also need some basic information that influences costs. Among these are:

- Date(s)
- Locations
- Number of attendees
- Allowable speaker expenses
- Number of speakers
- Type of food, beverages, and special events
- Promotional requirements
- Costs to be paid by the event's sponsor
- Costs to be paid by the attendee
- Financial objective (profit, break even, host pays all)

This gets us to revenue, and you had better know where that is coming from. Corporate planners usually use money allocated from the company's budget. For associations, revenue is generated from registration fees, exhibition fees, advertising fees, sponsorships, grants, or host underwriting. Less significant, but worth considering, are interest on deposits, cancellation fees, credit card processing fees, late fees, special program or event fees, one-day-only fees, and guest fees.

In-kind donations—services in lieu of money, such as printing, personnel—while not direct cash revenues, serve the same purpose by offsetting costs. This is a particularly effective option in a bad economy where there may be lots of volunteers and not so much cash.

Now that you have all that information, you must organize your budget into categories. My traditional budget is organized by the categories shown in the Quick Reference Guide. These are divided into income items and expenditures. Other schemes include organization by day, by fixed and variable costs, by profit centers (such as children's or spouse programs, exhibits, or events with add-on fees), or by internal accounting codes. Whatever the format, your job is to list every possible expense item and the estimated cost.

You must then explain exactly how you arrived at each cost figure—for example, 2,000 four-color, eight-page advance program announcements; or 200 lunches at $15 plus 21 percent tax and gratuity times three days. This explanation will be valuable in your monitoring and final accounting, to say nothing of your own learning.

Clearly, some areas are easier to budget than others, such as signs, furniture, office equipment, and any of those areas directly controlled by the planner. Audiovisual is one of those areas not easily controlled by the planner, especially if you leave all options open to speakers. Actually, I run into a conflict here because in programming, I want speakers to have whatever it takes for excellence, but when budgeting I'm likely to say you will have a lectern mike, a 35mm. projector, screen, and overhead—too bad if you want a video setup; we don't have the budget for it!

Budget for "unanticipated extras," but also give staff and speakers deadlines for additions to the budget. If you are on a tight budget, additions may also mean cuts. The video monitors may cut into food and beverages or decorations. A quick trip back to your purpose (goals and objectives) may provide guidance in additions and cuts.

Once your budget has been prepared and approved, attach a page for explanations of budget adjustments, with additional space for dates, changes, and approval signatures.

BUDGETING TIPS

BUDGET FORMS AND CHECKLISTS

Because no two meetings or people are exactly alike, you may never find a form or checklist directly applicable to your needs. The secret is to utilize another's experiences in developing your own system and cost items. I also have an "oops" list of unique items (easy to forget) that I reference when planning my budgets. This includes overtime for setups, extension cords or other electrical supplies or labor, lack of local recognition of nonprofit tax status, special insurance requirements, and union versus non-union rates and minimum calls.

BUDGET FORMULAS

There are formulas for almost everything, and many are included in this book. But formulas are guidelines applicable to the masses. Again, I stress the importance of knowing your own group and meeting, because ultimately you have to translate formulas to your situation.

For example, while the average per-person consumption of alcoholic drinks for one hour is 2.5, consumption at a reception before dinner may be less, at a hosted bar it may be more; a group of ministers may drink less; a "free-pouring" bartender with a heavy hand can make your group look worse than it is. The size (ounce capacity) of glasses or cups can influence how many of anything are in a gallon. The per-person square-footage allowance for a particular room setup may be inaccurate if there are posts, rear-screen projection, or a dance floor. (These and other formulas are discussed in Chapter 12.)

Use the formulas as a beginning point, discuss them with your suppliers, then clearly define your formula. For example, at one event you may allow 3.5 drinks per person; at another event you may consider one drink per person adequate.

Just remember: Everyone can read the operating instructions for your car, but on a cold snowy day not everyone could start it as well as you. The combination of knowledge, experience, and intuition gives meaning to the formulas.

BREAK-EVEN BUDGETING

The key to break-even budgeting is the division of costs into two categories: fixed and variable. Simply put, *fixed costs* are those that do not change with the number of attendees, such as promotion, signs, speakers, and insurance. *Variable costs* are those that vary with the number of attendees, such as food and beverages, on-site materials, room rental (if based on guest room pick-up), and so on.

Fixed costs are figured on a gross amount; they are the costs to hold the conference if nobody came. Variable costs are figured on a per-person basis. By combining both types, as outlined in the Quick Reference Guide for Chapter 15, you can identify the number of people required at a specified fee to break even. For accurate budgeting, do not overlook indirect costs such as staff time, telephone equipment and calls, copying, and insurance, or hidden costs such as labor and setup charges, electrical hook-ups, union requirements of minimums and overtime, taxes, and gratuities.

COMPETITIVE BIDS

The rule of thumb is to always get bids from three suppliers for each item or service (be they hotel, audiovisual, catering, and so on). The trick is to make sure all bids are based on the same specifications. A request for proposal (RFP) should be submitted to suppliers in writing; likewise, each supplier's proposal or bid should be returned in writing. The more information you provide, the better the quality of the bid will be. It is not a test to see who can second-guess your needs most accurately, although that may be a side benefit if you allow questions. Questions can be very revealing in evaluating technical knowledge.

If you are looking only for price comparisons or negotiating areas, and only plan to consider one proposal, remember that formal bidding is an expensive process for suppliers. A telephone interview is not expensive and can be equally helpful in justifying your "already made" decision. Be considerate: No one minds preparing or even losing a bid if the process is fair. Clearly, it is good business to have a back-up suppliers and cost comparisons; just don't misrepresent your actions.

There is a federal price-fixing regulation that prohibits one supplier from asking you what a competitor has bid, but you are not prohibited from voluntarily disclosing other bids.

An often-forgotten courtesy is a thank-you letter to bidders that also advises them of your decision. That small detail reaffirms your professionalism.

MASTER ACCOUNT BILLS

The most dreaded of all meeting planning responsibilities is deciphering the master hotel bill. The accompanying joke is that the hotel wants payment in thirty days. Who can even figure it out in thirty days? Some hotels claim to be addressing this problem. In the interim, here are several suggestions to assist you.

Require each event to be written on a separate check; for example, the morning coffee break should be listed separate from the afternoon coffee break—they should not be lumped together. At a minimum, you can match your event order to that check. Don't sign anything unless you have compared it with your order, written all charges and totals in your specifications book, and finally received a copy and stapled your receipt in your spec book. Review all your checks once a day, and make sure the adjustments are reflected before the hotel accounting department ever sees them. Because convention services and ac-counting personnel do not routinely speak to one another, reconciliation of differences is almost impossible.

The hotel system is intimidating. Hotel personnel may interrupt you in mid-conversation with the keynote speaker to sign the check, with half the crowd still in the room. You feel a brief rush of power as you blithely sign a check for $25,000, and off goes this potentially error-laden bill to accounting, only to reappear on some mysterious form that the hotel staff doesn't even understand. Do not get caught in this trap. You may save a few minutes on-site and add hours when you get home.

While hotel bills are the worst, any billing process can be confusing. If your order is complex, you can assume the bill will be. Ask to see a sample of the supplier's bill in advance of signing the contract. If the supplier won't provide one, be sure to ask your references how they found the billing system to work. If you still want to work with that supplier, schedule a pre-event meeting with the credit department. Explain your accounting needs, and prearrange a system that works for you both.

FINAL ACCOUNTING

Finally, compare your final costs with your budget. Where were you over or under? This is essential, because your bottom line totals may be on target, but the expenses within each category may differ widely. If you translate your over/ under numbers into percentages, you can spot trends that can help in future planning. A final accounting worksheet can help in this respect.

PROBLEMS AND STRATEGIES

PROBLEM: The executive director expects us to operate within the budget, yet waives registration fees and approves first class air fare and high-priced speakers.

Strategy 1: If there is a history of these additions and changes, add them to the budget. They are real costs.

Strategy 2: For greater emphasis, if the costs are high, take them out of their rightful categories and create a separate category called "Executive Director's Discretionary Funds." List *all* costs normally obligated by this person. Some-times it helps to see the dollar impact of one's casual decisions.

Strategy 3:   Document all costs not in the approved budget with the name of the person who approved the costs. Remember, lost revenues such as waived fees become a cost.

Strategy 4:   If these items are accurately reflected in your approved budget, don't worry about it. Position has its prerogatives. But don't lose your job because your budget overruns were out of your control.

PROBLEM: We have a champagne appetite on a beer budget.

Strategy 1:   Consider scheduling your event during the "shoulder" seasons (the first or last months of an area's "peak" or "high" season) or including a Friday or Saturday night stayover. This not only benefits room rates, but usually food-and-beverage costs are more negotiable. Areas with weekend attractions may vary in the days they are negotiable, so always ask.

Strategy 2:   Do not order more than three types of hors d'oeuvres, but order lots of those. People tend to try one of each before deciding what to go back for. Good buys are a baron of beef (looks expensive but goes a long way), cheese boards, and vegetable or crudite's (an upscale version) trays.

Strategy 3:   Block your meeting rooms and schedule your program so labor changes are not in overtime periods.

Strategy 4:   Plan your printing early enough to "piggy-back" other similar print runs.

Strategy 5:   Consult the "Cost-Saving Ideas" throughout the Quick Reference Guides in Part II of this book.

PROBLEM: Our organization refuses to pay deposits; that limits the number of suppliers we can use, and their charges are less negotiable without a deposit.

Strategy 1:   Find out *why* the supplier needs a deposit, and *why* your organization refuses to pay it. If you understand both thought processes, you may be able to find a point of negotiation. Agreement to pay in full on site may satisfy both parties, especially if a contract including this term has been signed.

Strategy 2:   Provide credit references for your company or organization and a payment history on a similar meeting. (If your record is slow, there may be valid reasons for a deposit.)

Strategy 3:   Offer to have a check cut for payment at time of service, either in full or for out-of-pocket expenses. This, at a minimum, allows the supplier to pay for required purchases, such as food, and to pay labor costs.

Strategy 4:   Consider an escrow account to protect your organization. All too often, deposits are used to pay a supplier's overhead costs rather than to purchase the items necessary for your event.

Strategy 5:   Always have a written contract and outline specifically what deposits or advances can be utilized for. Protect your organization, but be fair with your suppliers.

PROBLEM: Revenues are never sufficient to cover expenses.

Strategy 1:   Prepare the expenditure portion of the budget before you set the fees.

Strategy 2:   Try the break-even budget formula to determine your minimum number of attendees and your minimum fee to break even. (See Chapter 15.) If you can't meet these minimums, it is time to evaluate the cost effectiveness of holding the event.

Strategy 3:   Evaluate other revenue sources if the attendees cannot bear the full costs.

Strategy 4:   Evaluate the competition, especially those with similar topics and attendees. Is the market saturated? Are others offering incentives such as continuing education credits? Does your organization have national credibility in the subject of the seminar? Be objective in your evaluation. Plenty of organizations underwrite part of the costs of their meeting because the event is more important than profit. That is fine as long as the decision is made up front. Don't promise a profit you can't deliver.

PROBLEM: No matter how well we budget, there are always surprises that we didn't anticipate.

Strategy 1:   Pay attention to your past surprises, and add them to future budgets.

Strategy 2:   There are no stupid questions, only stupid people who don't ask questions. Ask a lot of "what if" questions, talk to other meeting planners and suppliers, read your professional publications and books.

Strategy 3:   Allow at least 1 percent of your budget for miscellaneous expenses, and more if your group is crisis oriented.

Strategy 4:   Keep good records, dissecting all bills. Records of previous years' expenses are the best planning tools for future years.

Strategy 5:   Put all agreements and costs in writing, and have both parties initial or sign and date them. Misunderstandings are the most expensive of all supplier costs.

Strategy 6:   Keep your budget in front of you before, during, and after the event. Updates and constant monitoring will keep you on target.

15

MATH FOR MEETING PLANNERS

There are two dreadful assumptions about meeting planners. One is that they either don't know, or possibly don't need, good math skills. The other is that people skills are all that is really important. The people skills issue is covered in Chapter 17; here let's talk about math.

The pocket calculator has made it a lot easier to perform basic calculations—simple addition, subtraction, multiplication, division, and percentages. But there are other math problems that require a little knowledge in conjunction with proper use of the calculator. There are also numerous formulas that meeting planners use—or should use—for each event they plan. Do you know how many ounces are in a gallon? How about how many cups of coffee in a gallon? Now how many ounces in a glass of juice? How many ounces in a liter? How many square feet in a 24-foot-by-36-foot room? It gets a little more complex as we convert from metric to U.S. equivalents.

If your attendance increased or decreased, can you easily figure the percentage of change? Can you easily translate an $11\frac{3}{8}$ square-footage allowance per person to the room size needed for 315 people? Can you easily figure how many 6-foot-by-5-foot tables are combined to form a 48-foot-by-60-foot conference table? How about how many buses it takes to transport 5,000 people from point A to Point B (10 miles away) in thirty minutes? In an hour?

Well, the point is, an awful lot of what we do is mathematical. I'm not a mathematical person. It isn't easy for me to figure out how much I will earn on an investment at an interest rate of 1.5 percent per year. Personally, it may never be important to me. But professionally, if I'm investing $100,000 in registration revenues for three months, I need to know what that will do to my total revenues versus a one-time annual rate of 13.5 percent.

Math skills are critical to your success as a manager of meetings and special events. The whole process is a lot easier if you have formulas, and if they are all in one place where you can quickly look them up. That is the purpose of the Quick Reference Guide in Part Two. The formulas are not all-inclusive, but they do provide you with a start.

If you will use the industry formulas in conjunction with the basic math formulas, you should see the benefit in your enhanced ability to plan based on facts. By the way, please note that I said industry formulas—not industry standards. To my knowledge, there are few standards if any.

GETTING IT ALL TOGETHER

Because math is based on numbers, the first thing you have to do is get your numbers and facts together as they relate to your meeting and your attendees. For example, if you have 300 attendees and only 75 percent attend the luncheon on day two, you need a room for 225. Then you look up the formula for square-footage allowance for a banquet setup (see the Quick Reference Guide for Chapter 14). If you determine you will allow 15 square feet per person, you will need a room size of 3,375 square feet. If you need a staging area without AV, there is an additional formula of 3,375 square feet × 1.7; if audiovisual is included, use 1.5 as your multiplier.

If the mathematics of the example are not clear, refer to the Quick Reference Guide for this chapter (Guide 15). The combination—your group plus industry formulas plus basic math guidelines—should get you on your way.

Regardless of the number, you have to add common sense and good judgment. The industry formulas may not match your preference. You may prefer a very spacious setup allowing 17 square feet per person or a close group with only 12 square feet per person. You may decide to put only forty people on a passenger bus designed to hold forty-seven people. You can adjust these formulas to meet your group's needs.

You also have to evaluate the appropriateness of the formula. If a room has lots of posts, you may have to throw out the formula; if you presume twenty-two cups in a gallon and your caterer uses 10-ounce mugs instead of 8-ounce cups, your formula will have to be adjusted.

From here you begin to establish trends. If you begin to regularly require setups allowing 15 square feet per person, over the years that becomes your formula. If your attendance increases by 10 percent each year, that becomes a trend and will assist you in planning for growth. If, for several years, 50 percent of your budget is spent on food and beverage, that is a trend.

As you begin to use the formulas and math, you will begin to see your group in terms of hard numbers. You can save dollars in your budgeting by planning based on facts and trends. But you must always translate your actual numbers to percentages. It is these percentages that provide a consistent evaluation.

MATH TIPS

FOOD AND BEVERAGES

Food and beverages make up the easiest area to figure, using almost no formulas at the beginning. For example:

You are providing lunch for 300 people at a cost of $15.95 per person. To compute the total cost of the meal, you would perform the following calculations:

$15.95/person × 300 people	$4,785.00
$4,785 × 15% gratuity	717.75
$4,785 × 7% sales tax	334.95
Total	$5,837.70

The variables are the tax and gratuity rates and whether the gratuity is figured before (as above) or after the tax. In some states it is allowable to pay gratuity on the tax.

The difficulty is figuring out how many meals you can safely guarantee. If you don't know your organization's history and trends, you may end up literally throwing your profits into the garbage. You have to keep records on each event and compare actual attendance with projected figures. To properly guarantee, you need to know what percentage of your attendees come to each food-and-beverage function. If the pattern is 75 percent, you will guarantee meals for 75 percent of your total attendance. The hotel will then set for 3 to 5 percent over your guarantee. The math (again for 300 people) is:

300 attendees × 75% guarantee	225
225 guaranteed × 5% overset	11.25
Total room set	236

Note: If your room is set in rounds of ten, the hotel will most likely set for 240, rounding up to the next full table.

LIQUOR

If you are planning a cash bar, little math is required, other than budgeting for the bar costs if you do not reach the minimum sales for each bar. Host bars are more difficult, but there are formulas to help you. First is to determine the number of drinks each person will consume the first hour: 2.5 is the accepted average. Thus, if you have 200 attendees for a one-hour reception:

$$2.5 \text{ drinks/person} \times 200 \text{ people} = 500 \text{ drinks}$$

500 drinks is your estimated consumption. If liters are the bottle size used, you can expect 33 1-ounce drinks per liter; thus:

$$500 \text{ people} \div 33 \text{ drinks/liter} = 15.15 \text{ liters}$$

Round up to 16 liters. Keep in mind that if even 1 ounce is poured out of a bottle, you will have to pay for the whole bottle. You may request that a small-size bottle be placed on the bar, such as a fifth or a quart. It is not the hotel's or caterer's responsibility to adjust bottle sizes; you must make a specific request, just as you would if you wanted premium, deluxe, or house brands. Also, when buying by the bottle—which is the best buy for more than 100 people—

each bar will have to be stocked. Therefore, you will have more "partials" left over. Clearly, it's easier to control costs when you have fewer bars, but service may suffer.

The math will also help you in evaluating charges. If you figured 500 drinks and were charged for 700, either an error occurred on the hotel's part or you have a group of heavy drinkers. It may not help your current budget, but your estimates for the future will be more accurate. (See Chapter 12 for a more detailed discussion of liquor and other food-and-beverage issues.)

HOTEL PICKUP

Often, the hotel requires you to utilize 75 percent of your room block or you are required to pay a meeting-room charge. Use your math here to save money. Let's assume you blocked 200 rooms and have to use 75 percent of them or incur a $500 meeting-room charge:

$$200 \text{ rooms} \times 75\% = 150 \text{ rooms}$$

Say the guest room rate is $100, and your actual pickup is 148 rooms. You can purchase two rooms for $200, saving $300 by avoiding the room rental. It pays to watch your counts on a daily basis and know in advance exactly what 75 percent means to your meeting.

INTEREST RATES

Simple interest is figured by multiplying the dollar amount times the interest rate:

$$\$1,000 \times 10\% = \$100$$

If you have $4,000 in a six-month certificate of deposit, your formula would be:

$$(\$4,000 \times 10\% \times 6 \text{ months}) \div 12 \text{ months} = \$200$$

Your total after six months will be the principal of $4,000 plus the interest of $200 equaling $4,200.

The process is more complex when compounded on a daily or monthly basis, especially if the balance fluctuates based on new deposits or withdrawals. *Compounded simple interest* means that you earn interest on the interest. If you are holding registration in an account that compounds interest, ask the bank to provide you with a compound interest table for the percentage interest you are earning and consistent with the compounding frequency (daily, quarterly, semiannually, or annually). You will still have to apply interest math based on your balance, the rate, and the length of time your money has been earning.

MEASUREMENTS

Meeting planners deal in square feet with an allowance of x square feet per person, per type of setup, or per other factors such as audiovisual, staging, or dance floors. You will note that hotel specifications give you the length, width, and total square feet per room, but those figures are not always correct. If space is tight, you will want to measure the room yourself; the length multiplied by the width is the square footage for a square or rectangular room. In an odd-shape room, be aware that certain areas (for example, the point of a triangle) are unusable. If an odd-shape space is usable, first measure the consistent (square or rectangular) area as described above; then measure the usable inconsistent area (inserts and offsets) and add those figures to the total.

The basic formula for arriving at the square footage of a triangle is:

$$\text{Square footage of triangle} = \frac{1}{2}\text{base} \times \text{height}$$

For the perimeter of a room, which is often needed when laying out exhibit booths, you add all four sides:

$$\text{Perimeter} = \text{length} + \text{width} + \text{length} + \text{width}$$

Remember to subtract areas along a wall, such as access doors and emergency exits, if the space is not usable. You can use graph paper to aid you in room layout by assigning a scale to each small square, although it is rarely necessary to be that precise. The formulas in this book should be sufficient to guide you once the room is accurately measured.

Decorators are skilled in preparing "to-scale" floor plans, so if needed utilize this resource. Your standards are still important, so you must work with the decorator, hotel, or audiovisual company to inform them about your specific group. The corners they may cut include aisle width, distance between chair rows, number of people at a 6-foot table, and the distance from the first row to the screen. These are requirements that you must establish in advance for the comfort and safety of your attendees.

Audiovisual measurements are equally important, especially if you want the presentation to be seen by all attendees. Once you have measured your room, draw a rough sketch allowing the distances from the screen to first row of chairs and the last row of chairs, leaving side-aisle space on either side. Box in the audience area and remeasure to determine total audience capacity.

The screen height is determined by measuring the distance from the screen to the back of the room and dividing by eight. In a 400-foot long ballroom, the screen size would be prohibitive; therefore, several screens may have to be set up with dual or triple projection. The general rule is to place chairs no closer to the screen than one-and-one-half to two times the height of the screen, and the last row no more than eight times the height of the screen. That formula should give you the placement of a second screen, if one is necessary. The math for a 10-foot screen is:

$$
\begin{aligned}
10 \text{ ft.} \times 1.5 &= 15 \text{ ft. from screen to first row} \\
10 \text{ ft.} \times 8 &= 80 \text{ ft. from screen to last row} \\
80 \text{ ft.} - 15 \text{ feet} &= 65\text{-ft. depth for seating}
\end{aligned}
$$

PERCENTAGES

Basic percentages are simple to compute. If the gratuity is 15 percent and the cost of the dinner is $10 per person the meal plus the gratuity is $11.50:

$$\$10 \times .15 = \$1.50$$
$$\$10 + \$1.50 = \$11.50$$

The difficulty usually comes when figuring percentage increases or decreases, and sometimes in finding the percentage.

Finding the percentage: If food costs are $3,000, what percent of your $15,000 total budget is that? Divide your food costs ($3,000) by total budget costs ($15,000) to equal .2; then move your decimal two places to the right (from .20 to 20) to arrive at the percentage (20 percent). Your proof of accuracy is to multiply $15,000 times .20, which equals the $3,000.

Costs ÷ total budget costs × 100 = Percentage

Finding the percentage increase (comparing the oldest figure to the current figure): Say the total income for the previous year was $50,000 and for the current year is $60,000. Deduct the prior year ($50,000) from the current year ($60,000), then divide the amount of difference ($10,000) by the prior year ($50,000) which equals .2; again, move the decimal two places to the right. The increase is 20 percent.

(Current cost − prior cost) ÷ prior cost × 100 = Percentage increase

Finding the percentage decrease: Say the total income from the previous year was $50,000, and the current year is $45,000. Deduct the current year ($45,000) from the prior year ($50,000), then divide the amount of difference ($5,000) by the prior year ($50,000). This equals .1; move the decimal two places to the right (.10 to 10) and the decrease is 10 percent.

(Prior cost − current cost) ÷ prior cost × 100 = Percentage decrease

FRACTIONS

An example of when fractions would be used would be computing the number of drinks in a quart when a ⅞-ounce jigger is used or an employee's wages at 7¾ hours times the rate. The goal in fractions is to get them translated to decimal figures. For example, if you have ⅖ × ⅝, multiply the top numbers (numerators) then the bottom numbers (denominators):

$$\frac{(2 \times 5)}{(5 \times 8)} = \frac{10}{40} = \frac{1}{4} = .25$$

If one number is a whole number, such as $10, convert it to fraction form (¹⁰⁄₁),then follow the same process as above.

AVERAGES, MEDIANS, MODES

This understanding is particularly useful in presenting meeting statistics. To find the *average* (mean), add all numbers and divide by the number of items added.

The *median* number is the middle number in a series; in the series 1–2–3–4–5, the median would be 3.

The *mode* is the number that appears most often in the series. If you are evaluating the attendance at breakout sessions and the numbers of attendees were 25, 25, 86, 35, 85, 42, 18, and 40, the mode would be 25 and the average would be:

$$25 + 25 + 86 + 35 + 85 + 42 + 18 + 40 = 356 \div 8 = 44.5$$

This would be rounded to 45.

The mode would be 25; that's the number most often attending. The difference between 25 and 45 (the mode and the average) is important to consider in selecting the size of meeting rooms ordering food and beverages, or in other areas, such as identifying the age of your attendees.

METRIC CONVERSIONS

The ability to convert American to metric system, and vice versa, is particularly useful for international meetings. A chart of conversion tables is in the Quick Reference Guide. Generally, metric measures—meters versus yards, kilometers versus miles, liters versus quarts—are slightly larger or longer than the similar U.S. measure. The metric system uses 10 as a base; the U.S. system uses 12; thus, conversion within the metric system is easier. (Incidentally, 35 mm film is 1.37 inches wide.)

READING NUMBERS

Did you ever get confused about the number of zeros in a million or a billion? Just remember that each group in this sequence—hundreds, thousands, millions, billions, trillions—has groups of three zeros or digits. Thus one million has nine zeros, a billion has twelve, and so on.

BREAK-EVEN ANALYSIS

The break-even concept is described in Chapter 14. To find the break-even fee with a set number of attendees:

1. Determine the fixed costs.
2. Determine the total variable costs, which equals variable costs per person times the number of attendees.
3. Add fixed costs and total variable costs to find total costs.
4. Divide the total costs by the number of attendees to find the break-even fee.

$$\text{Fixed costs} + \text{variable costs} = \text{Total costs}$$

$$\frac{\text{Total costs}}{\text{Number of attendees}} = \text{Break-even fee}$$

To find the break-even number of attendees where there is a set fee:

1. Determine the fixed costs.
2. Determine the variable cost per person.
3. Determine the contribution, which equals the fee less the variable costs.
4. Divide the total fixed costs by the contribution.

$$\text{Fee} - \text{variable costs} = \text{contribution}$$

$$\frac{\text{Total costs}}{\text{Contribution}} = \text{Break-even number of attendees}$$

PROBLEMS AND STRATEGIES

PROBLEM: Guarantees are often required before we have our final registration count.

Strategy 1:   Keep daily or weekly preregistration numbers so you can establish preregistration trends. If you know that an average of 75 percent of attendees preregister, base your guarantee on the preregistration number + 25 percent, which equals 100 percent.

Strategy 2:   Keep in mind that you can always increase your guarantee, but you can't lower it. So go low, then increase as soon as you have a more accurate count.

Strategy 3:   Try to schedule your first meal function for the second day. That gives you a chance to count all registrants one day prior to the function.

Strategy 4:   Keep records of session attendance and function attendance and convert your figures to percentages. Those percentages will be your most valuable guide.

Strategy 5:   Use good judgment. Always consider that there may be a change in the program structure, that bad weather may keep attendees inside, or that distractions, such as a casino location, may reduce attendance. These and a host of other variables can influence your figures up or down.

PROBLEM: What is the best way to present data?

Strategy 1:   Convert all numbers to percentages. Numbers may change but percentages are consistent. The numbers 300, 400, 500 don't tell you much; but an annual increase of 20 percent per year is very informative—that becomes a measure for future planning.

Strategy 2:   Graphs and charts are excellent methods for visual presentations. A budget presented in a pie (circle) graph clearly shows where money is spent. A bar graph is an excellent way to compare attendance over a several-year period.

Strategy 3:   Computer software systems can assist greatly in preparing various types of graphs. But you still have to know what you are looking for and how to interpret the data.

16

LIABILITY AND INSURANCE

Liability and insurance can be translated to their most basic meanings, which are responsibility and protection. Lawsuits are the result of a person's or organization's negligence in carrying out responsibilities in a reasonably cautious way, especially if there is harm done to people or property.

The meeting industry has had relatively few claims in the past, certainly compared with other professions, such as the medical field, but claims are increasing. Organizations risk their very existence by failing to address their potential liabilities. Yes, insurance is expensive, policies are confusing, and the value is elusive—until you need it. My advice to you is to consult an attorney regarding the liability laws, to consult an insurance agent about your insurance needs, to follow disclaimer and other protective legal measures, and to learn all you can from as many resources as possible.

GETTING IT ALL TOGETHER

ASSESSING RISKS

The first area meeting planners should address is potential problems or risks—the "what ifs." What if an attendee trips on a loose audiovisual cord, falls, and breaks an arm? Is that the audiovisual company's negligence or your negligence for not checking the work of your contractor? What if the attendee is a surgeon and not an opera singer, does that make a difference? What if the audiovisual company failed to obtain insurance or to keep its payments up-to-date?

The planner has to dissect each activity, event, contractor, and site, exploring the "what ifs" for that particular situation. Children, teenagers, the elderly, and the handicapped may require different considerations from the "average" conference attendee. Hot-air ballooning is a much higher risk activity than a hotel theme party. Poor lighting on stages or stairs or uneven surfaces are a risk. Heavy boxes that can strain the backs of staffers are a risk. And we are all exceedingly aware of the risks associated with alcohol. These subtle issues of potential negligence haunt me more than the more common suits resulting from cancellation, theft, or property damage.

Once you have a thorough list of the possibilities, you should explore your organization's current insurance coverage and the coverage of each of your suppliers as related to their contractual responsibilities. It is not enough to know that they have insurance; you must know what types of policies they have, check what the coverage inclusion and exclusions are, and, under certain circumstances, require their insurance company to notify you of any lapse in payment.

Insurance agents are a great resource and will assist you in evaluating high-risk areas and suggesting types and levels of coverage. But your attorney is the legal expert and knows where the burden of liability is likely to fall.

REDUCING RISK

In conjunction with good legal counsel and reasonable insurance coverage, thorough and thoughtful preparation is your best defense—not the only defense, but the best. In other words, avoid problems. Don't book your meeting in a high-crime area or where seasonal weather could cause cancellation. If you can't completely avoid risks, maybe you can minimize them or possibly even share them. You might minimize the risk of a person tripping over the audiovisual cord if you instruct the company in writing of your organization's specific requirements and inspect its work.

You can also in your contracts decline certain risks. These clauses are usually "hold harmless" or "indemnification" clauses, which basically say that one party is not responsible for negligence of the other party. If a chandelier is improperly hung and falls on the guest, you the planner are not liable for any claims. The facilty might in turn decline responsibility for theft of your meeting equipment that was not securely stored.

Thoroughly written contracts set the terms of suppliers' liability, often establish the manner of settlement (courts or arbitration), and create a disincentive to filing frivolous claims by requiring the losing party to pay all attorney and court fees.

The process of monitoring liabilities and protection alternatives is ongoing. Insurance coverage changes; new trends or new technologies create new risks; state laws are revised; court interpretations and rulings broaden or become more focused; and rates may become prohibitive. Beyond these issues, each meeting has its own unique qualities—facilities are different and services and contractors approach their responsibilities in unique ways.

LIABILITY AND INSURANCE TIPS

TYPES OF INSURANCE

Insurance options range from broad comprehensive general policies for one year to specific one-day policies for a piece of art on display. (See the Quick

Reference Guide for a comprehensive listing.) The broad liability policies cover:

- Contracts
- Government regulations and laws
- Personal injury
- Property damage
- Other general occurrences

Within each clause there are inclusions, exclusions, coverage limits, and deductibles. These four factors are the essence of your policy and the cost determinants.

Umbrella policies can be added to extend the coverage limits of an already existing liability policy, especially if you move from a low-risk situation to a higher-risk situation. An example would be a planner moving from an employee position within a company to an independent consultant position.

Meeting Cancellation or Interruption Insurance

Other popular meeting-related insurance is cancellation or interruption-of-convention insurance. This is particularly valuable for large meetings dependent on revenues for their operating expenses. This policy goes into effect only if there are circumstances beyond the sponsoring organization's control, such as fires, strikes, weather prohibiting access to the meeting site, or civil unrest. Poor attendance or failure of your organization to conduct the meeting as a result of financial difficulties are not normally covered reasons. As in all policies, the fine print is critical. If they are paying revenues lost, you need to know in the beginning how this figure will be established.

Planners' Professional Liability

Planners' professional liability policies are on the increase. As such positions are recognized as professional and industry standards are set, such as the certified meeting planner status, the planners' personal liability will increasingly be at risk. Presuming a company hired you as an expert, and you hired the AV company, if an attendee trips over an improperly taped cord you may be partially or completely at fault. If you are an employee of a company, check your coverage when acting on its behalf; you may want to increase your own personal coverage.

Eventually, there should be established a standard of conduct in relation to meetings for AV companies, hotels, caterers, transportation, and other suppliers. In the interim, you will have to prepare your own and have them signed by the various parties. In court, the strongest weapons you have are written, dated, and, if need be, signed documents, from letters to contracts.

LIQUOR LIABILITY

Liquor liability for the host is another new insurance trend among planners. Here the key word is "host" or free liquor. If a person is paying for his drinks and continues to be served after some vague interpretation of "intoxication," the liable party would be either the intoxicated individual, the serving establishment, or, more recently, the event host. As rulings have changed quickly in this area, it is wise to control drinking by reducing bar hours, types of liquor available, and adding security at doors checking for possible intoxication. State laws vary, as do local rulings. (The hotel or bureau can brief you on these.)

WORKERS' COMPENSATION

Workers' compensation is required by law in most states, which require companies to insure their employees in the event of job-related injuries. The risk to planners can be contract or temporary employees. Your contract with the company providing such employees should clearly state that it is the employer (the agency providing the personnel) that is responsible for this insurance and any related taxes or withholding.

TRANSFER OF RISKS

In the above situation and many others, contracts commonly transfer the risk to the primary party responsible through "hold harmless" or "indemnification" clauses. In some cases, the planner assumes the risks or shares them. While the language of the clause is standard, the areas covered are negotiable. Even with such clauses, you may have to defend your actions and show that you had sufficiently carried out the full extent of your part of the responsibility.

CERTIFICATES OF INSURANCE

Many organizations require proof of insurance from all suppliers in addition to a contract clause. This will limit your organization's liability up to the limits of the holder's policy. Claims over that limit may revert to your organization. Require that certain limits be carried by the suppliers. The certificate of insurance is a signed form that lists the insurance companies, types of coverage held by each, policy numbers, effective or expiration dates, and liability limits. Your company may require that it be named as an "additional insured" on the policies for the period covering your event.

BONDING

Bonding of workers handling cash or valuables has been a part of the meeting industry for a longer time than other types of insurance coverage. Most companies providing contract employees for registration and security bond their own employees; you will have to bond your own if large cash amounts or equipment responsibility are involved. (Your insurance company can provide you with information on bonding.)

STATE AND FEDERAL REQUIREMENTS

Codes, permits, and licenses are variable requirements of each service industry. State and federal laws determine what these standards will be. While less common than certificates of insurance, it is reasonable to require contractors to produce proof of valid licenses and permits.

SAFETY

General safety precautions should be adhered to by the service provider and by the planner. From the service provider they include properly operating equipment, security systems (such as fire alarms or security locks in guest rooms), and healthy food-preparation conditions. The planner must monitor safe placement of easels, safe candle holders and/or slow-burning candles, first aid emergency assistance, obstructions in aisles, and—one of the more dangerous—the practice of attendees angling chairs to reserve tables. Planners should address these issues in safety memos provided to suppliers or inserted in attendee packets. Preventive measures are in fact the best insurance.

ADMONITIONS, RELEASES, AND WAIVERS

These slips of paper, signed by attendees, are designed to alert attendees to certain risks and release the sponsor of liability should a claim arise. While the release may protect you from a first-party claim, the dedicated will find a party liable and that party may in turn sue you.

PROBLEMS AND STRATEGIES

PROBLEM: We have been unable to obtain insurance for short-term valuable displays such as art and jewelry.

Strategy 1:   Locate an agent who is willing to go to the added trouble of obtaining these unusual coverages for you. Your best approach is to let one agent handle all your insurance needs if they are qualified in the various areas.

Strategy 2:   Attempt to have the exhibit or display sponsored by a company that carries the type of insurance you need. Often, large companies have their own insured art collection and can add a rider to their policy for minimal, if any, additional costs.

Strategy 3:   If you must proceed uninsured, hire a security staff during all hours of public display and otherwise store in a top security area.

Strategy 4:   Cost versus risk must always be evaluated. Don't hesitate to cancel the display if you cannot afford the loss.

PROBLEM: Our most successful meetings have included sporting events, but we are concerned about injuries.

Strategy 1:   While it's not foolproof, require all participants to sign a waiver or release prior to participation.

Strategy 2:   Coordinators of professional sporting events carry insurance for personal injury. Require that you be listed as an additional insured and that a certificate of insurance issued.

Strategy 3:   If you are still uncomfortable, cancel the event or limit the activities to low-risk games.

Strategy 4:   Be vigilant in checking the site and equipment for safety and the history of your coordinators for conducting injury-free events. While this may not prevent a claim, your personal liability will increase if you hire a company with a reputation for negligence.

PROBLEM: When renting cars, should we purchase the rental company's insurance or not?

Strategy 1:   Your company's policy should indicate the inclusion or exclusion of rental or leased cars. Review that policy, and if you're still in doubt discuss your concerns and policy with your agent. If your company's policy includes rental cars, rent the car in the company's name, not yours.

Strategy 2:   Predetermine who the drivers will be; even with additional insurance, be sure they are included as covered drivers.

Strategy 3:   If in doubt, pay for the coverage.

Strategy 4:   Many states are reviewing the laws and placing limits on rental agencies. Follow the legislative activity in this area.

PROBLEM: Registration workers are careless about securing their personal items, yet they expect us to assume the cost of lost or stolen items.

Strategy 1:   Have all workers sign releases from claims against your organization for lost or stolen items.

Strategy 2:   Provide workers with a secure area for coats, purses, and other personal items. You may ask the hotel for use of safety deposit boxes for each worker. If the numbers are great, explore the possibility of using a locker system.

Strategy 3:   Require workers to leave unnecessary items at home, such as large amounts of cash, credit cards, checkbooks, jewelry, and other valuables.

17

PEOPLE MANAGEMENT

Meeting planners are expected to manage—lead—a mass of highly divergent people, from the chairman of the board to laborers (who might not even speak English) to highly skilled technicians, bringing them together as a team with a finished product in three to twelve months. It is truly mind-boggling. Yet few if any professional publications or seminars address this subject, beyond a procedural level of working with volunteers, setting up committees, or using Robert's rules of order to "run" a meeting.

Meeting planning is a "people business," and most meeting planners are people-oriented. The irony is that "people likers" are often flawed by the need to be liked as well, and therefore have difficulty in objectively selecting, assigning, and leading the people not only below and beside them, but above them. In other words "people likers" are not necessarily good "people managers."

No one organizes a meeting alone; planners are all very dependent on others. The more effective they are in working with the variety of people and in providing leadership, the more successful the event will be.

GETTING IT ALL TOGETHER

The first step is always the same, getting to know your project—but here the emphasis is on the people. Look at the existing structure (this will be the "chance" group, because you get them regardless of their skills or interest, in contrast to the "chosen" group, which you obviously selected) and identify the skills and expertise available. This group often requires your greatest people skills because you didn't pick the members, and usually you have less control over them. Included in the group are board members, committees, volunteers, VIP spouses, and the various people in your organization who are usually overworked before they get the added assignment of your meeting. However, people in this group have a working knowledge of the organization, are committed to a successful event, bring their diverse experiences to the job, and are usually available at no additional costs to the organization.

While your goal is to include everyone as part of the team, your approach with the "chance" group should be one of working *with*; others who are paid respond in a more controllable way, because they are working *for* you. Your homework should include a clear definition of what each person wants to do, what they are expected to do, how much time they can give, and other commitments and deadlines that may influence their ability to perform according to your planning schedule. Ask these people what you can do to help them, what information they need, how they like to be communicated with, what they have liked, disliked, or would like to see changed about past meetings.

Regardless of the group—those you have been given or those you have chosen—you need to understand people management. Motivation is the key. It is not simply what you do to motivate your team, but understanding what the internal motivator is within each individual. Some motivators are power, authority, money, recognition, credit, quality, position, involvement, creativity, and skill development.

People also respond differently to different management styles. There are the team members who need to see the whole picture. There are those who want only the facts—if you gave them the whole picture you would lose them before you got to their responsibilities. Some will only respond by knowing who else is involved (credibility) and others need to believe that the project is worthwhile. Some people will probably prefer written reports; others will want frequent verbal contact; still others prefer a combination—and you must figure out what each person wants.

One approach is to write a one-paragraph or one-page job description for the key people on your team. You might even ask them to read it and make corrections where you are off base.

It should be noted here that, regarding who you get versus whom you select, this is more of an issue for associations than for corporations. Corporate planners tend to use outside suppliers for certain work rather than expecting a committee to handle it, whereas associations often must use the existing organizational structure.

Regardless, the key to people management is understanding your project and your needs, understanding your people, communicating frequently (both verbally and in a written format), and, ultimately, ensuring that the thank-you they get is responsive to their motivation. Think about what you would want; it won't be the same for others, but it will give you clues.

PEOPLE MANAGEMENT TIPS

MANAGEMENT STYLES

There are, of course, experts and texts that deal on a scientific level with this subject, but if you are having problems, consider two issues: (1) You can certainly lose more time and energy fighting the problems than investing up-front money in identifying management styles and preferences. (2) Think of your own style. If your body language is communicating rushed, hassled, and frazzled, others will perceive problems where they probably don't exist. Calm versus frantic is your best look.

COMMUNICATIONS

You have already been given one excellent communication method, which is the planning schedule (Exhibit 1-1). If given to everyone, it tells them who, what, and when about everything they need to know. It is a simple format, easy to use, and a great management tool.

The telephone (which normally grows out of meeting planners' ears anyway) is another tool for keeping in touch.

For written communication, design a format that identifies all "paper" sent by you regarding this event or your department's activities. I have an "Action Request Form," which is salmon-colored and is attached to a request or memo if a response is required. Some people have their action form printed on a two-part carbonless form. You send a copy and keep a copy, so you don't forget what you asked for. You can add this to your "tickler" file according to the date the action or response is due.

Whatever you do, keep it simple for yourself and the receiver. And give people a reasonable advance notice. The "I want it yesterday" approach never wins a popularity or professionalism contest, and it usually ensures that deadlines will be missed.

COMMITTEES AND COMMITTEE MEETINGS

Understand the types of committees and committee members, and know which you are dealing with. There are basically three roles: the workers, the dreamers, and the endorsers. The workers actually accept assignments and complete them on time. The dreamers have great ideas, but you are the implementer. (If a dreamer accepts an assignments, be sure to ask who you should follow up with, because you can count on the fact that the work *will* be delegated.) Then there are the endorsers, who are most often found on committees that require fundraising. These committees usually meet only once or twice and are made up of community leaders, movie stars, professional sports players, politicians, and so on. This is a caviar-and-cocktails crowd, not a danish-and-coffee group. Their involvement most often means they will sign a letter and you can put their name on your letterhead or in promotional pieces.

Committee meetings should always have an agenda and a report. The committee agenda should be short, listing major topics to be discussed or reports to be given. Assign a name to each topic or report and a time. Try to be realistic, leaving discussion time where it is needed. If decisions are needed at the meeting, list them under each topic with a subheading ("Decision Needed"). This also helps keep discussions focused. With regard to reports, experience has taught me to always tape record meetings and to make the tapes available to those who need the details. I then write a condensed report of one or two pages. The report should include changes, upcoming or missed deadlines, and decisions made. If you format your report along the agenda structure with a subheading for these three areas, you can write it during the meeting. If need be, use what you have written to summarize the meeting. This gives the committee members a chance to add important points you might have missed. Mail the report as soon as possible, and always include the next meeting date and location.

VOLUNTEERS

While corporations do utilize volunteers, it is a labor source most frequently used by associations and other nonprofit groups. Associations utilizing volunteers who have been recruited from within their own ranks have a wide selection of well-qualified, well-informed people from which they may draw. These volunteers arrive equipped with a large fund of association-related information. They usually have attended enough similar meetings to have acquired a knowledge of services needed by attendees and an understanding of how these services are most effectively delivered. If you plan to use volunteers in any capacity at your meeting, you must provide them with the same guidelines and materials you would give to any other team member.

Among the important sources for volunteers are the policymaking people within the organizational structure who will bear the ultimate legal and financial liability (board members) or will serve as committee volunteers in decision-making roles for matters involving possible legal consequence. Such services are invaluable.

Corporate spouses are another source of volunteers and are essentially drawn only from the hierarchy of the corporate structure at the levels of CEO, president, and vice-president. Spouses can and do make valuable spontaneous contributions as volunteers, serving in a resource capacity, on committees selecting spouse programs, special event themes, children's programs, etc. (I automatically assume that all spouses will be female, because I have yet to encounter a male spouse serving in a volunteer capacity.)

Beyond people who have a personal commitment to your organization, use volunteers with caution and great thought. The guidelines in the Quick Reference Section may be helpful in planning volunteer involvement.

OUTSIDE SUPPLIERS

If you are a control person, you will love this group. The power to hire, pay, or fire is a very clear way of working. Of course, you still have to motivate suppliers, but you don't have to live with dead wood. Once you have explored all the "professional approaches" to selecting a contractor (credentials, experiences, references, licenses, insurance, and so on), conduct a "gut" evaluation. Are they interested in your project for the right reasons? Remember, you can choose these people!

Suppliers, just like volunteers, also require a clear understanding of your expectations. An audiovisual presentation may be technically perfect, but a poor setup may be the first thing you see when you walk into the room. If you don't ask for draping and define the setup location, you may not get what you want. You should also define setup times. If you are unclear in your instructions, you can't complain about what you get. In areas that are too technical or specialized for you to be the expert, ask for advice from people you trust. The guidelines given in the Quick Reference section will help ensure a smooth planner–supplier relationship.

PROBLEMS AND STRATEGIES

PROBLEM: What is the best way to assign volunteers?

Strategy 1:   Develop a questionnaire for volunteers so you can find out what each individual likes to do and how much time he or she can commit and when. If some want to attend specific sessions, assign them as door monitors to the preferred sessions. If others want people interaction, assign them to registration. A volunteer with a legal background may be most effectively used reviewing contracts on weekends in the planning stage. The more closely assignments meet volunteers' interests, the more reliable and effective their participation will be.

Strategy 2:   Don't assume a volunteer's interest will necessarily fall in that person's area of professional expertise. I personally am much more likely to accept a volunteer position that doesn't involve meeting and event planning.

Strategy 3:   Spend the time to personally discuss a person's assignment with him or her. Walk volunteers through the procedure, setting the pace and identifying the end result. People may perceive registration solely as an area of interpersonal activity—unless you tell them they have 45 seconds to process each person and they can't leave their posts until they balance their receipts. Appearance and reality are often very different. Door monitors need to know that they have to stand in one spot for two hours; volunteers working on legal issues need to know whether three or thirty contracts will be assigned; committee members need to know how many meetings are required. We tend to think people won't accept if they know the reality; the fact is, if they get more than they bargained for, they will either quit mid-stream or won't come back.

PROBLEM: Unfortunately, we have found many volunteers to be unrealiable. What can we do?

Strategy 1:   At the risk of repetition, you must define the parameters of each person's responsibility.

Strategy 2:   Be considerate of other people's schedules in the planning stage and be patient with schedule changes.

Strategy 3:   Keep in mind that your priorities are not the same as everyone else's. Prepare alternatives and backups for absent or irresponsible volunteers. Though rather morbid, I always ask myself, "What would happen if "x" person died?" (including me). Once you have dealt with the worst-case scenario, you have a reserve of alternatives to draw from.

Strategy 4:   Back to motivation. Don't be a bore to work with, make it fun! And don't forget to give credit, praise, and a continuing dose of thank-yous.

Strategy 5:   If you give people responsibility, let them do it and do it their way. Follow up, retain final control, and provide assistance, but don't stand over their shoulder.

PROBLEM: No one cares as much as we do.

Strategy 1: Accept it. That's life. It's cold, it's hard, and it's disappointing. The truth is, someone else's sick dog is not as compelling as your sick dog. Don't expect what can never be.

Strategy 2: Some people *do* care as much, but for different reasons. You may be obsessed with perfection in registration procedures, while someone else is focused on the welcoming/greeting aspect. Allow and encourage different perspectives.

18

ON-SITE MANAGEMENT

The day of the meeting or event is the time when all the pieces come together. Months, sometimes years, of preparation begin and end so quickly the days become a blur! Ironically, your many hours of preparation go unnoticed if the event is a success. It all looks so easy, as if everything just fell into place naturally. If you're ill prepared, however, you will find problems and rough edges at every turn. The meeting will become a nightmare as the disasters grow. Once the meeting begins, there is very little you can do to compensate for errors and omissions in preplanning.

My concept of the role of the planner on-site is that of a highly skilled manager. You have put together your team which includes suppliers from the hotel staff, audiovisual company, decorator, florist, tour company—essentially every company or individual who has a part in your event. The well-prepared manager will have provided each team member with written instructions, outlining the who, when, where, and how of each one's responsibilities. The objective is to communicate clearly and in great detail, so that there is no confusion and all members can easily merge together as your staff.

Chapter 17 on people management touches on many of the skills you will need on-site. The most successful planners take great care in building, motivating, and inspiring each person to do his or her best. The planner must remember that many of these people do one or more meetings every day. Thus, there is a danger of their tasks becoming routine and their attention to detail casual. It is up to you to make them feel differently about your event.

But motivation alone is not enough. The balancing point is your thoroughness in thinking through every moment and detail, recruiting experienced, high-quality people, and clearly communicating the details of their responsibilities to each as individuals who must interact with a team.

Incidentally, I would never agree to plan a meeting if I could not be on-site to "manage" it. But I also plan it as if I were *not* going to be there. While

Portions of this chapter are drawn from articles by the author previously published in *Convention World*, a Bayard publication.

I have never been too ill to stay away, there is always that risk. The written instructions should be so thorough that almost anyone could pick them up and run the meeting. Maybe not as easily as you, but without glitches noticeable to the attendees.

GETTING IT ALL TOGETHER

The process usually begins with a vision of what the end product will look like. Everything you do is oriented toward this ultimate experience: city selection, facility selection, supplier selection, agenda design, and speaker selection. It is much like a pyramid, where you begin with a broad base and refine each element to its finest point.

THE SPEC BOOK

To successfully build such a pyramid, the planner prepares a "spec book," otherwise known as a specifications book or staging guide, containing the detailed requirements. This staging guide is often called the "bible." There are several approaches for the preparation of this book, but the focus of this chapter will be not only on what has worked for me, but also on what has been well received by suppliers.

The important issue is that the planner prepare the instructions. All too often, the planner relies on the facility to write up the requirements, which within the hotel structure are called event orders, banquet event orders (BEOs), or some similar term. Their purpose is to communicate your needs internally to each of the hotel's departments outside suppliers and staff members responsible for making your event happen. You will receive a copy of the hotel BEOs to review, approve, adjust, and return to the hotel. This should all happen about four to six weeks before you arrive on-site. While the spec book should be the document they use to prepare their internal communications, your specifications extend beyond the facility requirements to all suppliers' requirements. Relying on the hotel's internal system leaves wide gaps in the detail needed by other contractors.

My process for checking supplier's orders is to have one of my staff read their (the hotel's and other supplier's orders while I compare with my requirements (spec book). Errors, omissions, and changes are marked on their sheets in red and returned by overnight mail. You want your corrected copies back to them before they are given to the internal staff. The biggest errors occur when these sheets are distributed to the hotel staff with incorrect information. Changes after this point are also highly risky. Be sure to ask your hotel coordinator how these changes are communicated. While I understand that changes and adjustments are a part of our job, the fewer you have, the greater your chance for success.

Now back to the timing and structure of your spec book. Ideally, it should be in the hands of your suppliers four to six weeks prior to the meeting. A month is the minimum time needed for their review, preparation of orders, review and approval by you, and distribution, ordering, and so on within each department.

The structure of your spec book may vary from meeting to meeting or according to the individual who prepared it, but the following information should be included.

General Information

Section I of the requirements does the following:

- Provides a profile of the group.
- Identifies your staff by name and responsibility areas (such as conference manager, exhibits manager, registration manager).
- Outlines the guest room block in each hotel with rates.
- Provides instructions on master account billing, authorized signatures, and charges.
- Lists VIP, staff, and complimentary accommodation requirements as well as any other complimentary items negotiated.

This section should not be filled with new information, but should provide a summarization of information that should have been communicated to all departments or suppliers. It also provides an opportunity to review agreements that may have been made many years ago or by a salesperson who has since left the organization. Although such agreements should be reviewed frequently, this will serve as a reminder and stimulate questions, if further clarification is needed.

Special Instructions

The instructions in Part II are specific to each responsibility area in a hotel or by outside suppliers, contractors, including:

- Convention services, food and beverages, reservations, front desk, accounting
- Bell station, PBX/switchboard, package receiving and shipping
- Housekeeping, housemen (or room setup crews), audiovisual, security, and engineering

The purpose is to provide guidance regarding the group's patterns, such as heavy early morning breakfasts in restaurant outlets and room service or the percentage of walk-in registrants that may be anticipated (who may require rooms that weren't reserved).

In this section, also specify your expectations and special needs, which include:

- Procedures for review and signing of function bills
- Advance setup times for inspection of function rooms
- Receipt and delivery of shipments and equipment
- Paid-out amounts
- Flower holding areas
- Fire evacuation procedures
- Personnel on duty and their hours
- On-site historical report requirements

The two sections of the spec book that have the greatest impact on the success of your meeting are the special instructions and the detailed event requirements discussed below. While the detailed event requirements vary with each meeting, the special instructions are largely generic. Your expectations as a professional meeting planner are established and consistent. The difficulty in writing this section is identifying those specifics that are important to your meeting. With each meeting, new issues will emerge that you can add. This section will help you learn about yourself, and assist the hotel in anticipating and planning for the unique requirements of your meeting.

Meeting Purveyors

We have all had those moments of standing on the street waiting for the buses, with one thousand impatient people behind you, watching rush-hour traffic creep by and not a bus in sight, and no time to search the files for the telephone number of the bus or tour company. In all such cases, Section III, containing the name of the bus company, a contact person, the telephone number, and the address is a quick and valuable reference for you. Included in this section is such information for each of the following:

- Audiovisual
- Security
- Decorator
- Equipment
- Office machines
- Special events
- Photographer
- Entertainment
- Secretarial service
- Florist
- Personnel
- Convention bureau personnel
- Headquarters and overflow hotels
- Audiotaping
- Official airline
- Official car rental
- Telephone company
- Quick-print companies

You can be sure the telephone number you felt was too insignificant to be listed will be the one you need and the most difficult to find in your files.

Detailed Event Requirements

When you receive the infamous BEOs from the hotel outlining all of the requirements that you must approve, sign, and live with forever, how do you double check their accuracy? When checking meeting room setups, how do you remember absolutely everything that goes in the room? This is when you turn to the final and largest section of the spec book: Section IV. Listed here are the detailed requirements that outline each event by date, time, room assignment, and supplier.

All aspects of the event are included at this point. Information relevant to the hotel is listed first and specifies the room set (with diagrams, where appropriate), audiovisual equipment to be provided by the hotel, food and beverages ordered (with serving time), the number of people anticipated, and the price and quantity of each item.

This is followed by a list of all other purveyor services or equipment necessary for the event. Each item ordered from outside the hotel should be identified with the name of the company you have contracted with for the service.

List all items and personnel requested, indicate the delivery, pickup, or duty schedule, the quantity, the price, and the specific location, such as placement of the banner.

THE ROLE OF THE MEETING PLANNER ON-SITE

The role of the meeting planner on-site is one of manager, teacher, accountant, recorder, historian, host/hostess, mediator, problem solver, morale booster and often general laborer. This is not always easy and not always fun, yet the energy generated by this menagerie of roles is what the meeting planner thrives on.

The meeting planner arrives at the convention a few days early and spends that time in countless meetings with the hotel's staff, suppliers, personnel, and individuals reviewing the unique responsibilities of each and building the on-site team. Interestingly, this "team" is not necessarily the one you have been working with in the planning stage. You now have to get to know the front-desk staff, the setup crew, and the registration workers. A list of the activities of the meeting planner from arrival to departure is in the Quick Reference Guide. While it is not comprehensive, it will give you some ideas for structuring your on-site time.

In addition to building the team, you have boxes to unpack and systems to organize. You are building the base that will allow you to operate efficiently and effectively during the meeting. Once the meeting begins, you will be busy checking rooms, providing guarantees, communicating changes and adjustments, recording critical information almost as it happens for your historical files, balancing registration monies, and assisting attendees with their many needs. You may have the additional responsibilities of coordinating attendees' arrival, distributing gifts, and supervising an array of special events. Following the meeting, tired though you may be, you will have to review bills, have wrap-up meetings and critiques with hotel and suppliers, and pack remaining materials for shipment back home. Ideally, you will have built strong bonds of friendship that will be a part of the memories, experiences, and learning that took place. It is hard to find a meeting planner who does not experience a rewarding sense of tiredness and an exhilarating sense of accomplishment at the end of a meeting.

ON-SITE MANAGEMENT TIPS

PRE-/POST-MEETINGS

I am amazed at the number of hotel managers who tell me that most meeting planners don't have a pre-convention ("pre-con") meeting and that virtually none have a post-convention ("post-con") meeting.

Pre-Con Meeting

The purpose of the pre-con meeting, as far as I am concerned, is for everyone to meet each other and for the hotel to learn the incoming group's needs, expectations, and special requirements.

The hotel staff needs to have a sense of who the meeting planner is. Does the planner expect perfection without flexibility? Is the planner experienced, confident, and well prepared? Is this the planner's first meeting? Does the planner have a sense of humor? Is the planner a team player? Will the planner be receptive to suggestions, or will he or she demand things be done one way?

It is also an opportunity for the hotel staff to ask questions of the planner that the sales or convention services managers may not be qualified to answer. Such questions often center on usage by attendees of restaurants and room service at various hours, the number of late check-out requests, and walk-in and no-show percentages. The hotel managers generally want to know what they can expect so they can schedule staff appropriately. I appreciate those questions and try to be as honest as possible, although even groups with the best histories have atypical years. One year the hotel's lounge may be the center of all after-hour activities; the next year the lounge may be a ghost town.

For some reason, hotels usually think the pre-con is their show. As a planner, I think it is mine, and I like to run it. If the hotel wants to have its own internal briefing, that's fine, but the pre-con is the planner's meeting.

The hotel's upper management may be unsure of the reason the planner is running the meeting because it is traditionally the responsibility of sales or convention services managers. If you want to take charge of your pre-con, be sure to explain your philosophy to the hotel staff. Most people accept things if they understand them.

The pre-con may be held earlier if you have a complex meeting, but it is usually held after you arrive at the site. The meeting usually takes place the day before the first day of your event. If Sunday or Monday is your opening day, you will have to arrange the meeting two days before—a weekday is a must so that key staff will attend. Ask whether the department personnel who will be staffing your meeting will be in attendance. (I had the unfortunate experience of a key person being on vacation at the time of the pre-con and showing up the next day with no briefing. Had I known in advance, I would have either requested that the employee come back early for the meeting or scheduled an individual briefing the next day.)

Within the hotel, the front desk is the most difficult department to communicate with. Somehow, key information never makes it from one shift to the next—and somehow the uninformed shift is the one working your peak arrival period. Once you identify areas that consistently cause problems, you can develop alternative strategies. To counterbalance the "front desk" problem, I try to meet with and brief each shift the first day.

Who should attend is fairly straightforward: the hotel sales manager, convention services manager, and department heads or their designated representative (if that person is responsible for your meeting). And since organization charts vary among hotels, include any subsections of departments that will in any way touch your meeting. I also always invite the general manager. Last but not least are the other suppliers who will be a part of your team.

The agenda usually begins with the necessary around-the-table introductions, which are extremely confusing if you are meeting behind-the-scene managers for the first time. At my most recent pre-con meeting, the convention services manager prepared place cards with everyone's name and department, which was extremely helpful. To facilitate communication, the meeting planner should have a list prepared with the name and number of a key staff member in each department (see Exhibit 18-1).

Regarding the agenda, first, I explain generally who the group is and provide its relevant history and behavior patterns. (Because my company is an independent planning company, I explain who we are and what our role is.) Second, I review the department-by-department instructions with the exception of convention services and food and beverages, which are too detailed and lengthy for other departments to endure, not to mention irrelevant to their responsibilities.

Among the points I make are:

- If there is a problem with an attendee's reservation, I must be contacted prior to any action being taken.
- Shipping must notify me immediately upon arrival of any packages.
- Security must contact me before taking any action with an attendee registered for the conference.
- The catering department will not deliver checks to the planner during the meeting. I will come to the catering office each afternoon to sign the daily checks.
- Each food-and-beverage event must have its own separate banquet checks—events must not be combined.
- All room setups must be approved by me before the crew leaves, regardless of the hour.

Among the things I ask for are:

- A daily printout of the guest/sleeping-room pickup.
- A review of fire procedures.
- A review of other groups in-house and their program.
- A schedule of staff on duty during my meeting.
- A review of light- and thermostat-control procedures.
- Current staffing levels (including temporaries, part-timers, or trainees) in the various departments. For example, are three of the five PBX operators at home with the flu? Will a local transit strike prohibit employees from arriving at work on time? Am I getting an exhausted staff that has just worked three major meetings in succession?

Communication lines are stressed and crisis management discussed. Above all I let people know that I don't like surprises. I want to be the first to know everything.

The flip side of this coin is that I will return the courtesy to the hotel staff. If I know of an attendee's cancellation, if my registration is drastically up or down, or if there is a detail of particular importance to my client, I will alert the hotel.

The pre-convention meeting is the ideal forum for communicating the feeling that while you will demand a great deal from the hotel, you are also willing to give in areas that help. In essence, your meeting is just another group to the switchboard, housekeeping, front desk, and probably 99 percent of the other departments. For this reason, demands must be presented as challenges. Try to create a feeling among the staff for your group and motivate people to see your attendees as unique, special, and worth the extra effort. Above all, establish a relationship that is honest. We have to be a team, and honesty is the only way to achieve that.

That's why the pre-con is the planner's meeting. You have at best sixty minutes to communicate all this, which is critical in developing the required rapport.

Post-Con Meeting

The post-con meeting is my favorite, tired though I may be. The post-con meeting brings everyone from the pre-con back, doors closed, guards down, and future sales forgotten, to ask, "What could we have done differently to make it better?"

This wrap-up meeting must be discussed at the pre-con meeting. The staff has to know in advance that everyone will have a critique opportunity, but the planner must be open and receptive to new ideas and must not be defensive. As the client, the planner must set the tone of the post-con meeting and make it clear that he or she is receptive to a critique by hotel staff.

The purpose is not to point fingers or place fault, but to seriously evaluate the process, the strengths and weaknesses, good and not so good, why certain things happened, and what was or wasn't done that did or didn't help.

I encourage you to add a post-con session to your meetings. I have found them to be helpful, honest, and a completion of the full circle of meeting planning. When the master bill arrives, we each return to our court to negotiate and mediate the disputes. Honesty and fairness have long since been established and validated, and we are eager to work with one another again.

MONITORING ON-SITE ATTENDANCE

One of the most surprising facts about a meeting is the number of people who actually attend sessions. If your attendance is 500, planners usually assume there must be space in every session for this number, either as a combined total in breakouts or as a total for a general session. In some situations this may be the case, but usually it is not. My experience is that session attendance may be as low as 40 to 50 percent of the total attendance, and for many groups is never in excess of 80 percent. But the only way to "know" is to count the attendees in each room. This is the purpose of the room-count form that door monitors fill out as soon as the session begins. (See Exhibit 18-2.)

If the sessions are longer than an hour, a new form should be completed each hour, following a break, or at a time when the door monitor notices a significant change in attendance. Often a room is filled to hear one speaker and after that presentation the "population" in the room experiences a dramatic change. Such additional counts are important for after-the-fact interpretive value. I ask door monitors for comments as well so I can have an even better perspective on what happens in each room. They are then asked to staple all the session-count forms for their room together and turn them in to the staff office or to their supervisor. Prior to turning them in, they must write on the top sheet the peak attendance, low attendance, and average attendance. This gives me a summary at a glance.

These data are then recorded on the Function Attendance Summary (Exhibit 18-3) by date, time, location, and function name. Much of the information on the summary sheet can be filled out in advance, but be sure to leave space for any last-minute additions. (Incidently, I also prepare room-counts for committee meetings and any other rooms used for my group.)

If the door monitors have counted the number of chairs in the room, you will have an accurate count of the number of seats the room was set to accommodate. While counting the empty seats is usually quicker, you may prefer to have door monitors count the number of people. You will have to let monitors know whether or not you want the stage area counted and, if so, whether the final number should be a combined total. (I am not usually interested in speakers for this count, and so prefer that only an audience count be taken.) For purposes of the summary form, I usually want the peak number recorded, as long as I have my back-up room sheets available to check any rooms that have great inconsistencies.

The information goes into the final report and into adjustments for future meetings. For psychological reasons, I do not want meeting rooms to look empty; if attendance counts are low, I reduce the space requirements for the next year. If sessions are closed or standing room only, I increase the requirements. The data will also assist you in placing sessions/speakers of high interest in larger rooms, and the reverse for low-interest topics. You may even decide to cancel topics in future years if interest is minimal. You will also have better insight into attendance patterns: Are early-afternoon sessions filled and late-afternoon ones sparsely attended? You may also begin to tell when attendance is dropping from early check-outs or building from late arrivals; or even the impact of a big party night on the next morning's session and meal-function attendance. The assumptions are mind boggling if you study the data you now have at your fingertips.

An additional consideration is that you may find you do not need as much meeting space and can expand your site choices. The key is always to maximize your organization's dollars and evaluate the hard data. Tough decision making is the most effective tool you have that doesn't affect the quality of the program or event. Of all the cost-saving ideas in this book, the most important ones are those that result from collecting and analyzing data and making adjustments to match the new information gained.

GUARANTEES

Guarantees are covered in Chapter 12, but are a major on-site activity. You must keep close count of the number of people who have registered, cancelled, or have not shown up at all (no-shows); then compare those figures with the history of your group for attending these functions. If 20 percent usually don't show up, you will take your total number of attendees and reduce it by 20 percent. You can also consider the hotel's overset policy and reduce the number by that percent. Remember, hotels have an overset policy to allow you a little leeway for errors in your guarantees. When you reduce the guarantee by that number, you are in effect allowing yourself no room for error. I do not like to see a lot of empty seats in a room, and I do not like to pay for uneaten meals—but it is even worse to have attendees arrive at a function where seats are not available. Use good judgment and pay close attention to the patterns of your group.

Fortunately, for corporate meeting planners guarantees usually do not pose a problem. The number of attendees is usually fixed, and at corporate meetings attendees have less flexibility in declining to attend a function.

HOTEL PICKUP POST-CONVENTION REPORT

The hotel reservations pickup report (see Exhibit 18-4) is important, especially if your attendees make their own hotel reservations and have a habit of doing this late. Hotel managers become very nervous if you have blocked a certain number of rooms and the reservations are not coming in. As has been stated earlier, hotels make their profit on guest/sleeping rooms, so their goal is to have these rooms filled. The planner's goal is to have every attendee in the major hotel at the convention rate. If I can "prove" to the hotel staff that my people may be slow, but they always meet my block, they will be a little more relaxed and flexible in holding the rooms for me. Thus, the purpose of this form is to document the number of rooms utilized and the date or pattern by which reservations are typically made.

The process begins in the contract phase; the hotel agrees to record the information, starting with the first day a reservation is received, on a weekly basis at first, then on a daily basis as the cutoff date and conference grow closer. On the day my brochure is mailed, I send a copy of the brochure along with a copy of this form to the reservations manager and sales manager with a short note alerting them to the possibility of reservations arriving and reminding them of their "contractual" responsibility. In addition, my meetings secretary calls the hotel every Friday for a count to put on our form.

Completing the form is very easy to do. You first must complete the upper portion of the form, paying particular attention to the date of your first mailing, since that becomes your yardstick. I put the dates of the meeting down the left-hand column and the date of my follow-up calls across the top. On the date of the call, I record the reservations for each day of the meeting, allowing for early arrivals and late check-outs. Once on-site, I require a daily printout of my attendees and a daily recording on the hotel pickup report. I record walk-ins (people who did not make advance reservations) and no-shows. For many groups, I have found that these numbers offset each other. Therefore, my last pre-conference numbers, even with changes, remain pretty stable. There are two very good financial reasons for generating these reports. First, meeting-room changes often go into effect if you drop below a certain, prenegotiated, percentage. Thus, overbooking in guest/sleeping rooms can cost you in meeting-room rental charges. Second, the room pickup determines the number of complimentary rooms or credits you will have. If you are one or two short, you may choose to "buy" those rooms to meet the required number to earn a comp suite. At any rate, be sure to get credit for every room utilized. Errors do occur, and a planner can usually pick them up by reading the printout.

You can make the form more complex by adding types of reservations (single, double, suite) if your group has a high mix in room type or rate—just one of the many reasons why you cannot easily use someone else's form other than as a guideline. You always have different requirements for information. The form is a starting point, and discussions with your hotel reservations department will be invaluable in redesigning it to meet your mutual needs in a realistic way. Although preparing the forms may be tedious, the preparation pays off—both in dollars and in enhanced reputation for you within the facility and in your own organization. Be sure to leave a space where the reservation manager must sign and date the "final" form. Your credibility with other hotels when they evalute your history will be measurably increased.

The key to successful data collection is finding a simple system that works for you and making it part of your daily pattern. To the extent possible, back-up systems, such as double collection by the hotel and the planner, will minimize gaps when someone simply forgets. Finally, if you don't use the data as decisionmaking tools, they are worthless. And, as I emphasized in Chapter 6 in the section on data collection, numbers must be converted to percentages so you know what percentages you can expect to receive after the first week, second week, and so on. If your organization is growing, the number will be higher, but the percentage should be consistent.

SHIPPING

Shipping is one of those areas that, if casually handled by meeting planners, can become a nightmare on-site. The problems begin in the shipping department when workers cannot identify your boxes, and escalate when you are unable to locate items or don't know where (staff office, registration, information center) to have the boxes delivered.

There are many solutions, but the most efficient system uses boxes that are all the same color and size for easy identification. (Be sure the size is acceptable by your shipper.) Number each box and label it according to the area it will be delivered to: SO #1, SO #2, and so forth, for boxes delivered to the staff office. Boxes should be numbered consecutively so that you know how many total boxes were actually shipped and received. You can develop your own codes, but include the registration area, exhibit area, resource center, and those you want in your private room. You can further identify boxes according to what they contain, such as program books, gifts, office supplies. In addition, you should inventory each box, listing the number and content. You can then simply check your inventory lists and immediately find the stapler—or whatever your crisis item is at the moment.

Some organizations have refined this system to the point that labels are one color for the staff office, another for registration, making on-site deliveries easy, especially if language is a problem. To expedite return shipments, the labels should be prepared before you leave for the conference—and bring along plenty of tape to seal them up for the return shipment. Save all boxes as you unpack them, storing them for packing for the return trip. You should be equally cautious with the return shipment inventories, in case boxes are lost.

If you have the luxury, I suggest you assign a very detailed staff person to the shipping tasks. That frees you, the planner, to oversee wrap-up responsibilities that no one else can handle.

TIPPING

Over the past twenty years tipping has been edging its way into the meeting industry to the extent that, today, most professional meeting planners have an automatic gratuity line item in their budgets. If you have had trouble deciding whether to tip or not to tip, an appropriate response might be *sometimes*. The decision depends on the complexity of the meeting and the quick response of the hotel's staff to the unexpected. Also consider the length of the meeting, the total meeting budget or master account billing, the size of the meeting, and the number of employees who will provide services to the meeting.

For example, a theater set for any number, from 10 to 5,000, that will remain set for a length of time, be it one or five days, may not be a candidate for a gratuity. The influencing factors should be fast turnovers, complex setups, numerous breakouts, or frequent refreshing of meeting rooms or public areas. The list will vary with each meeting, but the experienced planner recognizes the elements that make the meeting complex.

The planner is also aware of those people within the system who either make things happen or who interfere with the success of a meeting. But the meeting planner also has a responsibility to clearly state in writing, and with diagrams if necessary, just what the requirements are. An entire hotel staff can appear incompetent if the planner's needs are vague and poorly thought out.

Whom to Tip

Within the meeting industry, the gratuities can be divided into three simple categories: (1) those paid by the attendee, as in tipping the bell staff, (2) automatic food-and-beverage service charges, and (3) those paid to the hotel's meeting services staff. While there may be some overlap, it can be minimized if you know your attendees' tipping patterns and level of service required.

I rarely provide additional gratuities to doormen and bellmen unless they have provided a service directly to the meeting, such as moving registration boxes, delivering mail, or delivering flowers. Nor do I usually include the food-and-beverage personnel, who receive a portion of the automatic 15 to 17 percent gratuity. My dilemma is with the third group, the hotel's meeting services staff. Highest on my list are housemen, PBX operators, and convention services managers. Depending on the meeting requirements, variables include housekeeping, security, shipping, audiovisual technicians, the front desk, bartenders, and, finally, management (sales managers).

The greatest risk is using gratuities indiscriminately. Beware of asking the hotel staff members to present you with a list of their suggestions. You can all too easily end up giving each houseman $10—when you can remember only four of them. Ask the hotel for the names of employees who worked especially hard on your meeting, such as night setup crews that you have not had the opportunity to meet. Otherwise, a suggestion is not to tip anyone you do not know and or cannot remember as having contributed above and beyond the call of duty.

How Much to Tip

The hardest question is how much to tip. The Quick Reference Guide offers suggestions, although these can and should be viewed only as guidelines. Again, the complexity of the meeting and the service level of the employees should be the determining factors. My basic rule of thumb has been 1 to 3 percent of my estimated final master account bill, although some low-budget meetings can be very complex. Other planners suggest less, and some are reputed to go as high as 5 percent. Many planners base the amount on a dollar amount per attendee, while others have complex formulas. Regardless of your own system for budgeting for gratuities, distribution should be selective, personally handled, and documented with receipts. In presenting the gratuity, be sure to reference the conference sponsor so that it does not appear to be a gift from you personally.

In certain instances—especially for departments such as the front desk, PBX, reservations, and sales office—a gift that can be shared is appropriate. A gift may also be suitable for managers in lieu of cash, though my preference for managers is a gift certificate from one of the nicer local stores. And there are now catalogs that can be sent directly to recipients allowing them to make their own gift selections.

Letters of appreciation that mention individual employees and specific ways in which they were helpful beyond their normal duties are likely the most treasured of gifts, as are heartfelt thank-you letters and/or personal notes.

When to Tip

As for when and how, some prefer to distribute tips in advance, others throughout the meeting, and the vast majority—who have a wait-and-see attitude—distribute them as the last official act prior to leaving the hotel. The process is equally varied. Some planners use individually prepared checks, some prefer individual envelopes with cash, and others less personally leave the distribution up to management. Some planners even require a signed receipt from each recognized employee and are no doubt the best prepared for an IRS audit.

PROBLEMS AND STRATEGIES

PROBLEM: The internal hotel communication system—getting messages and having them delivered in a timely manner and to the right person—is our biggest on-site frustration.

Strategy 1:   Meet personally with the PBX staff (in-house operators) and tell them who you are and what your needs are. You need them on your team.

Strategy 2:   Send daily gifts (candy, flowers, cookies) thanking them for the great effort the prior day. It is lonely in that little room, and being remembered makes a lot of difference.

Strategy 3:   Most convention services managers are on beepers. Ask for the beeper number and a promise of a quick response, especially when you have a message for them.

Strategy 4:   Because so many meeting activities, from reception to room setup, occur after normal business hours, require that you have home phone numbers of key people.

Strategy 5:   Rent walkie-talkies for your key people. Their advantage over beepers is that you can talk directly to the person; beepers require a separate telephone call.

Strategy 6:   Set up your staff office as an information and message center for staff and suppliers, especially if your meeting is not too large.

PROBLEM: My staff and the suppliers are usually excellent. The volunteers are always a problem.

Strategy 1:   To the extent possible, limit the activities of volunteers to hospitality or some other area that does not threaten the success of your meeting.

Strategy 2:   In addition to hands-on training, provide very clear written instructions and post detailed assignments with hourly schedules.

Strategy 3:   Always have a 10 to 20 percent back-up crew. You can't fire volunteers easily, but you can reassign them.

Strategy 4:   Make your best volunteer the overall supervisor. It is much easier for a volunteer to be strict and demanding with other volunteers than for you to be. You may be perceived as ungrateful.

PROBLEM: One person can't be in ten places at once, and as a result many sessions and events aren't checked out in advance.

Strategy 1:   Require the hotel or suppliers to have all rooms set up a minimum of one hour prior to the event for standard setups; complex setups may require four to twenty-four hours, especially if rehearsals are scheduled.

Strategy 2:   Have a "sweep" patrol in charge of checking rooms and reporting problems to a central location. Door monitors and ticket-takers are usually willing to accept this additional responsibility.

Strategy 3:   Be sure the setup crews have room diagrams drawn exactly as you want the room set. Pictures are not only clearer, but some of your workers may not speak or read English.

Strategy 4:   Anticipate major problem areas and times and request extra setup personnel to handle the problems.

Strategy 5:   Offer incentives for perfectly set rooms. If you have a gratuity allowance of $10 per room setup, advise the staff that $10 will be removed for each improperly set room. But be sure to measure performance against your instructions—don't penalize the staff for your own mistakes.

PROBLEM: Shipments to the facility are late, lost, and, at best, confusing.

Strategy 1:   Ask the hotel coordinator or decorator how labels for shipments should read. Often, correct addressing allows the boxes to be internally processed to meet your requirements.

Strategy 2:   Hotels have limited storage space for holding meeting shipments. If you plan for your shipment to arrive three to five days before the event, there is less chance for getting lost.

Strategy 3:   Inventory all boxes by number and contents. That helps the hotel know when all have arrived and helps you locate your materials and have them delivered to the appropriate location.

Strategy 4: Color-code your shipping labels. There are several options, such as using pink for those going to the convention site and blue for those going back to your office. Or code them based on delivery location: pink to staff office, green to registration, yellow to resource or information center.

Strategy 5: Be sure the address is correct, legible, and securely attached.

Strategy 6: Purchase look-alike boxes so your shipment is easily recognizable. When 100 white 12-by-15-by-18-inch boxes arrive, it is certainly obvious that someone has taken great care and places a high value on materials.

Strategy 7: Use a reliable service. Check references if you haven't used it before.

Strategy 8: If your shipment is going out of the country, hire a customs broker, working with that company exactly as you would work with the hotel's staff. Be aware of the unique per-county regulations and extra time required.

PROBLEM: Our attendees always seem to get lost—they're out looking for sessions, functions, and so on.

Strategy 1: Place signs on easels at least 6 feet or higher in corridors. Otherwise, such signs are too low to be seen if crowds are large.

Strategy 2: Add a "schedule-at-a-glance" to the inside cover of your program so it is quick and easy to reference.

Strategy 3: Announce directions to upcoming functions at the end of each session. If you have audiovisual equipment already set up in the room, add a directional slide or two.

Strategy 4: Consider placing TV monitors with session information and directions at strategic locations. This is much easier if the hotel already provides this service at major entries and in guest rooms.

Strategy 5: Provide easy-to-read maps or floor plans in the program book or as a pullout in the attendees' packet. Include meeting-room names, telephones, restrooms, stairways, escalators, elevators, registration area, and so on.

Strategy 6: To encourage people-to-people interaction, have staff members available and wearing "ask me" type buttons.

Strategy 7: Color-code sessions, tickets, and signs so the attendee only has to look for green or orange. For a real upbeat group, you can even have door monitors in T-shirts color-coded to the session, or a red, orange, or "yellow brick road" leading to the sessions. With a little creativity, a mundane problem can be turned into a fun addition to the meeting.

19

EXHIBITS

Exhibits have been viewed by sponsoring organizations primarily as a necessary source of revenue. They are also an important part of the meeting. Hands-on product information and new technologies have added depth to the educational program, and the activity in the hall enhances interaction among attendees and suppliers alike.

Exhibits are not for every organization or for every meeting. To some, they are a necessary ingredient; to many others, they are distruptive to meeting goals. As in all aspects of your planning, the first measure is the extent to which the activity supports what you want to accomplish. The potential benefits must be measured against the time and financial investment necessary for success.

Planners unfamiliar with marketing and management of exhibits must also be prepared to spend many hours learning not only the obvious but the more subtle skills involved. Exhibits require excellent detail and organizational talents, much like the meeting portion of the program. But beyond the basic details, you are on new turf, unless you are highly skilled in marketing and selling.

This chapter provides some guidelines to those who have the dual challenge of meeting planning and exhibits management. The focus here is on an exhibition that takes place as an adjunct to the meeting—not the large trade shows that often fill an entire convention center and for which there is a separate exhibits manager.

GETTING IT ALL TOGETHER

SELECTING A SITE

Presuming you have evaluated the potential for an exhibits program and decided to proceed, your first step should be to locate a site. Preparation of a budget is equally important, but the site influences the budget because of the facility charges and revenue potential based on available space for booths.

The most appropriate site for a small exhibits program is in the facility where the meeting is being held. The advantages are greater participation among attendees and lower costs, especially if in a hotel. Often, planners choose to place exhibits in the areas surrounding the meeting room, forcing attendees to move through the booths or tables to get to the sessions. Refreshment breaks are also planned in the area to further encourage interaction between attendees and exhibitors. Because the hotel is a "finished" facility, charges for such things as carpeting are costs that do not have to be incurred. It is also wise to remember that, because hotels make their profit from guest rooms, their rental charges for exhibit space are less than convention centers' charges whose major revenue source is hall rental. The negative factor in a hotel is limited space for shows with more than thirty to sixty booths, although there are exceptions depending on the space requirements for the meeting portion of your program.

While many of the site considerations are the same for meetings and trade shows, other considerations include:

- Freight-dock location, size, and accessibility to show area
- Security
- Lighting
- Access to electrical outlets
- Union jurisdictions
- Per-booth daily charges
- Move-in and move-out times allowing for setup and tear-down
- Insurance
- Damage deposits
- Janitorial services
- Fire or other safety restrictions

The facility and the decorator or service contractor are valuable resources, as are planners who have used the space in a similar way.

As you move into the contract stage, be very specific in covering the details influential in selecting the site—costs, restrictions, guaranteed twenty-four-hour holds (of the exhibit room), approved floor plans, and freight-elevator access should be included with a myriad of other protective clauses. A convention center requires a more complex contract, so don't assume your familiarity with hotels will necessarily serve you well with other types of facilities.

BUDGET CONSIDERATIONS

There is a world of difference between the budget for an exhibit or trade show and a traditional meeting budget. The requirements of outside contractors alone can boggle the mind, and union regulations confuse the most experienced planners. In addition, some costs are transferred to the exhibiting companies; others belong to the show's sponsor. Usually, the show's sponsor provides the booth and basic furniture, e.g., table and chairs and a sign. Other items are ordered through the decorator by the exhibitor and paid for by the exhibitor. Possible contractors include decorators, electricians, plumbers, audiovisual technicians, security staff, florists, photographers, rental furnishing companies, and sign makers. Decorators usually provide many of the services, including storage and carpeting, even though some of those are subcontracted out. Review each of these areas with your decorator. Many activities require special permits or licenses, which you must check to prevent possible fines on-site.

With regard to space rental, there are a variety of price options, the most common based on usage (exhibits versus meetings) and total square footage. Some facilities may impose a per-booth charge and additional service charges based on your use of the services they provide, such as security and janitorial.

Marketing an exhibition requires additional printing, mailing, and telephone costs and general overhead costs to include added staff time (sales, show management, and secretarial services).

On the revenue side, you must consider the number of booths that can realistically be sold and at a competitive price. From this base, you can add early incentives, late fees, multibooth rates, prime location rates, or past-participation benefits. Whatever your choices, consider those when preparing your revenue estimates. This is an ideal place to use break-even budgeting, so you know when you have at a minimum recovered your costs.

Additional revenues may also be realized from exhibitors' advertising in the program book, exhibitors' sponsorship of events, sale of lists of attendees' names or mailing labels, a percentage of publications' sales, and fees from sales seminars offered to exhibitors. With regard to revenue-producing sales such as publications, consider the effect on the nonprofit status of the sponsoring organization, if it applies, and be prepared to comply with local rules pertaining to sales tax. You are only limited by your creativity, especially if your attendee participation is high and those attendees are either purchasers or influencers in purchasing decisions.

MARKETING

The marketing plan for an exhibition is a double-edged sword. You must maintain a balance between the number of booths sold and the attendance. The bottom line for exhibitors is exposure to a high number of qualified buyers, but the number of attendees alone is not enough if the interest level is low or if too few attendees have authority to purchase. And obviously, a hall full of sold booths but no people is not a success. While a balance is most desirable, given a choice between too many or too few booths, your future show potential is greater with more people and fewer booths.

A "prospectus" or announcement must be prepared for exhibitors. This is your primary marketing piece and includes all of the information necessary for a company to decide on its participation. While the costs, the sponsoring company's credibility, conflicting shows, dates, and location are factors, the most important selling point is accurate statistics on the attendee; prospective exhibitors want data concerning the participation level of qualified buyers.

When I talk about a "buyer," the definition extends to a variety of situations. If the show is for colleges, the buyer may be college-bound high school students. The attendee must be able to respond to the exhibiting company's objectives, and exhibitors must be consistent with your organization's concept of who it wants to bring together. The buyer concept for companies is less directed to "floor" sales and more focused on identifying prospects, leads, and heightened public awareness among their targeted markets. In fact, direct sales from the booths are usually prohibited.

The prospectus also includes rules and regulations for exhibitors. While rules vary from organization to organization, exhibitors must be notified of them before a contract is signed. Ideally, the rules should be printed on the back of the contract, ensuring that the exhibitor is aware of and agrees to the terms. Regulations include:

- Eligibility
- Booth sizes
- Equipment items included, such as table or chairs
- Payments
- Deposits
- Cancellation
- Contractors' services
- Allowable or restricted activities (such as direct sales)
- Hours (including setup, tear-down)

- Personnel
- Security
- Liability
- Insurance
- Construction and cleanliness of booth space
- Space application and assignment procedures
- Shipping and storage
- Registration and badges
- Enforcement

The contract itself can be relatively simple, even combining the application and agreements in one document. In addition to basic company information (company name, contact name, address, telephone, and products), booth location preferences should be requested and full payment or a deposit required.

A prospectus can range from a very sophisticated four-color brochure to multiple sheets of internally copied pages. In planning your approach, be aware of the increasing number of show-participation opportunities being offered to companies and their need to be selective. Also not to be forgotten is the image you are presenting of your organization.

Direct mail pieces combined with print ads placed in industry trade publications are most effective in building trade show participation. In addition, most organizations market to past exhibitors prior to general marketing. You will know you are successful when past exhibitors fill your hall and waiting lists.

ADMINISTRATIVE ISSUES

There are a number of administrative issues that meeting planners must consider when dealing with exhibits. Those discussed below are in no way meant to be comprehensive, but are intended to spark your thinking in systematic planning for your organization, your exhibitors, and your decorator or service contractor. These three entities have a very interdependent relationship throughout the entire planning process, and communication among them in a concise but complete and timely manner is the key to success.

It is essential to clearly communicate critical information, such as the location, dates, exhibit hours, and move-in and move-out times. A form such as the exhibitor's schedule (see Exhibit 19-1) is easy to complete, read, and follow. This should be sent to the exhibitor when the booth number is confirmed. Keep in mind that the information sent to the company requesting the space is different from that sent to the booth personnel. Therefore, be sure to send forms and instructions to the appropriate people or department. A complimentary program or exhibition book listing form may be sent to the marketing department to complete. (See Exhibit 19-2.) The form serves two purposes. First, it provides copy that will go into your on-site program book or possibly an exhibition book, if your numbers warrant that special publication. List the exhibiting companies' names alphabetically, followed by lists organized by categories of products, such as all data processing exhibits, and so on. Second, the form can be used to help in your evaluation by asking what the exhibitor hopes to accomplish and how the attendees will benefit. It is always easier to measure accomplishments when the goals have been identified prior to the opening of the show.

An exhibitor registration form should also be included in your packet to the exhibiting company. (See Exhibit 19-3.) It asks for the names of all the people who will be attending the conference as exhibitors. Names are important for badge preparation and for controlling people allowed on the exhibit floor. The space allowed for names of booth personnel should be limited to the number allowed per your rules and regulations. The general rule is two to three complimentary registrants with the price of the booth. You may have problems if you give one booth more comps than another—such unequal treatment will be perceived as favoritism and may decrease attendance in future years.

If guest room space is not a problem and if you do not control the assignment of hospitality suites, you will probably not need to concern yourself with housing arrangements for exhibitors. But if you are using more than one hotel, exhibitors may be limited to a certain number of guest rooms and room types in each facility. If that is the case for your organization, you may require exhibitors' hotel accommodation requests (see Exhibit 19-4) to come directly to you for approval before they are forwarded to the housing bureau or the appropriate hotel.

Finally, as the show manager or meeting planner, you should take the same care in preparing the written specifications for the exhibition as for the meeting. Hold on-site briefing meetings with suppliers, and conduct walk-throughs of the hall with any public officials responsible for enforcing fire and safety regulations. Once the show is open and all is running smoothly, it is critical for you to be visible and available to exhibitors. That helps you identify problems, check booth visitation (attendees' interest), and begin the selling process for the next year. If you require exhibitors to evaluate the show before leaving—and you should—try to personally pick up the evaluations from each booth and review exhibitors' comments with them. This personal attention to your exhibitors is the trademark of successful show managers.

EXHIBIT TIPS

THEMES

The addition of a theme to promotional materials and the exhibit hall have proven successful in building participation among both exhibitors and attendees. Decoration, food-and-beverage events, costumes, giveaways, and entertainment all add to the excitement and overall ambiance. Themes may be historical, such as those developed around founding dates; industry related, such as using lasers, robots, and other high-tech or futuristic devices; or tied to the meeting site, such as beach, Hollywood, casino, or international themes. Mini-themes can be used in low-traffic areas to encourage movement of attendees. The purpose of theme events is to encourage contact between attendees and exhibitors. Loud music or show-stopping entertainment may attract bodies to the area, but it might also distract them from the exhibits. Timing is critical, in terms of both how such entertainment is scheduled during show hours and the performance length.

THEFT

Theft at trade shows is increasing as more valuable products are brought in for display. Unfortunately, you have to plan for theft in order to avoid it. Security of the site or hall is the first consideration. If access to the area cannot be controlled during show hours and completely secured during closed hours, your best efforts may have little impact.

After facility security, the next most common preventive measure is providing twenty-four-hour guard service from the moment the first item is moved in until the last box is carted out. Security check-out and check-in stations (similar to airport security systems) may be set up, particularly for show personnel, laborers, and other service and support personnel. Badges distributed at this point (even to hotel staff) aid in controlling unauthorized entry and assist guards in identifying "stray" people. While control is primarily the responsibility of the show's sponsor, the exhibitors, security company, and facility should be held liable contractually for any theft resulting from their negligence.

Security guidelines should be provided to exhibitors, suppliers, and the facility, and briefings should be held to go over key points. To minimize the risks, encourage your people to become aware of and report suspicious people, to secure personal items (such as purses and briefcases) and high-priced items when not in use, and to engrave ID numbers on all items. If items are lost at a show that may result in a negative attitude among exhibitors and decreased attendance at future shows. An "it's not my responsibility" attitude may cost you in the end.

BOOTH ASSIGNMENT

The booth assignment process is very important to exhibitors because of the clear advantage in visibility and traffic some locations have over others. It is important that this process be presented to exhibitors in the prospectus. Fairness and adherence to the policies set by your organization are important to exhibitors. The most popular procedure is to assign booth locations by date of receipt of the application and deposit. If exhibitors have been asked for three preferences, the first exhibitor would receive the first choice. Once that booth has been assigned, the next request for that booth would be denied and the second choice assigned, if that booth is available. As the hall becomes filled, exhibitors will have to revise their priorities based on the remaining unassigned booths.

Another system assigns points to exhibitors based on the number of years, number of shows, and number of booths occupied in the past. An exhibitor with fifty points is more likely to get first choice than one participating for the first time. To further encourage repeat participation, an exhibitor unable to participate one year may lose points and have to begin at zero when participation resumes. If the point system is not for your organization, an alternative is to mail to past exhibitors three to four weeks prior to the general mailing, giving them a clear advantage in responding early.

Any system can work if it is well thought out and prudently enforced. A small show of ten or fewer booths may not require strictness in booth assignment, but as you grow you should anticipate adding a fair system to your procedures. Booth selection does require you to provide exhibitors with a copy of the floor plan with numbers for each space easily visible and special notations such as food stations, rest rooms, and entry doors to help exhibitors in selecting their preferred location.

BOOTH SIZES AND CHARGES

The standard booth sizes are 8 feet by 10 feet (80 square feet) and 10 feet by 10 feet (100 square feet). Size variance is not permitted, other than by purchasing two or more booths. Larger shows add additional charges for corner booths, booths exposed on three or more sides, raised booths, or booths with any other prominent feature, design, or location. Often, exhibitors are prohibited from adding any design features that will obstruct, detract, or interfere with other exhibitors' activities. In assigning prices to booths, show size, number of attendees, and qualified buyer status are the main factors.

SALES BY EXHIBITORS DURING THE SHOW

Usually, the meeting planner or show manager does not allow the exhibiting company to sell directly to attendees. Licensing compliance with local sales tax regulations and inventory concerns are but a few of the complications encountered when allowing such sales. Investigate what direct selling would entail before deciding whether to include it in your plan.

WORKING WITH THE DECORATOR

Decorators for your exhibits area offer a variety of services and are your best allies in planning and implementing your show. Their traditional services include floor plans, exhibits and registration booths, furniture, signs, materials handling (storage of materials and delivery to show site), and subcontracting for other services such as photography, security, electrical, or audiovisual. In addition to handling your requirements, they will receive orders directly from exhibitors for extra chairs, tables, carpeting, or electrical hook-ups, and are there to see that all is set up and moved out according to your schedule. Full-service companies are also often qualified to consult with you on your show's structure and marketing objectives.

Prices charged by decorators are based on a per-booth package that includes booth-frame steelwork (pipe), background and side fabric (drape), a sign with the exhibiting company's name, a table, one or two chairs, and a wastebasket. The show's sponsor pays these costs from the exhibitors' fees, sometimes eliminating the table, chairs, and wastebasket, or upgrading to a better quality or more items. The booth, sign, and aisle carpeting (if required) must be ordered by the sponsor for a consistent appearance. The decorator then provides you with order forms to send to exhibitors for additional items needed and for which the exhibitor must pay. (That is often the decorator's major profit area.)

Complimentary to the sponsor, or available at a prenegotiated price, are registration counters, information or message centers, entry banners, handling of several hundred pounds of freight, and any other items or services for the exclusive benefit of the sponsor.

Labor, which is supplied by the decorator, is over and above package and complimentary services. Labor required to set up and tear down the show will be billed to you. Labor requested by exhibitors is billed to them. Labor is expensive, often union, with minimums and overtime particularly when you are dealing with a convention center as opposed to a hotel. While the hourly rate may not be negotiable, hours counted as overtime may be. Be aware of union restrictions. To comply with work rules, you may find that you would have to hire five different people for one hour's worth of work, each with a four-hour minimum call. That one hour gets very expensive.

Always get competitive bids, as prices seem to vary considerably among decorators. Service may also vary accordingly, but your reference checks should reveal that information.

SPONSORSHIPS

Frequently tied to an exhibits program is the opportunity for exhibitors or other supporters to contribute full or partial funding for various special events and activities during the program. The types of activities open for sponsorship are most frequently food-and-beverage (social) events, although some groups have found sponsors for transportation, keynote speakers, multimedia presentations, program book printing, gifts, and just about anything you can think of. (The term "sponsorship" should not be confused with the use of the word "sponsor" throughout this book. "Sponsor" refers to the organization that is the initiator of the meeting or event.) Sponsorships may come from the corporate world, nonprofit organizations (such as universities, cities, government departments), or interested individuals from any segment of the population. Most sponsorships come from those with an altruistic interest in your organization, a desire to promote their product, public image or cause, or a need to increase visibility and profits by direct marketing to your attendees. Caution should be exercised in accepting money without a clear understanding of the benefits and limitations.

In the corporate world, a sponsor may underwrite an entire event, such as the "Coors Classic" bicycle race, or a portion, such as "official" sponsors of the Olympics. In many situations, a city or county will underwrite some of the costs for major events, from sporting events to conventions, if it feels that such an incentive is needed to lure the organization or event to the area.

PROBLEMS AND STRATEGIES

PROBLEM: Our meeting is in one place, the exhibits are in another; thus attendance at exhibits is always low.

Strategy 1: If the exhibits won't fit in the hotel, try moving the meetings to the convention center.

Strategy 2: Add door prizes and giveaways to your show. It's amazing what people will do for a free pair of socks or a mechanical pencil.

Strategy 3: Use food as another motivator. Free lunches, coffee breaks, or receptions are sure attendance-builders, but attendees must know about them.

Strategy 4: Provide shuttlebus service between the hotels and the exhibit hall.

Strategy 5: Allow exhibitors to contact registered attendees, personally inviting them to visit their booths. You will have to provide exhibitors with a list of attendees' names or with mailing labels.

PROBLEM: Our problem is keeping exhibitors happy.

Strategy 1: When assigning booths, keep major competitors apart. You may have to break your own rules, but everyone is happier in the end.

Strategy 2: If your problems are primarily from exhibitors in low-traffic areas, add attractions to draw interest (food, giveaways) to those areas, or revise rates to reflect likely traffic.

Strategy 3: Reevaluate your promises to exhibitors. If they continually go unmet, soon you won't have angry exhibitors—you'll have no exhibitors.

Strategy 4: Spend time on the floor observing and talking to exhibitors. If an absent exhibitor's crates are blocking aisles, if too many booths are empty, or if electrical service is not provided when ordered, your exhibitors will become frustrated—and with good reason. If you're there to pay close attention to details, you can resolve issues before they become problems.

PROBLEM: Our show was nearly ruined when the fire marshal closed us down.

Strategy 1: Meet with the fire marshal early in the planning process so that you clearly understand the regulations. Then follow them!

Strategy 2: Invite the fire marshal to walk through and check your show after setup is complete and before it is open to your attendees. It's better to open late than to close early.

Strategy 3: If the problem is that there are too many people, give door monitors counters to control the number allowed in each room. (What a nice problem!)

20

SELECTING A MEETING MANAGEMENT FIRM

GETTING IT ALL TOGETHER

Meeting managers find themselves with a variety of job titles and in any one of several departments within an organization. For example, hospitals employ continuing education directors; universities have conference services departments trade magazine publishers have seminars and exhibition divisions; corporations employ sales and marketing managers, special events coordinators, travel managers, public relations personnel; large associations assign meeting management functions to the meetings and conferences department; and, in small associations, the executive director along with a staff of one or two people manage the meetings. All are performing some or all of the meeting management functions described in this book for the employing organization.

Skilled planners have left the security of these positions to become independent meeting planners, consultants, or managers, and to form meeting management firms. They contract their services to corporations and other organizations, and for a fee will plan and implement some or all meeting activities. The contract can be for a one-time-only event, for a series of events, or for a multi-year assignment. The Quick Reference Guide lists types of companies offering meeting planning services.

IN-HOUSE VERSUS OUTSIDE SERVICES

One of the most difficult decisions for an organization is whether to handle meeting planning in-house (either by hiring a full-time planner or assigning the responsibility to a staff member) or to contract all or a part of the responsibilities to an outside firm. Issues to consider are:

- *The volume of work:* Can you keep a full-time staffer busy all the time? If you can, but only if you assign a variety of different tasks, will the skill requirements be comparable? Is there too much work for a staff member who has other responsibilities?

- *The level of skill:* Can you afford the cost of a highly experienced full-time planner, or will you have to settle for less than what you really want? Does your in-house staff member have all the skills needed to do the job?
- *The cost:* Have you analyzed the costs, beyond salary, of handling the operation in-house—your contribution to employee and other required taxes, benefits, office space, equipment, supplies, telephone lines and charges, professional dues, and many other overhead items, including internal support personnel?

Once you have all this information, compare it with the cost of the professional planner whose fee will cover all of the necessary tasks and responsibilities, but only to the extent that they are needed. The decision is not always an automatic yes for the outside service. Many companies not only need full-time in-house employees, but can afford them. The Quick Reference Guide provides a list comparing situations and indicating whether an outside planner or an in-house person would be best in each case. Often, an organization's preferred management style is the determining factor. An employer has greater daily control over in-house employees, but contractors are often more responsive when asked to jump, and usually ask only, "How high?" and not, "Why?"

TYPES OF OUTSIDE SERVICES

The companies involved in meeting management cover a wide range of types of businesses, including:

- Meeting management firms, which are exclusively engaged in meeting planning services, such as:
- Destination management companies, which are primarily involved in providing local services, such as transportation, theme events, and tours, to groups coming into their city
- Multi-association management firms that manage small associations
- Incentive houses, which produce sales incentive and reward programs for corporations
- Travel agencies, which obviously arrange and book travel
- Exposition management companies, which primarily produce major trade shows
- Public relations firms, which are primarily engaged in advertising, promotion, and media relations

While all these have links to the meeting profession and a similar client base, the meeting management firms are the only ones solely dependent on that service for their profits.

TIPS FOR SELECTING A MEETING MANAGEMENT FIRM

HOW TO FIND MEETING MANAGEMENT FIRMS

If an outside firm is the way to go, then your next step is to locate some likely candidates or companies. Many people begin with the Yellow Pages, but that may be the most difficult route to take. The generic "convention services" listing includes everything from hotels to dog-sitting services for conventioneers. I'll bet you don't pick your attorney, doctor, or even plumber from the Yellow Pages except as a last resort. The ideal way is to use referrals from people you know and respect. Hotel sales or convention services departments have usually worked with planners and know who the best ones are. But ask several, don't rely on one opinion. You can also ask business colleagues who have used outside meeting management companies. Contact the professional associations listed in "Appendix C: Resources" in this book and ask for the independent meeting planners who are members of their association and from your region of the country.

Actually, it is not necessary for the planner to be from your region of the country. It is not unusual for the planner to be in one city, the client in another city, and the meeting in yet another city. The disadvantage is that the distance prohibits frequent face-to-face meetings, but with telephones, fax machines, and overnight mail, communications do not have to suffer. I have found that I can bid a job more competitively if the client does not have headquarters locally, because of the time saved by not attending frequent meetings. When I do go to the cities of out-of-town clients for planning meetings, the agenda is well thought out and time is efficiently used.

CHOOSING A FIRM

The first step in choosing a firm is to prepare a list of services that you would like to delegate to the company. You may then choose to contact each company by telephone, or you may prefer to prepare a written request for a proposal (RFP or prospectus). The RFP puts the details in black and white and allows the planner to more accurately bid the project. I would recommend first contacting the planner by telephone, then sending an RFP or holding a meeting. Personal phone contact gives the planner a sense of the style and "rhythm" of the project and allows a better bid to be prepared.

Beyond the "paper bid," you will want to evaluate the planner's base of knowledge and experience, creativity, enthusiasm, and the personality match to you and your company. There are many variables beyond price and what planners say they can do. Be sure to ask for references and to find out how long planners have worked with individual clients. Repeat business is the best reference. The Guide has a list of suggested questions to ask the companies you are interviewing. It will get you started.

SELLING YOUR PROJECT TO THE PLANNER

In the early years, planners were fighting for any piece of meeting business they could get. But as the market has grown for professional planners, so has their selectivity in accepting clients. Meetings are labor intensive and planners cannot afford to incur the high costs of running a meeting that will not generate profits for them. Therefore, there is a need on your part as the client to present the project in an efficient and organized manner to the planner.

You must also realistically assess the costs associated with conducting a meeting and of hiring a meeting planner. You must honestly discuss your budget and trust that planners will not take advantage of the information. (You must also trust yourself to notice it if they do.) To help you prepare for meeting the planner, a series of questions which the planner is likely to ask you has been included in the Quick Reference Guide.

THE NEGOTIATION PROCESS

Once you have selected a meeting management firm, you will enter the negotiation process. This stage is not defined only in terms of money, it is also a time to clarify any questions that have emerged during the bid process and to clarify the details of the working relationship, from communication to processing payments. As a general rule, I include a statement in my bid saying that "Within the spirit and content of the outlined tasks, we will coordinate all activities necessary for a successful conference, even though such tasks may not be specifically mentioned." Such a statement reflects the flexibility of the planner, and is the type of issue you should discuss in negotiation. You do not want to be "nickle and dimed" for minor items not specifically mentioned in the contract. Such omissions during negotiations can be far more costly than many fee items negotiators spend far more time on.

There are also a variety of support services you can offer the planner to reduce out-of-pocket expenses, such as your company's billing account number for overnight mailings and 800 numbers to save on long distance charges. One of my clients gave me two interns to assist with clerical work and to serve as runners for the numerous pickups and deliveries the project required. That type of assistance and recognition of the time miscellaneous activities take allowed me to concentrate on the "professional" activities that I had been hired to do. If costs are an issue in negotiations, and they always are, consider what you can do more efficiently than the planner and delegate only those things you cannot do at all or as well. Do not price the job so low that the planner loses motivation, or you may find yourself out of a planner before the job is done.

THE CONTRACT

The contract ties the legal knot connecting the client and the planner and should not be taken lightly. Details negotiated but not in the contract are potentially lost. Good faith may come in to play and save you but, if so, consider yourself lucky. As with any contract, oversights can be expensive in dollars and in time.

As you will note in the sample contract in Exhibit 21-5, not only should the contract begin with the legal parties named, it should also limit disclosure of the information in the contract. (I also include this in my proposals.) The meeting planners' systems, creativity, and prices are private information, just as proprietary information about your company should be. Such information should be mutually confidential.

The "Scope of Work" section outlines the tasks the meeting planner has agreed to do for the contracted fee. If you include a "within the spirit of" clause you can limit this list to general categories with tasks broadly identified; for example, you can say, "Process mailings," without having to say, "Lick the stamps." But if the process is assumed to be affixing labels and you want them hand-addressed, you should specify the preferred procedure. Other sections include fees, payments, examination of records, indemnification, insurance, cancellation, and government regulations which must be followed such as equal employment opportunities.

Obviously, any contract you draw up should be reviewed by your own attorney. Once you have the blessings of legal counsel, the contract should be signed by parties having the authority to sign. When in doubt, have the parties in question sign a statement saying they are authorized to sign on behalf of their company.

THE END AND THE BEGINNING

If you have not already notified other meeting management companies who submitted bids, now is the time to thank them (bidding is time consuming and expensive) and let them know which firm you selected and why. With that bit of courtesy wrapped up, you are ready to begin to build a strong relationship with your new meeting management firm.

PROBLEMS AND STRATEGIES

PROBLEM: We are unsure how our in-house people will respond to an outside company working on something as important as our meeting.

Strategy 1:   Include key people in the decision and selection process.

Strategy 2:   The first year, you may want to delegate only those tasks that are not someone else's pet project.

Strategy 3:   Explain the need for and contributions of an outside firm. Often, the time and money saved are the factors that gain internal support.

Strategy 4:   Select a planner whose personality matches that of your organization and who can win the confidence of key people involved in the meeting.

Strategy 5:   Carefully outline the problems or areas targeted for change and explain how an independent planner can respond more effectively than an in-house person.

PROBLEM: Our budget is tight and the additional cost of a professional planner does not seem affordable.

Strategy 1:   Ask the planner to review your past financial reports to try to find areas of potential cost savings. Add any such cost savings to the funds available for a planner's fee.

Strategy 2:   Review the costs of your current system, including salaries, benefits, and other employment and overhead costs that may be either reduced or more efficiently reallocated.

Strategy 3:   Evaluate the long-term benefits of a more professionally managed meeting. Increased revenue through better marketing and promotion, or cost savings that may be used to increase the program quality may increase overall profits.

Strategy 4:   Contract for only those services that you can afford and that will provide the greatest assistance in reaching your goals.

PROBLEM: Meeting planning takes a great deal of time and we are not sure a meeting management firm with multiple clients can give us the time we need.

Strategy 1:   You may find the time required is greatly reduced when professional planners are involved in the process. They are skilled in scheduling activities and their experience expedites the implementation of various tasks.

Strategy 2:   If you know you will need specific blocks of time, include that information in your initial requirements. If you need the planner to work in your office the month before, say so. (You may be charged more for that service, but most planners will accommodate such requests.)

Strategy 3:   Require your consultant to submit a planning schedule and monitor it regularly; you will be able to tell if your meeting is being neglected.

Strategy 4:   Meet regularly, personally or by telephone, with the planner to discuss his or her progress and yours, as well as to go over upcoming deadlines.

Strategy 5:   Establish an open and honest relationship with the planner regarding your schedules and commitments. You should both be considerate of the other's projects and periods of heavy activity in other areas.

PROBLEM: If there are personnel or organizational changes in the meeting management firm, that can affect the progress and final outcome of our meeting.

Strategy 1:   Changes in the project manager can be disruptive to the planning process. Find out in advance if there is a backup person within the firm who will be familiar with your group and your meeting.

Strategy 2:   Partnership breakups are the most difficult type of change and should be addressed in the contract. One partner should be designated as the primary contact during any organizational changes and should be designated to handle your contracted services.

Strategy 3:   You may choose to have an added statement in the cancellation section of the contract that allows you to cancel if a change is not satisfactorily made. You may also consider a provision in the contract that allows for cancellation if personality conflicts inhibit the working relationship. You will find meeting planners resistant to such clauses, because such problems are not easily documented and can be loosely interpreted, allowing the contract to be broken. Most meeting planners will in fact want the reverse, which is a guaranteed contract even if management changes occur.

Strategy 4:   A meeting planning firm cannot offer guarantees that there will be no changes, any more than you can do so for your organization. Plan with your consultant, as you would within your own company, for these possibilities.

PROBLEM: Often the "professional" comes in and begins changing things so that the project becomes theirs more than ours.

Strategy 1:   Structure the services and role of the planner to meet the requirements of your organization. Discuss your needs in depth, and before contracting be assured that you have been understood.

Strategy 2:   Check references and ask if the planner's style was one of high control. Often, confidence and competence can be mistaken for control, but the reverse may be true.

Strategy 3:   The planner should have a clearly designated supervisor, although that person should be equally careful not to control the planner. The proficient planner will respond well to supervision and guidance; but, remember, you have hired that person for their knowledge of industry practices and the mechanics of meetings. If you are too controlling, you may lose these benefits.

Strategy 4:   If a planner is more interested in telling you what you should be doing than asking what you have been doing, you may find you have a problem. Good planners ask more questions about you than you do about them.

PROBLEM: Our CEO's secretary has been handling these details for years, and we're not sure why we should change.

Strategy 1:   If you are satisfied with the meeting, you may not be a candidate for a meeting management firm. But you should look beyond your internal operations for increasing or stabilizing attendance, solvent financial operations, proper management of your liabilities and risks, and the up-to-date format of your program.

Strategy 2:   Evaluate the time an in-house person spends away from primary responsibilities and assess the value of that person's meeting planning responsibilities versus primary responsibilities.

Strategy 3:   Encourage the secretary to participate in the training offered by professional meeting planning organizations to upgrade the skills needed to protect you and to enhance those responsibilities.

21

ESTABLISHING YOUR OWN MEETING MANAGEMENT FIRM

GETTING IT ALL TOGETHER

The decision to start your own business is a major one, especially when statistics indicate that one in ten new businesses will fail in three years or less. Although it is difficult to face these realities amid the excitement of making a dream a reality, it is prudent to carefully evaluate why businesses fail. The reasons are usually lack of planning prior to opening the doors, lack of capital, lack of business experience, and unplanned growth. Starting a business is often an emotional decision rather than a business decision. In such cases, the reality can be devastating, especially once the romance is over and the long hours and stacks of unpaid bills remain.

SETTING UP YOUR BUSINESS

The most exciting part of the process is naming your company. Tied to the name is the logo, colors, and paper for letterhead and business cards; all of which are building your company image. You will decide what services you will offer—and no matter what's on the list you come up with, the reality is you will make a 100 percent effort to do anything and everything a client wants.

Speaking of clients, your next task is to begin the search for your first one(s). If you are lucky and smart, you will have your first client the day before you leave the security of your salaried position.

You must decide whether to work out of your home. If you decide not to, you will have to begin the process of finding and furnishing an office. Next, you must evaluate and make decisions regarding equipment, staffing, and the general range of other operating costs that are a part of any business. Once you have established what your operating costs will be, you must use those costs to set your fees and to project your monthly and annual need for revenue—not only to survive, but to be profitable.

Once the basics have been determined, you are ready to tackle the most difficult parts of the process: writing a business plan, creating a marketing plan, setting up the books, reviewing government regulations—in short, addressing the numerous daily concerns of running a business.

THE BUSINESS PLAN

Preparing a business plan is probably the most important exercise for thinking through all of the issues necessary to the establishment of a new business. Many people mistakenly wait to prepare this plan until they are looking for financing, but the value of the plan extends far beyond that single purpose. It should be *your* plan for what *you* hope to accomplish; your yardstick for measuring your success; your guide to managing your growth.

In preparing the business plan, you may find yourself reviewing and assessing the meeting planning profession as a whole. Ask yourself how your company can overcome the clerical and administrative image of meeting planning and demonstrate instead the value of the professional meeting planner's knowledge of financial and personnel management, contract negotiations, risk management, and creativity. You might consider the matters of continuing education and certification if you think these will be important criteria to your prospective clients. Information on certification is available from the Convention Liaison Council. (See Resources.)

The plan is a multipurpose document because it presents your company from a financial position (costs, revenue, profits), a market position (your sales potential, your "target" clients, your competition), a management position (staffing needs and skill levels), a philosophical position (your goals, values, style of doing business), and a differential position (what makes you different, better, unique).

THE MARKETING PLAN

The marketing plan is a part of the business plan, but can also be a separate, more detailed version of the section in the business plan. Gathering the statistics alone is enough to deter even the heartiest among you from founding your own business, but it is those very facts that will guide you to your target market, help you define your services, and determine your marketing approach.

Once you have your plan, you are in many ways back to the issue of image and packaging. You will have to determine what you must do to sell your services, from preparation of printed materials to how you will find and contact potential clients. There are some ideas in the Quick Reference Guide which may spark your thinking.

SELLING YOUR SERVICES

Selling a service is always more difficult than selling a product. It is an intangible. Therefore, the more "products" you can show prospective clients, the easier the sale. Your products may be program books and photographs of past events, copies of reference letters, sales brochures, or documents or reports you have prepared for previous clients.

You must also assure clients that you are working on their behalf, that you will always represent their best interest, and that you will carry out their requirements in a manner consistent with their company's values and image. Your clients must feel as secure with you—your knowledge and skills, and your ability to represent them—as they would with one of their own staff members.

You must be honest in your pricing, your ability to deliver the required services, and your representation of your qualifications. The first sale is the hardest, but with this up-front approach you will ensure easier sales: repeat business.

STAFF

Whether you're working alone or managing a large staff, you will have staff. Your staff may consist only of part-time clerical help and subcontractors, or you may have full-time employees, but you will need to hire, train, and manage them. Think carefully about your personnel needs and the costs. While more staff allows you to handle more projects, it is also the most expensive of all your costs, greatly increases your administrative hours, and reduces your hours of direct client contact. There are pros and cons, but staffing level is certainly an important consideration in planning your company's structure. Staff can be your greatest joy or your most painful agony. And being the boss is not always easy.

ADMINISTRATIVE SYSTEMS

There are several administrative systems that must be set up for your business. First you must establish a system for managing the various costs and hours of each project. (In doing so, pay careful attention to the difference between soft profit and hard profit. *Soft profit* is what is left after all direct project costs have been accounted; *hard profit* is what remains after the apportioned share of operating costs have been deducted, and that is the real profit.) To set up an internal project-accounting system, each meeting or event must be given an account code. I use an abbreviated form of the client's name, followed by a project code that identifies the meeting or event. For example, if the client were Events Extraordinaire and the project the 1992 annual meeting, the code would read: EE/AM-92. All activities and expenses related to the project would carry that designation.

BILLABLE HOURS

Next you need to set up a system to control your various projects, a system your staff uses to record hours billable to a client. Unless you attain a certain threshold number of billable hours, you will not be able to cover your operating costs, and therefore will not achieve a profit. The required number varies with your operating costs and your hourly rate, but it is a critical factor that you should have addressed in your business plan.

The number of potential billable hours per year for a full-time employee is computed as follows:

5 working days/week $\times$ 52 weeks/year = 260 working days/year
260 working days/year − (5 holidays
  + x vacation days + x sick days)* = 255 days (at most)
255 working days/year $\times$ 8 hours/day = 2,080 billable hours per year

You must use this formula for all employees having project responsibility. (Salaries of other administrative employees, such as those in areas of personnel and acounting, are considered as overhead.) Then look at your total operating cost and determine what hourly rate you must charge and what percentage of billable hours you must have to reach a break-even and a profit position.

Time sheets are a popular system used by law firms, public relations firms, meeting management firms and others, to track the time spent on specific client projects. Even if you are not billing your clients on an hourly basis, it is important to keep records of the number of hours a certain project takes. Analyze the information to find out when you are underbidding projects, what rate of pay you are actually receiving, and what types of projects or clients are most profitable for you. A sample time sheet is shown in Exhibit 21-1. If you can afford it, computerization of timesheets will help you avoid the administrative nightmare that they can pose.

The traditional method is to record the client and project code (from our earlier example, EE/AM-92), then the activity, which, for meeting planning, might be site selection (SS), then the time in fifteen-minute segments. A brief phone call is recorded as fifteen minutes, because of the interruption factor. The rule of thumb is that it takes fifteen minutes to get back to the productivity level prior to the call. (If that were true, I would never get anything done—but that's how it works.) As you work through your day, you record each client, project, activity, and time on a single line. (See the Quick Reference Guide for this chapter.)

In order to cope with the bookkeeping, I revised the system to one time-sheet per client/project; my staff uses the sheet on a weekly, not daily, basis. That way, I can put each client's sheets together and total the weekly hours. I then give the sheets to project managers to tally and record. They are also responsible for controlling project costs and hours. This puts responsibility where it should be and reduces my administrative costs greatly. Systems are necessary and wonderful, but you have to control them rather than letting them control you.

PROCEDURES MANUALS

One of the most important documents in a well-managed office is a procedures manual. Preparing one is a time-consuming project, but it's well worth the effort. A three-ring notebook is ideal, because you can add, refine, and remove sections as things change. The best place to begin is with a statement of company values. Then prepare a section on employees, covering everything from office hours,

---

* Will vary according to your personnel policies.

holidays, and benefits, to copies of forms that must be completed by employees for the government and for your records.

I also have employees sign a confidentiality-of-information agreement. It covers some of the same ground as a agreement not to compete, which prohibits an employee from going into business or working for anyone in competition with your business. However, the confidentiality agreement is easier to enforce in that it prohibits employees from using client or other job-related information for their personal benefit, for the benefit of your competitors, or for the benefit of your clients' competitors.

The manual should have a section on general office procedures that covers opening and closing the office, processing mail, handling telephone calls, attending staff meetings, filing, handling rush projects, and dealing with the many routine and crisis situations that are common in a meeting management company.

Next prepare a section on accounting procedures: invoicing clients, project expense accounting, staff expense reporting, and reimbursement to the petty cash account.

This should be followed by a fairly major section on project management that includes the assigning responsibility, relations with the client, handling requests for services not contracted for, preparing reports (both internal reports and those for clients), and project evaluation forms.

There should be a section on sales that basically follows the same format as the project management section because each prospect is its own project. This should be followed by a how-to section on everything from computer operations to overnight mail, with simple operating instructions for every piece of equiment in the office. There should also be a list of every approved supplier for the administrative operations of the company and where services can be billed, whom to call when equipment breaks and where supplies can be ordered or purchased.

In my company, the procedures manual is given to each new staff member who must read it and know the information by the end of the first two weeks of employment. (I no longer answer questions that are covered in the manual, and when a question about an area not covered is asked, the question and answer go into the manual.)

CLIENT EXPENSES

There are two other forms that you will find useful: One is for postage/fax expenses that are billable to the client (see Exhibit 21-2) and the other is for photocopying expenses that are reimbursable (see Exhibit 21-3). You should use one sheet per client per month, simply entering the number of copies or the dollar amount of postage in the appropriate daily column. Put the sheets in a file folder near the copy/postage machines and make entries each time they're used. (For large amounts, number the entry and footnote the purpose.) At the end of the month, information goes into each client's billing file for invoicing.

It is wise to select a long distance carrier that provides account billing codes. You can then internally assign an account code, usually two digits, to each project. When the telephone bill comes in, project managers approve those calls accounted to their projects, the account listing goes into the client's billing file, and the file is ready for invoicing.

INVOICES

Try to keep all administrative procedures simple, efficient, and cost effective. My invoice for fees and expenses are line items on one sheet, with receipts attached. I run a calculator tape, staple, and mail. Errors in invoices delay payment, which is why I always attach a calculator tape. I try to contractually require payment on the first of each month, regardless of when clients get the invoice, because work for clients often takes priority over administrative tasks. But because billing is the most important administrative task, it is never more than a day or two late.

The Client's Expense Record (see Exhibit 21-4) is stapled to each client's billing file, and the expenses are written in the appropriate category along with the invoice date and invoice number. Invoice numbers are usually assigned in hundreds or thousands, such as client/project A-1000, B-2000. Then each invoice is subnumbered 100$\underline{1}$, 100$\underline{2}$, and so on. To assist in record-keeping, you may also add the year (1001-89). That also aids clients in recording invoices paid and provides an easy reference system for questions.

FEES

Setting fees is one of the most difficult tasks facing independent meeting planners. There are a variety of options listed in the Quick Reference Guide, but the most common seems to be a flat fee. Most planners cannot afford to take the risk of the per-attendee fee structure unless the minimum number guaranteed is very high. An hourly fee would probably be ideal for the planner, but clients are rarely willing to commit to the unknown. Charging a percentage of gross billings also has a negative side for the client, who may be concerned that planners will not be as cost conscious if they benefit in direct relation to the amount they spend. Accepting commissions may cast doubts on planners' commitments to negotiate the best rates again if they stand to benefit.

It seems that planners will have to learn to live with the fixed fee, but they must document the hours it takes to do a meeting more carefully and bid projects accordingly. Those who are not efficient will not be able to bid competitively, and those who bid low will ultimately have to increase their prices or will be out of business.

Many variables influence the fee, such as (from the perspective of the project) length and complexity, level of service required, number of attendees, and, I have found, number of suppliers. (If I have to negotiate with twenty suppliers versus ten, the time expended is dramatically different.) The variables from the planner's standpoint are the operating costs, the costs that are reimbursed, the profit margin needed, the prevailing local rates of your competition, and the intensity of competition. Other factors are the client's ability to pay and the planner's need for the business. Just like hotels, meeting planners have slow seasons and fees are more negotiable during those times. Start-up companies, which are trying to build their client base and experience level, are also more negotiable.

If you want to stay in business, the key is to know your operating costs, the cost to you of doing the meeting, and your profit need or goal. The fees you charge will never be consistent, but your product should be.

OTHER CONSIDERATIONS FOR MEETING PLANNERS

STANDARDS

As in any new profession a lack of standards exists. Standards are emerging in a random and disorganized way, and the industry's lack of emphasis on standardization of basic principles is frustrating. While the variables will change in each situation, there are guidelines that will allow planners and suppliers to communicate their expectations in a consistent way and to measure their group or personal preferences against the norm. The Quick Reference Guide puts forth some perceptions of needed standards in a variety of categories, both for the reader to begin to test and ultimately for the industry to arrive at what the "accepted standard" should be.

CERTIFICATION

Much of my own frustration about standards began when the issue of certification emerged. In theory, I agree with the need for certification; in reality, I believe that first the standards should be grappled with and then the test prepared. Even the "study materials" are contradictory, depending on who writes selected articles and what that person's values are. But it will improve; it probably already has.

For those interested in certification, a written request for an application should be sent to the Convention Liaison Council. (See the Resources at the end of this book.) A minimum of three years' experience is required to apply, along with other qualifying factors.

ETHICS

An important topic among professional meeting planners is ethics. Some favors and gifts extended to meeting planners have been interpreted as bribes. Some meeting planners accept nothing—not even a complimentary room when conducting a site inspection—while others call hotels in resort locations during high season and ask for a free room for their family's vacation. Some properties offer expensive gifts for booking roms. The "bribe factor" is obvious in extreme cases, but in its more subtle form, in which suppliers offer incentives or negotiate commissions to entice the planner to select them, it poses the real threat to our professionalism. I believe that I must always represent my client's best interest; my fees should be paid by the client. On the one occasion where I accepted a commission, the full amount was disclosed to my client. Any commission agreement with suppliers should be disclosed in the contract between the planner and the client.

PROBLEMS AND STRATEGIES

PROBLEMS: Payments are always late, causing a continual cash-flow problem for our company.

Strategy 1:   In the contract, specify dates that payments are due. Charge a high interest rate for late payments and reduce the time from thirty days to ten days when the rate goes into effect. Charge delinquent parties the penalty the first time they are late. A stated penalty that is not billed or collected is, in effect, no penalty at all.

Strategy 2:   Check the references of the party you are contracting with. I usually call hotels where the client's past meetings were held or call suppliers who have dealt with that client, asking about payment history.

Strategy 3:   If you are collecting a portion of the conference fees, require that all payments be held in an escrow account until all bills are paid.

Strategy 4:   Require a large advance deposit.   .

Strategy 5:   Stop work on the project until payment is received.

Strategy 6:   When in doubt, walk away.

PROBLEM: In the bidding and contracting stages, we have trouble getting to the decisionmaker.

Strategy 1:   Early in the initial stage, find out how and by whom the decision will be made.

Strategy 2:   An "influencer" can be as important as a decisionmaker. Ask the person you are dealing with about the decisionmaker. If the two of them meet, lunch, or golf together, you may be all right. If they never see or talk to each other, you might ask some more direct questions, especially geared to the decisionmaker's knowledge of the staff person's interests in subcontracting the meeting planning responsibilities.

Strategy 3:   The process increases in difficulty if you do not have an inside contact. Often the secretary, with a little special attention, will help you get in the door. Persistence can be annoying, but is often a trait of the successful.

Strategy 4:   If the decisionmaker has delegated the decision, don't try to get past the person who now has the responsibility. You really don't want to get to the top, you want to get the contract.

PROBLEM: Clients seem to be very casual about missing deadlines, which hampers our ability to complete our work on schedule.

Strategy 1:   Impose contractual penalties for missed deadlines (but use reasonable judgment).

Strategy 2:   Send frequent written reminders to those with responsibility for meeting deadlines and memos to your contractor when deadlines are missed. Documentation will be valuable in alerting your client to problems that may affect the success of the meeting.

Strategy 3:   Build in a little "fudge" factor.

Strategy 4:   Explain the importance of key deadlines and the affect failure to meet them may have on the rest of the project. Some deadlines are more flexible than others.

Strategy 5:   Evaluate the client organization's tendency to work in a crisis situation rather than in a systematic style. You may have to adapt to the client's sense of urgency.

PART TWO

QUICK REFERENCE GUIDE

Guide 1

Overall Planning Structure

Preliminary Considerations

✔ **Analyze the meeting:**
  - Purpose of meeting/event?
  - Who will attend?
  - Why will they attend?
  - What do they want to accomplish?
  - When will the meeting/event be?
  - Where will it be held?
  - How will it be financed?
  - How will it be marketed?

✔ **Assemble the planning team:**
  - Meeting planner
  - Clerical support
  - Decision makers
  - Technical staff (e.g., program, accounting, public relations, legal)

✔ **Identify tasks:**
  - Program design
  - Speaker selection
  - Site selection
  - Budgeting and financial management
  - Marketing
  - Press relations
  - Printing
  - Exhibits
  - Hotel and supplier arrangements
  - Transportation
  - Registration

- Materials preparation
- Mailings
- Other (identify)

✔ **Organize tasks:**
  - To be done before event
  - To be done on site
  - To be done after event

✔ **Assign tasks:**
  - Identify department, committee, or specific person responsible for each task.

✔ **Communicate:**
  - Submit completed schedule to all individuals with planning responsibilities and to their supervisors for review and approval.

Helpful Hints

Never consider the schedule complete.
Insert completion dates when known.
Add new tasks as they are identified.
Delete unnecessary tasks.
Be aware of relationship of tasks.
Follow up regularly with staff members regarding their responsibilities.

Record Keeping: Forms and Correspondence

Your record-keeping systems may be organized by:

✔ **Project name**

✔ **Subject heading**

✔ **Meeting components**

✔ **Account codes**

✔ **Contracts**

Forms

- Registration forms
- Hotel reservation forms
- Timetables
- Function sheets
- Speaker forms
- Evaluation forms
- Audiovisual equipment specifications
- Employee time sheets
- Printing specifications/ timetables
- Sponsorship forms
- Advertiser forms
- Exhibitor forms
- Telephone time logs
- Bar reading forms
- Function attendance forms
- Food and beverage forms
- Other (identify)

Correspondence

- Hotel/facility
- Official airline
- Speakers
- Entertainers
- Printer
- Sponsors
- Exhibitors
- Advertisers
- Transportation company
- Audiovisual supplier
- Photographer
- Decorator
- Outside caterers
- Other purveyors and suppliers

Policies and Procedures

General

✔ **Eligibility of registrants**

✔ **Complementary registration**

✔ **Preregistration**

✔ **Cancellations**

✔ **Refunds**

✔ **Deadlines**

✔ **Exhibitor eligibility and other rules and regulations**

✔ **On-site sale of merchandise**

✔ **Spouse, children, and guest attendance fees**

✔ **Speakers:**
- Travel expenses
- Lodging expenses
- Per diems
- Fees
- Releases

✔ **Hotel suite assignments**

✔ **Hospitality suites**

✔ **Private parties**

✔ **VIP services**

✔ **Ticket exchange for special events**

✔ **Controls for session/event attendance**

✔ **Volunteer participation/utilization**

✔ **Program advertisers**

In-House

✔ **Financial accounting/deposit/payments**

✔ **Promotional mailings**

✔ **Speakers' commitments and confirmations**

✔ **Exhibitor/advertiser commitments**

✔ **Registration payment processing**

✔ **Printing**

✔ **Shipping**

✔ **Staff:**
- Travel expenses
- Lodging expenses
- Per diems

1-1 | Planning Schedule Example

Dates and tasks should be adjusted according to the specifics of your meeting.

Date Completed	Task	Assignment (Person/department/committee)
	36–48 Months Prior	
_____	1. Establish conference goals and objectives.	_____
_____	2. Identify desirable months and days of weeks for conference.	_____
_____	3. Prepare preliminary conference outline to include program session blocks, social program blocks, exhibits, sleeping-room requirements, and a brief description of each.	_____
_____	4. Begin site research of cities meeting the conference criteria.	_____
_____	5. Send conference requirements to selected sites with requests for written proposals.	_____
_____	6. Obtain meeting dates and sites from other related organizations to avoid conflicts and potential tie-ins.	_____
_____	7. Review site proposals; select potential sites.	_____
_____	8. Begin site negotiations with potential cities and properties.	_____
_____	9. Conduct site visits as required.	_____
_____	10. Finalize and sign hotel contract.	_____
_____	• Add deadlines and requirements to timeline.	
	18–24 Months Prior	
_____	1. Select and appoint local conference committee(s) as required.	_____
_____	2. Establish two-year marketing plan and implementation schedule.	_____
_____	• Add deadlines and requirements to timeline.	_____

(continued)

1-1 Planning Schedule Example
(*continued*)

Date Completed	Task	Assignment (Person/department/committee)
	3. Prepare and mail letters to potential event sponsors requesting consideration in next year's budget.	
	4. Evaluate current and potential markets, and identify target market(s).	
	• Review, update, and obtain mailing lists based upon evaluation results (e.g., registrants, sponsors, advertisers, exhibitors).	
	5. Prepare preliminary budget categories.	
	6. Review and evaluate past, current, and potential revenue sources.	
	• Specify "needs" areas for funding requests.	
	• Match program needs to dollar needs and potential funding sources.	
	7. Prepare and mail funding request prospectus.	
	8. Review conference timeline for adjustments and update as required.	
	• Review all tasks (internal and external requirements).	
	• Identify needs for outside consultants, and specify requirements.	
	9. Request proposals from potential consultants.	
	10. Establish conference theme and preliminary graphics.	

18 Months Prior

	1. Select conference consulting firms and/or individuals.	
	2. Establish registration-fee structures and policies. Make sure cancellation procedures are included.	

Date Completed	Task	Assignment (Person/department/committee)
_____	3. Review, update, and prepare all policies and procedures governing conference, and distribute them to all staff, consultants, committees.	_____
_____	4. Identify areas of need for outside suppliers; outline specific requirements, and begin selection (e.g., decorator, security, official airline, and car rental, audiovisual, entertainment, registration services).	_____
_____	5. Follow up on item 4, and identify new sources for conference support funding.	_____
_____	6. Review and establish guidelines for submission, review, and selection of papers.	_____
_____	7. Prepare master schedule of all known printing requirements to include specific items, anticipated quantity, coding system, deadlines, and potential printers.	_____
_____	8. Assign program issue area responsibilities.	_____

12 Months Prior

Date Completed	Task	Assignment (Person/department/committee)
_____	1. Review hotel contract deadline dates.	_____
_____	2. Review, update, and finalize conference budget.	_____
_____	3. Review and revise conference accounting procedures, and assign appropriate meeting codes.	_____
_____	4. Prepare and forward a tentative conference schedule to hotel.	_____
_____	5. Finalize materials and mail "call for papers."	_____
_____	6. Begin preparation of conference brochure (copy, layout, design).	_____
_____	7. Update all speaker forms (e.g., releases, travel, housing, audiovisual).	_____

(continued)

1-1 Planning Schedule Example
(*continued*)

Date Completed	Task	Assignment (Person/department/committee)
	8. Establish awards selection criteria and categories.	
	• Update all materials and mail.	
	9. Prepare 12-month media schedule.	
	• Begin identifying specific media sources.	
	• Finalize media lists.	

10—12 Months Prior

Date Completed	Task	Assignment (Person/department/committee)
	1. Prepare list of available hotel function space and capacities.	
	• Compile master list of suggested program topics and speakers.	
	• Refine master format for general sessions, workshops, luncheons, youth conference.	
	• Begin incorporating topics and speakers into format.	
	• Compare hotel space and capacities and make tentative room assignments of conference functions and activities.	
	2. Begin confirming program speakers and topics as available.	
	• Obtain bios and photos as finalized.	
	• Promote conference via appropriate announcements.	
	3. Finalize selections of all remaining suppliers.	
	4. Identify and begin preparation of nonconference sale items.	
	5. Follow up on "call for papers."	

Date Completed	Task	Assignment (Person/department/committee)
	6. Reevaluate target markets and mailing lists in preparation for brochure mailing.	
	7. Continue publicity in newsletter.	
	8. Identify conference functions and activities available for sponsorship.	
	• Begin specific sponsorship solicitations.	
	9. Prepare and mail exhibit prospectus and related materials.	
	10. Establish procedures and controls for session and event admittance via tickets or badges.	
	• Establish monitoring process.	

8–10 Months Prior

Date Completed	Task	Assignment
	1. Continue follow-up on "call for papers."	
	2. Begin final selection process on papers.	
	3. Promote conference in identified professional publications.	
	4. Follow up on exhibit mailing.	
	5. Mail first conference brochure.	
	6. Begin finalizing awards nominee list.	
	7. Determine and implement badge preparation process.	
	8. Identify final reporting and analysis requirements.	
	• Develop data collection system(s).	
	• Prepare data collection documents.	
	9. Prepare expanded conference brochure for second mailing.	
	10. Prepare and mail second exhibitor solicitation materials.	
	11. Review and update hotel function-space assignments and communicate to hotel.	

(continued)

| 1-1 | **Planning Schedule Example** (*continued*) |

Date Completed	Task	Assignment (Person/department/committee)
_____	12. Begin preparation of hotel function-space diagrams (e.g., registration, general sessions, workshops, social functions).	_____
_____	13. Begin exhibit space assignment.	_____
_____	• Mail confirmations, update on conference activities, function sponsorships, and conference program advertising information.	_____
_____	14. Begin processing registration forms as received.	_____
_____	• Prepare and mail preregistrant confirmation notices.	_____
_____	15. Implement monthly registration reporting system.	_____
_____	16. Identify and communicate on-site responsibility areas for committees and volunteers.	_____
_____	17. Begin active solicitation of advertisers for program book.	_____
_____	18. Finalize conference program and schedule (e.g., youth conference, speakers, workshops).	_____
_____	19. Combine all relevant policies and specific procedures into how-to manual for on-site use.	_____

4—6 Months Prior

_____	1. Mail second conference brochure.	_____
_____	2. Finalize selection of awards recipients.	_____
_____	3. Identify materials included in registration packets.	_____
_____	• Select and order conference packet.	_____
_____	4. Design and print all function-admittance tickets.	_____

Date Completed	Task	Assignment (Person/department/committee)

5. Continue solicitation and follow-up of exhibitors, sponsors, advertisers.

6. Begin all food-and-beverage menu selections.

7. Order all on-site office equipment and furniture.

8. Order Awards and related Awards materials.

9. Review registration returns based upon targeted market.
   - Prepare and mail targeted registration invitation letters.

10. Identify and assign staff's on-site responsibilities.

11. Select and order speaker gifts.

2—4 Months Prior

1. Prepare special conference issue of newsletter.

2. Request camera-ready ads for conference program.

3. Review hotel sleeping-room pickup.

4. Review and finalize function-room diagrams with hotel and appropriate outside suppliers.

5. Continue follow-up with exhibitors.

6. Review conference budget, and adjust as required.

7. Order special decorative items for conference functions.

8. Prepare and print conference evaluation forms.

9. Prepare and print on-site registration forms.

10. Begin preparation of written requirements to hotel and suppliers.

11. Implement weekly registration reporting system.

12. Select printer for conference program book.

13. Review badge-preparation process.

14. Prepare sign list and order.

(continued)

1-1	**Planning Schedule Example** (***continued***)

Date Completed	Task	Assignment (Person/department/committee)

1–2 Months Prior

1. Reconfirm all speakers and their requirements.
2. Review exhibit floor plan.
3. Print and mail special event invitations.
4. Finalize all food-and-beverage selections.
5. Reconfirm all sponsored events.
6. Communicate final agenda to exhibitors, and request booth personnel list.
7. Continue follow-up with outside suppliers.
8. Finalize and mail detailed requirements to hotel and all on-site suppliers.
9. Prepare up-to-date exhibit floor plan, exhibitor listing, and schedule for conference program book.
10. Arrange for all staff and VIP travel and housing.

1 Month Prior

1. Print conference program book.
2. Prepare and print preregistrant list.
3. Finalize on-site accounting requirements (e.g., on-site payments, deposits, cash-out procedures).
4. Order all amenities for speakers.
5. Finalize exhibit layout, and update exhibitor list.
6. Schedule on-site media activities.
7. Begin preparation of registration packets.

Date Completed	Task	Assignment (Person/department/committee)

2 Weeks Prior

1. Pack and send all conference materials for early shipment.
2. Prepare badges for all nonregistered attendees (e.g., speakers, exhibitors, staff, complimentary registrants).
3. Communicate all last-minute changes and new requirements to hotel and affected suppliers.

1 Week Prior

1. Set up all on-site individual preconference supplier review meetings.
2. Finalize time and agenda for hotel and supplier preconference meeting.
3. Provide required early guarantees to hotel.
4. Complete proofing of badges and preparation of packets.
5. Follow up on on-site media activities.
6. Establish on-site staff meeting schedule and required attendance list.
7. Verify VIP arrivals, and schedule airport pickup.

On-Site

1. Receive and inventory all shipments, equipment, and supplies.
2. Review all VIP arrangements.
3. Set up conference offices.
4. Conduct individual review meetings with suppliers and hotel departments.
5. Conduct personnel instructional briefings (e.g., for registration staff, data collectors, volunteers).
6. Conduct preconference and daily staff meetings.

(continued)

1-1 Planning Schedule Example
(*continued*)

Date Completed	Task	Assignment (Person/department/committee)
_____	• Review each day's requirements, and highlight following day's requirements.	_____
_____	• Review responsibilities, procedures, and overlap areas (e.g., registration, food guarantees, speakers, VIPs, media, room setups, data collection, youth conference, exhibits, sponsors).	_____
_____	7. Reemphasize communication lines and authority and responsibility levels to staff, suppliers, hotel, and volunteers.	_____
_____	8. Arrange daily invoice review with hotel.	_____
_____	9. Consult with conference support personnel as required for issuance of gratuities.	_____
_____	10. Confirm and monitor pickup of all rental equipment and supplies.	_____
_____	11. Arrange for return shipment of materials.	_____
_____	12. Conduct postconference wrapup meeting with hotel departments and suppliers as needed.	_____

1–2 Months Post

Date Completed	Task	Assignment (Person/department/committee)
_____	1. Prepare list and mail all thank-you letters.	_____
_____	2. Prepare and mail final attendance list.	_____
_____	3. Collect and organize data for final conference reports.	_____
_____	4. Obtain evaluations from conference support personnel (staff, volunteers, consultants).	_____
_____	5. Prepare summary report(s) of all evaluation forms.	_____

Date Completed	Task	Assignment (Person/department/committee)
	6. Review each invoice received, break each one down into appropriate conference categories, and schedule payment.	
_____	7. Prepare preliminary financial report(s).	_____
		_____
	2–3 Months Post	
_____	1. Finalize financial report(s). • Break them down into appropriate subcategories for final conference report documents, internal and external (e.g., sponsors, funding sources).	_____
_____	2. Finalize conference report documents and distribute.	_____
_____		_____

1-2   Preplanning Questionnaire

Sponsoring Organization and Staffing

1. Number of years in existence: _____ Tax status: _____
2. Number of years conducting meetings: _____
3. Current staff size: _____
4. Average number of staff available to work on the planning of meetings: _____
5. Average number of staff who attend each meeting: _____
6. Is other personnel support available? _____
   If *yes*, check all that apply:
   - ☐ Cosponsoring organization ☐ Local/host ☐ Subcontractors
   - ☐ Technical committee ☐ Students ☐ Convention Bureau
   - ☐ Other _____

(explain)
7. Please briefly describe your organization and staff in relation to meetings:
   _____
   _____
   _____

(continued)

1-2   Preplanning Questionnaire
(*continued*)

Attendance

1. Average number of attendees per meeting: _____
   Largest: _____   Smallest: _____
2. Desirable number of attendees per meeting: _____
3. Number of attendees requiring handicapped equipped facilities: _____
4. Why do you think people attend your meeting (note in priority order):
   _____ Credibility of the organization   _____ Subjects   _____ Speakers
   _____ Dates/location   _____ Social   _____ Networking
   _____ Other _____
                     (explain)

Date and Site Selection

1. Number of meetings conducted per year: _____
2. Cities/geographic areas where previous meetings were held:
   _____
   _____
   _____
3. Type of facility:
   ☐ Suburban/airport hotel   ☐ Resort
   ☐ Downtown hotel   ☐ University campus
   ☐ Conference center   ☐ Other _____
                                        (explain)
4. What factors influence the selection of meeting location?
   ☐ Special features appropriate to subject   ☐ Cost
   ☐ Proximity of staff   ☐ Proximity of speakers
   ☐ Proximity of targeted attendees   ☐ Climate
   ☐ Ease of air travel   ☐ Other _____
                                        (explain)
5. Who makes the final decision on the location of the meeting?
   _____
6. Who signs the facility and supplier contracts?
   _____
7. Percentage of attendees who stay at the contracted meeting facility:
   _____%
8. Average length of meetings: _____ day(s)
9. Number of additional days for pre- and postactivities (e.g., committees, board meetings): _____
10. Is there flexibility in time of year meetings are held? _____
11. Is there flexibility in the day of the week meetings are held? _____
12. Time period between decision to conduct meeting and actual meeting date:
    _____ to _____

Financial

1. Average total *costs* accounted to meeting: $ _____
   Does this include staff time and overhead cost? _____

2. Average *revenue* accounted to meeting: $_____
   Largest: $_____   Smallest: $_____
3. Major source of funds to support meeting (indicate as percentage):
   ____% Budgeted (corporate)   ____% Registration fees
   ____% Grants   ____% Cosponsorships   ____% Exhibits
   ____% Other _____
   <small>(explain)</small>
4. Financial goal:
   □ Break-even   □ Profit-making
5. Is a budget prepared for each meeting? _____
   If *yes*
   Is the budget prepared prior to establishing registration fees? _____
   Is the budget compared to final expenditures/revenues? _____

Program

1. Purposes of meetings (rate in priority order):
   □ Motivational   □ Informative   □ Decision-making
   □ Exchange of ideas   □ Networking   □ Social
   □ Other _____
   <small>(explain)</small>
2. Average number of speakers per meeting: _____
3. Percentage of speakers who receive:
   ____% Reimbursement for expenses   ____ Honorariums
   ____% Complimentary registration   ____ No compensation
   ____% Other _____
   <small>(explain)</small>
4. Percentage of meetings that require audiovisual equipment: _____%
5. Other special meeting requirements (e.g., proceedings, taping):
   _____
   _____
6. Normal program format (check all that apply):
   □ General sessions   □ Breakouts   □ Meal functions   □ Exhibits
   □ Committee meetings   □ Spouse program   □ Cocktail receptions
   □ Other: _____
   <small>(explain)</small>
7. What terms best describe your meetings (check all that apply):
   □ Seminar   □ Workshop   □ Conference   □ Training
   □ Continuing education   □ Annual meeting
   □ Other _____
   <small>(explain)</small>
8. Meeting materials provided to attendees (check all that apply)
   □ Badges   □ Comprehensive on-site program book
   □ Agenda only   □ Registrant list   □ Portfolios
   □ Copies of speeches/position papers   □ Evaluations
   □ Promotional materials on organization/future meetings
   □ Meal/event tickets   □ Other _____
   <small>(explain)</small>
9. Are credit house (continuing education units—CEUs) available to attendees?
   _____

(continued)

1-2   **Preplanning Questionnaire**
(*continued*)

Marketing

1. Type of meeting announcements (check all that apply):
   ☐ Memos   ☐ Telephone calls
   ☐ Professionally printed brochures   ☐ In-house–prepared brochure
   ☐ Letters   ☐ Ads
   ☐ Other _____
   (explain)
2. Number of mailings per meeting: _____
3. Average number of people receiving mailings: _____
4. Number of weeks prior to meeting first announcement is mailed: _____
5. Methods of mailing:
   ☐ First-class   ☐ Bulk
   ☐ In conjunction with other material
6. With whom do you compete for meeting attendees? _____
7. What are the advantages of attending your program over the competitor?
   _____

Evaluation

1. Is there an evaluation process for each meeting? _____
2. If *yes*, is this evaluation process for (check all that apply):
   ☐ Attendees?   ☐ Staff?   ☐ Speakers
3. Method of evaluating meeting:
   ☐ Formal   ☐ Informal
4. Which of the following areas are included in the evaluation?
   ☐ Technical program content   ☐ Speakers   ☐ Meeting site/dates
   ☐ Future topics of interest   ☐ Logistical arrangements
   ☐ Other _____
   (explain)
5. Are the evaluation results used for future planning? _____

Guide 2
Program Design

Steps in Planning a Program

✔ **Prepare a general statement on the purpose of the program:**
- To educate or inform
- To disseminate information
- To solve problems
- To produce reports/documents
- To reach consensus/decisions
- To introduce products/services
- To recognize/reward individuals
- To build support
- To increase visibility
- To conduct corporate/organizational business
- To elevate organizational status
- To build constituency
- To exchange ideas
- To learn new skills
- To create group camaraderie
- To generate revenue

✔ **Prepare a profile on attendees:**
- Total size of group
- Age range
- Men/women ratio
- International participation
- Spouses/children/guests attending
- Children's age range
- Sophistication level
- Education level
- Group personality (e.g., serious, fun)
- Response of group to previous events

✔ **Prepare a budget listing all program costs:**
- Meeting-room rental
- Speaker fees and expenses
- Attendee materials
- Audiovisual costs
- Equipment and furniture rental to support format
- Signs, tent cards
- Door monitors

✔ **Determine time for program activities:**
- Time of year
- Number of days
- Hours per day
- Arrival/departure days

✔ **Determine location for program:**
- Type of environment (e.g., resort, airport, downtown)
- Type of facility (e.g., hotel, conference center, resort)
- Amenities required (e.g., golf, athletic club, shopping)

✔ **Convene staff or program committee if broader input is required.**

✔ **Create a theme, if appropriate:**
- Related to anniversary date
- To motivate/challenge
- To demonstrate past progress
- To project future goals

✔ **Prepare a master list of required topics/activities:**
- Committee or board meetings
- Awards presentations
- New/outgoing officer introductions
- VIP recognitions
- Product introductions
- Keynote addresses
- Official welcomes
- Pending legislation

✔ **Prepare a list of educational topics:**
- Important issues re meeting purpose
- Important issues for organization
- Important issues for profession
- Important issues for attendees
- Special-interest topics

✔ **Assign a format to each topic:**
- Site visits
- Debates
- General sessions
- Workshops
- Small group discussions
- Exhibits or product displays
- Multimedia presentations

✔ **Rough out program agenda:**
- Time
- Sequence
- Topic
- Format
- Activity

✔ **Match preferred speaker/program participant to role on program.**

✔ **Prepare a list of fun/recreational/networking activities:**
- Receptions
- Meal functions
- Theme breaks
- Sporting activities
- Tours
- Parties

✔ **Set time allowances for each topic/presenter.**

✔ **Determine meeting-space requirements and select site:**
- Number of attendees
- Preferred per-person square-footage allowance
- Type of presentations/activity
- Meeting space requirements for each format
- Audiovisual space requirements

Programming for Adult Learning

✔ **How adults learn best:**
- Adults learn best in pleasant surroundings.
- Retention is highest with participant involvement.
- Adults can and will learn when the need to know is there.
- Adults learn best when an association is made to already known information (examples, real problems).
- Adults' learning is increased by *3* when they both see and hear.
- Adults learn best by doing.
- Adults learn best when they are not forced to reveal inadequacies.
- Adults learn best when they are not treated like children.

Average Retention Levels

10% of what we read
20% of what we hear
30% of what we see
50% of what we see *and* hear

✔ **Retention improvement techniques:**
- Combining sensory faculties
- Repetition and reinforcement
- Note taking

Selecting Presentation Formats

Format	Description
General or plenary session	• All registrants attend topics of general interest.
Breakout	• Usually topics follow theme or keynote topics. • Simultaneous discussions occurring in groups of 8–12 people
Workshops	• Usually to produce documents or arrive at concensus
Concurrent sessions	• Multiple simultaneous topics covering wide range of interest • Sometimes can be a large group.
Lecture/papers	• One speaker • One topic
Panel	• 2–3 speakers • Different perspectives
Talk show	• Moderator interview • 2–3 experts • Different perspectives
Debate	• Two speakers • Opposing perspectives
Case study	• Simulated situation • Attendees work with others in group to practice skills.
Labs	• Replicate working environment with equipment to practice or learn new skills.
Round tables	• 8–10 attendees • Usually has group leader. • Idea exchange • Informal discussion of issues
Exhibits	• Booths or tabletops sold to industry suppliers for product promotion
Demonstrations	• One or more persons showing how a particular thing is done
Tours/site visits	• Trips to actual sites or points of interest.
Audiovisual	• Slides • Video • Film
Poster sessions	• Display boards placed around room with visual informational presentations • Usually prepared by attendees.

Time Allowances

Time Allowances for Program Scheduling

Single speaker:	20–30 minutes plus 15 minutes Q&A
Panel (maximum 3 speakers):	10–15 minutes each, plus 15 minutes Q&A
Lunch with speaker:	90 minutes
Lunch without speaker:	40–60 minutes
Unscheduled lunch break:	2 hours
Breaks after each 1½ hours of program:	*See* Guide 12, Time Requirements under "Food-and-Beverage Guidelines"

Time Allowances for People Movement Between Sessions

0–100 people:	10–15 minutes
100–500 people:	15–20 minutes
500–1,000 people:	20–30 minutes

Time Allowances for Meeting Activities

Structured program:	50–60%
Product viewing/exhibits:	20–30%
Meals/social events:	25–30%

Guide 3

Speakers and Other Program Participants

Resources for Locating Good Speakers

- ✔ Colleagues

- ✔ Experts in the field

- ✔ Staff/management

- ✔ Professional speakers bureaus

- ✔ Academic institutions

- ✔ Local personalities

- ✔ Noted authors in field

- ✔ Organizational membership

Types of Program Participants

Speaker	Role
Program moderator/master of ceremonies	• Introduces plenary topics. • Provides cohesiveness. • Summarizes as necessary. • Makes general announcements and those relative to next item on agenda. • Is responsible for program from first to last session.
Plenary/keynote/general-session speaker/presenter	• Provides overview of subject and trends. • Introduces theme. • Raises key problems and issues. • Provides a change of pace.
Panel moderator	• Provides overview of subject and smooth transition between panelists. • Introduces panel members. • Raises key problems and issues that have not been addressed. • Maintains time schedule. • Fields questions from floor. • Gives brief summary at end of session.
Panelist	• Provides brief overview of designated topic, with emphasis on current issues, problems, and solutions.
Workshop leader/trainer/facilitator	• Guides participation. • Prevents or discourages domination of session by one or more people. • Initiates technical issues and questions to resource people. • Stimulates discussion. • Keeps discussion on key issues. • Summarizes as necessary.
Workshop speaker	• Provides in-depth look at selected issues. • Offers solutions and alternatives.
Workshop resource person/expert witness	• Answers questions of a technical nature. • Raises points not covered in discussions. • Should give 3–4-minute comment on own credentials.

Guidelines for Working With Speaker

✔ **Identify points/questions to be covered in speech.**

✔ **Provide individual time allotments and program schedule.**

✔ **Check references for strengths/weaknesses.**

✔ **Establish fee and expense-reimbursement policies.**

✔ **Review participant background.**

✔ **Put guidelines in writing.**

✔ **Provide detailed conference information.**

✔ **Communicate regularly—*in writing*!**

✔ **Conduct an on-site briefing meeting for speakers.**

✔ **Provide speakers with a summary of attendee evaluations.**

Cost-Saving Ideas

Seek sponsors for speakers.
Do not use speakers' photographs in printed promotional materials.
Request 9" × 12" photo from each speaker to post at entrance to meeting room.
Utilize expertise of attendees.

| 3-1 | **Speaker Requirement Form** |

One page per section allows greater flexibility in organizing according to your internal system.

FOR OFFICE USE ONLY

Session: ———————————————
Day: ————— Time: ——————
Room: ———————————————

Section I: General Information

Please return by: ———————, 19———

Name: ———————————————————————

Title: ———————————————————————

Company: —————————————————————

Address: —————————————————————

City: ————————— State: ———— ZIP: ————

Home address: ——————————————————

Telephone

   Work: ————————————————————

   Home: ————————————————————

Emergency Telephone: ——————————————

For our planning purposes, please check the following food-and-beverage events you will be attending:

   ☐ Thursday reception   ☐ Friday luncheon
   ☐ Friday reception   ☐ Saturday luncheon
   ☐ None of the above

Badge Information

Name: ————————————————————————
     print or type exactly as you want name to appear on your badge

Title: ————————————————————————

Organization/office: ——————————————————

Do you want your business address and phone number listed in the program?
   ☐ Yes ☐ No

(continued)

3-1   Speaker Requirement Form
(*continued*)

Section II: Biographical Information

In an effort to make biographical sketches in the on-site program book consistent, we have structured the following format. If more space is needed, please use the back of this form. Your listing will be limited to 50 words.

Name as it should appear in the biographical sketch: _____

_____ Title: _____

Education (if applicable): _____

_____

Special awards or recognitions: _____

_____

Field or specialization; include number of years' experience: _____

_____

Key qualifications that will be of interest to attendees at this conference: _____

_____

Please enclose photo:

☐ Black-and-white   ☐ Color   Size _____

Section III: Presentation Information

Brief synopsis of topic issues included: _____

_____

_____

_____

Presentation   □ will
               □ will not   include question-and-answer session.

Agreements and Releases

I agree to limit my presentation information and materials to those directly relevant to the session topic, and will not promote in a commercial way my products or services or the products or services of any organization.

_____ / _____
                             signature   date

Taping Release

I hereby authorize _____ at their option to make a video/audiocassette of my presentation at the _____
meeting in _____ . I understand that, upon request, I will be entitled to a copy of my presentation.

_____ / _____
                             signature   date

(continued)

3-1	**Speaker Requirement Form**

Speaker Requirement Form
(*continued*)

Section IV: Audiovisual and Other Requirements

Projector
- ☐ 35mm slide carousel
- ☐ • Remote control
- ☐ • Slide trays _____
- ☐ 16 mm sound/film
- ☐ Other (specify) _____
_____

Video Equipment
- ☐ ½″ tape cassette player
- ☐ ¾″ tape cassette player
- ☐ 19″ screen monitor
- ☐ 5′ large-screen monitor

Microphone
- ☐ Lectern
- ☐ Standing
- ☐ Table
- ☐ Lavaliere (neck)

Recorder
- ☐ Cassette
- ☐ Reel-to-Reel
- ☐ Eight track

Other
- ☐ Chalkboard
- ☐ Flip chart
- ☐ • Black marker
- ☐ • Color markers
_____
_____
_____
specify color
- ☐ Posters
- ☐ Pointer
- ☐ • Electric
- ☐ • Stock
- ☐ Lectern
- ☐ Projector operator

Handout Material
Approximate number of
pages _____
- ☐ Distribute prior to presentation.
- ☐ Distribute following presentation.
- ☐ No materials will be provided.

Material Information
- ☐ All materials are enclosed and may be distributed to press and registrants.
- ☐ All materials will be mailed by _____ , 19____ .
- ☐ A copy of my presentation will be available for duplication and distribution.

Section V: Speaker Financial Agreement

Terms of agreement should be completed by meeting planner prior to mailing.

Name: _____   Session title: _____

     _____   Session date: _____

     _____   Presentation: _____

     _____ ZIP: _____   _____

  ( ) _____ EXT: _____   Time: _____ to _____ Room no.: _____

1. It is understood that the honorarium paid for my presentation at the _____
   _____ session on _____ , 19____
   in _____ will be $_____ .
2. It is also understood that the following expenses will be paid for or reimbursed
   as shown:
   _____ air fare to be
                  specify fare class
        □ paid for   □ reimbursed
   by _____ .
   Lodging for _____ nights and food to be
        □ paid for   □ reimbursed
   by _____ .
3. Other provisions (specify airport/hotel transportation, complimentary tickets,
   spouse accommodation, etc.—if none, state NONE) _____
   _____ .

   These terms are acceptable to me.

_____ / _____ , 19 ____
          signature   date

Return to: _____

          _____

          _____

          _____ ZIP: _____

     ( ) _____ EXT: ____

3-2   Program Moderator Worksheet Example

This memo is intended to provide the program moderator with a detailed description of the program goals, content, format, schedule and their roles.

Name and full professional
title: _____

_____

_____

_____ ZIP: _____

(   ) _____   EXT: _____

Name of meeting organization: _____

Meeting title: _____

Meeting facility: _____   City: _____   State: _____   ZIP: _____

Meeting dates: _____ , 19 ____ through _____ , 19 ____

Purpose of Meeting

[*A brief statement of meeting goal(s) and subjects to be addressed*]: _____

_____

_____

Meeting Design

[*A brief description of all speaker topics, session issues and problems to be addressed, formats (panels and workshops) to be utilized during course of meeting*]: _____

_____

_____

Meeting Structure

[*Attach copy of agenda*]:

Responsibilities:

General announcements
Introducing plenary topics and speakers
Making announcements regarding next item on agenda
Summarizing when it is deemed appropriate or necessary
Providing cohesiveness for and between all programs presented during course of
    meeting

Other

During general announcements of each plenary session, request program moderator to include information regarding the meeting facility such as:

- *Location of restrooms nearby*
- *Exits for handicapped*
- *Location of other sessions*

- *Other*
- *Location of restaurants in facility or nearby*
- *Telephones nearest meeting area*

Other information and courtesy closing remarks of letter/memo writer:

_____

_____

Attach appropriate sections on:
  Speaker financial agreement
  Speaker audiovisual requirements and taping release
  Speaker travel and hotel request form

| **3-3** | **Panel Information Worksheet Example** |

This memo, to be completed by planner, is intended to provide panelists with a detailed description of the panel, format, content, schedule, and their roles as panel members.

MEMO TO: _____ / _____ / _____ / _____
                       panel members   title of panel   title of meeting   date and time

FROM: _____

DATE: _____ , 19 _____

SUBJECT: _____
                  panel description

Purpose of the Panel

Please give a brief statement of subject(s) to be addressed and the audience's interest in and knowledge level regarding the subject: _____

_____

_____

Time Structure

The panel will last _____ minutes/hours.
Panel moderator's opening remarks _____ to _____ minutes.
Panelists' presentations _____ to _____ minutes for each presentation.
Panel moderator's summation _____ to _____ minutes.
Question-and-answer period _____ to _____ minutes.

(continued)

| **3-3** | **Panel Information Worksheet Example** (*continued*) |

Organizational Structure

1. _____
   panel moderator's name, title, company, address, phone

   _____
   _____

   a. General announcements: _____
   b. Introduction of panel members
      (1) _____
      (2) _____
      (3) _____
   c. Overview of panel subject, problems, and issues: _____

      _____
      _____
      _____

   d. Key questions and issues not addressed by panelists: _____

      _____
      _____
      _____

   e. Summary of session: _____

      _____
      _____
      _____

Panel Structure

To allow each panelist to know who other panelists are and what they will cover to avoid duplication.

1. _____
   panelist's name, title, company, address, phone
   a. Topic: _____
   b. Key issues to address:
      (1) _____
      (2) _____
      (3) _____
2. _____
   panelist's name, title, company, address, phone
   a. Topic: _____
   b. Key issues to address:
      (1) _____
      (2) _____
      (3) _____

3. _____
   panelist's name, title, company, address, phone
   a. Topic: _____
   b. Key issues to address:
      (1) _____
      (2) _____
      (3) _____

Include appropriate sections on:
   Speaker financial agreement
   Speaker audiovisual requirements and taping release
   Speaker travel and hotel request form

3-4   Workshop Information Worksheet Example

This memo, to be completed by planner, is intended to provide the workshop team with a detailed description of the workshop format, content, and schedule and to clarify their roles as members of the workshop team.

TO: _____ / _____ /
       speaker, leader, resource person   title of session/meeting

       _____ , 19 ____ / _____
              date   time

FROM: _____

DATE: _____ , 19 ____

SUBJECT (Supply workshop description, e.g., "Participant groups of eight, working at tables."):

       _____

       _____

Purpose of the Workshop

(Give a brief statement of the issues and problems to be addressed and resolved.)

_____

_____

_____

(continued)

3-4   Workshop Information Worksheet Example
(*continued*)

Time Structure

The workshop will last _____ hours.
Speaker's presentation and introductions _____ to _____ minutes.
Resource person's presentation of credentials _____ to _____ minutes.
Leader/trainer remarks _____ to _____ minutes.
Participants' group project work time _____ minutes/hours.
Participant group reports of conclusions, solutions/alternatives _____ minutes per group.
General discussion period _____ to _____ minutes.
Workshop speaker's summary _____ to _____ minutes.

Workshop Structure

1. _____
   leader/trainer name(s)
   a. Introduction of self and workshop team members and their roles.
   b. Brief overview of workshop subject, key problems and issues to be addressed:
      _____
      _____
      _____

   c. Brief explanation of how participants will work (small groups or other):
      _____
      _____

   d. Summation of conclusions, solutions, and alternatives; closing observations and remarks: _____
      _____
      _____

   e. Other: _____
      _____

2. _____ / _____
   resource person's name(s)   area of expertise
   a. Is available to participants for technical information.
   b. Will raise issues or questions not covered in participant discussion.

3. Responsibilities:
   a. Guides participation
   b. Stimulates group discussions.
   c. Guides discussion toward key issues involved.
   d. Intervenes if discussion is dominated by an individual.
   e. Refers needs for technical information to resource person.

Other information and courtesy closing remarks: _____
_____
_____

When workshop immediately follows a panel, panel members frequently serve as members of the workshop team.

Workshop Team Members

(List names and full professional titles for each member.)

Speaker: _____

                  _____

                  _____

                  _____ ZIP: _____

                  ( ) _____ EXT: _____

Leader/trainer(s): _____

                  _____

                  _____

                  _____ ZIP: _____

                  ( ) _____ EXT: _____

Resource Person(s): _____

                  _____

                  _____

                  _____ ZIP: _____

                  ( ) _____ EXT: _____

Include appropriate sections on:
   Speaker financial agreement
   Speaker audiovisual requirements and taping release
   Speaker travel and hotel request form

3-5 | **Speaker Confirmation Letter**

This letter should be sent immediately upon confirmation.

[Date]

[Inside address]

Dear _____ :

We are pleased that you have agreed to be a part of the [date] [sponsor] [meeting]. If the dates are not already on your calendar, please mark [date] at the [hotel] [address]. Additional information will be forthcoming regarding a meeting, prior to the conference, for presenters.

For your convenience, we have enclosed a Speaker Information Memo [Exhibit 3-6], outlining details relevant to your participation.

To assist us in making the proper arrangements for you, there is also a Speaker Requirement Form that we would like you to complete and return no later than [date]. It is critical for us to have this information by that date to ensure the inclusion of your biographical sketch in the on-site program book.

If there are any changes in your audiovisual requirements, those may be called in prior to [date] at [phone number].

Please make a copy of the form you return to us for your files so that you can review your requests prior to the cut-off dates.

We are committed to another successful conference. Your assistance in providing information will ensure a well-managed conference for [organization name].

If we can be of assistance, please do not hesitate to call.

Sincerely,

Conference Coordinator

enclosures: Speaker Information Memo
            Speaker Requirement Form

| **3-6** | **Speaker Information Memo** |

This memo provides general information to reconfirm speaker details one to two weeks prior to the event.

[*Conference name*]
[*telephone number*]

DATES: _____

SCHEDULE: _____

LOCATION: _____

DRIVING DIRECTIONS: _____

_____

YOUR SESSION: _____

        Name: _____

        Date: _____

        Time: _____

        Track: _____

        Title: _____

Check-In

At least 30 minutes prior to your session, even if you may already be at the hotel attending other sessions:

1. Report to the registration desk to pick up your badge, packet, and room location.
2. When you reach the assigned room, please check in with the door monitor.
3. Check the room to be sure your required audiovisual equipment is in place. Report any problem to the person monitoring the session.

Deadlines

Return Speaker Requirement Form: _____ , 19 _____
Return final changes of audiovisual equipment: _____ , 19 _____

Guide 4
Site Selection

Site Selection Process

- ✔ **Be prepared to provide hotel with basic information regarding your meeting.**

- ✔ **Have ready the key questions you will want to ask the hotel.**

- ✔ **Prepare a prospectus, or request for a proposal (RFP), to send to hotels of interest, outlining your requirements (*see* Exhibit 4-1).**

- ✔ **Conduct a site inspection of the hotels that have responded to your RFP and that best seem to meet the needs of your meeting (*see* Exhibit 4-2).**

- ✔ **Select a minimum of two hotels—and more if they are viable sites for your meeting—and begin the process of negotiating the details of your agreement (*see* Chapter 5 "Negotiation and Contracts" and Exhibit 5-1).**

- ✔ **Prepare contract and sign (*see* Chapter 5 "Negotiation and Contracts" and Exhibit 5-2).**

- ✔ **Follow up with all responding hotels, thanking them for their time, interest in your group, and bid. Also, be sure to let each one know which hotel(s) was selected and some general reasons why.**

Site Selection Decisions

✔ **Preferred dates and arrival/departure pattern**

✔ **Number of participants, including spouses, speakers, and staff**

✔ **Number and size of meeting rooms required, along with approximate hours**

✔ **Number of sleeping rooms required**

✔ **Number and types of food-and-beverage events (*see* Guide 12)**

✔ **Audiovisual equipment required (*see* Guide 13)**

✔ **Transportation needs of your participants. Will they require air travel arrangements, parking, taxis, buses, limousines?**

✔ **General level of acceptable guest/sleeping-room rates**

> Example:

> *Single rooms:*
> Low—$40–$60
> Moderate—$60–$80
> High—$80+

✔ **General level of acceptable meal costs**

> Example:

> *Lunch:*
> Low—$7–$10
> Moderate—$10–$15
> High—$15+

✔ **Special requirements, e.g., government per diem rates, handicapped-equipped facilities, whether facilities are locally owned, union/nonunion, and so on**

✔ ***Citywide meetings*—large meetings requiring use of multiple hotels and involving other services, businesses, and local government departments**

✔ **Space for exhibits (*see* Chapter 19, Guide 19, and Exhibits 19-1–19-4)**

Site Selection Questions

✔ **Are sleeping rooms available for your group during the dates desired?**

✔ **What are the hotel's rack rates, including taxes (*see* Rate Categories under "Guest/Sleeping Rooms," this section)?**

✔ **Are required meeting rooms available during desired dates?**

✔ **Will there be a meeting-space rental charge? How much?**

✔ **Can space be held on a tentative basis during your decision-making process?**

✔ **What is the reservation cutoff date?**

✔ **What is the deposit policy?**

✔ **What is the complimentary-room policy?**

✔ **What is the cancellation policy?**

✔ **What is the distance from the airport?**

✔ **What parking facilities are available? At what costs?**

✔ **Are any other groups meeting in the hotel during your dates? What groups are they?**

✔ **Are restaurants/lounges located in the hotel or nearby?**

✔ **What gratuity percentage is charged on food-and-beverage service?**

✔ **What are the state and local taxes?**

✔ **Are there any union requirements, e.g., for setups, audiovisual operators, electricians?**

✔ **Can outside contractors be used, e.g., as audiovisual suppliers, florists?**

✔ **Is audiovisual equipment available through the hotel? What equipment?**

✔ **What is the capacity for placing outgoing telephone calls and for handling incoming calls. What are the surcharges and house charges for local and long-distance outgoing calls?**

✔ **What other services are available at or near the site?**

Meeting Prospectus Preparation

A meeting prospectus is a formal request for proposal (RFP). Prepare a series of statements describing the unique features, general requirements, and history of your meeting. The information should be based on as many years' data as are available. The prospectus is the first step in site selection and should be submitted to the cities/hotels under consideration. A three- to four-week response time should be allowed.

Guest/Sleeping-Room Information

✔ **Number, type, and rate of sleeping rooms (*refer to* the options listed under "Guest/Sleeping Rooms," this section).**

✔ **Room/block requirements and arrival/departure pattern (*see* "Room Block/Pattern," this section).**

✔ **Method by which attendee reservations will be made (*see* "Room Block Pattern," this section).**

✔ **Preferred date for reservation deadline (*see* "Room Block Pattern," this section).**

✔ **If bed size is important, especially with shared-bed sleeping arrangements, ask hotel to specify bed sizes (*see* "Formulas and Standards," this section).**

Meeting-Room Information

✔ **Number of meeting rooms, number of people in each room and the required setup for each room (*see* "Formulas and Standards," this section).**

✔ **Furniture, equipment, and/or staging that will be in each room (*see* "Formulas and Standards," this section; similar guides may be found in Chapters 12 and 13).**

✔ **Estimates on the total square footage needed for each room (*see* "Formulas and Standards," this section).**

✔ **Specific allowances you prefer for such things as aisles, distance from stage area to first row of seats, handicapped requirements, and fire safety (*see* "Handicapped Requirements," "Fire Safety Considerations," and "Formulas and Standards," this section).**

Meeting Prospectus Contents

See also Exhibit 4-1.

Section I: General

✔ **Descriptive statement about your organization, membership, and/or attendees**

✔ **Any unique requirements and requests**

✔ **Overview of past meetings relative to current requests**

✔ **Preferred dates**

✔ **Guest/sleeping-room-block pattern, rates, and cutoff date**

✔ **Complimentary requirements, such as:**
  • One complimentary guest/sleeping room per fifty rooms used by your attendees or "picked up"
  • One or more complimentary suites
  • Complimentary meeting rooms
  • Complimentary local calls from staff office
  • Complimentary shuttle service from airport for attendees

See also Exhibit 4-2.

Section II: Specific Guest/Sleeping- and Meeting-Room Requirements

✔ **Public meeting-room requirements**

✔ **Food-and-beverage and special-function requirements**

✔ **Exhibits**

✔ **Program schedule**

Section III: Past History

✔ **Actual meeting registration**

✔ **Registration and hotel reservation patterns**

✔ **Hotels/cities used**

✔ **Former meeting dates**

✔ **Room rates obtained**

✔ **Public meeting-room utilization**

✔ **Exhibit booths (total square feet/sizes of booths)**

Guest/Sleeping Rooms

Approximately 60 percent of a hotel's revenues come from guest/sleeping rooms.

Rate Categories

✔ **Rack rate**
- Current advertised rate per room.
- Established by hotel management.

✔ **Convention/group rate**
- Specific negotiated room rate for a group.
- Agreed-upon in advance by group and hotel.

✔ **Government rate**
- Low rate, limited in number.
- Available only to government employees who have government ID card.
- Seldom available to groups.

✔ **Corporate rate**
- Usually higher than group rate, but lower than rack rate.

✔ **Flat rate**
- Priced at an average figure between minimum and maximum room types for groups.
- Applies to all available rooms except suites.
- Room assignments generally made on "best available" basis.

✔ **Range rate**
- Based on a mix of minimum-, middle-, and maximum-rate rooms, which vary in size and/or quality.
- Ask how many rooms you will have in each rate category.

✔ **Day rate or "use rate"**
- Usually half of regular rate for daytime use.
- Check-out time generally 5:00 P.M., but may vary.

✔ **Complimentary rate**
- Room extended free-of-charge to meeting organization.
- Sales tax on room must be paid by guest or hotel.

✔ **Run-of-house rate**
 • Same as flat rate.

✔ **FAP (full american plan)**
 • Includes three meals.

✔ **MAP (modified american plan)**
 • Includes breakfast and dinner.

Room Block Pattern

Anticipate the number of rooms to be utilized each night by your group, according to room type: singles, doubles, or suites. The arrival/departure pattern of staff, speakers, attendees, and others staying at the hotel during your event will determine the room block.

Example:

If your event begins on Sunday and ends on Wednesday, will the anticipated number of rooms required remain consistent during each night of that period?

Will any preevent activities—such as staff, committee, or board meetings—planned on site require early guest-room accommodations?

Ways Reservations Can Be Made

• Hotel reservation cards
• Telephone (800/# or direct dial)
• Rooming list prepared by planner
• Housing bureau (often provided by local convention bureau)

Reservation Cutoff Date

Designate a date when rooms in the room block are to be returned to the hotel for public sale. The hotel contract should specify that "group rates will be honored after cutoff date on a space-available basis." A three- to four-week cutoff date is preferred by hotels. Occasionally, two weeks or less can be negotiated.

Formulas and Standards

Standard Hotel Bed Sizes	
Single/twin:	38″ × 75″
Double:	53″ × 75″
Queen:	60″ × 80″
King:	76″ × 80–84″

Term	Code*	Definition	Sq. ft. per person (min./max.)
		Meeting-Room Setups and Square-Footage Allowances	
Theater	T	Chairs in a row, as in movie theater	9–6
Banquet	B	Round tables seating 8 or 10	12–20
Classroom or schoolroom	CR SR	Tables place in front of chairs	9–16
Reception/ hospitality room	R	Primarily stand-up occasion, scattered tables as found in bar or lounge	8–9
Conference	C	One large table, or several joined together, with chairs placed around perimeter	25–45
Hollow square	HS	Tables joined to form a	25–45
U-shape	US	rectangle or a square with an open center	

Furniture Sizes and Capacities

6' tables	• *Classroom, schoolroom*—72" long × 18" wide, 30" high—will tightly seat three people per table. • *Regular*—72" long × 30" wide, 30" high—will tightly seat three people along each side of table (30" table preferable).
Cocktail table	• 15"–30"—will seat four people per table—also called cabaret or club table.
Rounds	• 60" (5') diameter—will seat eight people per table. • 72" (6') diameter—will seat ten people per table.
Chairs	• Standard conference stacking chairs, 18"–20" wide.
Lectern	• Stand for holding notes.
Podium	• A low platform or stage, also called a dais or rostrum.

★ Codes are used to advise hotel of room setup. T-60 = Theater for sixty people.

Formula to Determine Square Footage

Total square footage   = width × length
Room size ÷ number
   of people   = square feet available per person.

Example:

500 square feet ÷ 30 people = 16.66 square feet per person.

Determining Square-Footage Requirements

Example:

Of 300 attendees, 75% will attend an event.
An audiovisual presentation will be shown.
The per-person allowance is 15 square feet.
The established staging multiple is 1.7.
The established AV multiple is 1.5.

How many people will attend, and what size room is required?

300 × .75 = 225 people

225 × 15 sq. ft. = 3,375 sq. ft.

3,375 × 1.5 (AV multiple) = 5,062.5 sq. ft.

Formula to Determine Dance Floor Size

$$\frac{\text{Number of event attendees}}{4} = \text{average number of couples who will dance at one time.}$$

Allow 10 square feet per each dancing couple.

Example: $\dfrac{200 \text{ attendees}}{4} = 50$ dancing couples.

50 dancing couples × 10 sq. ft. = 500 sq. ft. required.

Variable: If attendees are classic style ballroom dancers, allow 20 square feet for each dancing couple.

Minimum Layout Allowances for Open Space/Aisles

Speakers' table to first row of chairs:	6' wide
Center aisle:	4' wide
Side aisles:	3' wide
Back aisle:	4' wide
Midsection aisle per every 15 rows of chairs:	3' wide
Midsection aisle dividing front and back half of room:	5–6' wide
Classroom set, center to center of table (table width 30"; chair depth 34"; movement 20'):	84" wide

Increase aisle widths by 1' if there are over 400 people. Recommended aisle width for handicapped accessibility is 4'–5', 7' between rounds (*See* also "Handicapped Requirements").

Special Considerations

- Local fire regulations
- Hotel's experience in setting up room

Handicapped Requirements

During your hotel-site inspection, note the following features for handicapped or disabled persons.

✔ **Exterior:**
- Passenger loading zone
- Parking, designated by sign RESERVED FOR HANDICAPPED OR DISABLED
- Hard-surface driveway or path connecting parking lot to entrance; must be obstruction-free (no curbs, steps, or level changes in excess of ½")
- Outside ramp to elevated entrances

✔ **Entrances:**
- Swinging or automatic sliding door a minimum of 36" wide
- Revolving door or entrance equipped with specified alternative

✔ **Lobby, corridors, and public areas:**
- Carpet depth does not preclude easy use of wheelchairs, walkers, or other similar devices.

✔ **Elevators:**
- Raised or braille indicators, located a maximum of 54" above floor
- Call buttons
- Obstruction-free walls
- Large enough for wheelchairs to enter, turn, and exit
- Access to all floors

- Conveniently and centrally located
- How many elevators; how many elevator locations
- Equipped with light-up and sound signals to announce arrival
- Waiting areas, corridors, and halls similarly equipped

✔ **Public restrooms/toilets:**
- Restroom entrance a minimum of 36″ wide.
- Doors easily opened.
- Easy access to toilet-room area (no narrow vestibule or powder room).
- One or more toilet stalls designed for handicapped and disabled.
- Toilet stall equipped with grab bars and a minimum width of 36″.
- Door swings *out* of stall.
- Door a minimum of 33″ wide.
- Washbasins with lever or push-button handles
- Ample (30″ minimum) knee space beneath wash basin.
- Soap dispensers (maximum 48″ above floor) easily reachable from wheelchair.
- Towel dispensers (maximum of 48″ above floor) easy to reach.
- Mirrors hung no more than 40″ above floor.

✔ **Guest/sleeping rooms:**
- Doors a minimum of 36″ wide, swinging *out*.
- Flashing lights for telephone and alarm system.
- Bathroom large enough to provide easy access to all fixtures.
- Bathtub equipped with grab bars or shower that will accommodate entering and exiting.

Fire Safety Considerations

General

✔ **Is building equipped throughout with fire detection equipment?**
- Smoke and/or heat detectors?
- Computerized heat detection system.   Does system:
  —Set off alarm in room and/or corridor of floor?
  —Set off alarm in designated area of hotel?
  —Set off alarm at designated fire station?
- Other?

✔ **Whatever the system, how does it operate? What does it and does it not do?**

✔ **Are all floors equipped with fire-alarm box (with axe)?**
- Location of fire alarm boxes?
  —By elevator bank?
  —One per floor?
  —One for each corridor per floor?

✔ **Are all fire exits marked with lighted fire exit signs?**

✔ **Are fire exits clearly marked on posted floor plan maps in each sleeping room?**

✔ **Does meeting facility give fire drill education to employees? How often?**

✔ **Are revolving doors banked by standard outside exit doors?**

✔ **Are standard building exit doors kept unlocked 24 hours per day?**

✔ **Are all fire exits clear of obstacles? On all floors?**

✔ **Are emergency exit stairwells well-lighted?**

✔ **Do emergency stairs exit on both roof and first floor?**

✔ **Is reentry possible, or do roof doors automatically lock to outside?**

✔ **How many outside exits does facility actually have?**

Kitchen

✔ **Do fire safety measures meet fire and safety codes?**
  • Number and location of fire extinguishers
  • Hoods and vents
  • Other
  • Waste baskets/receptacles metal?

Meeting Rooms

✔ **What are the location, number, and types of doors?**
  • Double doors?
  • Multiple standard doors?
  • Two or more exits?
  • All exits unlocked?
  • Doors open *into* corridor?

✔ **Are the aisles wide and unobstructed? Are there cross aisles leading to exits?**

✔ **Does the seating plan provide for easy exit?**
  • Even from center of row?
  • Is there adequate space between rows?

✔ **Do theater rooms (with anchored chairs) conform to fire code?**

Public Areas

✔ **Are there adequate exits in each area?**

✔ **Is access to exit(s) unobstructed? (Small, intimate cocktail lounge areas merit a good check for this.)**

✔ **Are there lighted exit signs for all exits?**

✔ **Are there lighted directional signs to emergency exits in all corridors?**

Guest/Sleeping Rooms

✔ **Are all rooms equipped with fire safety equipment?**
  - What?
  - Where?

✔ **Is fire exit information posted in all rooms?**

✔ **Do lighted directional signs point to emergency exits in all corridors?**

✔ **Do windows open?**
  - If so, do they work properly (try one)?

✔ **Are ashtrays ample in number and size?**

Room Setup Diagrams

Conference-Style Setups

Hollow Square Open-Centered Table

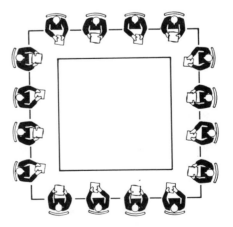

U-Shaped Open-End Table

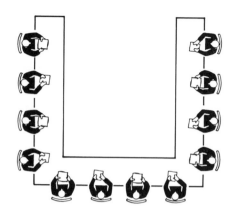

Banquet

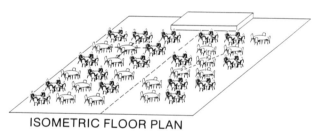

ISOMETRIC FLOOR PLAN

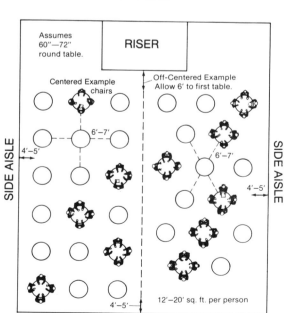

Schoolroom/Classroom

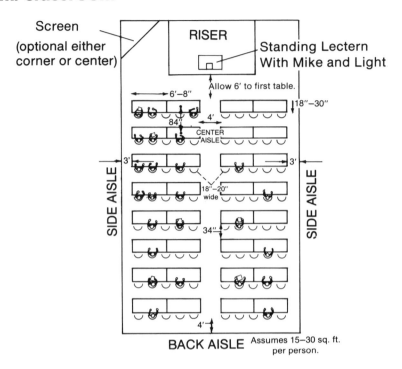

Theater

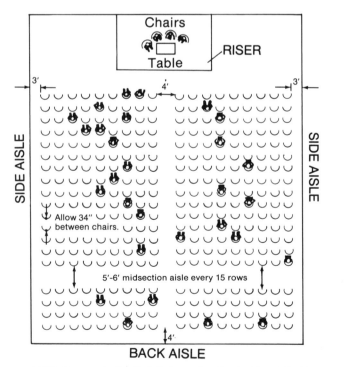

NOTE: Create aisle after 15 chairs in any direction (to side or to back).
Square footage allowance: 9–16 square feet per person.

4-1   Meeting Prospectus Example

_____, 19 ____ NATIONAL CONFERENCE PROSPECTUS

INTRODUCTION

_____ is a national,
nonprofit organization representing _____
_____. Its _____ members include more than
_____ students from chapters in schools and colleges
around the country and _____ professional scientists,
engineers, corporate, and individual members. In the
past, attendance at the National Conference has been
_____% students, _____% general members, and
_____% corporations.

This National Conference is held each year in November.
Sites are balanced geographically in locations west of
the Mississippi.

GENERAL

The _____ National
Conference Contract will be negotiated by _____
_____, who is acting as agent for
_____ on a noncommissioned
basis. All communications will be directed to _____
_____ unless otherwise advised.

The following _____
National Conference requirements will provide a basis
for selected facilities to submit proposals. Proposals
must fall within these guidelines to merit serious
consideration. Please note the detailed history of this
conference in Appendixes 1-10.

Please enclose with your proposal three client
references from meetings held at your property since
December 19X5.

(continued)

4-1 | Meeting Prospectus Example
(*continued*)

DATES

The preferred dates for the 19X7 _____
_____ National Conference are _____, 19 _____,
and _____, 19 _____, with limited preconference
requirements beginning _____, 19 _____.

ROOM BLOCK, RESERVATIONS, AND PATTERN

A minimum of 200 guest rooms are required with major
arrival on Thursday, and major departure on Sunday. Of
these, approximately 50 will be triples and quads (for
students). Current rack rates must be quoted. Strong
consideration will be given to properties that can
confirm room rates. An agreement to hold this conference
in a property will not be considered final until hotel
guest-room rates or a percentage under rack has been
established. It is requested that 5 staff rooms, 30
teacher rooms, and the 50 student rooms be quoted at a
lower than group rate.

Teacher, student, and staff reservations will be
coordinated through _____,
and a housing list will be submitted. The balance of the
reservations will be made by individuals returning a
hotel reservation card. Bulk hotel reservation cards
will not be required, although the hotel is requested to
submit one sample card with the final contract.

Student check-in will be handled at a special desk in
the registration area jointly staffed by _____

_____ and the contracted facility. Guest-room
floorplans will be provided for assignment of student
rooms.

Because a large number of rooms must be triple and/or
quads, bed sizes in inches must be specified as well as
your total house breakdown by bed category (e.g., king,
queen, double, single, and twin), with number of beds
per room if more than one.

COMPLIMENTARY POLICY

_____ requires a large
suite for the Executive Director and one for the
Chairman of the Board. This is to be provided above the
complimentary commitment of one (1) guest room per 50
based on total room nights utilized.

PUBLIC MEETING ROOMS

See tentative meeting schedule. _____
_____ normally uses theatre-, classroom-, and
conference-style setups and requires setups and meeting
rooms to be provided at no charge. Please provide to-
scale floorplans of all meeting space.

All space will be held on a twenty-four-hour basis for
the exclusive use of _____ .
Space may be released only with written permission
from _____ to the
facility.

A staff office is required in close proximity to the
major meeting area. Parlors on guest-room floors may be
used for committee meeting rooms. _____
_____ prefers all exhibits, major and concurrent
sessions, to be on the same level.

Please indicate group bookings immediately preceding,
during, and following the dates you are proposing for
this meeting.

We occasionally allow individuals to operate audiovisual
equipment for smaller program sessions. When submitting
a proposal, please advise us of hotel and union policies
that might restrict or otherwise affect our use and/or
operation of audiovisual equipment in the hotel.

EXHIBITS

A large room is required for thirty 8'-by-10' exhibit
booths. The exhibit booths should be located near the
major session areas.

(continued)

4-1 | **Meeting Prospectus Example**
(*continued*)

FOOD FUNCTIONS

During this conference there will be *no* liquor served.
Menu selections will be geared to the high school- and
college-age food preferences. There will be a
continental breakfast on Friday, Saturday, and Sunday, a
luncheon on Friday and Saturday, a major dinner and
party on Saturday, with informal parties on Thursday and
Friday evenings. All breaks are scheduled in the exhibit
area. Please enclose menus with your proposal (include
room service). Food prices must be confirmed one year in
advance for the purpose of budgeting.

ROOM RESERVATION CUTOFF

A two-week cutoff is required for 100 individual
reservations. The room list block (85 rooms) will be
provided three days prior to the major conference
arrival. Close contact will be maintained with the
hotel, and unoccupied rooms will be released to the
hotel for resale.

BILLING

A credit application should be enclosed for Master
Account billing.

UNIONS

Please advise of any union contracts with your facility,
with the contract expiration dates.

ADDENDUM I

TENTATIVE MEETING SCHEDULE

DAY	TIME	FUNCTION	SETUP	NO. PEOPLE
TUES.	24 HOUR	2-3 COMMITTEE MEETINGS	CONFERENCE	15-20
	24 HOUR	STAFF OFFICE		
	24 HOUR	STORAGE ROOM		
	8A.M.-5P.M.	TEACHERS TRAINING	CLASSROOM	30
	10-11A.M.	PRE-CONVENTION MTG.	CONFERENCE	TBA
WED.	24 HOUR	2-3 COMMITTEE MEETINGS	CONFERENCE	15-20
	24 HOUR	STAFF OFFICE		
	24 HOUR	STORAGE ROOM		
	24 HOUR	REGISTRATION	FLOW	
	8A.M.-5P.M.	TEACHERS TRAINING	CLASSROOM	30
	8A.M.-5P.M.	BOARD OF DIRECTORS MEETING & LUNCHEON	CLASSROOM	20
	Evening	DECORATOR MOVE-IN	(30 8' × 10' booths)	
THURS.	24 HOUR	2-3 COMMITTEE MEETINGS	CONFERENCE	15-20
	24 HOUR	STAFF OFFICE/PRESS		
	24 HOUR	STORAGE ROOM		
	24 HOUR	REGISTRATION	FLOW	
	24 HOUR	EXHIBITS	FLOW	
	8A.M.-5P.M.	BOARD OF DIRECTORS MEETING & LUNCHEON	CONFERENCE	20
	8A.M.-10P.M.	TEACHERS TRAINING	CLASSROOM	30
	12-3P.M.	PERSONNEL BRIEFING	CONFERENCE	20
	7-8:30P.M.	ORIENTATION	THEATRE	175
	8:30P.M.-12A.M.	STUDENT SOCIAL	RECEPTION	200
FRI.	24 HOUR	2-3 COMMITTEE MEETINGS	CONFERENCE	15-20
	24 HOUR	STAFF OFFICE/PRESS		
	24 HOUR	STORAGE		
	24 HOUR	REGISTRATION	FLOW	
	24 HOUR	EXHIBITS	FLOW	
	7-8A.M.	CONTINENTAL BREAKFAST IN EXHIBIT AREA	RECEPTION	300
	8-10A.M.	OPENING/WELCOME	THEATRE	400
	10-10:30A.M.	BREAK IN EXHIBIT AREA	FLOW	300
	10:30-12P.M.	6 CONCURRENT WORKSHOPS	THEATRE	5(@40) 1(@75)
	12-1:30P.M.	LUNCHEON	ROUNDS	400
	1:30P.M.-5P.M.	CORPORATE TOURS OUTSIDE HOTEL		
	6:30-8:30P.M.	DINNER	ROUNDS	400
	8:30-10P.M.	STUDENT CAUCUS	THEATRE	100
	10P.M.-12A.M.	STUDENT DANCE	RECEPTION	200

(continued)

TENTATIVE MEETING SCHEDULE (*continued*)

DAY	TIME	FUNCTION	SETUP	NO. PEOPLE
SAT.	24 HOUR	2-3 COMMITTEE MEETINGS	CONFERENCE	15-20
	24 HOUR	STAFF OFFICE		
	24 HOUR	STORAGE		
	24 HOUR	REGISTRATION	FLOW	
	24 HOUR	EXHIBITS BREAKDOWN		
	7-8A.M.	CONTINENTAL BREAKFAST	RECEPTION	300
	8-11A.M.	GENERAL SESSION	THEATRE	400
	11-11:15A.M.	BREAK IN EXHIBIT AREA	FLOW	
	11:15-12:30A.M.	6 CONCURRENT WORKSHOPS	THEATRE	300 5(@40) 1(@75)
	12:30-2P.M.	LUNCHEON	ROUNDS	400
	2:15-3:30P.M.	6 CONCURRENT WORKSHOPS	THEATRE	Same
	3:30-4P.M.	BREAK IN EXHIBIT AREA	FLOW	300
	4-5P.M.	GENERAL SESSION	THEATRE	400
	6-9P.M.	TRADITIONAL DINNER	ROUNDS	500
	9P.M.-12A.M.	DANCE	RECEPTION	500
SUN.	24 HR.-10P.M.	2-3 COMMITTEE MEETINGS	CONFERENCE	15-20
	24 HR.-10P.M.	STAFF OFFICE/PRESS		
	24 HR.-10P.M.	STORAGE AREA		
	24 HR.-10P.M.	REGISTRATION		
	8-9A.M.	CONTINENTAL BREAKFAST	ROUNDS	300

ADDENDUM II

_____ NATIONAL CONFERENCE HISTORY

Indicate information not available.

APPENDIX 1: MEETING DATES

1980-October 24-25
1981-November 09-12
1982-November 17-20
1983-November 10-12
1984-November 14-17
1985-November 07-10
1986-November 06-09

APPENDIX 2: PUBLIC MEETING ROOMS USED CONCURRENTLY (AT PEAK)

1980-1
1981-1
1982-9
1983-*
1984-4-5 breakout rooms and suites for small meetings
1985-5 breakout rooms and small committee rooms
1986-6 breakout rooms and small committee rooms

APPENDIX 3: EXHIBIT BOOTHS

1980-0
1981-0
1982-0
1983-42
1984-35
1985-27
1986-30 (estimate)

APPENDIX 4: ACTUAL MEETING REGISTRATION

1980-*
1981-*
1982-300
1983-approx. 300
1984-274
1985-418
1986-

* Information unavailable

(continued)

APPENDIX 5: HOTELS USED

1980-[*Hotel name*]	Denver, Colorado
1981-[*Hotel name*]	Phoenix, Arizona
1982-[*Hotel name*]	Oklahoma City, Oklahoma
1983-[*Hotel name*]	Albuquerque, New Mexico
1984-[*Hotel name*]	Los Angeles, California
1985-[*Hotel name*]	Minneapolis, Minnesota
1986-[*Hotel name*]	Denver, Colorado

APPENDIX 6: HOTEL ROOM BLOCK

1980-*
1981-*
1982-100
1983-120
1984-175
1985-180
1986-190

APPENDIX 7: HOTEL PICKUP (AT PEAK)

1980-*
1981-*
1982-100
1983-151
1984-172
1985-173
1986-205

APPENDIX 8: ROOM RATES

	single	double	triple	quads	suites
1980-	*	*	*	*	
1981-	*	*	*	*	
1982-	*	*	*	*	
1983-	*	*	*	*	
1984-	$55.00	$65.00	$70.00	$70.00	
1985-	$69.00	$69.00	$69.00	$69.00	
1986-	$70.00	$70.00	$70.00	$70.00	
1986	$44.95	$44.95	$44.95	$44.95	(Students, staff, teachers)

* Information unavailable

APPENDIX 9: RESERVATION CUTOFF

1980-*
1981-*
1982-2 weeks prior
1983-3 weeks prior
1984-2 weeks prior
1985-2 weeks prior
1986-2 weeks prior

APPENDIX 10: FINAL MASTER ACCOUNT HOTEL CHARGES

1980-*
1981-*
1982-*
1983-*
1984-$40,000
1985-$55,705
1986-$60,250

* Information unavailable

4-2 | Site Selection Checklist

Site Comparative Data Summary—Sleeping Rooms

	HOTEL		
Name: Address: Telephone: Contact person:	1. _____	2. _____	3. _____
Room rates and room tax			
When will room rate be guaranteed?			
Type rate offered (e.g., government, flat, range)			
Condition of rooms			
Dates block is available			
Number of sleeping rooms in hotel			
Number of stories			
Percentage breakdown of room types (e.g., single/double)			
Number of sleeping rooms available in block			
Number of suites available			
Are sleeping rooms equipped with TVs?			

Site Comparative Data Summary—Functions

	HOTEL		
	1.	2.	3.
Number of meeting rooms in hotel			
Number of meeting rooms available			
Number of meeting rooms if all movable walls are open			
Prime space			
Size and shape of room			
Daily charge			
Setup charge			
Location			
Storage area location			
Kitchen location			
Obstructions?			
Number of breakout rooms available			
Proximity to major meeting area			
Number meeting rooms with sound systems			
Number meeting rooms with screens			
Location/type temperature control			
Condition of rooms			
Tax and gratuity rate on food and beverage?			
Average number of covers per waiter			
Average price of lunch			
Average price of coffee per gallon			

(*continued*)

4-2	**Site Selection Checklist**
	(***continued***)

Site Comparative Data Summary—Policies

	HOTEL		
	1.	2.	3.
Preferred reservation policy			
Policy for late arrivals			
Policy for late checkout			
Complimentary-room policy			
Will convention rate apply after cutoff date on space available basis?			
Can space be held on tentative basis during the decision-making process?			
Reservation cutoff date			
What is gratuity percentage?			
Hotel credit card and check-cashing policy			
Hotel cancellation policy			
Hotel billing policy			
Deposit policy for master bill and sleeping rooms			
Unusual rules/policies?			

Site Comparative Data Summary—Services

HOTEL

	1.	2.	3.
Services provided by hotel at no charge?			
At what charge?			
Number of hotel employees; ratio to rooms			
Is room service available?			
Hours?			
Is in-house audiovisual equipment available?			
Is there an audiovisual repairperson on site?			
Who will hook up outside telephone?			
Are in-house services available? Contact?			
For audiovisuals			
For security guards			
For decorators			
For florists			
Others			
Is security available for hotel guests, attendees, materials?			
What union contracts or restrictions exist?			
Date union contract renewed			

(continued)

4-2	**Site Selection Checklist**

(continued)

Site Comparative Data Summary—Transportation

	HOTEL		
	1.	2.	3.
Airline service offered in or near hotel			
Distance to hotel from airport/driving time			
Hotel/airport shuttle bus frequency and cost			
Availability of taxis and cost to airport			
Hotel/city shuttle bus frequency and fare			
Convenience of car rental and return			
Hotel parking facilities and cost			

Site Comparative Data Summary—Miscellaneous

	HOTEL		
	1.	2.	3.
Other groups in hotel at same time			
What size?			
What activities and when?			
Music/entertainment and when?			
Does hotel offer any special rate packages during your stay?			
Two-for-one drinks/ free hors d'oeuvres during time of your cash bar reception			
Breakfast/dinner special rates for hotel guests			
Other (specify)			

Site Comparative Data Summary—Miscellaneous (*continued*)

	HOTEL		
	1.	2.	3.
How long has general manager been with hotel?			
Percentage of other staff turnover			
Is there a convention service manager?			
Is hotel equipped for handicapped?			
Number of elevators in hotel			
Access to meeting rooms (e.g., stairs, escalator, elevator)			
Names of three comparable groups meeting at facility recently			
Is hotel under renovation? When completed?			
Percentage of state and local taxes on food and beverage			
Gratuity rate			
Number of public restaurants in hotel			
Capacity of public restaurants			
Outside-of-hotel dining options and local activities in close proximity to hotel			
Special events in city during your stay?			
What?			
When?			

Guide 5
Agreements and Contracts

Negotiation Guidelines

✓ **When to negotiate:**

Negotiation may begin during the initial contact with the hotel and should be completed prior to signing a legally binding agreement or contract.

✓ **Who should negotiate?**

The person who is responsible for coordinating the meeting arrangements and a designated member of the hotel sales department should be responsible for the negotiations. Depending on the size and type of event, the hotel general manager, sales manager, or the food/beverage director may be designated by the hotel.

✓ **Some factors under your control in negotiation:**

- Flexibility in dates, time of year, and days of week (shoulder/low season, weekend occupancy)
- Arrival pattern and length of stay
- Ratio of sleeping rooms to meeting space
- Multiple booking options (i.e., having more than one event to book (repeated bookings) at either the same hotel or with the same chain)
- The dollar value of your business, including spending habits of group members
- Availability of advance deposits/payments
- Extensive food/beverage requirements
- Sleeping rooms paid by cash or checks (saving the hotel 3–7% in credit card charges)
- Guarantee of personal checks
- Full payment prior to departure after event
- Long lead time (e.g., 2–10 years); short lead time (e.g., 1–3 months)
- Previous history

✔ **Some factors under hotel's control in negotiation:**
  - Extra staffing services (housekeeping, bellman, front desk, waiters per cover)
  - Late check-outs/early check-ins
  - Cutoff date for reservations
  - Guarantee deadline for food and beverages
  - Airport pickup
  - Use of hotel van/limousines
  - Amenities
  - Room location, type, quality
  - Complimentary rooms, staff rooms, speaker rooms
  - Twenty-four-hour holds/all space holds
  - Compensation for overbooking
  - Materials furnished for attendance promotion
  - Specific meeting-room commitment
  - Assignment of preferred hotel convention coordinator
  - Rates and rate structure/spread
  - Deposits/payments
  - Gratuities/service charges
  - Meal and meal-plan prices
  - Extra labor, meal surcharges, service charges (e.g., bartenders, carver, bars)
  - Table decorations (e.g., carvings, flowers, color of linens, props)
  - Menu items
  - Room service charges
  - Price structure for liquor (per person, per drink, per bottle)
  - Liquor brands
  - Hors d'oeuvres
  - Exhibit charges
  - Audiovisual charges
  - Parking fees
  - Recreational activity fees
  - Electrician fees (lighting)

✔ **If guest/sleeping-room rates are not quoted:**
  Request one of the following:
  - A fixed percentage increase over the current group rates
  - A percentage off the rack rate at the time rates are confirmed
  - A dollar reduction off the rack rate
  - Net increase not to exceed consumer price index

Cost-Saving Ideas

During negotiations with a convention bureau request:
  - *Free on-site registration personnel*
  - *Free typewriters (usually bulletin type) for badge inserts*
  - *Free information desk personnel*

For large, citywide meetings only:
  - *Request similar complimentary services, equipment from local Chamber of Commerce and host-city government management departments.*

Facility Contract

Elements of a Hotel Contract

✔ **Parties entering agreement**

✔ **Dates**

✔ **Guest/sleeping rooms:**
  - Number of rooms
  - Room rates
  - Confirmation policy
  - Guarantees, deposits, cancellation policies
  - Check-in/check-out policy
  - Complimentary and other negotiated agreements
  - Reservations/reservation cutoff procedures
  - Credit arrangements

✔ **Food-and-beverage functions:**
  - Function space, setups
  - Price guarantees
  - Date of functions

✔ **Function space:**
  - Meeting schedule with meeting rooms and hours specified, and approval requirements if changed
  - Hotel's equipment provided at no charge
  - Setup time
  - Exhibit space and charges
  - Services, service level, staffing level

✔ **Audiovisual equipment:**
  - Equipment to be supplied, dates, costs

✔ **Renovations/construction:**
  - Construction schedule and penalty for failure to meet deadline
  - Postpone/reschedule construction when it interferes with meeting or guest comfort

✔ **Safety, handicapped-equipped**

✔ **Level of service:**
  - Compensation for substandard performance

✔ **Parking and airport service**

✔ **Special instructions**

✔ **Insurance/liability**

✔ **Signatures of parties**

✔ **Other items that do not appear in the body of the contract (as an addendum)**

Cost-Saving Ideas

Request information on any complimentary decorations/backdrops/plants/costumes, etc., or those available at reduced costs. Negotiate if available (but not complimentary).

Negotiate free staff parking, reduced room rates for staff, suite at reduced or single occupancy rate for VIPs.

5-1 | Negotiation Form

What You Want	What You Must Have	What You Will Give Up

5-2 | Hotel Contract Example

Suggested clauses may vary depending on negotiated terms and following review of legal counsel.

<u>YEAR/SPONSOR/MEETING</u>

ENGAGEMENT:

This Contract confirms the following agreement between
_____ (SPONSOR) and
[*official hotel name*] (HOTEL) and its staff for
SPONSOR's [*date*] [*meeting*], and HOTEL agrees to furnish
same as on the enclosed terms.

DATES:

Meeting dates: _____, 19 _____
Primary arrival date: _____, 19 _____
Primary departure date: _____, 19 _____
Approximate number of attendees: _____, 19 _____

SLEEPING-ROOM BLOCK

SPONSOR estimates that the attendees at the [*date*]
[*meeting*] shall require and HOTEL shall provide the
following number of sleeping rooms:

Day	Date	General Block	Staff/VIP Block	VIP–Suite Block
Tuesday	11/4		20	2
Wednesday	11/5		20	2
Thursday	11/6	135	65	2
Friday	11/7	135	65	2
Saturday	11/8	135	65	2
Sunday		c/o	c/o	c/o

Following the room block cutoff date of _____,
19 _____, all rooms under SPONSOR's room block shall
revert to HOTEL, and attendees' room requests will be on
a space-available basis at the contracted convention
rate.

(continued)

| **5-2** | # Hotel Contract Example |

(*continued*)

ROOM RATES (plus % tax)

135 general—block single/double/triple/quad: $_____ flat
 65 staff block: $_____ flat

Rates are based on single, double, triple, and quad occupancy, and are noncommissionable. The applicable state/city sales tax will be added to the room rates.

RESERVATIONS

Reservations will be on an individual basis with SPONSOR providing a rooming list of staff, VIPs, and general block 3 days prior to the conference. HOTEL will provide reservation cards. Upon receipt of reservations, HOTEL shall confirm the reservations to the individual. HOTEL will accept reservations by telephone.

To guarantee an individual reservation past 6:00 P.M., an amount equal to $_____ must be received by HOTEL within 7 days from date of reservation. HOTEL will accept deposits and payments in the form of cash, credit cards [*specify VISA, MasterCard, American Express*], traveler's checks, company checks, or personal checks.

If HOTEL is unable to provide a sleeping room to an attendee holding a guaranteed reservation, HOTEL shall provide to each such attendee the following as liquidated damages, and not as a penalty, for each night the attendee is not accommodated.

1. A free sleeping room at a comparable nearby hotel;
2. Free transportation to and from the substitute hotel and HOTEL as needed.

All room, tax, and incidental charges are the responsibility of the individual attendee unless otherwise indicated in writing to HOTEL.

Within two weeks following the conference, HOTEL agrees to furnish SPONSOR with a final occupancy report including the number and type of rooms occupied each day of the conference.

CHECK-IN/CHECK-OUT

Check-in time is 4:00 P.M. and check-out time is 1:00 P.M. SPONSOR may designate early check-in or late check-

out for selected staff and/or VIPs, the number of which
will not exceed 25.

COMPLIMENTARY ROOMS

HOTEL will provide one complimentary room for every 50
rooms utilized with specific assignments designated by
SPONSOR. HOTEL also agrees to provide, over and above
the one per 50 rooms, one 2—bedroom presidential suite
for SPONSOR's Executive Director and one 1—bedroom
presidential suite for SPONSOR's Chairperson.

All space listed will be held on a 24—hour basis for the
exclusive use of SPONSOR. Space may be released only if
in writing from SPONSOR to HOTEL. Final room assignments
shall be mutually agreed upon by SPONSOR and HOTEL two
months prior to conference period. After this date, room
assignments can be changed only upon the mutual written
agreement of SPONSOR and HOTEL. HOTEL must notify
SPONSOR of any other activities or groups booked in the
facility immediately prior to, during, or overlapping,
and advise SPONSOR of activities that may interfere with
this meeting.

SETUP TIME

All meeting rooms will be set no later than 30 minutes
prior to a scheduled event. Those rooms requiring 24—
hour hold shall not be dismantled, reset, or adjusted by
HOTEL or its authorized personnel without permission
from SPONSOR's meeting planner.

CANCELLATION POLICY

This Agreement may be canceled by mutual agreement at
any time or by _____, 19 ____ without penalty
upon giving written notice to HOTEL prior to August 8,
19X6.

Cancellation of the contracted Agreement may be subject
to penalty based on the following scale provided by
HOTEL:

Cancellation within	Percentage of estimated revenue	Not to exceed
_____ days	_____ %	$ _____
_____ days	_____ %	$ _____
_____ days	_____ %	$ _____

(continued)

5-2   Hotel Contract Example
(*continued*)

HOTEL shall undertake all reasonable efforts to resell canceled rooms and will credit those revenues against liquidated damages in an amount not to exceed the full amount of damages. Liquidated damages, if any, shall be due and payable 30 days after the convention period, provided HOTEL provides proof of its efforts to mitigate damages and proof that rooms being held for SPONSOR's attendees were unsold.

The performance of this Agreement by either party is subject to acts of God, war, government regulations, disaster, fire, strikes, civil disorder, curtailment of transportation liability preventing and/or reasonably delaying at least 25% of attendees from attending, or other similar cause beyond the abilities of the parties, making it inadvisable, illegal, or impossible to hold the meeting or provide the facility. This Agreement may be terminated for any reasons by written notice from one party to the other. In addition, this Agreement may be terminated upon breach of any material term of this Agreement, provided written notice of such termination is given.

This Agreement may be canceled by _____, 19___, without penalty if there is any change in management or ownership of HOTEL, any remodeling or renovation that interferes with any portion of SPONSOR's planned meeting.

Any controversy or claim arising out of or relating to this Agreement or the breach thereof shall be settled by arbitration in accordance with the rules of the American Arbitration Association, and judgment upon the award rendered by the arbitrator(s) may be entered in any court having jurisdiction thereof.

FOOD-AND-BEVERAGE FUNCTIONS (plus % gratuity, % tax)

SPONSOR shall provide HOTEL with an estimate of the number of persons attending each food-and-beverage function at least 72 hours in advance of the function and a guarantee of the number at least 24 hours in advance. HOTEL agrees to set for 5% over the guarantee and to indicate on each food and beverage invoice the number served as well as the number guaranteed. HOTEL will provide SPONSOR with a separate food and beverage function bill for each event.

Current prices as of ＿＿＿＿＿＿, 19 ＿＿ for food-and-beverage functions shall be in effect for SPONSOR's conference. Added to these prices will be the applicable sales tax and gratuity. [*Attach dated signed menus.*]

SPONSOR's conference is a NON-ALCOHOLIC meeting. HOTEL has agreed to move the complimentary alcoholic bar from the convention center and provide a nonalcoholic bar for SPONSOR from ＿＿＿＿＿＿, 19 ＿＿ to ＿＿＿＿＿＿, 19 ＿＿ each day from 4:30 P.M. to 6:30 P.M.

HOTEL agrees to send SPONSOR a copy of each food-and-beverage order two weeks prior to the conference period for review.

Three references must be provided to SPONSOR prior to confirmation of this Agreement and one month prior to event. References must have met in this facility 4-6 weeks prior to date provided and have had an event/meeting of similar requirements.

HOTEL SERVICE

HOTEL will provide adequate staffing for SPONSOR's conference. A manager will be on duty and available throughout the SPONSOR conference period.

The following service level is required at food and beverage functions:

Breakfast:	One waitperson per 20 covers
Lunch:	One waitperson per 15 covers
Dinner:	One waitperson per 10 covers
Reception:	One waitperson per 50 people
	One bar per 50 people

Based on HOTEL's promise of quality service, an incidence of poor service will require an automatic deduction off SPONSOR's master account charge of ＿＿＿＿%. An incidence of poor service may be defined as delay in meeting/session start time, ＿＿＿＿% of attendees documenting facility/service-related complaints, ＿＿＿＿% of attendees' guest rooms unavailable one or more nights, rooms improperly set up, improperly working equipment, or any other contracted facility and/or personnel failure of which direct responsibility belongs to the facility.

(*continued*)

5-2	**Hotel Contract Example**

(continued)

HOTEL EQUIPMENT

HOTEL agrees to provide a reasonable amount of meeting equipment/decorations complimentary to SPONSOR (e.g., tables, chairs, chalkboards, lecterns). There will be one complimentary microphone provided for each meeting room. Audiovisual equipment will be provided by an outside supplier. HOTEL will provide SPONSOR with a complete list of equipment and decorations that HOTEL has in-house, indicating prices and no-charge items. HOTEL has agreed to provide complimentary pipe and draping for SPONSOR's use if needed.

EXHIBIT AREA

HOTEL will, at its own expense, contract with [*name of security company*] to provide security to the SPONSOR exhibit area during all hours exhibits are not open. A schedule of exhibit hours will be provided to HOTEL.

MASTER ACCOUNT

HOTEL will establish a Master Account for SPONSOR to cover activities during the meeting as indicated in the final meeting specifications provided by SPONSOR. The Master Account should read:

    [*Sponsor name*
    Address
    City, State, ZIP
    Telephone]

SPONSOR accepts exclusive responsibility for payment of the final mutually agreed-upon Master Account charges. Interest charges will not be billed to SPONSOR if the disputed amount results from HOTEL's error or if payment is delayed because of slow billing by HOTEL, or if the bill is presented in a disorganized and confusing manner requiring excessive time for review and approval. SPONSOR requires 30 days for review and payment.

    [*Tax exempt number*]

SAFETY

HOTEL represents and warrants that it complies and shall
comply during the Conference period with all local,
state, and federal fire, safety, and building codes.
HOTEL further represents and warrants that it maintains
procedures and policies concerning fire safety and other
safety issues, and HOTEL shall provide all such
procedures and policies to SPONSOR for inspection upon
reasonable notice.

INSURANCE/LIABILITY

HOTEL hereby releases, relinquishes, dscharges, and
agrees to indemnify, protect, and hold harmless SPONSOR
from any and all claims, demands, liabilities, costs and
expenses, for any injury to, including the death of,
persons and any loss of or damage caused by, growing out
of, or happening in connection with the provision of
services or equipment by HOTEL.

HOTEL shall secure and furnish to SPONSOR upon demand,
and maintain during the conference period, a policy of
comprehensive general liability insurance, in a form
satisfactory to SPONSOR, issued by an insurance company
authorized to transact business in the State of [*State
name*], in which SPONSOR and its successors are named as
insured [coinsured]. The limit of liability of such
policy shall be not less than $500,000 combined single
limits covering bodily injury and/or property damage in
any one occurrence. The policy shall provide that it
will not be canceled or materially altered prior to the
termination of the conference period or until SPONSOR
has been given at least 30 days' written notice of such
cancellation or alteration.

* Note: Both cancellation and damages/liquidation
figures + reclaimation procedures do not include block
of _____ rooms held for conference attendees.

SPONSOR and the HOTEL state that the signatures below
have the authority to sign and commit SPONSOR and the
HOTEL to the provisions as outlined in this Agreement.

[*SPONSOR NAME*]: _____

[*TITLE*]: _____ [*DATE*]: _____

[*HOTEL NAME*]: _____

[*TITLE*]: _____ [*DATE*]: _____

(continued)

ADDENDUM I

TENTATIVE MEETING SCHEDULE

CODES: T — THEATRE   F — FLOW   C — CONFERENCE   R — RECEPTION   CR — CLASSROOM
B-8 — BANQUET TABLES OF 8   B-10 — BANQUET TABLES OF 10

DAY	TIME	FUNCTION	ROOM	NUMBER AND SET
TUES.	24 HOUR	2-3 COMMITTEE MEETINGS	SUITES	12/C
	24 HOUR	STAFF OFFICE	LOWER BR	
	24 HOUR	STORAGE ROOM	LOWER BR	
	8A.M.-5P.M.	TEACHERS TRAINING	PLAZA	30/CR
	10-11A.M.	PRE-CONVENTION MTG.	CONFERENCE	TBA
WED.	24 HOUR	2-3 COMMITTEE MEETINGS	SUITES	12/C
	24 HOUR	STAFF OFFICE	LOWER BR	
	24 HOUR	STORAGE ROOM	LOWER BR	
	24 HOUR	REGISTRATION	E LOBBY*	400/F
	24 HOUR	DECORATOR MOVE-IN/	E LOBBY*	300/F
		EXHIBITS	BR 5,6*	
	8A.M.-5P.M.	TEACHERS TRAINING	PLAZA 3,4	30/CR
	8A.M.-5P.M.	BOARD OF DIRECTORS MEETING & LUNCHEON	PLAZA 2	20/C
THURS.	24 HOUR	COMMITTEE ROOMS	SUITES	12/C
	24 HOUR	STAFF OFFICE/PRESS	LOWER BR	
	24 HOUR	STORAGE ROOM	LOWER BR	
	24 HOUR	REGISTRATION	E LOBBY	400/F
	24 HOUR	EXHIBITS	E LOBBY/ BR 5,6	300/F
	8A.M.-4P.M.	HOSPITALITY	LOWER BR	30/B-8
	8A.M.-5P.M.	BOARD OF DIRECTORS MEETING & LUNCHEON	CONFERENCE	20/C
	8A.M.-10P.M.	TEACHERS TRAINING	PLAZA	30/CR
	12-3P.M.	PERSONNEL BRIEFING	LOWER BR	20/C
	12-10P.M.	INFORMATION/MESSAGES	E LOBBY	
	7-8:30P.M.	ORIENTATION	BR 4	175/T
	8:30P.M.-12A.M.	STUDENT SOCIAL	BR 2,3*	200/R
FRI.	24 HOUR	COMMITTEE ROOMS	SUITES	12/C
	24 HOUR	STAFF OFFICE/PRESS	LOWER BR	
	24 HOUR	STORAGE	LOWER BR	
	24 HOUR	REGISTRATION	E LOBBY	400/F
	24 HOUR	EXHIBITS	E LOBBY/ BR 5,6	300/F
	7-8A.M.	CONTINENTAL BREAKFAST	E LOBBY	300/B-10
	8-10A.M.	OPENING/WELCOME	BR 3,4*	400/T
	10-10:45A.M.	BREAK IN EXHIBIT AREA	E LOBBY	300/R
	10:45-11:15A.M.	6 CONCURRENT WORKSHOPS	PLAZA 1-6*	30-70/T
	11:30A.M.-12P.M.	6 CONCURRENT WORKSHOPS	PLAZA 1-6	30-70/T
	12-1:30P.M.	LUNCHEON	BR 2,3,4*	400/B-10
	2-5P.M.	CORPORATE TOURS	OUTSIDE HOTEL	
	6:30-8:30P.M.	DINNER	BR 2,3,4	400/B-8
	8:30-10P.M.	STUDENT CAUCUS	THEATRE	75/T
	10P.M.-12A.M.	DANCE	BR 3,4	250/B-10

* HOTEL to supply SPONSOR with to-scale floorplans.

DAY	TIME	FUNCTION	ROOM	NUMBER AND SET
SAT.	24 HOUR	COMMITTEES	SUITES	12/C
	24 HOUR	STAFF OFFICE	LOWER BR	
	24 HOUR	STORAGE	LOWER BR	
	24 HOUR	REGISTRATION	E LOBBY	
	24 HOUR	EXHIBITS	E LOBBY/ EMPIRE 5,6	
	7–8A.M.	CONTINENTAL BREAKFAST	E LOBBY	300/R
	8–11A.M.	GENERAL SESSION	BR 3,4	400/T
	11–11:15A.M.	BREAK	E LOBBY	300/F
	11:15A.M.–12:30P.M.	6 CONCURRENT WORKSHOPS	PLAZA 1–6*	30–70/T
	12:30–2P.M.	LUNCHEON	BR 2,3,4	400/B–10
	2:15–3:30P.M.	6 CONCURRENT WORKSHOPS	PLAZA 1–6	30–70/T
	3:30–4P.M.	BREAK	E LOBBY	300/F
	4–5P.M.	GENERAL SESSION	BR 3,4	400/T
	6–9P.M.	DINNER	BR 2,3,4	400/R
	9P.M.–12A.M.	DANCE	BR	400
SUN.	24 HR–10P.M.	COMMITTEE ROOMS	SUITES	12/C
	24 HR–10P.M.	STAFF OFFICE/PRESS	LOWER BR	
	24 HR–10P.M.	STORAGE AREA	LOWER BR	
	24 HR–10P.M.	REGISTRATION	E LOBBY	
	8–10A.M.	CONTINENTAL BREAKFAST	BR 3,4	300/R

* HOTEL to supply SPONSOR with to-scale floorplans.

Guide 6

Data Collection
Evaluation, and Reporting

Elements of Historical Data Report:

✔ Types of information:
- Dates, locations, hotels, attendance, and room figures of past meetings
- Past budgets, financial reports, attendee lists, evaluations, programs
- Records of hotels and other suppliers
- Current data needs

✔ Methods for collecting data:
- Update general files regularly.
- Design forms for collection of specific types of data.
- Make use of observation/interviews.
- Make notations on calendar.
- Consult official documents.
- Review reports (e.g., committee, status).

✔ Guidelines for presentation of data:
- Always use hard data and percentages.
- Include pictures (e.g., charts, bar graphs, circle graphs, line graphs).
- Present your analysis in narrative form.
- Make sure data are easy-to-read and to follow.
- Round to nearest whole numbers or tens.
- Make sure that real numbers are documentable.

✔ Source of evaluation information:
- Attendees
- Hotel and suppliers
- On-site staff
- Internal planning staff
- Observation

Questions to Ask Focused on Observation

Process

- Were there long lines of attendees waiting to register?

- Was the program on-budget?

- Were meal guarantees accurate and the breaks on time?

- Were signs well-anticipated and well-placed?

- Did the flowers make it out of the hotel refrigerator the second day and back on to the hospitality desk?

- Were the rooms set on time—and correctly?

- Did speakers appear at the right time and in the right place?

- Were the buses on schedule?

- Was the room block filled?

Program/Attendees

- How soon after the first mailing did phone calls and registration forms start coming in?

- Is attendance growing each year?

- Is the percentage in the various categories changing?

- Was attendance consistent with other similar meetings?

- Were there more people in the sessions or the prefunction, or were they attending the cocktail parties?

- Were the breaks noisy?

- Did attendees arrive on time for sessions? Did they listen responsively to speakers? Take periodic notes? Stay until the end?

- Did attendees clean their plates? Were the hors d'oeuvres eaten?

- Was there lots of trash on the exhibit hall floor at the end of the day?

Staff

- ✔ **Were the staff well-briefed on their assignments?**

- ✔ **After the opening rush of registration, were workers encouraged to talk to and/or listen to attendees for feedback and note comments?**

- ✔ **Was a postconference meeting held with members of the hotel staff to collect their evaluations of your meeting?**

- ✔ **Did you ask attendees if they had problems unrelated to the program?**

- ✔ **Were you calm, cool, and collected in the face of disaster?**

- ✔ **Did you take your badge off and ask, "How's it going?"**

- ✔ **Are *you* evaluated by your peers? Staff? Hotel? Other purveyors?**

- ✔ **Whom do you evaluate formally? Informally?**

- ✔ **How do you use the evaluation data collected?**

6-1 Function Data Collection Form

Group name: _____

Meeting: _____

Meeting dates: _____

Hotel: _____ City: _____ State: _____

- -

DOOR MONITORS: Please fill this form out accurately, as the information is used for our historical data collection. If you have any questions, please ask the Conference Coordinator before you go on duty.

Today's date: _____ , 19 _____ Session time: _____
Room name: _____
Type of function (specify, e.g., luncheon, workshop, banquet): _____
_____

Time data collected: _____
Number of chairs in room: _____
Number of empty chairs in room: _____
Number of people in function room: _____
If tickets, number collected: _____

Comments: _____
_____
_____
_____
_____
_____
_____
_____
_____
_____
_____
_____

Data collected by: _____

6-2 Registration Data Collection Form

	Confirmations per Last Report		Confirmations This Week		Total	
	Number	Amount	Number	Amount	Number	Amount
As of _____ , 19 _____						
Tables:	_____	_____	_____	_____	_____	_____
Seats:	_____	_____	_____	_____	_____	_____
Contributors:	_____	_____	_____	_____	_____	_____
Total:	_____	$_____	_____	$_____	_____	$_____

Announcements mailed: _____
Responses received: _____
Responses outstanding: _____

6-3	**Conference Evaluation Form**

——————— , 19 —— **CONFERENCE EVALUATION**

Please help us improve the quality and value of our future meetings by completing this form.

Registration Information

1. Affiliation:
   ☐ Corporate ☐ Member ☐ Nonprofit association ☐ Government
   ☐ Academia ☐ Other _____
   explain
2. Past conference attendance:
   ☐ 1988 ☐ 1987 ☐ 1986 ☐ 1985
3. Registration fee:
   ☐ Fee paid by me personally, not reimbursable
   ☐ Fee paid/reimbursable by my employer
   ☐ Fee complimentary/sponsored

Do you feel the registration fee was appropriate to the value received and items/ meals included?
   ☐ Yes ☐ No
If not, please explain: _____
_____
_____
_____

Hotel

Check-in
   ☐ Excellent ☐ Good ☐ Fair ☐ Poor
Guest/sleeping rooms
   ☐ Excellent ☐ Good ☐ Fair ☐ Poor
Meeting rooms
   ☐ Excellent ☐ Good ☐ Fair ☐ Poor
Food
   ☐ Excellent ☐ Good ☐ Fair ☐ Poor
Overall
   ☐ Excellent ☐ Good ☐ Fair ☐ Poor

Please explain any problems or compliments that relate to the hotel: ————
_____
_____
_____
_____

Conference Location

City was:
☐ Excellent   ☐ Good   ☐ Fair   ☐ Poor

Please explain any problems or compliments that relate to the city: _____
_____
_____
_____
_____

Program Content and Speakers

Favorite sessions were:
1. _____
2. _____
3. _____

Least favorite were:
1. _____
2. _____
3. _____

The MOST VALUABLE part of the conference was:
(Please place a *10* in the blank preceding those features that were most valuable, ranging down to an *0* for those least valuable.)

_____ Educational programs   _____ Corporate tours—Infomart
_____ Cultural programs   _____ The people who attended
_____ Social/meal times   _____ Recruiting/employment
_____ Exhibit program   opportunities
_____ Other _____
                 please explain

To assist in planning future programs, please offer any suggestions/ideas (use back of page if more space is required):
_____
_____
_____
_____
_____
_____
_____
_____
_____
_____
_____
_____
_____
_____
_____
_____

Program/Session Evaluation Form

PROGRAM EVALUATION

Session/event name: _____ Meeting room: _____

Registration Category

☐ Corporate   ☐ Nonprofit   ☐ Member   ☐ Guest

☐ Exhibitor   ☐ Other _____

                                       specify

	Session Content			
	Excellent	*Good*	*Fair*	*Poor*
Speaker/leader	_____	_____	_____	_____
Content	_____	_____	_____	_____
Format	_____	_____	_____	_____
Overall value	_____	_____	_____	_____

	Food and Beverages			
	Excellent	*Good*	*Fair*	*Poor*
Food quality	_____	_____	_____	_____
Service	_____	_____	_____	_____
Presentation	_____	_____	_____	_____

Additional Comments

_____

_____

_____

_____

THANK YOU!

Data Collection Report Format

All numbers should also be expressed as a percentage of total.

Report	Dates Collected	Variables/Options	Supportive Documents
Financial (profit/loss)	Budget-final accounting	1. Current year 2. Cumulative	1. Original budget 2. Final bills/payments 3. Internal charges
Cash flow	First-last payment in/out	1. Income by date received 2. Bank deposits summary by date 3. Expenses by date paid 4. Current year 5. Cumulative	1. Income records 2. Deposit records 3. Payment records 4. Post reports
Revenue	First-last payment in/out	1. By date received 2. By registration category 3. By other categories/exhibitors/sponsors/tickets 4. Pre/on-site/post 5. By method of payment (check, cash, credit) 6. Current year 7. Cumulative 8. By price (fee) category 9. Per person	1. Payment records 2. Post reports
Expenditure	First-last expenditure	1. By date bill received/paid 2. By budget vs. actual 3. By functional categories 4. Per-person average 5. Current year 6. Cumulative	1. Final bills 2. Budget(s) 3. Post reports
Discrepancy	Final accounting	1. Due but uncollected 2. Amounts under dispute 3. Category/date unidentifiable 4. Accounting adjustments 5. Indirect cost not accounted to conference	

(continued)

Data Collection Report
Format (*continued*)

Report	Dates Collected	Variables/Options	Supportive Documents
Attendance	First-last registration received	1. By date registered 2. By cutoff date(s) 3. By registration category 4. By state/county/zip 5. By company/organization 6. By session/function 7. By official airline usage 8. By hotel room usage 9. Current year	1. Final registration report 2. Hotel pickup report 3. Official airline report 4. Function attendance report
Attendee profile	On registration form or on site	1. By company budget 2. By individual income 3. Specific brands/product used/owned 4. By transportation mode 5. By age/gender/nationality 6. By education level 7. By marital status 8. By family size 9. By job title 10. By past conference attendance 11. Current year 12. Cumulative	1. Attendee questionnaire 2. Questionnaire summary reports 3. Post reports
Function attendance	On site per-person square footage	1. By session 2. By special event 3. By tour 4. By meal function 5. By day 6. By exhibit hours 7. Liquor consumption 8. Current year 9. Cumulative	1. Room counts 2. Function summary 3. Food/beverage reports 4. Post reports 5. Bar reading reports

Report	Dates Collected	Variables/Options	Supportive Documents
Supplier(s)	On-site and final bills	1. By supplier 2. By staffing level 3. By session 4. By meeting room 5. By committee or 6. Current year 7. Cumulative	1. Individual bills 2. Cost per session reports 3. Budget 4. Financial reports 5. Post reports 6. Food/beverage reports
Hotel	From first reservation on site, final bill	1. Total hotel charges to sponsor 2. Total estimated hotel revenue from guests 3. Guest room utilization (type/rate/number) 4. Meeting room utilization 5. Reservations by date 6. Average costs per person 7. Current year 8. Cumulative	1. Final bill 2. Hotel pickup report 3. Public services restaurant utilization report 4. Room service usage report 5. Post reports
Personnel	From first activity to final report completion and on site	1. By responsibility/function 2. Average rate 3. Total hours 4. Paid vs. volunteer 5. By supplier/agency 6. Waitpersons/servers per event	1. Personnel schedule 2. Final bills 3. Time reports 4. Check-in/-out logs
Program		1. Speaker-to-attendee ratio 2. Session evaluations 3. Per-person costs 4. Event/activity evaluation 5. Attendance level 6. Speaker evaluations (by attendee/speaker) 7. Facility evaluations 8. Average attendance by type/event 9. Current year 10. Cumulative	1. Agenda 2. Session evaluations 3. Attendee evaluations 4. Function attendance reports 5. Speaker evaluations 6. Post reports

(continued)

6-5 Data Collection Report Format (*continued*)

Report	Dates Collected	Variables/Options	Supportive Documents
Printing	From rough to delivery on site, final accounting	1. By type of items printed (# & $) 2. By time from rough to delivery 3. Per-piece/per-person costs 4. Ordered vs. used 5. Response rate (mailed vs. registered) 6. Current year 7. Cumulative	1. Printing schedule 2. Final bill 3. Post reports 4. Attendance report 5. Attendee evaluations 6. Post reports
Mailing	From date of mailing to conference opening	1. By mailing list 2. By mailing date vs. first/last response date 3. By returns/undeliverables 4. Coded response 5. Costs per person 6. Current year 7. Cumulative	1. Mailing list 2. Mailing schedule/deadlines 3. Registration reports 4. Undeliverable report 5. Financial reports 6. Post reports
Exhibits	From first mailing on-site to final accounting	1. Income/expenses 2. Profit/loss 3. Cost per booth 4. Attendance per booth, per hour 5. By date sold (#/size/type) 6. By type of company 7. Other participation levels (sponsor/ads/full registration) 8. Total facility square footage 9. Current year 10. Cumulative	1. Financial reports 2. Exhibitor prospectus 3. Function attendance reports 4. Exhibitor evaluation 5. Post reports

Guide 7
Marketing and Promotion

Types of Promotion and Publicity

- ✔ **Promotional materials by direct mail:**
  - Letters
  - Brochures
  - Mailing inserts
  - Postcards

- ✔ **Promotion and publicity in publications:**
  - Meeting sponsor's magazine, newsletter, house organ
  - Allied organizations' publications
  - Trade and professional magazines and journals
  - Newspapers and magazines in host city

- ✔ **Publicity in other media:**
  - Television and radio

- ✔ **Telephone solicitation**

Promotional Materials Considerations

- ✔ **Your budget**

- ✔ **Image you want to create**

- ✔ **Number and frequency of mailings:**
  - Teaser
  - Program

- Follow-up
- Ongoing (as in 12 different courses spread over one year)

✔ **Total number of pieces:**
- Pages per item
- Total pages

✔ **Paper-stock quality**

✔ **Number of colors**

✔ **Printing process required**

✔ **Lead time**

✔ **Availability of stock**

✔ **Number of items included in one mailing**

✔ **How it will be mailed:**
- Envelope (size)
- Self-mailer

✔ **How to address:**
- Hand
- Labels (type)

✔ **Who will process mailing:**
- You
- Mailing house
- Volunteers
- Other (specify)

✔ **How person receiving mailing will respond:**
- Return envelope
- Other

✔ **Postage costs (*see* "Mailings"):**
- Your mailing, based on total weight of piece mailed
- Return envelopes, stamped or unstamped

✔ **Postage method, original mailing and reply envelopes:**
- Metered
- Stamps applied by hand
- Use of mailing house

✔ **Any international pieces:**
- Additional postage required
- Additional time required for mailings, including response

Brochure Copy

- ✔ **Program title**

- ✔ **Logo**

- ✔ **Dates (month, day, year)**

- ✔ **Location (hotel, city, state)**

- ✔ **Hotel address and phone number**

- ✔ **Name of contact for further information, address, and phone number**

- ✔ **Agenda (program content)**

- ✔ **Identity of sponsors/cosponsors**

- ✔ **Identity of principal speaker (name, title, affiliation)**

- ✔ **Registration information such as fee, cutoff date, attendee limit, and payment procedure**

- ✔ **Tax deductible information**

- ✔ **Detachable registration return cards**

- ✔ **Continuing education credit**

Policy statements communicated to attendees should include:

- ✔ **Statement of policy**

- ✔ **To whom policy applies**

- ✔ **Dates over which policy applies**

- ✔ **Restrictions**

- ✔ **Dollar amounts**

See also Attendees' Services.

Elements of Conference Registration Form

- ✔ **Number in party, names**

- ✔ **Name of registrant/name as to appear on badge**

- ✔ **Address and phone number**

- ✔ **Name of company or organization**

- ✔ **Title**

- ✔ **Address, phone number, and extension**

- ✔ **Registration category**

- ✔ **Any special requirements of registrant:**
  - Dietetic
  - Handicapped equipment
  - Child care

- ✔ **Workshop preferences**

- ✔ **Deadline for registration**

- ✔ **Payment**

- ✔ **Enclosure of return envelope, or if return side form:**
  - Name or organization to which form should be returned
  - Street address
  - City, state, ZIP
  - Line reading "Place stamp here. Post office will not deliver mail without postage."
  - Notice to "Make check payable to . . ."

Elements of Hotel Room Reservation Form

- ✔ **Name of registrant**

- ✔ **Address**

- ✔ **Name of business, company, or organization**

- ✔ **Address, phone number and extension, area code**

- ✔ **Final date reservation must be received**

✓ **Late arrival guarantee policy**

✓ **Deposit policy, if credit card provide space for card company, account number, expiration date, and signature**

✓ **Arrival day and time**

✓ **Departure day and time**

✓ **Check-out time policy of hotel**

✓ **Room rates (single, double)**

✓ **Type room requested**

✓ **Cut-off date for reservations**

✓ **Notice to "Cancel your hotel reservation if your plans change."**

✓ **Hotel name, address, and phone number**

✓ **If return side form is used:**
  • Name of hotel
  • Street address
  • City, state, ZIP
  • Notice "Attention: Reservations"
  • Line reading "Place stamp here. Post office will not deliver mail without postage."
  • Notice to "Make check payable to . . ."

Timetable

✓ **Number and frequency of promotions—depending on:**
  • The type of meeting
  • Overall marketing plan
  • Response patterns for previous events
  • Participants' travel considerations
  • Cutoff date for early registration discount and budget

✓ **Mailings:**

6 to 10 months:	A "teaser" may be sent in advance of first mailing
8 to 12 weeks:	First mailing of program outline
6 to 12 weeks:	Second mailing, with more details
4 to 5 weeks:	Reminder postcard (may follow second mailing)
3 through 16 weeks:	Promotional inserts accompanying regular mailing

✔ **News releases:**

Ongoing throughout year:	Meeting sponsor's publications
4 to 16 weeks:	Allied organizations' publications
3 weeks:	First release in local papers, first TV/radio ad
1 week:	Follow up of local paper release; follow up of TV/radio ad

✔ **Advertising:**

6 months before publication:	Trade/professional calendars
4 to 6 months before publication (or according to ad policy):	Trade and professional magazines/feature stories/ads

✔ **Telephone solicitation:**

Generally not recommended except for period just before the cutoff for early registration discount.

Mailings

✔ **Services of mailing service companies:**
Services may include part or all of the following:
- Folding
- Stuffing
- Sealing
- Labeling/addressing
- Sorting according to ZIP code
- Stamping or metering
- Delivery to post office, UPS, or other carriers
- Warehousing
- Data processing for response analysis

✔ **Types of mailing labels:**
- *Cheshire*: Computer-generated; machine-gummed, trimmed, and applied
- *Pressure sensitive*: Backed with pressure-sensitive adhesive requiring no moistening for application; usually hand-applied

Ad Sales (Program Book)

✔ **State specifications in contract.**

✔ **Define camera-ready art in contract.**

↙ **Discuss camera-ready requirements with your printer before you begin your ad sales campaign.**

↙ **Contact local newspapers or magazines with four-color ads to find out their standard specifications for space ads.**

↙ **Provide written instructions to advertisers and printer.**

Camera-Ready Art for Ads

True "camera-ready art" means art boards ready to be shot as negatives. Specifications/criteria MUST be spelled out with regard to what you will and will not accept or pay for.

> **Example:**

Specifications for a Black-and-White Ad:
- Sized and on one art board or velox.
- 85-line PMT photos, sized and in place.
- 85-line screens (must be composited with master velox art).
- Solid reverses must be reversed on master art board.
- Advertiser will be billed for additional stripping and camera preparation.

> **Example:**

Ad sizes for an $8\frac{1}{2}'' \times 11''$ Program Book to Allow Space for Margins:

Book dimension:	$8\frac{1}{2}'' \times 11''$
Full-page ad:	(w) $7\frac{1}{2}'' \times$ (h) $10''$
Bleedsize:	(w) $8\frac{5}{8}'' \times$ (h) $11\frac{1}{8}''$
Half-page ad:	(w) $7\frac{1}{2}'' \times$ (h) $4\frac{3}{4}''$ (horizontal only)
Quarter-page ad:	(w) $3\frac{1}{2}'' \times$ (h) $4\frac{3}{4}''$
Eighth-page ad:	(w) $1\frac{3}{4}'' \times$ (h) $2\frac{3}{8}''$

Cost-Saving Ideas

Request sample copies of all free promotional materials available from hotel; host city; chamber of commerce; convention bureau.
- *Evaluate materials.*
- *Select items desired.*
- *Request number required.*
- *Request one copy per attendee of each item and desired quantities to be dispensed from information desk.*

Minimize mailing costs by using handouts at meeting whenever feasible.

7-1 | Advertising Contract Example

Specifications

Camera-Ready Art—Black & White Velox—film in which the dark & light image values are the same as the original
- Due Date:
- Any photographs required must be camera ready and scaled to size (Screen: 85 lines or less)

Book Dimensions—$8\frac{1}{2}$″ × 11″ (3-color)
Full-page ad—w$7\frac{1}{2}$″ × h10″ (ad size) $8\frac{5}{8}$″ × $11\frac{1}{8}$″ (bleed size)
Half-page ad—w$7\frac{1}{2}$″ × h$4\frac{3}{4}$″ (ad size) (horizontal)
Quarter-page ad—w$3\frac{1}{2}$″ × h$4\frac{3}{4}$″ (ad size)
Eighth-page ad—$1\frac{3}{4}$″ × $2\frac{3}{8}$″ (ad size)

This contract certifies that _____
　　　　　　　　　　　　　　　company name
has agreed to advertise in the program book. All follow-up contact should be made to _____
　　　　　　individual's name
at (___) _____ .
　　　　　telephone number

We, the above-named, would like to purchase the following advertisement(s):
　　☐ Full page: @ $_____　　☐ Quarter-page: @ $_____
　　☐ Half-page: @ $_____　　☐ Eighth-page: @ $_____

If for any reason [*name of organization*] fails to run said paid advertisement(s), the organization agrees to reimburse the above-named company the total of the above payment.

If our artwork does not conform to the specifications outlined above, we agree to pay [*name of organization*] any and all charges incurred.

As a representative of the above-named company, I accept the above terms.

_____ / _____ _____
　　　　signature　　　　　　　　　　　title　　　　　　　　　　date

_____
　　　please type or clearly print name

_____ / _____ _____
　　organization representative　　　　　title　　　　　　　　　　date

Make check payable to [*name of organization*] and mail to [*address*].

Guide 8

Graphic Design
And Printing

Designing the Piece

✔ **Information graphic artist will need:**
  - Purpose of the piece
  - Who will receive it
  - Tone or mood you want to achieve: Describe this by using descriptive terms, such as:
    —Light
    —Serious
    —Modern
    —Conventional
    —Straightforward
    —Classy, but not extravagant
    —Unusual
    —Lots of copy or lots of white space
  - Desired method of production
  - Number of colors involved
  - Desired type of layout
    —Rough
    —Semicomprehensive
    —Comprehensive
  - Your budget

✔ **Preparing the copy:**
  - Use 8½" × 11" white paper.
  - Type copy on one side only.
  - Always double space.
  - Allow generous left margin (minimum of 12 pica spaces or 15 elite).
  - Use either pica (40 characters per typed line) or elite type.
  - Do not mix pica and elite in copy.

✔ **Changes and corrections:**
  • Write or print legibly.
  • Minimize handwritten corrections.
  • Avoid placing corrections/changes in margin if possible.
  • Added words should be inserted within typed line and above that line.
  • Use accepted proofreader's marks and editing symbols specified in most standard dictionaries.

Printing the Piece

✔ **Questions printer will ask before estimating or quoting your job:**
  • Number of pieces?
  • Size of piece?
  • Description of piece—booklet, brochure, folder, poster, other?
  • Number of pages, including cover? (A printer's page is one side of a leaf or one numbered page.)
  • Self-cover or plus cover?
  • Flat/open size?
  • Paper stock required?
  • Will photographs be used? How many? What size?
  • Special effects desired? (Reverses, bleeds, etc.)
  • Number of ink colors desired?
  • If four-color process, the number and size of each color photo or illustration to appear in finished artwork?
  • Is printer responsible for preparing camera-ready copy?
  • How is piece to be finished (folded, bound, die-cut, embossed, foil-stamped, stitched, engraved)?
  • What is your deadline for finished pieces and mailing?
  • Will printer be responsible for labeling, mailing, or shipping finished pieces?
  • Will graphic art services be required?

✔ **Items that can be printed:**
  • Promotional piece(s) and envelopes
  • Program book
  • Program-at-a-glance pocket cards
  • Badge card stock
  • Jacket for registration materials
  • Event tickets
  • Registration receipts (in triplicate or other)
  • Special letterhead and envelopes
  • Return envelopes
  • Response registration card
  • Special-issue newsletter
  • News release letterhead
  • Evaluation forms

- Local information (e.g., restaurants, sight-seeing, entertainment)
- Registration-packet items
- Banquet souvenir program and other special events book
- Exhibitors directory
- Exhibit prospectus

✔ Printing time sequence schedule:

Each of the following elements of the printing process will have an estimated deadline. Work with your printer to determine those deadlines. The time frame will vary from one to eight weeks if the process runs smoothly.

- Rough layout
- Rough copy
- Approval
- Completed layout
- Approval
- Final art, photography, graphics, final copy
- Typesetting/mechanicals
- Proofreading
- Corrections
- Proofreading
- Approval
- Bluelines or other prepress proofs
- Approval
- Printing
- Finishing
- Delivery

✔ Choices that affect the cost of each piece:

- Special effects (e.g., embossing, die-cutting)
- Quality of paper (e.g., grade, weight, finish)
- Number of ink colors
- Production time
- Number of printed pieces

✔ Selecting a printer:

- Determine whether you need "quick copy" or "commercial" (*see* Glossary).
- Can that printer handle all of your printing needs?
- Obtain references from printer:
  —Quality of work
  —Service
  —Dependability
  —Response time
- Request examples of printer's past work that is similar to your requirements.
- Does printer have necessary equipment to do your job?
- Will your delivery deadline date be met?
- Competitive quality of bid—competitively priced, but not necessarily the lowest bidder.

Printing Decisions—Binding

✔ **Need for bindery services will be determined by:**
  • Method of piece you desire
  • Your printer's ability/inability to provide desired binding service

✔ **Methods of binding include (from least to most expensive):**
  • Loose-leaf:
    —Notebooks and ring binders
    —Holes punched along left margin (two or three)
    —Pages held together by rings
    Advantages:
    —Opens 180 degrees.
    —Lies flat when open.
    —Permits addition of pages.
    —Inexpensive.
  • Saddle-wire:
    • Small booklets
    • 64–96 page maximum depending upon paper weight
    • Staples or wires (two to three) inserted through crease of spine
    Advantages: Low cost, lies flat when open.
    Disadvantage: Does not permit addition of pages.
  • Perfect bind:
    —Paperbacks, some hardbound
    —Pages folded and assembled
    —Spine edge of pages roughened
    —Adhesive applied to spine
    —Cover is applied
    —Durability depends on proper planning and use of materials
    Advantage: Cost is lower than sewn binding.
  • Spiral or coil:
    —Calendars, spiral notebooks
    —Holes or slots punched along left margin
    —Pages held together by wire or plastic coil
    Advantages:
    —Rotates to open 360 degrees.
    —Lies flat when open.
    —Moderate in cost.
    Disadvantage: Does not permit addition of pages.
  • Sewn:
    —High-quality hardbound
    —Edges sewn together
    —Sewn pages passed through rounding machine to produce conformity
      to contour of cover
    —Cover attached
    Advantage: Durability.
    Disadvantage: Most costly binding process.

Printing Decisions—Paper

🗸 **Classes of paper:**
- Cover-weight
- Text-weight

Postal regulations require a 7-point caliper thickness of cover-weight and stock for all postal reply cards and self-mailers after folding.

When printing on one side of a piece only, a text-weight paper is sufficient if it is at least 50- or 60-point offset. For printing on two sides, a 60- and 70-point weight paper should be used.

Standard Sizes for Minimum Paper Waste

8½″ × 11″:	Regular letter size
8½″ × 14″:	Legal size
5½″ × 8½″:	One-half regular letter size
6″ × 9″	
12″ × 9″	Standard brochure sizes
4″ × 9″	

🗸 **Color selection:**

The graphic designer and/or printer will have a PMS book. Select desired colors from that source and indicate choice.

Colors may look different on different paper stocks. Check with the graphic designer and/or printer to avoid disappointment.

Cold colors:	Blues, purples, greens
Hot colors:	Red, oranges, yellows
Four-color:	Magenta (red), cyan (blue), black, yellow with color separation

---

Printing Decisions—Finishing Options

"Finishing" is a catchall word to describe a variety of operations required following printing, such as:

🗸 **Varnishing:**
- Usually done on press or while piece is being printed.
- Increases contrasts in colors and shades.

- Enhances halftones.
- Increases durability by protecting product from finger marks and normal depreciation of images.
- Normally used only for high-gloss sheets.
- Wasted on rough-surfaced papers.

✔ **Plastic coating:**
- Provides higher gloss and longer protection than varnishing.
- Requires services of coating specialist and expensive equipment.
- Used only on high-gloss sheets.

✔ **Film laminating:**
- Using heated rollers, a thin layer of plastic is glued to sheet.
- Provides ultimate gloss and protection.
- Produces washable surface.
- Indicated only for items to be exposed to long-term, frequent use, such as menus.

✔ **Die-cutting:**
- A process of cutting shapes into a sheet of paper, usually to reveal a small portion of the following page.
- A simple die-cut frequently falls within the price range of a single-colored ink impression and can produce an attention-getting result.

✔ **Embossing:**
- Paper pressed into bas-relief.
- Requires special equipment and services of a specialist.
- Produces highly tactile three-dimensional effect.
- Slightly higher-than-average printing budget.

Printing Agreement

✔ **Name of client**

✔ **Date**

✔ **Job number or title**

✔ **Job description**

✔ **Quantity ordered**

✔ **Specifications:**
- Flat size
- Number of folds
- Size after folded
- Ink color(s)
- Paper stock and color(s)

- Photographs/other art graphics
- Halftones
- Duotones
- Bleeds
- Number of pages (printed on one side or two sides)
- Finishing and binding

✔ **Camera work**

✔ **Special effects and instructions**

✔ **If book or booklet, specify:**
  - Number of pages
  - Final size
  - Type cover

✔ **Proofing:**
  - Blueline
  - Color key
  - Other

✔ **Special processes:**
  - Specify

✔ **Special instructions**

✔ **Delivery instructions**

✔ **Billing name and address**

✔ **Delivery date**

✔ **Receipt date**

✔ **Cost of job**

✔ **Initials**

Helpful Hints

Never go to press without first seeing a final proof. Most quick copy companies do not furnish proofs.

If you have a firm deadline, plan your work in advance with your printer. Give advance notice if a rush job is coming.

Confirm your estimate when the order is turned in to your printer. Most companies will estimate based upon certain assumptions about your artwork, and will not commit until artwork is prepared. The price is more easily controlled if artwork is handled by the printer.

If your printer is given all or the majority of your work, he or she will be more motivated to accommodate your special needs, such as rush jobs.

Cost-Saving Ideas

Obtain firm written bids.
Provide clean copy to typesetter.
Use standard paper sizes.
Make multiple use of same paper stock.
Piggyback print items of same color.
Use standard ink colors.
Reuse graphics.
Avoid special effects.
Use dotted lines as cutting guide instead of perforations.
Coordinate printing of all items:
- *Tickets*
- *Badge stock*
- *"Gang" items*

Keep copy changes to a minimum.
Use self-mailers.
Avoid rush deadlines.
Use bulk mail instead of first class (see Mailings)
Presort first-class mailings if feasible (see Mailings)
Consider free promotional items:
- *Badge inserts*
- *Program jackets*
- *Hotel*
- *Host city*

Obtainable from:
- *Chamber of Commerce*
- *Convention bureau*

Use ready-made artwork from art supply companies.
Use art students from local colleges/trade schools.

Guide 9
Registration

Registration Categories

Each registration category may have a preregistration rate and an on-site or walk-in rate.

- Member (may be specific to field, such as a physician)
- Nonmember
- Companion/guest/spouse
- Child
- Student
- Government employee
- Corporate/supplier
- Allied industry or association member

- Complimentary
- Daily rate
- Early bird rate
- Late rate
- Reduced/special rate
- Exhibitor
- Retired member
- Emeritus member

Typical Registration Policies and Procedures

Consider the following, and determine which are appropriate for your event. All are accepted practices.

- Registration fee structure policy

✓ **Administrative fee covering cancellation-processing costs (penalty)**

✓ **Full or partial refunds; or no refunds for cancellations**

✓ **Cancellation refund cutoff dates**

✓ **Reduced early registration fee**

✓ **Complimentary policy (e.g., for speakers, press)**

✓ **Payment policy**

✓ **Billing policy**

✓ **Approval process for exceptions**

✓ **Badge replacement charge**

✓ **Exhibit hall/session passes**

Helpful Hints

If different forms are used for each registrant category, e.g., member, nonmember, color code forms.

Make sure registration forms are in duplicate or triplicate so as to provide copies for attendees, on-site receipts, accounting, and master registration files.

Design forms so that questions can be answered easily by circling or checking answers.

Factors to Consider in Selecting Registration Area Location

✓ **How many booths or tables are required for:**
  • Registration processing?
  • Message center?
  • Information booth?
  • Ticket sales/exchange?
  • Tour information and sales?
  • Supervisor/trouble-shooter?
  • Hotel check-in (limited to special groups arriving at same time)?
  • Conference sale items (e.g., T-shirts, posters)?
  • Cashier?
  • Staff office?
  • Nearby secure storage area?

✔ **Can setup remain in same location throughout meeting?**

✔ **Is this area a major traffic area for other hotel guests?**

✔ **Is there adequate space for lines to form during peak hours and number of registration lines required?**

✔ **Is lighting/ventilation adequate in area for staff and attendees?**

✔ **Can writing counters be placed away from registration lines allowing attendees to complete registration forms? Is space sufficient for number of counters required?**

✔ **Can registration booths or tables be located near major conference activities?**

✔ **Can signs be placed where they are visible and out of traffic flow?**

✔ **Are electrical outlets adequate?**

✔ **Is there access for the handicapped?**

Selecting Registration-Area Personnel

✔ **What types of personnel do you need?**
- Registration processors
- Registration supervisors
- Door monitors (to check badges)
- Security
- Ticket exchange and other service personnel

✔ **What sources of personnel are available?**
- Your organization staff/volunteers
- Independent meeting management company staff
- Outside personnel supplied through temporary personnel company or convention bureau
- Volunteers

✔ **What should you ask the company supplying personnel?**
- What is the hourly rate? Minimums?
- Is company bonded? Are individuals bonded?
- What is the experience/training of personnel? Are they computer literate?
- Are references available?
- Is standard uniform used? If not, can one be provided?
- Does company provide bulletin typewriters/computerized system for badges?

- Does company provide cash boxes?
- What is the procedure for terminating services of employees for unsatisfactory performance?
- Do you have an opportunity to screen personnel?
- Are supervisors provided?
- What are the cancellation and payment procedures?

Registration Personnel Training

The registration process, whether for the meeting or checking in at the front desk, should ideally take 30 seconds, and no more than three minutes for highly complex systems.

✔ Briefing booklet:
One or two days prior to the time registration begins, distribute booklets to personnel that contain the following:
- Information on organization and sponsors
- Schedule-at-a-glance
- Registration categories and fees
- Policies and procedures
- List of approved complimentary delegates
- List of frequently asked questions
- Facility floor plans
- Ticket-distribution/sales procedures
- Badge-preparation and distribution
- Cash handling

✔ Suggested elements of training session:
Allow a one-hour minimum for briefing. Introduce key organization staff. Provide an overview of organization and event. Review sections of briefing booklet. Review policies and procedures in detail. Review schedule. Review sign-in/sign-out procedures. Provide a step-by-step review of on-site registration process. Encourage questions from trainees.

✔ Role-playing scenarios with personnel:
- Attendee wants refund.
- Attendee says check is in the mail, but no such check has been received prior to on-site arrival.
- Attendee assures you that he/she is a member, but you have no record indicating this.
- Attendee wants to pay only for sessions he/she plans to attend.
- Attendee states he/she received approval to register at the preregistered fee.
- Someone states that he/she is entitled to a press pass, but name does not appear on press list.
- Attendee loses badge and wants a replacement.
- Attendee loses function tickets and wants replacements.
- Unregistered attendee wants pass to enter exhibit area.

On-Site Registration Supplies

- ✔ **Cash boxes**

- ✔ **Badge-preparation equipment (e.g., typewriter, KROY lettering system, computer/printer)**

- ✔ **Badge paper stock, badge holders, or lamination machine**

- ✔ **Preregistration list**

- ✔ **Complimentary and press list**

- ✔ **Membership list**

- ✔ **Exhibitor list**

- ✔ **VIP list**

- ✔ **On-site registration forms**

- ✔ **Delegate information packets**

- ✔ **Daily accounting forms**

- ✔ **Function/event tickets**

- ✔ **Receipts**

- ✔ **Signs**

- ✔ **Pens**

- ✔ **File system for on-site registration forms**

- ✔ **Check-deposit stamp**

- ✔ **Check-in/check-out book for registration personnel**

- ✔ **Brochures**

- ✔ **Personnel briefing book**

- ✔ **Survey and data collection forms**

- ✔ **Office supplies (e.g., scissors, tape, tacks)**

- ✔ **Industrial size wastebaskets**

✔ **Message pads**

✔ **Stapler, staples, staple remover, paper clips**

✔ **Calculator/adding machine**

✔ **Extension cords**

Badges/Badge Holders

✔ **Paper options (stock):**
- Sticky-back, self-adhesive, pressure-sensitive
- Card stock inserted into plastic holders (plain or imprinted with company-name logo, registration category)
- Single badge, with perforated strips for typewriter or computer strips for automatic feed

✔ **Badge-holder options:**
- Soft, pliable plastic (high quality)
- Hard, stiff plastic (most common)
- Laminated plastic (high quality)

✔ **Badge-fasterner options:**
- *Self-adhesive:*—Best for one day/one event, not reusable.
- *Pin (safety type):*—Most common, least expensive.
- *Bulldog clip:*—Clips to collars/lapels, does not damage fabric.
- *Pocket inserts:*—Inserts in suit pocket, not appropriate for women or casual dress.
- *String (around neck):*—Best for sporting or casual events.

Common Badge Sizes

$4'' \times 2\frac{1}{4}''$
$4'' \times 2\frac{1}{2}''$
$4'' \times 3''$

Smaller sizes are available, but trend is to larger badges.

9-1 | **Daily Check-Out Sheet**

One for each registration worker to use when balancing cashbox

Name: _____ Date: _____

Shift/time: _____ Assignment: _____
                                    specify category registered

Please fill in the blanks below from your individual registration forms.

Example:

Five registrations @ $600 = $3,000; one registration @ $175.00 = $175.00.

Actual Dollars Received	Registrants to Be Invoiced/Charge Cards
#_____ @ $_____ = $_____	#_____ @ $_____ = $_____
#_____ @ $_____ = $_____	#_____ @ $_____ = $_____
#_____ @ $_____ = $_____	#_____ @ $_____ = $_____
#_____ @ $_____ = $_____	#_____ @ $_____ = $_____
#_____ @ $_____ = $_____	#_____ @ $_____ = $_____
#_____ @ $_____ = $_____	#_____ @ $_____ = $_____
#_____ @ $_____ = $_____	#_____ @ $_____ = $_____
#_____ @ $_____ = $_____	#_____ @ $_____ = $_____
#_____ @ $_____ = $_____	#_____ @ $_____ = $_____
#_____ @ $_____ = $_____	#_____ @ $_____ = $_____
#_____ @ $_____ = $_____	#_____ @ $_____ = $_____
#_____ @ $_____ = $_____	#_____ @ $_____ = $_____
#_____ @ $_____ = $_____	#_____ @ $_____ = $_____

Subtotal   Subtotal
#_____ = $_____   #_____ = $_____

Total Registration for the Day
#_____ = $_____

9-2

Registration Personnel Check-In/Check-Out Sheet

Time In	Time Out	Total Hours	Position	Name
			Monday, September 23, 19X5	
_____	_____	_____	Registrar/typist 11A.M.–9P.M.	_____
_____	_____	_____	Registrar/typist 11A.M.–2P.M.	_____
_____	_____	_____	Door monitor 12:45–4P.M.	_____
_____	_____	_____	Door monitor 12:45–4P.M.	_____
_____	_____	_____	Door monitor 12:45–4P.M.	_____
_____	_____	_____	Door monitor 12:45–4P.M.	_____
_____	_____	_____	Door monitor 6:15P.M.–8:30P.M.	_____
			Tuesday, September 24, 19X5	
_____	_____	_____	Registrar/typist 7:30A.M.–12:30P.M.	_____
_____	_____	_____	Registrar/typist 7:30A.M.–12:30P.M.	_____
_____	_____	_____	Door monitor 9:00A.M.–5P.M.	_____
_____	_____	_____	Door monitor 9:00A.M.–5P.M.	_____
_____	_____	_____	Door monitor 11:30A.M.–5P.M.	_____
			Wednesday, September 25, 19X5	
_____	_____	_____	Door monitor 8:30A.M.–5P.M.	_____
_____	_____	_____	Door monitor 8:30A.M.–12:30P.M.	_____
_____	_____	_____	Door monitor 8:30A.M.–1:30P.M.	_____
_____	_____	_____	Door monitor 5:30P.M.–10P.M.	_____

| **9-3** | **Registration Form Example** |

FOR OFFICE USE ONLY

No.: _____

Date: _____

[*Name of Sponsor*]

FUNCTION/MEETING: _____ MEETING ACCT. I.D. **#** _____

Name: _____ Title: _____

Organization: _____

Address: _____

City: _____ State: _____ ZIP: _____

Business Phone: _____

FEE SCHEDULE

Type of Registrant	*Registration Fee*	*Amount Due*
Member	$	$
Business or other Private Representative	$	$
Speaker	$	$
Spouse	$	$
Other [*specify*]	$	$

TOTAL $_____
RECEIVED $_____
BALANCE $_____

Method of Payment:

□ Cash   □ Travelers check   □ Complimentary
□ Check **#** _____   □ Purchase order **#** _____

TYPE OF CHECK:
□ State   □ Business   □ Personal

Bill to: _____

Registered by: _____

Guide 10

Attendees' Services

Basic Communications

Broad information about services should be contained in an early mailing to prospective attendees to permit them an opportunity to make any additional special needs known to the meeting planner well in advance of the meeting date.

✔ **Travel:**
- To city
- To meeting facility
- Car rental
- Area map
- Ground transportation/limousine service
- Distance
- Costs

✔ **Check-in/check-out policy (specific times)**

✔ **Weather and climate**

✔ **Attire guidelines:**
- Gourmet dining (e.g., jacket and tie)
- Business meetings/sessions
- Banquets/special events
- Outdoors (e.g., boots, heavy coats, rainwear)

✔ **Credit cards honored:**
- American Express
- MasterCard
- VISA
- Other
- None

✔ **Check-cashing policy**

✔ **Tipping information:**
  • Service charge percentage (if any) added by meeting facility

✔ **Services and amenities available:**
  • Valet cleaning/laundry
  • Laundromat
  • Beauty salon/barber shop
  • Handicapped access
  • Shoeshine
  • Guide dog accommodations
  • Interpreters (specify type, hourly rates, advance notice required)
  • Child care (specify hours available and hourly rate)
  • Special diet (specify advance notice required)
  • Other

Special Needs

✔ **Health problems:**
  • Chronic problems (e.g., arthritis, diabetes, high blood pressure)
  • Sudden *minor* illness (adult or child)

✔ **Special diets:**
  • Health-related (e.g., diabetic, low-salt, fat-free)
  • Religious
  • Vegetarian
  • Canine

✔ **Emergencies:**
  • Personal injury
  • Sudden illness (adult or child)
  • Guide dog illness or injury
  • At-home family illness or injury
  • Auto accident
  • Robbery/loss of money
  • Lost articles (e.g., eyeglasses, hearing aids)
  • Business emergencies

✔ **Child care:**
  • Daytime/nighttime sitters
  • Group activities (organized and supervised)

✔ **Special events and activities:**
  • Spouse programs
  • Group tours
  • Group competitive sports

✔ **Special needs:**
  - Foreign-language speaking
  - Visually handicapped
  - Hearing handicapped
  - Wheelchair attendees

✔ **Wardrobe requirements:**
  - Formal dinner attire (men and women)
  - Dinner/dance attire   "   "   "
  - Reception   "   "   "
  - Theme parties   "   "   "
  - Sports activities (adult and children)
  - Weather requirements (specify by season)
  - In-room comfort requirements
  - Spouse activities

✔ **Financial needs:**
  - Cash requirements
  - Credit cards
  - Check cashing
  - Minibanks
  - Tipping/expectations/requirements
  - Local transportation costs

✔ **First aid:**
  - Services (personnel required)
  - Supplies:
    —Information desk
    —Message center

✔ **Facility comforts and amenities:**
  - Heat control (central heating or thermostat in room)
  - Recreational facilities, equipment, outside areas
  - Meeting rooms
  - Public restrooms
  - Floorplan maps
  - Facility rules and guidelines

✔ **City information:**
  - Recreational facilities
  - Equipment rental (sports) locations
  - Transportation (local bus, rental cars, taxi)
  - Religious services and locations
  - Local physician information

✔ **Housing:**
  - Staff coordination
  - Hotel services
  - Visitor/convention services housing bureau
  - Independent housing bureau

Special Considerations for Corporate/Incentive Attendees

✔ **Home-to-airport transportation/airport-to-hotel**

✔ **Baggage handling from pickup to hotel room (preprinted luggage tags)**

✔ **First- or business-class travel**

✔ **Being met and greeted at the airport**

✔ **Gifts on arrival with name badges and schedule**

✔ **Prearrival expedited hotel check-in**

✔ **Gifts each day in room or tied to theme activities**

Transportation Basics

✔ **Factors to review:**
  • Size of group
  • Routing of buses
  • Point of departure
  • Capacity of boarding and deboarding areas
  • Hour of leaving/returning
  • Local traffic patterns during these hours
  • Driving time each way
  • Distances to be traveled
  • Capacity, type, and age of buses provided
  • Liability responsiblity and insurance coverage

✔ **Making arrangements:**
  • For small groups, investigate availability of meeting facility's shuttle buses.
  • Use charter bus companies.
  • Use professional transportation companies (e.g., tour companies and "destination management" companies, ground operators). Professional companies are suggested when group is large and the area is unfamiliar.
  • Apply the same guidelines to evaluating these companies as are given for other purveyors.

✔ **Informing attendees:**
  • Supply boarding times and locations in Program Book.
  • Post these times and locations on lobby bulletin board.
  • Use directional signs to identify locations.

Busing

↙ Bus capacity:

> *For an Average 47-Passenger Bus*
>
> • Subtract two seats if there are restooms.
> • Subtract three backseats. Use for food and supplies. These are also undesirable locations for passenger visibility.
> • Subtract one seat for guide/staff.

↙ Average capacity:
  • 42–44 seats

↙ Types of service:

Road tours: 15+ miles
City tours: 5–15 miles
Continuous shuttle: Every 15–30 minutes
Quick shuttle: Mass group, 1–4 miles
Airport shuttle: Hour/half-hour schedule
Deadhead run: Empty one way

Note: Buses should arrive 15 minutes prior to report time.

↙ Variables to consider in planning schedule:
  • Crowd pregathered/not gathered
  • Bus report/leave time
  • Load/unload area, capacity/location
  • Bus queue/wait-area distance
  • Distance from bus drop-off to function area
  • Weather
  • Traffic (rush-hour/regular)
  • Travel route obstructions (parades, road repairs)
  • Single/multiple destinations
  • Driving time
  • Friends sitting together versus random seating

Bus Formulas

Average Miles per Hour	
Road:	45 mph
City:	15 mph
Heavy traffic:	5 mph

Shuttle/Waiting/Loading Allowances

No obvious passengers: 30 seconds–1 minute
Multiple mini stops: 1–3 minutes per stop
Major stops: 3–5 minutes per stop

Bump Loading

Per schedule: 5–20 minutes

Shuttle service begins with one bus at each destination. As bus 1 arrives at next shuttle stop, bus at that location is "bumped" and departs for next location. Process continues with each bus and destination, ensuring continuous and regular service.

Road/City Pickup Allowances

• 5 minutes per bus
• Multiple buses (three simultaneously loading)
  × 1.5 minutes

Average Shuttle Schedule

• Every 15–30 minutes

Example:

If you have 1,000 people to move, divide by bus capacity, figured here at 42 passengers:

$$1,000 \div 42 = 23.81 \text{ or } 24 \text{ buses needed}$$
$$24 \text{ buses} \times 1.5 = 36 \text{ minutes}$$

The 1.5 factor presumes that three buses will be loading simultaneously allowing 5 minutes from pull-up to pullout. A well-organized, on-time group may take less time, while a poorly organized group or multiple-destination loading may take three to four times longer.

Bus guides should use counters to make sure that all seats are filled and to avoid the delay of head counts on buses.

Loading begins:	8:00 A.M.
Last bus leaves at:	8:36
Travel time:	:45
Walk time to hall:	:03
Program/event start time	8:84 =
(adjusted to next hour):	9:24 A.M.

Bus Fee Structure

✓ **Flat fee (usually 4–5-hour minimum in city).**

✓ **Over minimum, charged on hourly rate.**

✓ **Road trips, flat fee plus mileage.**

✓ **Time may begin at point of pickup and end at point of drop-off or from garage to garage adding 30–45 minutes each way.**

✓ **Usually no charge for cancellations if made 24 hours or one day in advance (one day in advance could be 5 P.M. on day prior to 8 A.M. next departure; 24 hours means by 8 A.M. of day prior to next day's 8 A.M. departure).**

✓ **Spot charge is usually incurred if bus is cancelled after it arrives at point of pickup. Includes negotiated cancellation charge.**

Planning a Bus Trip

✓ **Staff requirements**

Spotter:	At bus queue area to send to load area
Dispatcher:	At bus load area to control load and departure
Guides:	To travel with bus (if desired)
Possible supplies:	Recognizable uniforms or badges
	Signs per bus, color-coded
	Walkie-talkies
	People counters

✓ **Agreements—timing**

Confirmation of charter order:	Date of confirmation
Full payment:	Three weeks prior
Total refund:	24-hour cancellation

Helpful Hints

Continuous shuttle loading is faster than loading for one-time movement of large groups.

Friends, groups, and couples slow bus loading (because of collecting group, saving seats, looking for lost group members)

Dividing city into halves or quadrants reduces the number of stops per bus and increases passengers-to-bus ratio. You may be operating four shuttle services each in a different part of town. Hotels with large numbers of attendees can have more buses available to handle their numbers, while still providing good service to hotels with lower attendee counts.

It helps to color code signs for various shuttle routes or destinations.
Standing on buses is never safe, although it may be permitted on short-distance
rides or shuttles.

On-Site Services and Amenities

Depending upon size of the meeting, many or all of these services can be offered in one general area. For large meetings, separate areas for registration and information and lounge areas are normally required.

✔ **Meet and greet:**
  • Airport welcome and transportation

✔ **Registration area:**
  • Preregistered participants
  • On-site registration

✔ **Information/message booth providing:**
  • Restaurant guide
  • Local entertainment guide
  • Recreation and fitness facilities
  • Churches and religious services
  • Local transportation schedules
  • Other

✔ **Publications center providing:**
  • Publications
  • Sponsor
  • Imprinted souvenirs
  • Displays

✔ **Hospitality center providing:**
  • Program books
  • Name badges
  • Facility floor maps
  • Area maps
  • Sign-up tables for recreational activities and excursions
  • Other

✔ **Shopping shuttle**

✔ **Lounge area with light refreshments**

✔ **Bulletin board for:**
  • Program schedules and locations
  • Special events
  • Other

✔ **Directional signs that are:**
- Clear
- Visible
- Appropriately placed

✔ **Child care**

✔ **Tuxedo rental**

✔ **Secretarial services**

✔ **Photocopy machines**

✔ **Daily newsletter**

✔ **Knowledgeable friendly staff**

✔ **Other**

10-1 | Attendee Needs Questionnaire

Your answers to the following questions will enable us to anticipate the services and amenities to provide throughout this meeting to most effectively meet your personal needs and interests.

1. Have you attended this meeting before?
   ☐ Yes ☐ No
   If *yes*, indicate number of years: _____

2. Do you have a chronic health problem?
   ☐ Yes ☐ No
   If *yes*, provide names and phone numbers for attending physician(s): _____
   _____

3. Do you have a special diet requirement?
   ☐ Yes ☐ No
   If *yes*, indicate type of diet: _____
   List your food preferences: _____
   _____

4. Will you require child care?
   ☐ Yes ☐ No
   If *yes*, indicate daytime/nighttime hours: _____
   Age(s) of child(ren): _____
   Sex(es) of child(ren): _____

5. In case of emergency, whom should we notify?

☐ *Family* (illness/personal injury): ☐ *Office*

Name: _____ Name: _____

Address: _____ ZIP: _____ Title: _____

Phone: ( ) _____ EXT: _____ Phone: ( ) _____ EXT: _____

6. Do you plan to arrive at meeting city by air?
    ☐ Yes ☐ No
  How will you travel to hotel?
    ☐ Via hotel airport limousine ☐ Taxi
    ☐ Private car ☐ Rental car
7. How will your registration fee be paid?
    ☐ Purchase order # _____
    ☐ Check ☐ Credit card # _____
8. Please rate the following services according to their importance to you.
    (1) Very important
    (2) Moderately important
    (3) Unimportant
    _____ Airport hotel limousine _____ Airport taxi
    _____ Hotel doorman _____ Bell captain
    _____ Express check-out _____ Safety deposit box
    _____ Room service _____ In-room bar
    _____ Daily newspaper delivered to room _____ Shoeshine
    _____ Valet service _____ Check cashing
    _____ Secretarial services _____ Photocopying services
    _____ Cellular phones availability _____ Telex/fax availability
    _____ Child care _____ Movie channel
    _____ Athletic club facilities _____ Beauty salon
    _____ Barber shop _____ Hotel nightclub
    _____ Nearby shopping _____ Fashion show
9. Do you usually come accompanied to meetings?
    ☐ Other staff/colleagues ☐ Spouse
    ☐ Children ☐ Guest
  Total number usually in your party: _____
10. Were the costs associated with attending this meeting an influential factor in your decision to attend? ☐ Yes ☐ No
11. Is this meeting tax deductible for you? ☐ Yes ☐ No
12. Would you have preferred to have this meeting held in a city that was:
    ☐ Larger? ☐ Smaller?
    ☐ More sophisticated? ☐ Less sophisticated?
13. What sports programs or activities do you prefer? Rank them from 1 through 7 in order of preference:
    _____ Golf _____ Tennis _____ Jogging
    _____ Walking _____ Aerobics
    _____ Other (specify) _____
    _____ None

(continued)

10-1	**Attendee Needs Questionnaire** (*continued*)

14. Average number of telephone calls received by you during the meeting: _____
15. Average number of telephone calls placed by you daily: _____
    From your room: _____ From hotel pay phones: _____
16. Number of nights you plan to dine outside hotel: _____
17. Rank the following evening events from 1 through 6 in order of preference:
    _____ Formal dinner _____ Dinner/Dance _____ Early reception
    _____ Hospitality suite _____ Theme party away from hotel
    _____ No planned activities
18. Rank preferred daytime activities during the meeting from 1 through 10 in order of preference:
    _____ Historical tours _____ Industry-related tours
    _____ General-orientation-to-city tour _____ Shopping tours
    _____ Scientific tours _____ Sporting activities
    _____ Scheduled breakfast _____ Scheduled luncheon
    _____ Free time _____ No tours

10-2	**Attendee Needs Chart**

From information obtained from the completed Attendee Needs Questionnaires (Exhibit 10-1), chart attendees' various needs and preferences; the related information, services, or solutions you are able to provide; and any actions required on your part. Save this chart to use for your program evaluation, and retain it as part of your group history file.

Information Needed	Questions to Ask Yourself re: Attendee Needs/Problems/ Preferences	What You Can Provide	Action Required
HEALTH PROBLEMS	• Illness/personal injury?	• Local doctor • Notification of personal doctor. • First Aid center	• Contact doctor.
SPECIAL DIET	• Religious or health-related?	• Type of diet required	• Notify food service manager.

Information Needed	Questions to Ask Yourself re: Attendee Needs/Problems/ Preferences	What You Can Provide	Action Required
CHILD CARE	• Hours required? • Number, age, and sex of children?	• Sitters or supervised group activity	• Obtain list of sitters from hotel. • Arrange qualified supervision for group.
OTHER EMERGENCIES	• Family- or business-related?	• Notification of family. • Notification of office.	• Contact family or office.
TRANSPORTATION	• *To meeting:* By air or car? • *At meeting:* By bus, taxi, limousine, private car?	• Obtain/supply information re cost/frequency. • Furnish city bus schedule, rental car information.	• Send airline information or city map. • Post bus schedule at meeting. • Furnish rental information.
SPOUSE PROGRAMS	• Special luncheon? • Fashion show? • Group tour?	• Luncheon tickets/ favors • Site for show and tickets • Transportation and tickets	• Order tickets from printer. • Notify food manager. • Buy favors or get them donated. • Order tickets. • Arrange for room. • Advise shop in hotel or outside haute fashion shop of need. • Contact local destination management or bus purveyor. • Order tickets.
SPORTS AND ACTIVITIES	• What specific types?	• Arrangements for tournaments or group games	• Determine availability and location of facilities (e.g., tennis courts, golf course).
HIGH-ACTIVITY/HIGH-RISK GROUPS		• Ambulance and paramedic on site	
GROUP TOURS	• What type?	• Arrangements for tour/tickets; transportation	• Order tickets. • Contact local bus purveyor.

(continued)

10-2	**Attendee Needs Chart** (***continued***)

Information Needed	*Questions to Ask Yourself re: Attendee Needs/Problems/ Preferences*	*What You Can Provide*	*Action Required*
FOREIGN-LANGUAGE-SPEAKING ATTENDEES	• Will interpreter/ translator be needed?	• Interpreter • Currency exchange • Multilanguage signs	• Obtain interpreter. • Arrange for currency exchange services. • Order and post signs.
SPECIAL PROBLEMS	• At-home family illness or personal injury?	• Message center to receive information	• Instruct message center to contact you personally. • Personally notify attendee of illness or injury. • Arrange for special transportation and other needs for attendee.
ROBBERY OR LOSS OF MONEY	• What happened?	• Contact with hotel security officer/ police. • Personal comfort	• Contact necessary authority. • Arrange for immediate check cashing, if indicated.
AUTO OR OTHER ACCIDENTS	• Nature of accident? • Has attendee been jailed?	• Notification of necessary persons. • Contact with family liaison service. • Notification of necessary persons	• Contact police, family members, insurance broker. • Relay messages between family and attendee. • Contact an attorney for attendee, if requested. • Contact bail bondsman.
LOST-AND-FOUND ARTICLES	• Nature of article? • Lost *or* found?	• Lost-and-found center at Message Center.	• Establish necessary service plan. • Post loss/reward/ return instruction on bulletin board.

Information Needed	Questions to Ask Yourself re: Attendee Needs/Problems/ Preferences	What You Can Provide	Action Required
HANDICAPPED REQUIREMENTS	• What are the requirements? • Wheelchair access? • Visual alarm system? • Braille elevator floor indicators?	• Facility offering special amenities such as wheelchair ramps, wide doorways	• These are normally available in all public buildings.
VISUALLY HANDICAPPED REQUIREMENTS	• Braille programs? • Will guide dog accommodations be required? • What are airport/ ground trans- portation needs? • Guide dog illness?	• Necessary programs • Dog food • Meeting site with adequate walking areas • Braille floor numbers in elevators	• Order and obtain programs from braille printer. • Advise hotel manager. • Give priority to grounds during site selection. • Require braille elevator numbers during site selection. • Advise airport and ground transport managers. • Call vet.
HEARING IMPAIRED REQUIREMENTS	• Special hearing devices? • Signer for the deaf?	• Meeting rooms with special audio equipment • Sleeping rooms with specially equipped phones • Arrangement for signer	• Advise hotel manager of special meeting rooms needed. • Advise hotel manager of need for special phones. • Obtain signer for meetings.
WARDROBE REQUIREMENTS	• Formal (tuxedo/ sequins, dark suit/ cocktail dress) for formal dinner or dinner-dance? • Sweaters, raincoat, swimwear, tennis attire or other clothing needs • Jacket and tie required in dining room?	• Specific information ("formal" means different things to different people) • Specific information re weather, events and activities • Hotel rules (e.g., no bathing suits outside pool area) • Recreation facilities available	• State actual dress code in registration materials. • State in registration materials.

(continued)

10-2 | Attendee Needs Chart
(*continued*)

Information Needed	Questions to Ask Yourself re: Attendee Needs/Problems/ Preferences	What You Can Provide	Action Required
CASH REQUIREMENTS	• Credit cards accepted? • Check cashing on site?	• Specific information	• State in registration materials.
	• Interstate/intrastate minibank available?	• Information	• State in registration materials.
	• Local tipping customs	• Information (e.g., whether hotel adds in surcharge for food service)	
	• Local transportation costs?	• Bus schedule and fares • Excessive taxi rates, if known	
FIRST-TIME ATTENDEES	• Any additional requirements other than above?	• Briefing session • First-timer badges	• All action stated above • Order badges. • Arrange for briefing site. • Give/arrange for briefing.
FACILITY GUIDELINES AND GENERAL INFORMATION	• Individual thermostats in sleeping rooms? If not:	• Information	• Advise warm robe for morning/ evening.
	—Public restroom locations?	• Information	• Hand out public-area floor maps.
	—Meeting room locations?	• Directional signs	• Order signs. • Post signs.
	• What recreational facilities exist at hotel?	• Specific information not covered in hotel brochure	• Send brochure with registration materials.
	• Rental recreational equipment available (e.g., scuba, ski)?	• Specific information	• Obtain rental equipment lists and charges.

Information Needed	Questions to Ask Yourself re: Attendee Needs/Problems/ Preferences	What You Can Provide	Action Required
CITY INFORMATION	• Miles to downtown area?	• Information	• State in registration materials.
	• Recreational facilities locations? • Equipment rental locations? • Special exercise programs?	• Information	• Obtain rate sheets for Information Desk.
	• Religious services available?	• Location and times of services	• Obtain service schedules from nearby churches and synagogues. Post near Information Desk.
	• Local physicians' names and locations?	• Yellow pages • Telephone number for local medical association	• Keep Yellow Pages at Information Desk. • Advise about services of house doctor.
FIRST AID INFORMATION	• Supplies *only*?	• Supply *only* materials (e.g., bandaids)	• Purchase supplies. • Keep supplies at Information Desk and Message Center.
	• First Aid *services*? (should be given only by qualified personnel, such as a nurse, paramedic, doctor, or *certified* first-aid personnel carrying current first-aid card)		• Arrange for qualified individual to be present.
MISCELLANEOUS	• What services are you unable or not planning to provide?		• Identify and state any unavailable services in registration materials.

10-3 | Child-Care Information And Release Form

Be sure to consult an attorney before issuing any release forms. State laws vary.

RESERVATIONS MUST BE RECEIVED BY JUNE 10, 19x8

Check activity child will participate in:

Monday, June 27, 19X8
    ☐ ARTS & CRAFTS   COST: $25
    ☐ PICNIC LUNCH & SHOW   COST: $25
Tuesday, June 28, 19X8
    ☐ PUPPET MAKING   COST: $25
    ☐ BICYCLE TRIP   COST: $25

Total amount must accompany payment. Please use one form per child.

Child's name: _____ Age: _____

Parents' names: _____ Home phone: _____

Address: _____

City: _____ State: _____ ZIP: _____

Please make checks payable and mail to:
[*name and address of sponsor*]

IN CASE OF MEDICAL OR OTHER EMERGENCY: I understand that an effort will be made to contact me before any action is taken. In the event that I cannot be reached, I hereby give permission to the physician selected by [*sponsor*] to hospitalize and secure proper treatment for my child.

_____ / _____
signature of parent or guardian   date

If neither mother nor father can be reached in an emergency, please call:

Name: _____ Relationship: _____ Phone: _____

We, the parents of _____ do, for ourselves, our child(ren), and our heirs, executors, and administrators, hereby release and forever discharge [*sponsor*] and its respective agents and employees from any and all claims and causes of action on account of injury or damage of any nature, occurring to the person(s) or property of said child(ren) during the [*sponsor*] program. We also affirm that we have read in full this information sheet and understand and agree to all provisions therein.

_____ / _____

signature of parent or guardian   date

CANCELLATION: Full refund, less $10 administrative fee, prior to June 20, 19X8. No refunds after June 20, 19X8.

Guide 11
Special Events

Types of Special Events

- Children's programs
- Cultural events
- Professional entertainment (e.g., singers, comedians)
- Recreational activities
- Sporting events
- Spouse/guest programs
- Theme events
- Tours
- VIP activities

Elements of a Special Event

- Music
- Entertainment
- Games (competitive/noncompetitive)

- ✔ **Tours**

- ✔ **Food and beverages**

- ✔ **Invitations**

- ✔ **Decorations**

- ✔ **Lighting**

- ✔ **Special audiovisual effects**

- ✔ **Favors/souvenirs/prizes**

- ✔ **Costumes**

- ✔ **Transportation**

Questions to Ask When Selecting Special Events

- ✔ **Does the event fit in with your program design and the purpose of the meeting?**

- ✔ **Will it introduce or carry out the meeting theme?**

- ✔ **Will it promote attendance?**

- ✔ **Will it motivate attendees?**

- ✔ **Will it provide relaxation and diversion for attendees?**

- ✔ **Will it offer an opportunity for social interaction and informal conversation among attendees of educational programs?**

- ✔ **Will it meet or enhance the goals of attendees?**

- ✔ **Do you have a sufficient budget allocation for the event?**

- ✔ **Is space available?**

- ✔ **What are the staging requirements?**

- ✔ **Is audio and lighting required and are qualified technicians available to operate equipment?**

- ✔ **Is affordable talent available?**

✓ **What are the union minimums for performers and technicians?**

✓ **What pertinent union regulations will you be subject to?**

✓ **What local laws bear on your event?**

✓ **What are the local liquor regulations?**

✓ **Is insurance coverage needed?**

✓ **Are special licenses/permits required?**

✓ **Can the space be secured?**

✓ **What are the costs?**

✓ **What is your budget allocation for the event?**

Determining the Kinds of Special Events Your Attendees Will Enjoy

✓ **What is your attendee profile?**
  - Age range
  - Men/women ratio
  - Spouses/companions/guests
  - Children, age range
  - Size of group
  - Sophistication level
  - Education level
  - Group "personality"
  - Response of group to previous events

Considerations for Special Events Sites

✓ **Which meeting facilities under consideration offer the kind of space required for the event? For example:**
  - Ballroom with stage or "stage area"
  - Theater
  - Large lounge area
  - Golf course
  - Tennis courts
  - Open grounds (or nearby park) for outdoor group games

Other questions to ask are:
- Is area safe?
- Is water available?
- Is electricity available?

✓ **What size room is necessary to present the event? If dancing is planned, what size dance floor is needed (*see* Guide 4)?**

✓ **Will weather be a factor in the event?**

✓ **Is required space available on date needed?**

✓ **What are the local liquor laws? Fire codes?**

✓ **Does meeting facility have the staff to meet your needs for catering, decorating, audiovisual and special effects, guided tours? If so, must you use its staff, or may outside purveyors be used?**

✓ **If an off-site event is planned, will it require group transportation? Is that transportation available?**

✓ **Will an off-site event require catering services? If so, check:**
- Business reputation of caterer
- Experience of caterer in serving similar events
- Host's liquor responsibility, yours or the caterer's?
- Possible conflict with local health department regulations
- Special local licenses required

Theme Parties

Theme Development

✓ **Promotional materials**

✓ **Program books**

✓ **Location of event or meeting**

✓ **Room and table decorations**

✓ **Gifts, favors, souvenirs, prizes**

✓ **Floral arrangements**

✓ **Menu and food presentation**

✔ **Music and entertainment**

✔ **Anniversary dates**

✔ **Special audiovisual effects**

Some meeting facilities offer theme party packages to fit your budget that frequently are advantageous from a cost point of view.

Professional party planners or special events companies are available and can be hired to handle or present all or parts of the event.

Staged Entertainment

✔ **Elements**
  • Master of ceremonies (frequently professional entertainers/comedians)
  • Celebrity speakers
  • New-product presentations
  • Award presentations
  • Celebrity performers or musicians/orchestra/band

Sporting Events

✔ **Examples:**
  • Golf tournaments
  • Tennis tournaments
  • Miniolympics
  • Volleyball tournaments
  • Rodeos

✔ **Meeting planner's responsibilities re sporting events:**
  • Scheduling the event
  • Reserving the site
  • Promoting the event
  • Writing up the specifications for the event (e.g., dates, times, scheduling, suppliers, equipment needed)
  • Participant sign-up sheet
  • Participant assignments according to skill levels
  • Providing for scorekeepers
  • Prizes and favors
  • Refreshments
  • Tournament "extras" such as
    —Videotaping
    —Celebrity professionals
    —Game clinics

- Insurance
- Safety
- First aid/paramedics on site

✔ **Special considerations:**
- Safety factors
- Availability of medical facilities (on- and off-site)
- Appropriateness of activity for age group of participants
- Obtaining waivers for safety for high-contact sports

Helpful Hints

Added audiovisual components enhance a meeting. Simultaneous video presentations and videotaping for later viewing are popular. Your AV producer can offer suggestions.

Midmorning and afternoon refreshment breaks can be enhanced by providing roving musicians or live background music (e.g., a piano player).

Arrange special programs for children according to age. Puppet shows, clown acts, and craft classes provide popular forms of entertainment. Have an adequate number of trained activity leaders at all times.

Such added activities, if financially feasible, will contribute substantially toward making your meeting successful and memorable and deserving of consideration.

Selecting a Photographer

Items to Discuss With Photographer

✔ **Purpose of photographs**
- Official conference archives
- Candid shots for newsletters/future publicity
- Sales of photos to attendees
- Press releases for new officers/awards recipients
- Multimedia presentations
- Advertisement inserts
- Exhibits and other special activity promotion
- Gifts/souvenirs

✔ **Dates, time, length, location of photographic sessions**

✔ **Types of photos (e.g., formal, staged, candid, still, action)**

✔ **Largest/smallest number of people to be photographed at one time**

✔ **Special staging, lighting, or backdrops required**

✔ **Estimated number of photos to be taken and number to be purchased/sold**

✔ **Type(s) of film required:**
  • Color (%)
  • Black-and-white (%)

✔ **Number, finish, and size required:**
  • Slides
  • Finish (e.g., matte, glossy)
  • Contact sheets
  • Processing time (especially if rush)

Working With Photographers

✔ **What you will need from the photographer:**
  • Training and past experience of photographer
  • Personality/attire/demeanor appropriate to your group
  • References/portfolio
  • Costs
  • Equipment (e.g., cameras, studio, processing)
  • Processing lab resources if not in-house

✔ **What the photographer will need from you:**
  • Contract
  • Policies and procedures
  • Detailed schedule and staging guidelines
  • List of key people to be photographed
  • Daily review meeting

Cost-Saving Ideas

Contact local colleges for:
• *Student bands, instrumental soloists*
• *Student teachers to supervise children's program*
• *Drama students for mime presentations, puppet shows, comedian acts during host receptions*

Note: Give credits to schools and performers. *Investigate possibility of union conflicts/ repercussions.*

Save floral decorations from all events for reuse in:
• *Reception areas*
• *VIP rooms*

- *Luncheon/dinner tables*
- *Host cocktail hours*

Utilize staff/talent from within your organization

Develop theme around easily available props

Select location that, in its current state, enhances the theme:

- *Football stadium for sporting event*
- *Ethnic restaurant/park to match ethnic theme*
- *Other*

Avoid special effects (e.g., lighting and smoke, which can be very expensive)

(*See also* Guide 12, under "Cost-Saving Ideas.")

Guide 12
Food and Beverages

Questions Caterer Will Ask You

- Number of food-and-beverage events required

- Dates and beginning/ending times of functions

- Budgeted amount for each function

- Number of people expected to attend

- Type of food preferred by attendees

- Room setup (e.g., rounds, head table)

- Whether there will be speakers, and if so, how many

- Whether handicapped people will be in attendance

- Purpose of the event (e.g., educational, social)

- Whether special preassigned seating is required for any or all guests

- Whether tickets will need to be collected

- What audiovisual equipment will be required

- What security services might be required

✔ **Whether cocktails/wine will be served, and if so, when:**
- Cash bar?
- Host bar?
- Hors d'oeuvres?
- With dinner?

✔ **Your organization's tax-exempt status**

✔ **Any special requirements (e.g., dance floor, head table, audio-visuals)**

Questions to Ask Caterer

✔ **Who is contact when planning the function? During function?**

✔ **Are printed menus with pricing available?**

✔ **Are you limited to the items on menu? If not, may you create your menu?**

✔ **What does the chef prepare best?**

✔ **Which entrees are fresh/frozen? Are vegetables fresh or canned?**

✔ **What size portion is served at lunch? Dinner?**

✔ **Can a pot of coffee be placed on each table before the speaker commences?**

✔ **Will current menu prices be confirmed for my function?**

✔ **Are substitutions available for people on special diets? How much advance notice is required?**

✔ **Can luncheon dessert be served at afternoon break?**

✔ **How much time should be allowed for meal service?**

✔ **What level of staffing can be expected (waitperson-to-cover ratio)?**

✔ **What percentage is overset?**

✔ **When must guarantees be final?**

✔ **When is payment expected?**

✔ **What is sales tax rate? Gratuity rate?**

✔ **Is the gratuity taxed?**

✔ **What percentage of gratuities go to the waitpersons? To others?**

✔ **What other charges might be expected (e.g., overtime charges, setup)?**

✔ **What time can you get in to set up for your function?**

✔ **What time do waitpersons arrive prior to functions? This is especially important for breakfasts.**

✔ **Are there signs for identifying smoking/nonsmoking sections? Reserved tables?**

✔ **Can tables be set for eight (60″) instead of ten (72″)?**

✔ **What linen colors are available?**

✔ **What table decorations are available at no charge?**

✔ **What will be preset on tables prior to guests being served?**

✔ **Is it possible to tour the kitchen? Meet the chef?**

✔ **Are lights and temperature controls in the meeting/dining room on a separate thermostat?**

✔ **Are facilities available for the handicapped?**

✔ **Is one (or more) microphone provided at no charge?**

✔ **What other groups are meeting in nearby rooms?**

Food-and-Beverage Formulas

Time Requirements

Breaks*:
- 15 minutes for 50 people or fewer
- 30 minutes for 50–100 people
- 30–45 minutes for 100–1,000 people

Allow 15 minutes for approximately 100 cups of coffee (5 gals.) to be served from a coffee urn. Less if waiters pour. Allow one coffee station per 50 people for groups under 500; one per 75 people for over 500.

Lunch:	45 minutes to one hour
Dinner:	20 minutes per course; when accompanied by an event or show, allow three–four hours
Buffet:	Allow one line per 50 people and 15–20 minutes per 50 people to go through the line.
Cocktails:	(Prior to dinner) 45 minutes to 1 hour
Reception:	(As part of program) 1 to 1½ hours

* Break is necessary following a session of one and one-half to two hours duration.

Types of Service

French service (white-glove):	Each food item individually served by waitperson.
à la Russe:	(plated service): Waitperson serves each guest a completely setup plate.
Buffet:	Assortment of foods offered at a table where one usually helps oneself.
Russian/butler:	Waitperson presents tray to guests, who then help themselves (most often at reception).

Staffing Requirements

Breakfast:	*French service*—one waitperson per every 15 covers
	Plated service—one waitperson per every 16–20 covers
	Buffet service—one waitperson per four tables
Lunch:	Same staffing as breakfast
Dinner:	*French service*—one waitperson per 8–10 covers
	Plated service—one waitperson per 16–20 covers
	Buffet service—one waitperson per four tables
Buffet:	One buffet table per 75 guests

Types of Room/Food Package Plans

FAP: Full American plan: Hotel rate includes three full meals each day and a sleeping room.

MAP: Modified American plan: Hotel rate includes breakfast, dinner, and a sleeping room.

EP: European plan—No meals are included in hotel rates.

Food Allowances

Cocktails:	(one hour duration): two and one-half–three per person
Hors d'oeuvres:	Five to eight pieces per person per hour (reduce by adding cheese or vegetable tray)
Nuts:	3 lbs. per 100 people (with major hors d'oeuvres)
	5 lbs. per 100 people (with minor hors d'oeuvres)
Dry snacks:	4 oz. per person
Cheese:	3 oz. per person
Lunch:	6 oz. meat portion per person
Dinner:	8 oz. meat portion per person

Cocktail Allowances per Person

Hour 1:	2.5 drinks
Hour 2:	1.5 drinks
Hour 3:	1.0 drinks
Total for three-hour reception:	5.0 drinks
Wine with dinner:	1.5–2.0 4-oz. glasses, or a 1 glass per course if a new wine is introduced

Bar Allowances

- One bar per each 100–125 people
- Three–four bottles of wine per 10 covers

Liquid Measurements and Yields

1 gallon (4 quarts):	22 6-oz. cups
1 fifth (25.6 oz.):	23 1-oz. drinks
1 liter (35.6 oz.):	33 1-oz. drinks
	6 6-oz. juice glasses
1 quart (32 oz.):	5 6-oz. glasses per juice pitcher
1 bottle of wine (24 oz.):	6 4-oz. glasses

Liquor Purchase Options

- By the bottle
- By the drink
- By the hour/per person

Cost-Saving Ideas

Schedule more continental breakfasts and few sit-down meals.

Give catering manager your food/beverage budget. Let catering manager create menus.

Request two or three food/beverage proposals for evaluation.

Hold cash bars. Do not tip when gratuity charge is included.

Arrange host-bar packages (e.g., a fixed cost per person for drinks for one hour).

For under 100 people the most economical bar is by the drink; for over 100 people, by the bottle.

Offer wine and cheese instead of cocktails and hors d'oeuvres.

Use 4-oz. champagne glasses for juice instead of 6–8 oz. glasses.

Reduce entrée-size portions (6 oz. luncheon, 8 oz. dinner). Use luncheon size at dinner.

Take advantage of 5% overset—under guarantee by 5%.

Schedule fewer coffee breaks; check per-gallon cost of coffee when evaluating hotel.

Save luncheon dessert for afternoon break.

Utilize ticket systems and collection.

The more crowded a reception, the less food consumed. Remember this when determining size of room for reception.

Use waitpersons to pass hors d'oeuvres (butler service).

Do not provide plates during reception; use napkins instead.

Order a small selection of hors d'oeuvres in large quantities and under guarantee.

Be creative. A beer and hot dog reception can be lots of fun and be cost-effective.

Offer sponsorship to organizations for coffee breaks, receptions, and other food-and-beverage events.

Keep good records on event attendance and consumption.

Instruct and remind hotel/bar personnel that unless personally extended by you, event is to end at time specified.

Avoid serving salty foods during host-bar events.

When possible, schedule free time in lieu of host events.

| 12-1 | Meeting Report—Food-And-Beverage Form |

Group name: _____ Meeting: _____

Location: _____ City: _____ State: _____

Meeting dates: _____ Person preparing report: _____ Today's date: _____

Date	Time	Room	Banquet Event Order Number	Function	Attendance Gtd.	Served	Food	Bev.	Grat.	Other	Total
							$	$	$	$	$

AND TOTAL

12-2   Bar Readings

Date: _____   Count taken by: _____

Bar location: _____   Bartender fee: _____

Function: _____   Gratuity: _____ % Tax: _____ %

Number of bars: _____

Count per bar: _____

Count combined bars: _____

Name	Size	Price	Start Number	Amount Used	Partial Carryover*	Notes

Guide 13

Audiovisual And Other Media

Information to Request From Audiovisual Company

Check out all bidding companies; compare bids and select the best bid. Check references. Whether services needed are sought by RFP or other (e.g., telephone request to company), the information outlined below must be obtained.

✔ **Equipment (in-house/outside)**

✔ **On-site maintenance availability**

✔ **Setup/breakdown schedule**

✔ **Rehearsal schedule**

✔ **Support equipment such as extension cords, projection stands**

✔ **Equipment rental cost and complimentary items**

✔ **Hourly rates, overtime charges, and a statement of what constitutes overtime**

✔ **Equipment/technician availability costs for all items**

✔ **Itemization of all union regulations**

✔ **Backup equipment/supplies**

✔ **Equipment delivery, storage, and pickup arrangements and costs**

✔ **Cancellation policy requirements, procedure, and penalty**

✔ **Insurance requirements:**
  • Certificate copy enclosed?
  • Where on file?

✔ **References**

Equipment

Prior to contact with the audiovisual supplier, determine what equipment is needed, based on program and speaker requirements.

Speaker Needs	Questions to Ask	Equipment Types	Equipment Purposes
Projector	• What type?	• Slide, carousel	• Projects 2 × 2 (35 mm) slides.
		• With or without remote control	• Allows speaker to advance slide from a distance.
		• With or without slide tray(s)	• Holds up to 80 slides.
		• Opaque	• Projects books, papers
		• Overhead, Vu-Graph	• Projects transparencies.
		• Movie, 8 or 16 mm	• Projects film reel.
Projector stand or cart	• What type? • What height?	• 32″ high, wheels • 42″ high, wheels • 54″ high, wheels	• For overhead projector • For 19″ TV • For 25″ TV, slide projector, movie projector
		• Folding "safelock" stand expands 24″ to 54″.	• Adapts to all projector needs, but requires more floor space.
Two or more projectors in same room	• For simultaneous use? • Front or rear projection?	• Call audiovisual company	
TV	• What size? • Color or black-and-white?	• 19″ screen • 25″ screen	
Video monitors	• What size? • Color or black-and-white? • Sound?	• 19″ screen • 5′ or 5′ large-screen	One 19″ per 15–20 people One 5′ or 7′ screen per 100–150 people

(continued)

Speaker Needs	Questions to Ask	Equipment Types	Equipment Purposes
Video recorder/ player (Complex programs (use of audio requires services of specialists)	• What type? • What size tape? • Color? • Black-and-white?	• Beta • VHS • U-matic	• Play ½" tape • Play ¾" tape • Records and projects videotape, with or without sound, of still or moving objects. • Capable of combining materials taken from other AV equipment (e.g., slides, filmstrips) on videotape. • Videotapes are easily duplicated and stored; duplicating is fairly inexpensive. • Material updating can be expensive and time-consuming.
Video projection	• Front or rear projection? • Size tape? • Black-and-white? • Color?	• Brand name (e.g., Betamax)	• Replaces video monitor for large-group use. • 24' maximum screen size • Projector can be hung from ceiling or project from floor level.
Screen	• What type? • What size?	• Call AV company to confirm most practical type and size for room setup. Larger than 12' × 12' requires special lens.	• Tripod—50", 6' and 8' • C-stand or roll-up (sits on table or floor) • FastFold, 12' × 12' and larger. Most have black or blue draperies available.
Recorder	• What type? Patch to house sound usually required for good recording	• Cassette (stereo/ mono) • Reel-to-reel (stereo/mono) • 8-track	
Microphone(s) (first mike per room is usually free)	• What type? • How many? If three or more are in same room, a mixer should be used. CALL AV COMPANY.	• Podium or table • Standing or floor • Lavaliere or "neck"	• Used on lectern or at tables where speakers are seated • Used when speakers are standing. Height is adjustable. • Fastens around neck. Permits speaker to move around with free use of hands.

Speaker Needs	Questions to Ask	Equipment Types	Equipment Purposes
Spotlight	• What type? • For what purpose?	• Track lights • Follow spot	• Highlight podium/lectern/exhibit, as used in entertainment.
Flip chart and stand	• With paper? • With marker?		• A large writing tablet for speaker's use. Frequently saved for subsequent lectures.
Electric pointer		• Sometimes called flashlight pointer	• Use in darkened room as pointer on projected images.
Lectern (often incorrectly called podium)	• Standing or table? • With light? • Mike?		• A stand for holding a lecturer's notes

High-Tech Equipment Guidelines

Equipment Type	Equipment Purpose/Use
Computer video graphics	• Computer receives and stores information for transfer and organization to produce desired formats (e.g., graphs, pictures, sounds).
Electronic transparencies	• Stores information on computer disc for projection through standard overhead projector. • Comes with or without remote control. • During presentation, information can be added or changed from the computer keyboard. • Eliminates need to make or store transparencies. • Versatile, space-saving, lightweight device at moderate cost.
Electronic writing board (also called electronic presentation, chalk, or white)	• Makes photocopies of materials written on any surface, or taped on surface, for immediate transmission to other locations. • Yields permanent, easily stored copies. • Replaces flip chart and chalkboard.
Lasers Obtain services of specialists	• Produces clear, vivid, multicolor images. • Projects on almost all surfaces. • Presents excellent graphic displays (still or moving). • Laser light pointers are commonly used.

Teleconferences

Frequent Uses

- Small business meetings
- In-company meetings
- Sales promotion meetings
- New-product orientation and launching
- Technical briefings
- Resolution of technical problems (e.g., production)
- Meetings requiring interaction and information exchange when teleconference costs are less than the combined losses of time, transportation, housing, and food costs of assembling participants
- To avoid time-delayed product loss

Premeeting Checklist

Prior to calling interconnect service to reserve time:

✔ **Check agenda for:**
- Meeting date, starting time, duration of meeting
- Name of chairperson, meeting style, and experience in chairing teleconferences. If you don't know chair's background, ask how he or she prefers to conduct teleconference meetings.

✔ **Be knowledgeable about assembly plan for each site location involved:**
- If all meeting participants at one site are assembled in one room, you will need *one speakerphone.*
- If participants are individually scattered throughout the site, you will need *one phone per person.* It's expensive, so double-check the number actually required.
- Repeat for each site location involved, *including your own conference originating site.*

✔ **Determine number of locations (ports) to be reserved:**

One speakerphone: One port
Each individual phone: One port

When determined and double-checked, total the number of ports.

✔ **Decide who will place the calls.**
Operator called (frequently impractical for on-the-road sales representatives):
- Obtain a list of phone number(s) for each site location to give to operator.
- All charges will be billed to location placing originating call to operator.
Attendees calling into a central number:
- Give each attendee the central number.
- Give each attendee the date and time of teleconference.

- Unless the number called is toll-free, billing will go to number from which call is placed.

Some interconnect companies accept only operator-placed calls. Check with your long-distance carrier for assistance.

🖊 **Become knowledgeable about your interconnect services:**
- Will conference calls be operator-monitored so that assistance is available when needed? If not, how is operator summoned?
- Is disconnection automatic at end of scheduled time?
- What is the procedure if call is accidentally disconnected? Procedures vary widely. Ask your interconnect service beforehand, and instruct all attendees on what to do if such a situation should arise.

🖊 **Learn how to summon operator (if not monitoring call) in cases of noise interference on the line.**

If you are an absolute novice in arranging for teleconference calls, or will be working with an unfamiliar interconnect system or service, request a conference with the interconnect company's service representative handling teleconferences.

Screens

Determining Correct Screen Size

Screen size is the most important audiovisual consideration. Square screens are preferable to rectangular ones.

- *When the room size is known:* Divide the distance from screen to back row of seats by 8 to determine minimum screen size/image height.

    EXAMPLE: $80' \div 8 = 10'$ high screen

- May vary with shape of room and obstructions.

Space Requirements When Using Screen

- *Necessary distance between screen and first row of chairs:* Screen height × 1.5.

    EXAMPLE: $10' \times 1.5 = 15'$ from screen to first row of chairs

- *Maximum distance between screen and back row of chairs:* Screen height × 8.

    EXAMPLE: $10' \times 8 = 80'$ from screen to back row of chairs

- *Required ceiling height:* Screen height plus 5' (absolute minimum, 4'8").

    EXAMPLE: $10' + 5' = 15'$ ceiling height.

- *Bottom of screen:* 5' from floor.
- *Screen coverage:* Side-to-side visibility based on 40° angle.
- *Rear screen projector:* 16'–35' allowance between wall and screen.

Audiovisual Formulas

Distance From Screen   Lettering Sizes

30'	=	1″ letters
45'	=	1½″ letters
60'	=	2″ letters

For every 15 feet, increase letter height by 1½″.

Video Monitor Coverage

- 19 inches will handle 15–25 people; if material is nontechnical, it will handle up to 50 people.
- 5–7 feet (large screen) will handle 100–500 people.

Correction of Sound Problems

No sound:	• Turn on microphone/amplifier.
	• Check cable connection.
Squeal/feedback:	• Lower volume.
	• Move mike so it isn't in line with loud speaker.
Ringing sound:	• Lower volume.
Hollow or booming sound:	• Lower volume.
	• Stand 5–8 inches from mike.
	• Get new mike.
Hum:	• Move mike cable away from electric cord, especially at connection.

13-1 | Audiovisual Supplier Request Form

Use one form per room. Then prepare summary.

Company: _____   Deliver to: _____

_____   _____

_____ ZIP: _____   _____ ZIP: _____

Phone: ( ) _____ EXT: _____   Phone: ( ) _____ EXT: _____

Contact: _____   Contact: _____

Event: _____ Date: _____ Time: _____ Room No.: _____

Item (specify types, brands, sizes)	How Many	Cost Each	Special Instructions	Operators Number	Rate	Total Estimated Cost
Projectors						
35 mm slide	_____	$_____	_____	_____	$_____	$_____
Remote control	_____	_____	_____	_____	_____	_____
Slide trays	_____	_____	_____	_____	_____	_____
8 mm film	_____	_____	_____	_____	_____	_____
16 mm film	_____	_____	_____	_____	_____	_____
Take-up reels	_____	_____	_____	_____	_____	_____
Opaque	_____	_____	_____	_____	_____	_____
Overhead	_____	_____	_____	_____	_____	_____
Other	_____	_____	_____	_____	_____	_____
Projector stands						
32" high	_____	$_____	_____	_____	$_____	$_____
42" high	_____	_____	_____	_____	_____	_____
54" high	_____	_____	_____	_____	_____	_____
Folding "safelock"	_____	_____	_____	_____	_____	_____
Screens						
Tripod	_____	$_____	_____	_____	$_____	$_____
C-stand or roll-up	_____	_____	_____	_____	_____	_____
FastFold	_____	_____	_____	_____	_____	_____
Video equipment						
½" tape cassette player	_____	$_____	_____	_____	$_____	$_____
¾" tape cassette player	_____	_____	_____	_____	_____	_____
19" screen monitor	_____	_____	_____	_____	_____	_____
5' large screen monitor	_____	_____	_____	_____	_____	_____
Recorder						
Cassette	_____	$_____	_____	_____	$_____	$_____
Reel-to-reel	_____	_____	_____	_____	_____	_____
Eight-track	_____	_____	_____	_____	_____	_____

(continued)

13-1 | Audiovisual Supplier Request Form (*continued*)

Item (specify types, brands, sizes)	How Many	Cost Each	Special Instructions	Operators Number	Rate	Total Estimated Cost
Microphones						
Table	___	$___	___		$___	$___
Podium	___	___	___		___	___
Standing	___	___	___		___	___
Lavaliere	___	___	___		___	___
Mixer	___	___	___		___	___
Flip chart and stand						
With paper	___	$___	___		$___	$___
With marker	___	___	___		___	___
Lighting equipment						
Electric pointer	___	$___	___		$___	$___
Spotlight	___	___	___		___	___
Lectern light	___	___	___		___	___
Lecterns						
Standing	___	$___	___		$___	$___
Table	___	___	___		___	___
Chalkboard						
Chalk	___	$___	___		$___	$___
Erasers	___	___	___		___	___
Video recorder/player						
Brand name	___	$___	___		$___	$___
Size tape	___	___	___		___	___
Video projector						
Front projection	___	$___	___		$___	$___
Rear projection	___	___	___		___	___

Guide 14

Budgeting and Financial Management

Essentials for Preparing Your Budget

- ✔ **Establish goals and objectives for the event.**

- ✔ **Periodically compare budget costs against actual costs.**

- ✔ **Compare final budget allocation against actual costs.**

Defining Costs

When preparing your budget, the estimated figure for each item should be broken down to per-person or per-piece cost *times* quantity *plus* surcharges such as tax and gratuity.

Budget Items

- ✔ **General income sources (revenues)**
  - Corporate internal allocations
  - Grants and contracts
  - Registration fees
  - Exhibits and sponsorships
  - Conference-related merchandise sales
  - Investment interest

- Special functions ticket sales
- Nonrefundable administrative and/or registration fees
- Program Book advertising

✔ **General expenditures categories**
- Administrative overhead
- Food/beverage functions
- Registration materials
- Promotion
- Speaker travel, expenses, and honoraria
- Audiovisual equipment
- Signs, posters, and banner
- Staff travel and expenses
- Public relations and press
- Gratuities and gifts
- Taxes
- Printing and photocopying
- Office furniture and equipment
- Telephones
- Room rental
- Insurance
- Decorations/flowers
- Supplies
- Car rental
- Labor charges (including AV operators)
- Personnel
- Shipping/freight charges
- Postage, mailing labels, addressing/mailing service
- Photography
- Session taping
- Complimentary and staff registrations
- Shuttle buses
- Entertainment
- Other

Expenses (With Sample Account Codes)

	Account Codes
100 series	Administrative expenses
200 "	Personnel fees/expenses
300 "	Food-and-beverage expenses
400 "	Registration expenses
500 "	Promotion
600 "	Speakers and other program participants
700 "	Audiovisual
800 "	Transportation
900 "	Hospitality

✔ 100 Administrative
- Gratuities
- Telephones and long-distance charges
- Miscellaneous postage
- Miscellaneous copies
- Secretarial services
- Office furniture (rental)
- Typewriters (rental)
- Computer/printer (rental)
- Copy machine (rental)
- Calculator (rental)
- Shipping to/from meeting
- Meeting-room rental
- Insurance
- Photography
- Decorations
- Signs
- Flowers
- Taxes

✔ 200 Staff/volunteers
- Professional fees
- Travel (air/ground)
- Accommodations
- Food and other miscellaneous expenses
- Complimentary registrations

✔ 300 Food and beverages (plus tax and gratuity)
- Opening reception
- Breakfast #1
- A.M. break #1
- Lunch #1
- P.M. break #1
- Dinner #1
- Breakfast #2
- A.M. break #2

. . . .

✔ 400 Registration expenses
- Advance registration forms
- On-site registration forms
- Envelopes for advance registration forms
- Postage for advance registration forms
- Confirmation-letter paper
- Confirmation-letter window envelopes
- Confirmation-letter postage
- Badge stock printing
- Plastic bulldog badge holders

- Computer ribbons for badge preparation
- Registration packets
- Reproduction of packet materials
- Reproduction of registration lists
- Tickets (meals, special events)
- Registration personnel
- Bulletin typewriters (rental)
- Cash boxes
- Registration booths (rental)
- Gifts/mementos
- Registration signs
- Setup labor

✓ 500 Promotion

- Program announcement (art, printing, paper)
- Mailing lists/labels preparation
- Program announcement envelopes
- Postage for program announcement
- Conference letterhead
- Chairman's letter preparations
- Chairman's letter envelopes
- Chairman's letter postage
- Ad preparation
- Advertisement placement
- Press release preparation
- Press release postage
- Posters
- Complimentary registrations

✓ 600 Program participants

- Speaker #1
- Hotel accommodations
- Travel expenses (air)
- Travel expenses (ground)
- Food and miscellaneous expenses
- Honorarium
- [*Repeat for as many speakers as you have.*]

✓ 700 Audiovisual

- Microphones
- Sound system
- Recording equipment (audio)
- Recording equipment (video)
- Technicians
- Spotlights
- Screens
- Slide projectors
- Overhead projectors

- Chalkboards
- Flipcharts
- Carts, stands, easels
- Mixers
- Remotes, dissolves, extension cords and other accessories
- Supplies (markers, chalk, transparencies, electrical tape)
- Setup labor

✔ **800 Transportation/shuttle service**
- VIP pickups
- Car rentals
- Tours

✔ **900 Hospitality/attendee**
- Meet and greet (airport)
- Welcome hospitality suite

Example of Budget Layout With Explanation

ACCOMMODATIONS		$15,960
Accommodations	$15,960	
(based on 50 attendees × 3 nights @ $95.00 per night single occupancy + 12% lodging tax)		
FOOD AND BEVERAGES		$15,428
Breakfast	$1,452	
(based on 50 attendees × 3 breakfast @ $8 per person per day + 21% tax & gratuity)		
Lunch	$2,723	
(based on 50 attendees × 3 lunches @ $15 per person per day + 21% tax & gratuity)		
Dinner	$9,075	
(based on 50 attendees × 3 dinners @ $50 per person per day + 21% tax & gratuity)		
Breaks	$2,178	
(based on 50 attendees × 2 breaks per day × 3 days @ $6 per person per day + 21% tax & gratuity)		
ROUND TRIP AIRPORT TRANSFERS		$1,160
Bus transportation	$800	
(based on group arrival/departure utilizing 2–30 passenger vehicles @ $200 each × 2 trips each)		
Airport signs	$50	
(based on 2 signs @ $25 each)		
Tips/gratuities	$310	
(based on 20% for bus drivers; and 50 attendees @ $1.50 per bag × 1 bag per person × 2 baggage handlings)		

Example of Final Accounting With Comparisons

List all items appearing in your budget (see Budget Items appearing in this Quick Reference Guide section) and carry out procedure outlined below.

	Budgeted	Actual	Over/Under	Percentage of Total
INCOME				
Paid Registrations				
Member 86 @ $175	$15,050.00	$14,700.00	($350.00)	54%
Nonmember 6 @ $250	1,500.00	1,750.00	+250.00	6
Public officials 8 @ $250	2,000.00	2,000.00		7
Industry 13 @ $500	6,500.00	6,500.00		24
Ticket sales	150.00	125.00	(25.00)	0
Contributions	2,000.00	2,400.00	+400.00	9
Total income	$27,200.00	$27,475.00	+$275.00	
EXPENSES				
Promotion				
Brochure preparation/printing	$ 2,250.00	$ 2,400.00	$ (150.00)	
Postage				
Brochure 1500 @ $.22	330.00	330.00	0.00	
Letter 400 @ $.22	88.00	88.00	0.00	
Miscellaneous	100.00	80.00	+20.00	
Press	20.00	20.00	0.00	
Total promotion expense	$ 2,788.00	$ 2,918.00	$ (130.00)	

Cost Categories for Break-Even Budgeting

✔ **Fixed costs**
Fixed costs are expenses that do not vary with the number of attendees, such as:
- Meeting room rental
- Speaker/staff travel and expenses
- Printing of promotional materials
- Equipment rental

✔ **Variable costs**
Variable costs are expenses that vary based on the number of attendees, such as:
- Food and beverage events
- Transportation
- Personnel
- Printing of attendee materials

Break-Even Budgeting

To find total costs:

$$FC + VC = TC$$

$$\frac{TC}{\text{number of attendants}} = \text{BE Fee}$$

To find breakeven number of attendants with set fee:

$$\text{Fee} - VC = \text{Contribution}$$

$$\frac{TC}{\text{Contribution}} = \text{BE number of attendants}$$

Definition of Terms

Breakeven point (BE or BEP):	Point where money is neither gained nor lost
Fee:	Dollar amount paid by each attendee
Total costs (TC):	All costs incurred, including those appearing as fixed and/or variable costs
Fixed costs (FC):	Costs that do not vary regardless of the number of attendees
Variable costs (VC):	Costs that vary in direct proportion to number of attendees
Per-person costs:	Dollar amount spent on each attendee
Administrative overhead:	Percentage of total expenses to be charged for the meeting
Profit:	Financial gain resulting from meeting
Loss:	Financial loss resulting from meeting

Any complimentary (fee-waived) attendees (guest speakers, VIPs, staff, others) who will not pay a registration fee must still be included in computing costs and/or expenses.

Cost-Saving ideas

Provide exact expense reimbursement guidelines to speakers and staff.
Limit the number of people authorized to sign master bill.
Watch for hidden costs, such as:

- *Labor surcharges*
- *Union requirements*
- *Tablecloths/linens*
- *Decorations*
- *Schoolroom setups*
- *Pads and pencils*
- *Easels*

Be flexible about dates; off-peak rates are less than those during the high season.

Guide 15
Math for Meeting Planners

Math Considerations

Detailed explanations for many of these are found in Chapter 15 and other chapters specifically related to their applications.

- ✔ **Percentages**

- ✔ **Measurements**

- ✔ **Interest rates**

- ✔ **Fractions**

- ✔ **Averages, medians, modes**

- ✔ **Breakeven analysis**

- ✔ **Metric conversions**

Break-Even Budgeting

- ✔ **Hotel Pickup:**

Example:

  Your room block is for 200 rooms.
  Room rate is $100 per room.

Hotel requires 75% occupancy to qualify for complimentary meeting room.
Meeting room rental is $500.
Your actual room pickup is 148 rooms.

Should you pay for the additional sleeping rooms to meet the 75% requirement occupancy or the meeting room rental rate?

$$200 \text{ rooms} \times .75 = 150 \text{ rooms}$$

$$150 \text{ rooms} \times \$100 = \$15,000$$

$$148 \text{ rooms} \times \$100 = \$14,800$$

$15,000 - 14,800 = $200 out of pocket to meet the 75% occupancy requirement.

(meeting-room rent)	$500
Unoccupied rooms	-200
Savings	$300

Dividend: Use these two rooms for staff or hospitality purposes.

✔ Simple Interest Rates:

> **Example:**

You have purchased a six-month certificate of deposit for $4,000 at 10% per annum yield.

How much money will your certificate earn?

$$\$4,000 \times .10 = \$400 \text{ per annum}$$

$$\frac{\$400}{2} = \$200 \text{ earned in one-half year}$$

$$\frac{\$200}{6} = \$33.333333 \text{ earned per month}$$

✔ Compound Interest:

Compound interest rates involve fluctuating amounts. If you are investing or borrowing monies that involve compound interest, ask your bank to furnish you with the compound interest table for the percentage interest involved.

✔ Determining a Gratuity:

> **Example:**

Ten people attend a luncheon, the cost of which is $10 per person. You want to tip 15%.

What is the total amount you should pay?

$$10 \times \$10.00 = \$100.00$$

$$\$100 \times .15 = \$15.00$$

$$\$100 + \$15 = \$115.00 \text{ including tip}$$

✔ Finding the percentage:

| Example: |

Total budget is $15,000.
Food costs were $3,000.

What percentage of the budget was spent on food?

$$\frac{\$3,000}{\$15,000} \ (3000 \div 15,000) = .20$$

Move decimal two points to the right: 20%

✔ Finding percentage increase:

| Example: |

Total previous year's income was $50,000.
Total current year's income was $60,000.

What was the percentage of increase?

$$\begin{array}{r} \$60,000 \\ -\ 50,000 \\ \hline \$10,000 \end{array}$$

$$\frac{\$10,000}{\$50,000} \ (\$10,000 \div \$50,000) = .20$$

Move decimal two points to right: 20%

✔ Finding Percentage Decrease:

| Example: |

Total previous year's income was $50,000.
Total current year's income was $45,000.

What was the percentage of decrease?

$$\begin{array}{r} \$50,000 \\ -\ 45,000 \\ \hline \$\ 5,000 \end{array}$$

$$\frac{\$5,000}{\$45,000} \ (5,000 \div 45,000) = .10$$

Move decimal two points to right: 10%

⌁ **Translating fractions to decimal amounts:**

How many ⅞-ounce drinks will one quart yield?

One quart = 32 ounces
One drink = ⅞ ounce

The decimal equivalent of ⅞ (⅞ or 7 ÷ 8) is .875.

$$\frac{32}{.875} \ (32 \div .875) = 36.57 \text{ drinks per quart}$$

Metric System

Although for centuries the United Kingdom (Great Britain) resisted acceptance of the metric system, now the United States is the only major nation that has not adopted it as its official measurement system.

Measurement	United States	Metric Equivalent
Length	Inch	2.54 centimeters
	Foot	.305 meters
	Yard	.914 meters
	Mile	1.609 kilometers
Area	Square inch	6.45 sq. centimeters
	Square foot	.093 sq. meters
	Square yard	.836 sq. meters
	Square mile	2.59 sq. kilometers
	Acre	.405 hectares
Volume	Cubic inch	16,387 cu. centimeters
	Cubic foot	.028 cu. meters
	Cubic yard	.764 cu. meters
Capacity	Liquid ounce	.029 liters
	Liquid pint	.473 liters
	Dry pint	.55 liters
	Liquid quart	.946 liters
	Dry quart	1.101 liters
	Gallon	3.785 liters
Weight	Troy ounce	31.103 grams
	Pound	.454 kilograms
	Ton (200 lb.)	907.18 kilograms
Temperature	1° fahrenheit	.555° centigrade
	1.8° fahrenheit	1° centigrade

Room Measurement Diagrams

To find a *perimeter*:

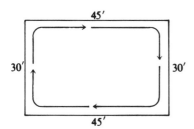

$$45' + 30' + 45' + 30' = 100 \text{ ft.}$$

To find an *area*:

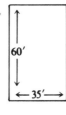

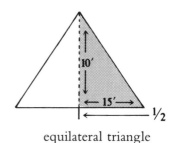

square   rectangle   equilateral triangle

$30' \times 30' = 900$ sq. ft. $60' \times 35' = 2,100$ sq. ft. $10' \times 15' = 150$ sq. ft.

Odd-Shaped Rooms

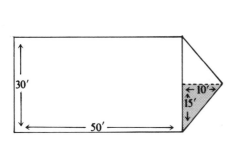

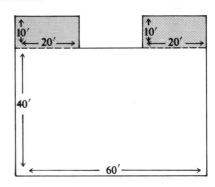

$50' \times 30' = 1,500$ sq. ft.
$15' \times 10' = \underline{150}$ sq. ft.
$\overline{1,650}$ sq. ft.

$60' \times 40' = 2,400$ sq. ft.
$20' \times 10' = 200$ sq. ft.
$20' \times 10' = \underline{200}$ sq. ft.
$\overline{2,800}$ sq. ft.

Guide 16
Liability and Insurance

Insurance

Be sure to discuss these insurance coverages with your insurance department, broker, or agent. Some types of coverage may depend on where the meeting is taking place. Ask which policies are required to meet your needs. Require suppliers to carry certain limits. For example:

Automobile (bodily injury): $500,000/person, $1 million/accident
Property: $250,000 or $1 million single limit

✔ **Comprehensive general liability insurance policy**
- Contractual liability
- Host/liquor liability
- Independent contractors liability
- Products liability pertaining to food service
- False arrest
- Wrong eviction
- Slander/libel
- Accidents

✔ **Automobile Insurance:**
- Protects against accidents involving an owned, leased, or hired automobile.

✔ **Workers' compensation:**
- Protects employees injured on the job.
- Pays for medical expenses and loss of income.
- Required in most states.

✔ **Errors and omissions:**
- Covers clients' financial loss resulting from errors, omissions, or negligence on the part of the meeting planner or planner's employees.

✔ **Property, real and personal:**
  - Covers loss or damage of property.
  - The policy should be written as "all risk" and include off-premises and in-transit coverage.

✔ **Crime coverage ("bonding"):**
  - Insures against losses from theft of securities, property, or money.
  - It should cover theft by employees of organization's (or planner's) funds, client funds, and any other funds for which the organization is responsible.

✔ **Cancellation/interruption:**
  - Covers loss of income resulting from cancellation or interruption of a meeting.

✔ **Medical payment insurance**

✔ **Accidental death and dismemberment**

✔ **Incidental medical malpractice**

✔ **Valuable papers and records**

✔ **Office contents (all risks of loss or damage)**

✔ **Entertainer's failure to appear**

✔ **Directors and officers liability**

Liability

Professional Considerations

A professional meeting manager is *expected* to recognize potential risk and take action to eliminate and reduce and/or inform participants of any risk, and could be held liable if such action were not taken. When a part-time or one-time, inexperienced meeting planner is acting on behalf of someone else, the latter assumes responsibility.

Many elements of the meeting require attention to potential risks. For example:

✔ **Site selection:**
  - Attendee safety and security (e.g., proper lighting, peephole in guest room door, location of facility)
  - Facility staff trained in emergency procedures (e.g., CPR)
  - Facility abides by laws and ordinances pertaining to sanitation, fire safety
  - Facility is properly insured (*see also* Guide 4)

✔ **Activities/sports/recreation:**
  • Proper grounds, safe equipment, appropriate supervision
  • Food service including alcoholic beverages
  • Weather factors
  • First aid, emergency procedures
  • Permits, licenses
  • Medical certification permitting participants to participate

✔ **Transportation:**
  • Air carrier safety record
  • Ground transportation (e.g., vehicle safety, licensed drivers)
  • Boating
  • Provider insurance properly in force
  • Proper licenses to engage in business

✔ **Other:**
  • Shipping company (past performance, problem procedures)
  • Audiovisual producer, experienced in the meetings area
  • Vendor insurance properly in force
  • Proper license to engage in business you are hiring for

Breach of Contract

Contracts should be carefully written and be as specific as possible. (*See* Chapter 5, "Agreements and Contracts.")

✔ **Facility Contract**

✔ **Cancellation clause**

✔ **Overbooking procedures**

✔ **Indemnification clause**

✔ **Renegotiation clause**

✔ **Signatural concerns (authority to sign on behalf of company/organization)**

✔ **Arbitration clause or procedures for dispute resolution**

Noncompliance with Laws and Ordinances

✔ **Health, sanitation**

✔ **Fire, electrical codes**

✓ **Liquor laws**

✓ **Copyright law, especially pertaining to reproducing presentations on tape and distributing written materials without written permission**

✓ **Workers' compensation**

✓ **Proper license to engage in business you are hiring for**

Reducing Risks

You may want to consult with an attorney with regard to the following suggestions.

✓ **Evaluate levels of safety and security during site inspections.**

✓ **Review safety records of airlines and bus companies.**

✓ **Evaluate injury possibility when planning for sports-related and competitive activities.**

✓ **Require waivers/releases from participants in potentially dangerous activities.**

✓ **Use facility staff to serve alcoholic beverages, and limit availability to prevent excessive consumption.**

✓ **Inform all attendees and staff of fire exits at the beginning of each event or session.**

✓ **Instruct staff and volunteers on procedure to follow in case of injury.**

✓ **Request that a "hold harmless" clause (protecting your organization) be contained or added to contracts with meeting facility.**

✓ **Have contracts approved by your legal counsel.**

✓ **Include "disclaimer" statement in all promotional packets (a statement of nonresponsibility for acts of God, strikes, floods, earthquakes, wars).**

✓ **Send copies of all important documents to your boss/client/ sponsoring organization's director.**

✔ **Verify in writing all authorized signatures.**

✔ **Prepare accident/"incident" reports on such occasions.**

✔ **Inform/instruct attendees about the limits of your responsibility regarding their personal property and encourage them to use the facility's safe.**

✔ **State NOT RESPONSIBLE FOR PERSONAL PROPERTY in appropriate places.**

✔ **Instruct staff and volunteers about procedures in case of injury.**

Cost-Saving Ideas

Buy additional insurance at the time you are buying your insurance.

Review existing policies with your broker to learn if endorsements can be added to policies you already hold instead of purchasing new coverage.

Investigate possibilities for obtaining specific types of on-site coverage, such as loss due to fire or theft, by being named as an "extra insuree" on policies held by meeting facility, bus companies, and other purveyors.

Review coverage with care to make sure limits of liability are sufficient.

Request certificates of insurance from contractors/exhibitors before signing contracts.

Ask to be named as additional insured on contractors/exhibitors policies.

Guide 17
People Management

Knowing Your People

"People" basically fall into three categories:

- ✓ **Internal staff, elected officers, committee members**
- ✓ **Volunteers**
- ✓ **Outside suppliers/professional consultants**

Chain of Command

- ✓ **Board of directors**
- ✓ **Chief executive officer**
- ✓ **Executive vice-president(s)**
- ✓ **Section heads**
- ✓ **Department heads**
- ✓ **Supervisors**
- ✓ **Staff with special responsibility/expertise**

Management Responsibilities

✔ **Legal responsibility (e.g., in signing contracts)**

✔ **Decision-making authority (e.g., in site selection)**

✔ **Responsibility for assigning staff**

Guidelines for Managing Volunteers

✔ **Identify and assess volunteers' skills and expertise.**

✔ **Determine amount of time volunteers can give.**

✔ **Assign tasks and responsibilities.**

✔ **Provide written job descriptions, instructions, and work schedules.**

Recognition to Volunteers

- Complimentary registration
- Ribbons for badges
- Program book acknowledgements
- Awards or certificates of appreciation
- Thank-you letters

Questions to Consider When Working With Volunteers

✔ **Who will recruit the volunteers?**
- The host organization
- The meeting planner
- The local committee

✔ **Where do you find volunteers?**
- Local organizations
- Friends of the organization (or friends of friends)
- Client generated (spouses, supporters, related interest groups)
- Students from local colleges, intern programs
- Other

✔ **What jobs can you safely assign to volunteers?**
- Greeters
- Runners
- Staff office (answer phone, take and post messages)

- Message Center (take messages for delivery *only to you or person assigned by you*)
- City Information Desk (make certain they really do know the city)
- Other (only in providing specific information on topics *you select*)

✔ **What jobs can you never assign to volunteers?**
- Anything that involves decision making or follow-up by volunteer.

✔ **How can you help volunteers to be effective?**
- Provide all volunteers with a thorough, comprehensive briefing.
- Give them *written* materials on:
  —Dress code while on duty
  —Job descriptions for each duty to be performed, including what they are not permitted to do
  —Days and times they are to report for duty
  —Location of area to which they are assigned
  —Name/title of individual to whom they will report for duty

✔ **How can meeting planners protect themselves against consequences of using volunteers?**
- Recognize that all legal liability arising from the use of volunteers rests with your organization.
- Ask your insurance broker if your liability insurance will cover actions or omissions of volunteers. Will it cover the consequences of misinformation given?
- Be as comprehensive in preparing written job descriptions for volunteers as you would be for paid employees.
- During the briefing session, allow ample time for questions and answers. This may be your only opportunity to assess them before they report for actual duty.
- Don't assume that they possess the knowledge to do the job assigned to them.
- Try to tie the personal aptitudes of the individual to the work to be assigned. For example, senior citizens make wonderful greeters; students make great runners.
- Consider all of the time and money costs involved in using them.
- Assign them only to "harmless" (to you) jobs.
- Never use them for duties that could result in injury or jeopardize your professional liability.

Types of Committees and Responsibilities

✔ **Finance and budget committee tasks:**
- Prepare overall meeting budget.
- Present budget for approval.
- Determine registration fee per person, per category, per event.
- Recommend payment, receipt policies, and procedures.

- Determine cancellation/refund policy.
- Determine expense approval procedures.

✔ Site committee tasks:
- Determine city for meeting and geographical rotation schedule if appropriate.
- Determine facility type required.
- Conduct site-inspection visit.
- Review and recommend final contract.
- Evaluate past attendance history and project growth for facility space requirements.
- Prepare budget for facility-related cost.

✔ Marketing/public relations committee tasks:
- Develop overall marketing plan.
- Recommend conference theme, graphics, brochure copy.
- Identify new attendee markets.
- Recommend news release and advertising placement.
- Support press activities on site.
- Prepare attendee surveys and meeting evaluations.
- Prepare budget for all marketing and public relations-related costs.

✔ Program committee tasks:
- Research topics and speakers appropriate for group.
- Prepare preliminary program agenda (times, format).
- Recommend/invite moderators/introducers.
- Host speaker/VIP hospitality.
- Recommend program design and schedule.
- Recommend procedures for contacting and handling speakers.
- Work with the groups/committees responsible for entertainment and guest activities.
- Prepare budget for all program-related costs.

✔ Entertainment committee tasks:
- Recommend and coordinate entertainment activities.
- Review contracts.
- Prepare budget figures.

✔ Exhibits/product display committee tasks:
- Recommend policies/procedures.
- Target market(s).
- Review supplier contracts.
- Recommend revenue/expenditure figures.

✔ Registration committee tasks:
- Recommend registration policies/procedures/fees/categories.
- Prepare revenue/expenditure figures.

✔ **Welcome and hospitality committee tasks:**
  • Evaluate attendee needs.
  • Recommend services.
  • Prepare budget figures.
  • Act as host to attendees on site.

✔ **Guest/spouse activities committee tasks:**
  • Recommend tours/programs/special activities for guests.
  • Prepare budget figures.

✔ **Special events committee tasks:**
  • Research local or theme events.
  • Conduct pre- and postconference trips.
  • Coordinate with other related committees.
  • Prepare budget figures.

Types of Outside Suppliers

✔ **Facility employees**

✔ **Graphic designer and printer**

✔ **Audiovisual producer**

✔ **Airline representative**

✔ **Ground transportation company**

✔ **Entertainment producer**

✔ **Decorator**

✔ **Convention and visitors bureau**

✔ **Travel agent**

✔ **Badge makers**

✔ **Drayage/shipping**

✔ **Sign printer**

✔ **Supplier of binders, gifts, awards**

✔ **Florist**

✔ **Security company**

Supplier Communications

Types of Communications

- Request for proposal (RFP)/specifications
- Contracts/letters of agreement
- Pre-/postplanning meeting
- Reports
- Detailed instructions
- Policy guidelines/procedures
- Work schedules
- Day-to-day memorandums/confirming letters/telephone conversation notes

Guidelines for Communicating With Suppliers

✔ **Outline in writing all needs in request for bid from suppliers (RFP or Prospectus), including reference checks (financial and from past clients).**

✔ **Prepare a written agreement outlining all needs, policies, costs, deadlines (supplier contract).**

✔ **Maintain frequent telephone meeting and follow-up with a written memo on content of call, decisions made, and changes agreed to.**

✔ **Log all calls made to suppliers, number of times called, date and time calls are returned, and with whom messages are left or name of person spoken to.**

✔ **Copy suppliers on key attendee materials and on internal memos related to responsibilities.**

✔ **Respond quickly to calls from suppliers.**

✔ **Provide regular "updates" on key attendee information such as number registered (e.g., attendees, exhibitors), major arrival/departure dates/times, and VIP attendees.**

✔ **Have suppliers sign an agreement to adhere to policies and procedures established after the contract is signed, with penalties for violations.**

✔ **Require supplier to provide proof of insurance, certificate of insurance, or additional insured proof; you should provide this if liability is accepted by your organization.**

✔ **Obtain copies of related health, safety, and other permits and licenses of certificates.**

✔ **Conduct preconvention meetings to review all requirements, organizational policies and procedures, and the on-site schedule to check areas such as staffing levels, equipment quality, general technical preparedness, emergency procedures, and supervisor availability.**

✔ **Conduct supplier evaluation and postreview meeting.**

✔ **Receive supplier reports if necessary for your reporting or data collection records.**

✔ **Prepare follow-up letters to company and exceptional individuals as thank-you letters for reference files, evaluation of strengths/weaknesses, and/or to resolve questions/disputes and adjustments regarding billing/payments.**

✔ **Close file when final payment is made, but keep records for future reference.**

Guide 18

On-Site Management

Preparing the Meeting Specification

The preparation of the detailed requirements is the first step in minimizing problems. Written instructions, room setup diagrams, event schedules and specifications are compiled into a master staging guide. Review these four sections when preparing your staging guide.

✔ **General information:**
This section is a summary of information about your group, staff, and event. It is appropriate to recap important aspects of your agreement in this section. Include such items as:
- Profile of the group
- Staff and responsibility areas
- Guest-room block and rates
- Master account billing instructions
- Authorized signatures
- Authorized charges
- VIP, staff, and complimentary accommodations
- Negotiated agreements, such as complimentary units

✔ **Special instructions:**
This section provides detailed instructions to each department in the hotel, specifying your expectations and needs. Include such items as:
- Procedures for review and signing of function bills
- Advance inspection of function-room setups
- Receipt and delivery of shipments and equipment
- Paid-out amounts
- Flower-holding areas
- Fire evacuation procedures
- Names and hours of personnel on duty
- Hotel reports required
- Requirements for handicapped attendees

✔ **Meeting purveyors:**
This section provides the name, contact name, address, and phone number of each supplier of a product or service to your meeting. Obtain information for each of the following, if applicable:
- Audiovisual
- Security
- Decorator
- Equipment
- Office machines
- Special theme events
- Photographer
- Entertainment
- Secretarial service
- Florist
- Personnel
- Convention bureau
- Hotel(s)
- Audiotaping
- Official airline
- Official car rental
- Telephone company
- Copying/quick print company
- Bus company

✔ **Detailed event requirements:**
This section outlines each of your function requirements by date, time, and room assignment. Include such areas as:
- Room setup requirements and diagrams
- Food/beverage selection, quantity, price, serving time
- Signs
- Audiovisual equipment and personnel
- Personnel schedule
- Delivery/pickup schedule
- Room setup diagrams
- Guarantees
- Flowers

The On-Site Process

Before Meeting

✔ **Arrive two to four days before meeting is scheduled to begin.**

✔ **Check arrival of shipments, and arrange for delivery to appropriate location.**

✔ **Follow up on equipment deliveries per date delivery due and per each area (e.g., staff office, registration, exhibit area, press room).**

✔ **Begin to set up staff office.**

✔ **Conduct preconvention meeting.**

✔ **Provide updates on counts and guarantees to hotel or outside caterers.**

✔ **Conduct other individual supplier meetings.**

✔ **Conduct separate in-hotel meetings with each department that will have unique responsibilities for your meeting:**
  - Front desk
  - Accounting
  - PBX operators
  - Security
  - Electrician
  - Bell staff
  - Other

✔ **Conduct personnel briefing for registration, staff office, door monitors, airport greeters, and any other personnel for your meeting, whether paid or volunteer.**

✔ **Set up registration area and oversee setup of other areas (e.g., exhibit hall, general session area).**

✔ **Distribute notes and gifts to front desk and PBX operators.**

✔ **Coordinate distribution of gifts/amenities to attendees' rooms.**

✔ **Do an advance check on hotel for cleanliness and correct functioning of elevators, restrooms, and other public facilities.**

✔ **Handle advance room check-in of VIPs and key organization officials.**

✔ **Walk around area surrounding hotel to locate emergency resources (quick copy and secretarial services, office supplies, florists).**

During Meeting

✔ **Check hotel reader board daily for accuracy.**

✔ **Conduct daily review meeting with key hotel staff.**

✔ **Check each meeting room for accurate setup by hotel and all other suppliers 30 to 60 minutes prior to your function; much more time should be allotted before a major session.**

✔ **Check all food-and-beverage areas for readiness and accuracy 30 to 60 minutes prior to your function; much more time should be allotted before a special event.**

✔ Remove cash from safety deposit box, and set up cash boxes for each registration worker.

✔ As large amounts of registration income are received, balance cash against registration records, and place in safety deposit box or local bank account.

✔ Conduct personnel check-in to make sure that all have arrived and are at assigned areas.

✔ Provide personnel with items needed for daily activities, such as function sheets and evaluations to door monitors.

✔ Place signs in proper positions.

✔ Place awards, gavels, and any other items in appropriate rooms.

✔ Check to be sure that all speakers have arrived and are in or moving to their appropriate sessions.

✔ Conduct counts of attendees in meeting rooms on a regular basis, and record counts on Function Attendance Summary.

✔ Check smooth functioning of each area on a regular basis.

✔ Pick up messages regularly from staff office, and maintain other regular communications with suppliers and personnel (pager numbers, beepers, and walkie-talkies are helpful).

✔ Set aside a time to review charges from hotel and suppliers, and record information on your Summary Sheet after approval and/ or adjustments.

✔ Pick up from the front desk the daily hotel printout of guest rooms used by your group.

After Meeting

✔ Have all cash transferred to your organization's at-home bank account, or request a cashiers' check for safe transport home.

✔ Prepare thank-you notes for hotel staff and suppliers, and distribute individual gratuities.

✔ Conduct postconference meeting with key hotel staff and suppliers.

✔ Pack all conference materials and equipment for return shipment home, and arrange for shipping.

✔ Inventory all equipment rented locally, and supervise pickup.

✔ Review final bill with accounting, and pay required payments on noncontested portion of bill.

Gratuity Guidelines

Unless part of the contractual agreement, tipping is never required. However, 1– to 2% of the total hotel bill may be budgeted in excess of the following recommended amounts for gratuities, to be distributed among those individuals who have contributed above-standard services to your event.

Recipient	Amount of Tip	Given By	When Given
Doorman	$1–$2	Individual	Time of service
Bell staff	50¢–$1 per bag	Individual	Time of service
House personnel	$3–$5 per day, per worker	Organization	End of stay
Waitpersons, captains, wine stewards	15–17% of food-and-beverage charges, usually before tax	Organization	Time of service
Cleaning staff	$1–$2 per night	Individual	Daily if change in personnel, or at end of stay
Guides	Maximum of $1 per person	Organization	Time of service
Bus drivers	$5 for 10 minutes of luggage handling only	Organization	Time of service
Limousine drivers	Minimum of $5	Individual or organization	Time of service
Sales/upper management	Gift or gift certificate	Organization	End of stay
Front desk	Gift or shared item such as candy	Organization	End of stay
Convention service coordinator	Gift or gift certificate	Organization	End of stay
Switchboard operators	Gift or shared item such as candy	Organization	End of stay

Previously published as "Tipping: An Expected or Earned Reward," in *Convention World*, A Bayard Publication, January/February 1987.

Helpful Hints

Ask hotel sales or convention services staff to provide a written breakdown on automatic gratuities and how they are distributed—e.g., to waiters, captains, maitre d', catering director.

Request a signed receipt for distribution of special cash gratuities.

Prepare thank-you notes on organization's letterhead or note cards. (These can be prepared ahead of time.)

18-1 | Facility Personnel

Information from this form is compiled onto master form, Exhibit 18-3.

Facility: _____

_____

_____

_____ ZIP: _____

( ) _____ EXT: _____

Personnel/Departments	Name	Pager Number	Phone Number
*Audiovisual			
Bell captain			
*Convention services manager			
Credit manager			
Electrician			
Food-and-beverage services			
Banquets			
Bar			
Catering			
Chef			
Dining room			
Restaurant manager			
Room-service manager			
*Front-office manager			
General manager			
Assistant general manager			
Housekeeping			
Executive housekeeper			
Head houseman			
Head cashier			
Head doorman			
Laundry/valet			
Maintenance			
Night manager on duty			
Receiving dock/packaging room			
Reservations manager			
*Sales director/manager			
Security chief			
Service superintendent			
Switchboard head operator			

* Also recommend getting home numbers.

| 18-2 | **Function Attendance Form** |

This form is to be completed by meeting planner, door monitor, or other personnel assigned to this responsibility. Information from this form is compiled onto master form, Exhibit 18-3.

Group name: _____

Meeting: _____

Meeting dates: _____ , 19 ____ to _____ , 19 ____

Hotel: _____ City: _____ State: _____

DOOR MONITORS: Please fill this form out accurately, as the information is used for our historical data collection. If you have any questions, please address them to the Conference Coordinator before you go on duty.

Today's date: _____ , 19 ____ Session time: _____

Room name: _____

Type of function:

☐ Luncheon   ☐ Workshop   ☐ Banquet

Time data collected: _____ Number of chairs in room: _____

Number of empty chairs in room: _____ Number of people in function room: _____ If tickets, number collected: _____

Comments: _____

_____

_____

_____

Date collected by: _____

18-3 | Function Attendance Summary Form

Group Name: _____ Meeting: _____

Location: _____ City: _____ State: _____

Meeting Dates: _____ Person Preparing Report: _____

Today's Date: _____

Date	Time	Location	Function	# Set	# Tickets	# in Room	Empty Chairs	Notes

18-4 | Hotel Reservations Pickup Report

Group name: _____

Meeting: _____   Meeting dates: _____

Day of first mailing: _____   Hotel: _____

City: _____   State: _____   Hotel cutoff date: _____

Hotel guest room rates: Single: _____ Double: _____ Suites: _____

Tax _____%   Gratuities _____%

Complimentary policy: _____

Group		RESERVATIONS TO BE FILLED IN ON DATES LISTED BELOW							On-Site		
Date	Block	Week 1	Week 2	Week 3	Week 4	Week 5	Week 6	Final	Walk-In	No-Show	Actual

Comments: _____
_____
_____
_____

Guide 19
Exhibits

Questions to Ask Before Deciding Whether to Have Exhibit

- ✔ Will an exhibit fit in with or enhance the meeting program?

- ✔ Will additional revenues be raised by offering an exhibit?

- ✔ Will attendance be sufficient to attract exhibitors?

- ✔ Can your organization attract enough exhibitors to make it worthwhile for attendees?

- ✔ Will an exhibit promote attendance at your meetings?

- ✔ Can enough income from an exhibit be generated to offset expenses and operate it at a profit?

Budgeting for Exhibits

Determine the revenue and expense generated that would not otherwise appear in your budget.

- ✔ **Exhibit income:**
  - Exhibitor registration fees
  - Sponsorships

- Booth rental
- Program book advertising sales
- Nonrefundable administrative fees/deposits
- Other

✔ **Exhibit expenses:**
  - Exhibit hall rental
  - Booth costs
  - Decorations (not included by decorator)
  - Registration materials
  - Promotion
  - Printing
  - Mailings/postage
  - Equipment
  - Electrical hookups/installations
  - Utilities
  - Labor (list by category)
  - Security
  - Shipping/delivery
  - Shuttle buses (if exhibit is held off site)
  - Insurance
  - Other

See also Guide 14.

Site Selection for Exhibits

Trade show/exhibition space is available in hotels and convention centers/exhibit halls. Unless otherwise stated, the following site selection criteria apply to both.

✔ **Proximity of exhibits to other meeting rooms.**

✔ **Width of hallways.**

✔ **Number of elevators and capacity.**

✔ **Escalators: Can directions be changed to provide for mass transit in either direction?**

✔ **Ceiling height of at least 35 feet. High ceilings provide better air flow and appear more spacious.**

✔ **Lighting that is ample throughout hall. Avoid having to assign a dim corner to any exhibitor.**

✔ **Floor load: Should be able to accommodate any needs regarding heavy equipment.**

✔ **Floor finish: Should be able to accommodate your needs regarding movement of heavy equipment during setup/tear-down.**

✔ **Efficient access for decorators and exhibitors: Includes freight elevators, receiving dock, and ramps for unloading and loading. This also affects scheduling of setup and tear-down time. There should be convenient truck access to dock(s).**

✔ **Availability and placement of sources for electricity, gas, water, and drains in relation to exhibit booths.**

✔ **Security: You should be able to close off areas such as service corridors, and control all access on a 24-hour basis.**

✔ **Union regulations.**

✔ **Storage availability.**

✔ **Facility's regulations.**

✔ **Rates: Determine inclusions and exclusions.**

Formula for Determining Minimum Exhibit Space

Multiply number of booths by square footage per booth, and multiply answer by 1.5.

Example:

10 booths × 8′ × 10′	= 800 sq. ft.
10 booths × 10′ × 10′	= 1,000 sq. ft.
(800 sq. ft. + 1,000 sq. ft.	= 1,800 sq. ft.)
1,800 × 1.5	= 2,700 sq. ft. (minimum required)

Marketing to Exhibitors

✔ **Identify exhibitors:**
  • List the kinds of services or products used by most of your prospective attendees. Identify by:
    —Manufacturers
    —Suppliers
    —Products
    —Services
    —Other

- Obtain a list of key suppliers.
- Add key suppliers who have exhibited at previous meetings you have attended or sponsored.

✔ **Prepare timetable for mailing to exhibitors.**

Suggested Timetable	
Prospectus:	6–9 months prior
Booth assignment and other confirming details (from sponsor):	2–3 months prior
Schedule:	Immediately following booth
Program book listings:	assignments confirmation
Registration:	" "
Housing:	" "
Service kit from decorator:	" "
Follow-up:	As needed

Identifying Exhibitors

✔ **List the kinds of services or products used by most of your prospective attendees. Identify by:**
- Manufacturers
- Suppliers
- Products
- Services
- Other

✔ **Obtain a list of potential exhibitors.**

✔ **Add key exhibitors who have exhibited at previous meetings you have attended or sponsored.**

Preparing the Exhibit Prospectus

Formats vary, ranging from one printed page to multipage bound copies. Contents must include the following:

✔ **A short descriptive statement, identifying:**
- Organization profile
  - —Purpose
  - —Scope (national, state, other)
  - —Date established
  - —Membership total
- Membership profile by category and number
  - —Professional members
  - —Corporate members
  - —Student members
  - —Other
- Exhibit attendance history by number
  - —Membership category
  - —Number per category
  - —Buying influence/authority
  - —Income levels

✔ **Outline of meeting schedule of events (emphasizing exhibition hours and support activities)**

✔ **Exhibit information:**
- Exhibit manager's name, address, and telephone number
- Exhibit theme
  - —Colors
  - —Decorations
- Limitations
  - —Types of products/services of interest to, or used by, attendees
  - —Any limitations for display of products or services
- Dates and location(s)
  - —Exhibit hall name/rooms
  - —Dates and hours (meeting and show)
- Move-in times
  - —Date and hours
  - —Completion deadline, date, and hour
- Move-out times
  - —Date and hours
  - —Deadline

✔ **Booth information:**
- Method of assignment
  - —First-come, first-served
  - —Point system
  - —Other
- Dates
  - —Deadline for application
  - —Booth assignment date
  - —Assignment confirmation
- Standard sizes
  - —8' × 10' (include cost)
  - —10' × 10' (include cost)

- Booth layout
  —Exhibit hall diagram
- Booth description, such as:
  —One 8′ × 10′ booth with 36″-high side dividers
  —One 8″ × 44″ identification sign
  —One 6′ skirted table
  —Two chairs
  —One wastebasket
  —Complementary registrations (give number)
  —Other
- Statement of nonrefundable policy

✔ **Exhibitor registration:**
- Advance registration deadline
- On-site registration
  —Dates
  —Hours
  —Location

✔ **Exhibitor housing information:**
- Hotel name, address, phone
- Mailing date for reservation application forms
- Guest room and hospitality suite information

✔ **Contract:**
- Exhibitors' application and agreement form

✔ **Decorator (exhibit services contractor):**
- Name, address, phone
- Types of services rendered
- Mailing date for Exhibitor Kit

✔ **Program book advertising (stating where advertisements will appear):**
- Advertising space available
  —Full page (include cost)
  —Half-page (include cost)
  —Quarter-page (include cost)
- Copy deadline

✔ **Sponsorship opportunities**

Exhibit Rules and Regulations

Rules and regulations may be included in the prospectus or in a separate mailing with the contract.

✔ **Booth display specifications:**
  - Appearance
  - Maximum heights
  - Draping
  - Signs
  - Booth numbers
  - Other

✔ **Labor:**
  - Costs
  - Types
  - Other

✔ **Delivery and removal allowances and restrictions**

✔ **Storage arrangements**

✔ **Exhibitor personnel:**
  - Booth staffing limit
  - Conduct
  - Canvassing
  - Sales demonstrations
  - On-site sales
  - Other

✔ **Food-and-beverage allowances and restrictions**

✔ **Unoccupied space penalties**

✔ **Subleasing of booth space**

✔ **Deposits:**
  - Amounts
  - Deadlines

✔ **Final payment deadline**

✔ **Insurance requirements**

✔ **Cancellation/refund policy**

✔ **Organization's insurance disclaimer for liability**

Exhibitor's Kit

Decorator sends kits directly to all exhibitors once the names are provided by the meeting planner or show manager. Kits usually include the following:

✔ **Name of exhibit manager, address, phone number**

✔ **Exhibit hall rules, regulations, and policies**

✔ **Shipping and delivery instructions**

✔ **Storage information and restrictions**

✔ **Setup times and requirements**

✔ **Dismantling/removal times and deadlines**

✔ **Local laws and tax information**

✔ **Health department regulations for food-and-beverage sales**

✔ **Fire department regulations**

✔ **Union regulations**

✔ **Exhibit hall requirements for use of employees**

✔ **Utilities required**

✔ **Purveyors/contractors request forms**

✔ **List of local contractors with service order forms**

✔ **Name of decorator's contact person, address, phone number**

Decorator Costs

Services and Charges to You

✔ **Booth package supplied:**
- Booth frame (of pipe)
- Background drape
- Side drapes
- One exhibitor sign
- Specified number of tables
- Specified number of chairs
- Wastebasket(s)
- Carpeting
- Order forms/kits to send to exhibitors
- Setup/dismantling

✔ **Charges:**
   • Based on per booth package

✔ **Cost adjustments:**
   • Deletion, reduction, or addition of booth package items
   • Downgrading or upgrading quality of booth items

✔ **Negotiable items at reduced cost complimentary to organization:**
   • Registration counters
   • Information/message center
   • Entry banners
   • Carpet quality (newness)

✔ **Additional costs:**
   • Labor requested by you
   • Storage off premises
   • Cartage/drayage
   • Subcontracted services and items

Services and Charges to Exhibitors

✔ **Billed directly:**
   • Upgrading of booth items by quality and number
   • Additional amenities
   • Any subcontractors required
   • Materials/equipment handling and storage
   • Move-in, move-out, and setup services
   • Florists, photographers
   • Electrical

Exhibitor's Contract

The Exhibitor's Agreement and Application Form usually accompanies your prospectus. It specifies:

✔ **Name of sponsoring organization**

✔ **Exhibit location, dates, and hours**

✔ **Booth sizes and costs (with space for exhibitor to identify selection and number desired)**

✔ **Booth signs (with space for exhibitor to supply exhibitor name, city, and state)**

✔ **Need for special services (with space for exhibitor to specify special needs)**

✔ **Cancellation policy**

✔ **Deposit requirement (usually 50% at time of application)**

✔ **Signature lines for:**
   • Exhibitor (name and title)
   • Application acceptance by organization

Exhibit Hall Contract

A contract will be furnished by the exhibit hall, or may be prepared by the planner (*see* Chapters 4 and 5). Review its contents thoroughly using the following as guidelines:

✔ **Terms and conditions clearly defined**

✔ **Services, equipment, basic decorating and props included in lease rate**

✔ **Facility's labor requirements**

✔ **Other requirements or restrictions**

✔ **Move-in/move-out policy, restrictions, and requirements**

✔ **Important dates and hours, clearly defined throughout contract**

✔ **Penalty charges**

✔ **Activity restrictions**

✔ **Security/damage deposit and refund requirements or restrictions**

✔ **Sales/excise taxes, percentage**

✔ **Condition-of-building guarantee**

✔ **Resetting charges**

✔ **Utilities included, limitations or restrictions**

✔ **Copy of operating conditions, rules, and regulations**

✔ **Cleaning (if not included), cost and union requirements**

✔ **Exclusive contractors required**

✔ **Telephones furnished, how many, and where**

✔ **Parking facilities, capacity, and proximity**

✔ **If facility is shared, provisions for move-in/move-out and for exhibit attendee traffic**

✔ **Signs provided by facility**

✔ **Security personnel to be provided by facility at no additional cost**

✔ **Additional security required to be hired from facility**

Decorator Contract

The contract between the decorator and the sponsoring organization outlines the terms of your agreement for your organization/exhibitors. It includes the following:

✔ **Floor plans for your brochure**

✔ **Registration area setup**

✔ **Booths, usually including:**
  - 8'-high black drape
  - 3'-high side dividers
  - One 7" × 44" identification sign showing company name, city and state, and booth number
  - Complimentary items

✔ **Special decorating services/masking/lounges**

✔ **Exhibitors service center**

✔ **Exhibitors manual forms for equipment and services**

✔ **Exterior traffic control during freight move-in/move-out**

✔ **Freight handling and storage**

✔ **Skilled union labor and supervision**

- Signs

- Association as additional insured on insurance coverage

- Terms/rates for all rentals and service

- Cancellation/performance clause

- Signatures of authorized conference official

Building Attendance During the Show

- Provide exhibitor list, booth, location, and floor plan in attendee packet.

- Provide exhibitor brochures/handouts at a convenient location throughout meeting.

- Post exhibit hours on or near bulletin board.

- Mention exhibit hours in daily newsletter.

- Announce exhibit hours during general and special sessions.

- Post directional signs to hotel exhibit area or to exhibit shuttle bus if held offsite.

- Hold light refreshment breaks/receptions in exhibit area of hotel.

- Announce exhibit door prizes and other giveaways.

- Encourage exhibitors to mingle with attendees during meeting hours.

- Include exhibitor-sponsored themes/events.

Exhibit Evaluation

From Exhibitors

The meeting planner/show manager should ask each exhibitor to evaluate the exhibition, as follows:

✔ **Determine attendance/traffic on each day of exhibition.**

✔ **Describe traffic flow (high, medium, low) at given times each day (e.g., 10:00 A.M. to 12 noon, 12 noon to 1:00 P.M., on Tuesday and Wednesday)**

✔ **Evaluate on a scale, from 1 to 5, attendee interest.**

✔ **Evaluate on a scale from 1 to 5 the worth of attendee inquiries (e.g., Was attendee a qualified buyer?).**

✔ **Give opinion on various types of giveaways and other attendance promotion activities.**

✔ **Rate services furnished by hall or show management, such as lighting, acoustics, security, janitorial, and food service.**

✔ **Ask, "Would your company exhibit at our show again?"**

Follow up with exhibitor on results of contacts made during exhibition.

From Attendees

✔ **Rate length of exhibition. Ask attendees if there was enough time to view exhibits/meet with exhibitors.**

✔ **Ask at which times they visited the exhibition. Did visits coincide with attendance promotion activities?**

✔ **Rate the location of facility and its convenience to other meeting locales.**

✔ **Ask if exhibits were educational, useful, and/or pertinent to their professions/jobs.**

19-1 | **Exhibitor Schedule Example**

For Booth Personnel

Meeting name/sponsor: _____

Meeting dates: _____   Booth number: _____

Exhibiting company: _____

Address: _____   ZIP: _____

Contact person: _____   Telephone number: (   ) _____

Exhibit location: _____

	Day of Week	Month and Year	Hours	
			From	To
Exhibit hours	_____	_____	_____	_____
	_____	_____	_____	_____
	_____	_____	_____	_____
	_____	_____	_____	_____
	_____	_____	_____	_____
	_____	_____	_____	_____
	_____	_____	_____	_____
Move-in	_____	_____	_____	_____
	_____	_____	_____	_____
	_____	_____	_____	_____
	_____	_____	_____	_____
	_____	_____	_____	_____
	_____	_____	_____	_____
	_____	_____	_____	_____
Move-out	_____	_____	_____	_____
	_____	_____	_____	_____
	_____	_____	_____	_____
	_____	_____	_____	_____
	_____	_____	_____	_____
	_____	_____	_____	_____
	_____	_____	_____	_____
Postmeeting critique (optional)	_____	_____	_____	_____

To be held at: _____

EXHIBITORS MUST REMOVE ALL EXHIBIT MATERIAL FROM THE
HALL BY: _____ .

Early move-out carries the following penalties:
- Loss of future priority/booth assignment status
- Loss of early receipt of registration-information status

Please direct any questions to:

_____

_____

_____

_____ ZIP: _____

(   ) _____ EXT: _____

19-2 | Program Book Listing Example

For booth personnel

Booth No. _____

Exhibitor company: _____
name as to appear in directory and on sign

_____

_____

_____ ZIP: _____

(   ) _____ EXT: _____

Contact person: _____

Supplying the following information will help us ensure a successful show for the exhibitors and will provide a guide for attendees in selecting booths to be visited.

1. Give a brief overview of the products or services your company provides. (_____ typed words or less): _____
   _____
   _____

2. In what way will your exhibit benefit attendees of this meeting? (_____ typed words or less): _____
   _____
   _____

(continued)

19-2	**Program Book Listing Example** (*continued*)

3. What do you hope to achieve by exhibiting during this meeting? (_____ typed words or less): _____

_____

_____

4. What products or services do you plan to highlight? (_____ typed words or less): _____

_____

_____

Arrangements for additional copy may be made at _____ rate with a $_____ minimum charge.

Please direct any questions and return this form to:

_____

_____

_____

_____ ZIP: _____

( ) _____ EXT: _____

Deadline for return: _____ , 19 _____ .

19-3	**Exhibitor Registration Form Example**

Exhibitor company: _____   Meeting title: _____

_____   _____

_____   Location: _____

_____

_____ ZIP: _____   Meeting dates: _____

( ) _____ EXT: _____   Booth no.: _____

Contact person: _____

Please list the names of *all booth personnel* who will be representing your company at the show and return it by _____ , 19 _____ . Badges may be picked up at _____ during _____ .

Name (as to appear on badge)   _____

Title (optional)   _____

_____

_____

_____ ZIP: _____

( ) _____ EXT: _____

Name (as to appear on badge)   _____

Title (optional)   _____

_____

_____

_____ ZIP: _____

( ) _____ EXT: _____

Name (as to appear on badge)   _____

Title (optional)   _____

_____

_____

_____ ZIP: _____

( ) _____ EXT: _____

Return to: _____

_____

_____

_____

_____ ZIP: _____

( ) _____ EXT: _____

Deadline for return: _____ , 19 _____ .

19-4 | **Exhibitor Housing Request Example**

Name: _____

Company: _____

_____

_____ ZIP: _____

( ) _____ EXT: _____

Please make the following room reservations: ☐ Single @$_____ per night
☐ Double @$_____ per night

Arrive: _____ , 19 _____
Depart: _____ , 19 _____

Company personnel requiring reservations.

_____ ☐ Single ☐ Double
name

Arrive: _____ , 19 _____
Depart: _____ , 19 _____

_____ ☐ Single ☐ Double
name

Arrive: _____ , 19 _____
Depart: _____ , 19 _____

_____ ☐ Single ☐ Double
name

Arrive: _____ , 19 _____
Depart: _____ , 19 _____

Special instructions: _____

_____

Payment by:
☐ Voucher ☐ Purchase order ☐ Check
☐ Credit card #_____ / _____
number   expiration date

_____
cardholder's signature

RETURN TO:

Name: _____

_____

_____ ZIP: _____

Attention: _____

DEADLINE FOR RETURN: _____ , 19 _____ .

Guide 20

Selecting a Meeting Management Firm

Types of Companies

With the exception of the first type listed, these companies offer meeting services as an adjunct to their main line of business.

✔ **Meeting management company:**
Primary business is all-inclusive, full-service, meeting management. Most independent meeting planners fall into this category.

✔ **Destination management company:**
Primary business is planning and coordinating local tours, parties, and special events that are activities within the meeting program.

✔ **Multiassociation management company:**
Primary business is full-service management, including meeting event management, for associations/organizations. Also offers meeting management services to corporations.

✔ **Incentive houses:**
Primary business is developing and implementing corporate incentive/reward programs, including incentive meetings and travel. Also offers meeting planning support for nonincentive meetings.

✔ **Travel agencies:**
Primary business is booking travel. May offer limited meeting support as a special service to clients.

✔ **Exposition management companies:**
Primary business is trade show management and sale of exhibit booths. May produce shows independently, or be hired by corporations/associations. May provide limited meeting planning services when assistance is required by client.

✔ **Public relations companies:**
Primary business is advertising, marketing, and media relations. Meeting planning is usually limited to special events and promotional parties for existing clients.

In-House vs. Outside Professional Meeting Services

In-house may be best:	Outside service may be best:
• Job is full-time year-round. • Your company requires multiple services from meeting staff (e.g., business travel, other general staff assignments). • Full-time meeting planner is needed in office on a regular daily basis. • Your company prefers (or needs to use) in-house personnel for reasons of confidentiality. • You can afford to pay professional planner's salary.	• In-house planner is too busy. • Organization needs to generate more profit from meeting dollars spent. • Meeting activities do not require a full-time position, but consistency is needed in overseeing from year to year. • Organization has no full-time or professionally trained planner. • There has been a work force reduction in middle management or meeting-planning staff. • Increased skill and efficiency are needed. • Expertise is lacking in-house. • Meeting history reveals ongoing problems (e.g., decreasing attendance, low enthusiasm level, communication gaps, other). • In-house management reorganization within department(s) interferes with schedule deadline requirements.

Services Provided by Meeting Management Companies

✔ **Long-range planning, consulting, and staff training**

✔ **Program design/speaker selection**

✔ **Budgeting and financial accounting**

✔ **Marketing and promotion**

✔ **Creative services, meeting themes, parties, and other special events**

✔ **Site selection, vendor selection, contracting, negotiations**

✔ **Attendee services, registration, housing, transportation**

✔ **Data collection, evaluation, and reporting**

✔ **Food-and-beverage event management**

✔ **Supervision and management of the project**

✔ **Personnel training/management**

Benefits of Professional Meeting Services

✔ **Cost savings and/or efficient use of money**

✔ **New approaches, creativity**

✔ **Efficiency from tested and/or in-place systems**

✔ **Knowledge of suppliers and suppliers' trade language**

✔ **Rate negotiation through power they bring to table in terms of total business, not just your meeting**

Where to Find Professional Independent Planners

✔ **Professional membership directories, such as *Meeting Planners International Directory***

✔ **Referrals from hotel sales and convention services staff**

✔ **Referrals from colleagues who have used independent planner services**

✔ **Referrals from local convention and visitors bureaus**

✔ **Yellow Pages listing, usually under catchall category of CON-VENTION SERVICES**

✔ **Contacts made through attendance at professional meetings**

Selecting a Meeting Management Company

✔ **Identify the services you want to subcontract and the dollar amount you have available to pay in fees.**

✔ **Identify the "first cut" of companies you want to talk to, and schedule a telephone or personal meeting. Request copies of background/promotional materials.**

✔ **Prepare an RFP (bid) either before or immediately after these conversations. Mail to those companies not eliminated.**

✔ **Review bids received by the stated deadline.**

✔ **Contact the references of all companies or those not eliminated in this stage.**

✔ **Conduct interviews with the finalists, including key people from both your staff and theirs.**

✔ **Ideally criteria should mainly include overall ability to perform the services, personality compatibility to your organization, stability as a company, and quality of reports from references.**

✔ **Negotiations should begin and be focused in the primary areas of services, fees, and terms of the contractual relationship.**

✔ **A contract should be drawn up, reviewed by your attorney, and signed by the authorized parties.**

✔ **Follow up with all companies, thanking them for their bids and advising them of your selection.**

Helpful Hints

Avoid giving sketchy or incomplete information in the RFP or prospectus. The less information a professional planner receives, the higher the bid in order to cover the unknowns.

If only one planner is being considered, do not request other companies to bid in the hope of achieving cost comparison. Not only is this unfair and discourteous to the additional planners, you will find yourself attempting a cost comparison while lacking information as resulting from the interview and evaluation process.

Consider hiring a professional meeting management consultant to assist in the interview and evaluation processes and to mediate or advise during contract and fee negotiations.

Questions to Ask a Meeting Management Company

✔ **How many years has the company been in business?**
  • Full time? Part time?
  • Size of present staff?
    —Planners
    —Clerical
    —Consultants used? For what?
  • Equipment capability?
    —Computer
    —Other
  • Support services available?
    —List of services

✔ **How many members of management firm's current staff will have direct contact with you?**
  • List of job titles, names, and experience

✔ **What is the experience level, educational and professional training, and credentials of staff members closely involved with your project?**
  • Length of tenure and/or turnover rate?

✔ **In what professional organizations is company a member?**
  • Name of organization(s)
  • Years of membership
  • Offices held

✔ **Can meeting management company provide all supplier resources required for your meeting?**

✔ **What jobs does the company perform in-house?**

✔ **What jobs are subcontracted out?**
  • Name of subcontractor to be used. (*Note:* Subcontracting can indicate either a lack of competent in-house staff or the desire to locate ultimate expertise in an area.)

✔ **Does meeting management company have a working knowledge of all subcontract requirements, such as:**
  • Service levels?
  • Average costs?
  • Purveyor contracts?
  • Negotiable points?
  • Contractual pitfalls?
  • Union requirements related to specific services?
  • Insurance requirements?

- Scheduling and deadlines?
- Ability to evaluate technical expertise?

✔ **Who within the company will do your work? If not the contact person, request to meet the person who will. Who will do work in case of illness or injury?**

✔ **What other bookings do they have during the dates of your meeting?**
- One month prior or following
- Two months prior or following

✔ **What is the staffing plan for handling these multiple commitments?**

✔ **What communication methods can be expected? How frequently?**
- Personal office visits
- Telephone
- Memos
- Fax, overnight, or regular mail

✔ **How will communication pattern(s) change during:**
- Planning phases?
- Periods immediately surrounding your event?

✔ **What is the fee? How is it computed (hourly or other)?**

✔ **If commissions are accepted, are they deducted from fee? Refused? A negotiation tool? Ask to see example of the contract used by the company.**

✔ **Can cost benefit to you be clearly demonstrated and supported?**

✔ **What types of insurance are carried by the company, and what are the coverage limits?**

✔ **Does the meeting management company have capacity to:**
- Respond quickly to your needs?
- Be flexible and adaptable to changes required?
- Create appropriate ideas for:
  —Expanding or enhancing your meeting?
  —Efficiency in systems?

✔ **Do you have an easy rapport with management company or planner assigned to work with you?**

✔ **Do you feel that there has been openness and honesty in communications?**

Questions the Meeting Management Company Will Ask You

✓ **What are your company's values, and what is its business philosophy?**

✓ **What are your company's meeting goals and objective?**

✓ **Can you supply an idea of your management style and preferences?**

✓ **What is the reporting structure (i.e., who will planner talk to)?**
  • One person only, or other designated in-house people
  • Communication procedures

✓ **What internal resources will be available to the planner? (Mention all, from accountant to coper.)**

✓ **Can you describe your company's policies regarding:**
  • Deposits?
  • Payments?
  • Expenditure approval?

✓ **Does your company have current or pending financial or legal actions in place that would interfere with its ability to conduct this meeting?**

✓ **Describe the meeting audience:**
  • Percentage men?
  • Percentage women?
  • Clients?
  • Employees?
  • Top producers?
    —Spouses?
    —Children?
  • Percentage married?
  • Percentage single?

✓ **Describe knowledge/education level of attendees.**

✓ **List themes, speakers, and/or agendas used in past meetings:**
  • Were they received with enthusiasm?
  • Do you wish to follow similar pattern or seek new ones?

✓ **What is your budget for this meeting?**
  • Tight or flexible?

✓ **What were the meeting budgets for the past three to five years? Do they indicate a stabilized pattern, growth, or reduction?**

Items You Can Negotiate With Meeting Management Company

Depending upon the policies of the independent meeting management company, varying numbers of these negotiable items will be attainable.

✔ **The bid fee (*see* Guide 21)**

✔ **Levels of service**

✔ **Areas of responsibility (meeting management company's and your own)**

✔ **Fee-setting structure changes (from per person to flat fee)**

✔ **Allowable expenses**

✔ **Overhead costs**

✔ **Company-provided personnel, interns, equipment**

✔ **Company-provided services:**
  • Credit cards
  • Overnight mail accounts
  • 800 numbers
  • Direct bill accounts

✔ **Administrative fees, service charges**

✔ **On-site rate vs. office time**

✔ **Frequency of payments and net days due**

✔ **Interest on late payments**

✔ **Profit margin**

✔ **Cancellation fees/penalties, cancellation terms, and key dates for cancellation**

Guide 21

Establishing Your Own Meeting Management Firm

Elements of Setting Up Your Business

- ✔ **Define the services you will offer.**

- ✔ **Decide on the company image you want to project.**

- ✔ **Develop your business and marketing plans.**

- ✔ **Identify your most likely market target(s).**

- ✔ **Prepare a realistic, comprehensive operating budget:**
  - First six months of operation
  - First year of operation
  - Projections for three to five years

- ✔ **Establish a realistic fee structure.**

- ✔ **Assess your legal liabilities and discuss with insurance broker:**
  - Professional
  - Operating
  - Contractual

- ✔ **Prepare your client contract, and submit it to an attorney for changes and approval.**

- ✔ **Hire your staff.**

- ✔ **Set up your management systems.**

The Ideal

✔ **Have enough capital to operate for six months with no income.**

✔ **Have enough capital to go without a salary for three years.**

✔ **Reinvest all profits in growth for three to five years.**

Operating and Start-Up Costs

✔ **Rent**

✔ **Utilities**

✔ **Equipment (e.g., desks, chairs, file cabinets, computers, printers, copier, postage meter)**

✔ **Printing (letterhead, business cards, sales brochure)**

✔ **Paper**

✔ **Postage**

✔ **Salaries (including yours)**

✔ **Supplies (from pencils, paper clips, and rubber bands to mailing labels, printer ribbons, and computer diskettes)**

✔ **Telephone (lines, equipment, long distance)**

✔ **Travel and entertainment**

✔ **Advertising**

✔ **Marketing and promotion**

✔ **Professional meeting expenses**

✔ **Professional dues**

✔ **Membership dues (e.g., in convention and visitors bureaus)**

✔ **Accounting**

✔ **Bookkeeping**

✔ **Legal fees**

✔ **Taxes**

✔ **Insurance**

✔ **Sales commissions**

✔ **Finder's fees**

✔ **Referral rewards/incentives**

Developing Your Business Plan

Components of a Business Plan:

✔ **Executive summary:**

Length: One page
Focus: Strengths and enthusiasm found within your company

Should be prepared last and tie all components together.

✔ **Overview of company:**

Length: Two to three pages
Focus: Company background, goals, services, and philosophy

✔ **Description of the market:**

Length: Two to four pages
Focus: General market, size, and conditions
              Your target market
              Your competition

✔ **Differential advantage:**

Length: Two to four pages
Focus: What you do that is different and/or better

✔ **Marketing plan:**

Length: Two to four pages
Focus: A specific statement on how you plan to reach your market

✔ **Financial plan:**

Length: Two to three pages
Focus: Current operations cost
              Capital needs
              Expansion costs
              Future projections

🗸 **Management plan:**

Length: Three to four pages
Focus: Staffing
             Résumés
             Job descriptions

Developing Your Marketing Plan

Examine these questions well and list all possible answers for each question. Your answers will form the foundation for your marketing strategy and decisions and will determine a significant number of your marketing costs.

🗸 **What are you going to sell (list all services)?**

🗸 **Is it needed?**

🗸 **Who will buy it?**

🗸 **How many will buy it?**

🗸 **How will you find them?**

🗸 **When will they buy it (peak season/low season)?**

🗸 **Who else is selling the same services?**

🗸 **Why should client(s) buy from you?**

Targeting Your Market

🗸 **Evaluate fields you know well:**
   • Scientific
   • Legal
   • Medical
   • Political
   • Corporate
   • Association
   • Other

🗸 **Research the companies and associations in these fields within your area (or *target* area) to determine the market potential, paying special attention to:**
   • Number and size of company(ies)
   • Products or services produced

- Corporate or privately owned/operated
- Financial condition
- Expansion plans
- Corporate structure
- Other

✔ **Identify secondary market suppliers serving primary market (e.g., pharmaceutical companies for medical firms, computer hard/software manufacturers for computer sales companies).**

✔ **Assess needs potential of targeted companies (e.g., current in-house talent, prior use of subcontracted services).**

Reaching Your Market

✔ **Develop supplier lead sources.**

✔ **Ask clients for referrals, repeat business.**

✔ **Consider additional products and services your clients may want.**

✔ **Become visible in local and professional communities. Join and become active in your professional associations.**

✔ **Ask friends and family for leads.**

✔ **Send out press releases regularly.**

✔ **Send monthly/quarterly newsletters.**

✔ **Write articles.**

✔ **Accept speaking invitations.**

✔ **Develop associations with public relations firms, travel agencies.**

✔ **Send thank-you notes regularly.**

✔ **Focus your attention on markets you know well and where people know you.**

✔ **Contact all leads at least four times within ninety days.**

✔ **Advertise to increase your name recognition.**

✔ **Don't be afraid to show enthusiasm for your company.**

✔ **Send direct mail pieces when you have a qualified list.**

✔ **Participate in networking. The more good ideas you bring to other people, the better you look.**

Putting the Marketing Package Together

✔ **What to include:**
- Well-written transmittal letter
- Staff bibliographies (including yours)
- A list and/or description of your company qualifications
- A list and/or description of services you can provide
- Samples of your work
- Copies of articles you have written
- Copies of articles written about your company
- Pictures from meetings you have managed
- Letters of appreciation received from clients
- Your business philosophy
- Advocate for your clients
- Integrity and ethics
- Track record
- Successes

✔ **Presentation options:**
- Personal presentation(s):
  - —Videos, slides, and photographs providing good illustrations of room setups, theme-party possibilities, and other creative work developed within your company
  - —Flip chart to reinforce points covered during meeting
  - —Scrapbook
- Mailable Items (these should be well-designed, attractively presented, and of high quality):
  - —Company brochure
  - —Presentation folder
  - —Business cards
  - —Letterhead

✔ **Important considerations**
- Consistent use of logo, color, theme:
  - —Letterhead
  - —Business cards
  - —Mailing envelopes
  - —Mailing labels
  - —Planner-to-client memo paper

—Brochures
—Presentation folders
—Other company mailing materials
- Paper quality (the best you can afford)
- Creative presentation (the greater the impact, the greater the result)

Hiring Staff

Look for people who have the following characteristics:

✔ **An ability to quickly assimilate information**

✔ **A wide range of job-related skills**

✔ **Flexibility regarding work schedules**

✔ **Good people skills (work well with others)**

✔ **Enthusiasm**

✔ **Energy (can usually deal well with deadlines and pressure)**

✔ **A reputation for being self-starting and self-disciplined**

✔ **Detailed and systematic approach to project**

✔ **Cost-consciousness**

✔ **Good personal skills:**
  - Well-spoken
  - Well-groomed
  - Well-read
  - Ability to write well

✔ **Self-confidence**

✔ **Good time-management skills**

Helpful Hints

Establish a dress/appearance code that projects the image you want to create for your company. See that you and your staff adhere to it.

Organize and maintain a work-flow pattern to avoid disorganization in your office.

Create a feeling of order and efficiency and a pleasant atmosphere for clients and your staff.

Preparing Bids

- ✔ **Provide full disclosure of your system to a client: how and when expenses and service, handling, and administrative fees are to be paid; and late-payment percentage charges.**

- ✔ **Select the fee-setting method that best serves the project, the client, and you. *Bid that method.* (Avoid any mention of additional fee-setting methods you may use. That can only muddy the waters.)**

- ✔ **Prepare a chart to illustrate the cost of one full-time in-house employee versus the cost of using an independent meeting management company.**

- ✔ **Answer any client questions fully and honestly, including those on how costs have been determined.**

Payment Options

- ✔ **Deposit with signed contract (always).**

- ✔ **One-third in advance, one-third midway, and one-third upon completion**

- ✔ **Actual hours worked, usually on a monthly basis**

- ✔ **Monthly percentage of total fixed fee or estimated total billing (e.g., twelve equal installments of balance after deposit)**

- ✔ **Final payment from 10 to 30 days after event or after final report/work submitted/completed**

Fee Variables

- ✔ **Client variables:**
  - Type of event
  - Length of meeting
  - Complexity of meeting
  - Level and type services required
  - Lead time for planning
  - Number of suppliers to recruit and coordinate
  - Number of attendees
  - Potential for repeat or upgraded business

- Client's ability to pay
- Group history

✔ **Planner variables:**
  - Overhead costs
  - Estimated contract hours required
  - Planner-covered costs vs. reimbursable costs
  - Profit margin
  - Rates in your own area
  - Competition
  - Experience, education, and qualifications of in-house employees
  - Inflation rate if long-term or multiyear contract
  - Your current schedule/staffing
  - The market/your need for business

Fee Structures

<table>
<tr><td colspan="2" align="center">Fee-Structure Summary</td></tr>
<tr><td>Fixed price (flat fee):</td><td>• By project/contract plus expenses. Average three-day meeting = $25,000–30,000.</td></tr>
<tr><td>Per person:</td><td>• Flat fee (nonvariable fixed amount). Average = $20–$30 per person.
• Sliding fee

$30 for first 1,000
$25 for next 500
$25 for next 500, . . .</td></tr>
<tr><td>Per hour:</td><td>• Fixed rate or based on professional vs. support hours. $40–$50 per hour average usually requires time sheets based on 15-minute increments.</td></tr>
<tr><td>Per day/per meeting attendee:</td><td>• A fixed daily rate or per-attendee rate</td></tr>
<tr><td>Commissions/split commissions:</td><td>• Average = 10% of gross supplier bill (for hotels, based on sleeping rooms only)</td></tr>
<tr><td>Retainers:</td><td>• Regularly scheduled payment for continuing services</td></tr>
<tr><td>Incentives:</td><td>• Sliding rate increased (number of attendees, booths sold)</td></tr>
<tr><td>Per diem:</td><td>• $250–$1,000 per day ($750 most common)</td></tr>
<tr><td>Gross billing:</td><td>• 20–30% × total cost of program</td></tr>
<tr><td>For trade show:</td><td>• $3–$5 per attendee/$50–$100 per booth</td></tr>
</table>

Fee-Structure Formulas

Formula for billable hours:

$$H = t - a - h.$$

where:
    H = billable hours
    t = total man-hours paid in one year. (40 × 52 = 2,080.)
    a = administrative (nonbillable) hours in one year. (22 × 40 = 880.)
    h = holiday, sick-day, vacation-day hours in one year. (3 × 40 = 120.)

| Example: | 2,080 (t) − 880 (a) − 120 (h) = 1,080 billable hours. |

Formula for hourly rate needed, R:

| Example: | $$R = \frac{g\$i}{e}.$$ |

where:
    $g\$i$ = gross income needed (overhead and profit).
    e = estimated percentage of H.

$100,000 ($g\$i$) ÷ 1,080 ($e$) = approximately $92 per hour (F).

Formula for per-hour structured fee charged to client (based on meeting time cards):

| Example: | Fee (F) = Rate (R) × Hours (H). |

$92 (R) × 20 (H) = $1,840 (F)

✔ Fixed price or flat fees:

A flat fee or fixed-price fee is usually determined by project/contract plus expenses.

    Average: $25,000
    Range: $15,000–$40,000, depending on complexity and variables

---

How to Figure Fees

- List all tasks.
- Put estimated hours by each.
- If appropriate, divide according to professional/clerical time/rate.
- Multiply hours by rate.
- Add a 20% error rate.
- Add profit.
- Set fee. Budget expenses separately.

✔ **Percentage of gross billing:**

> *Average:* 20–30%

Gross expenses for project + gross expenses paid by planner = gross billing

Example:

Meeting expenses:	$150,000
Planner expenses:	50,000
Gross billing:	$200,000
	×20%
Fee:	$ 40,000

✔ **Hourly or daily rate:**

In-office (8 hours per day):	$40–$75 (per hour) average
Out of office (8–10 hours a day):	$500–$750 per day suggested
On-site hours (12–16 hours a day):	$750–$1,000 per day suggested

Example:

600 in-office hours × *$40:*	$24,000
21 out-of-office days × *$750:*	15,750
Fee	$39,750

✔ **Per-person/registration fee:**

Planner charges per-person rate for each conference attendee, including speakers, guests, and staff. Viable only for very large groups.

> *Average:* $10–$30 per registrant planner fee

Example:

Registered attendees:	×500
Per-registrant fee:	$ 30
Planned fee:	$15,000

✔ **Sliding fees:**

The per-person fee increases/decreases on the basis of the number of attendees. The most common practice is to decrease, as first registrants must cover costs/ profit. A sliding fee is usually tied to the per-person fee. It tends to be higher for the first group in order to cover fixed service requirements. The fee is then systematically reduced as numbers increase to cover the additional but lessened work load resulting from higher attendance.

Average:	$30 for first 1,000
	$25 for next 500
	$20 for additional 500

Example:

(based on 2,000 attendees):

$30 × 1,000:	$30,000
$25 × 500:	$12,500
$20 × 500:	$10,000
Fee:	$52,500

✔ **Retainers:**

A retainer is usually based on the professional hourly/daily rate. The number of hours are guaranteed at a guaranteed rate, frequently over an extended length of time. They are often used for consulting, training, or other services requiring exclusive professional time. Clients should be billed at frequent and regular intervals, usually monthly.

> *Average:* $50–$100 per hour

Example:

Four hours per day × 20 days:	80
Hourly rate:	× 75
Retainer fee:	$6,000

✔ **Commissions:**

A commission is a fee paid by the supplier to the person or organization who books the sale. Hotels, airlines, travel agents, and other suppliers are the usual sources. A commission is frequently used to transfer payment of planner fees from the client to an attendee or an individual. This is the most common form of payment among travel agents.

> *Average:*   Usually 10%, sometimes negotiable to 15%

How to Figure Commission

Hotel room rate × total room nights =
      total revenue × commissionable percentage

Example:

Hotel room rate:	$100
Three total room nights (× 50 people):	× 150
Total revenue:	$15,000
Percentage:	× 10%
Commission:	$ 1,500

✔ **Phase billing:**

Phase billing is computed on the basis of intensity of professional staff involvement versus clerical involvement. For example, the registration phase may require professional time only in setting up the system and supervising personnel; the major time is taken up by clerical duties such as mail processing and data entry. Identify involvement by pre-, on-site, and post-times, or by menu of services.

Average: $40–$50 professional hourly rate
$30 clerical hourly rate

Example:

160 professional hours @ $40:	$6,400
20 clerical hours @ $30:	600
Fee for program design phase:	$7,000

Achieving Profits

Keys to Profit	Profit Eaters
• Staying within operating budget • Accurately computing man-hours spent on projects • Selling 90 percent of your possible billable hours • Accurately recording reimbursable expenses and billing for them at regular intervals	• Overstaffing • Underestimating project hours and hourly rate • Inefficient operation/doing more without producing more • Bad judgment during negotiation processes and/or lack of negotiation skill

Professional Liability

Liability and Liability Insurance Concerns

• Potential risks
• How to eliminate and reduce risk
• Areas in which you may be held liable

Guidelines in Protecting Yourself Against Liability

✔ **Obtain professional liability insurance coverage.**

✔ **Consult with your attorney and accountant regarding the advantages and disadvantages of incorporating your business to limit your liability. Federal and state taxes, however, may increase.**

✔ **Obtain certificates of insurance from suppliers/vendors (e.g., audiovisual production companies, caterers, temporary-help employment agencies, ground transportation companies).**

✔ **Note that certificates of insurance must include the name of the insurance company, coverage, inception/expiration dates, and limits of liability.**

✔ **Always require meeting/event host to pay liquor supplier directly.**

✔ **Require suppliers'/vendors' insurance coverage to include general liability, worker's compensation, and, in some cases, auto coverage.**

✔ **Protect the client's money, securities, and other property by using separate bank accounts, frequent bank deposits, and by implementing proper check-signing policies.**

✔ **Obtain insurance coverage protecting you, your company, and your client in case of theft by your (the independent meeting planner) employees. (*See* Chapter 16.)**

✔ **Sign contracts with your name, your title, and the name of your company, followed by "as agent for [*your client*]." Send copies of all such contracts, letters of agreement, and similar documents to your client.**

✔ **Apply high standards when conducting your business and professional affairs.**

✔ **Work closely with attorneys and insurance professionals to identify other risks, liabilities and protections.**

See also Chapter 16 and Guide 16 for more information on this topic.

21-1 Daily Timesheet Form

Actual Hours Worked: _____

Name: _____   Date: _____

Client	Project	Activity Code	#	Notes	Hours	Rate

21-2 | Postage Usage Form

Client: _____   Month: _____

Date Cost Incurred

1	2	3	4	5	6

7	8	9	10	11	12

13	14	15	16	17	18

19	20	21	22	23	24

25	26	27	28	29	30

31

Total: $_____

21-3	Copying Summary Form

Client: _____   Month/Year: _____

Date	Pages	× Copies	= #Total	Copier's Initial	Description (if necessary)

Total copies × Rate per copy $0._____ /Copy = Total Charge: _____

21-4 | Client Expense Summary Form

Client: ——————————————— Project: ———————————————————

Month Incurred	Date Billed	Date Paid	Invoice Number	Postage	Copies	Long-Distance Phone Calls	Travel	Misc.	Total
January				$	$	$	$	$	$
February									
March									
April									
May									
June									
July									
August									
September									
October									
November									
December									

Explanation: 1. ——————————————— 2. ———————————————
3. ——————————————— 4. ———————————————

21-5 | Independent Meeting Planner Contract Example

The following has been selected to illustrate the components of a full-service meeting management contract. Additional components may appear, and any of the components in the example shown may be deleted with the exception of the following:

Opening statement and disclosure agreement
Fees and payment
Indemnification
Termination
Acceptance of Agreement
Signatures

Please be sure to consult an attorney before drafting your own contract. State laws vary.

OPENING STATEMENT AND DISCLOSURE AGREEMENT

This contract contains the Agreement under which [*meeting planner company*] will serve as meeting management consultant for [*client corporation/ association*] for the [*name of meeting or event*].

This proposal contains ideas and descriptions that are considered to be of proprietary interest to [*meeting planner company*]. The contents of this document are intended for the exclusive review and consideration by [*client corporation/association*]. No redistribution or subsequent disclosure of the materials contained herein is authorized.

SCOPE OF WORK

This section may be attached as an addendum to add continuity to the body of the legal document.

A. Site Selection
   —Identify client site requirements for prospectus.
   —Conduct site inspection(s) of selected hotel(s).
   —Finalize site selection and negotiate hotel contract.
   —Prepare space utilization plan.
   —Other.
B. Financial
   —Prepare budget.
   —Establish purchasing and accounting procedures.
   —Monitor income/expenditures throughout planning process.

(continued)

21-5   Independent Meeting Planner Contract Example
(*continued*)

                               –Submit interim financial reports.
-Prepare postmeeting financial reports.
-Other.

C. Artwork, Printing, and Mailing
-Prepare and print conference timeline.
-Coordinate graphics design, printing, and mailing of brochure; registration materials; speaker/exhibitor packets; program book, badges, tickets.
-Coordinate all outgoing and incoming mailings.
-Other.

D. Program Design
-Consult on program design and speaker selection, as needed.
-Collect speaker requirements.
-Implement speaker needs, travel arrangements, audiovisual requirements, bios; obtain photographs.
-Monitor conference goals.
-Other.

E. Housing
-Design systems and forms to expedite hotel reservations and room assignments.
-Maintain close check on attendance and room uptake numbers.
-Other.

F. Transportation
-Negotiate contract for official airline.
-Coordinate all transportation related to parking, scheduling, group movement to and from off-site events, insurance requirements.
-Coordinate airport pickup/drop-off transportation for designated VIPs.
-Other.

G. Registration
-Establish registration-fee structure.
-Establish preregistration/on-site procedures and forms.
-Receive attendee registration forms and monies.
-Process all preregistrations.
-Prepare preregistration and final attendee lists.
-Train paid personnel/volunteers for registration duties.
-Other.

H. Conference Logistics
   —Prepare and update planning—schedule timeline.
   —Report planning progress at scheduled intervals to client.
   —Recommend and schedule all meetings required.
   —Prepare agendas; facilitate and moderate meetings.
   —Negotiate and follow up contractual agreements with suppliers.
   —Conduct premeeting briefings with hotel staff, suppliers, and client.
   —Other.
I. Exhibits/Sponsorship
   —Prepare exhibit plan and budget.
   —Prepare exhibitor/sponsorship brochure.
   —Coordinate advertising campaign for program book.
   —Establish exhibitor registration procedures, both pre— and on—site.
   —Receive registrations and monies.
   —Assign exhibit space.
   —Coordinate exhibitor setup and move—out requirements.
   —Other.
J. Optional Events
   —Research and develop special events and tours according to client requests and specifications.
K. Final Report
   —Maintain records required for historical and planning purposes throughout planning period.
   —Produce formal postmeeting reports, including historical, statistical, and financial data and recommendations.

FEES AND PAYMENT
—Specification of contract dollar amount
—Additional costs to be reimbursed for items, such as
  —Actual travel expenses
  —Printing/copying
  —Mailings and postage
  —Other
—Dollar amount of professional services fee to be paid at time contract is signed
—Payment schedule and dollar amounts to be paid at specified intervals
—Date final payment is due
—Reimbursement time and schedule requirements
  —Within 30 days of invoices
  —1 1/2% service charge to be added at end of 30 days

(continued)

21-5 | Independent Meeting Planner Contract Example (*continued*)

—15% service charge to be added to cost for all payments made to outside suppliers by meeting planner if paid within 60 days, or case-by-case negotiation basis if paid after 60 days

EXAMINATION OF RECORDS
[*Include a brief statement that an authorized person has right to examine and have access to all records relating to contract and/or compliance with its terms, for a specified period of time.*]

INDEMNITY
[*Include a brief statement that client corporation/association indemnifies meeting planner for any actions, liabilities, or claims arising from meeting activities or corporate employees or agents under terms of contract.*]

TERMINATION OF AGREEMENT
[*Include a brief statement of requirements for dismissal of planner for nonperformance by client corporation or association, specifying*
[*—Time (e.g., 45 days) advance notice to planner.*]
[*—That client is to be responsible for any cancellation charges/penalties imposed by outside suppliers resulting from termination of Agreement.*]
[*—Other.*]

EQUAL EMPLOYMENT OPPORTUNITY
[*Provide standard EEO statement.*]

ACCEPTANCE OF AGREEMENT
[*Include a brief statement that all terms and conditions of Agreement are accepted.*]

_____   _____
signature of meeting planner   date

_____   _____
signature of client   date

APPENDIX

A QUICK REFERENCE GUIDE FOR INTERNATIONAL AND FOREIGN MEETINGS

international meeting   A meeting comprised of attendees from two or more countries meeting for mutual reasons. May be held outside the national borders of both countries or within the borders of one of the participant nations.

foreign meeting   A meeting comprised of attendees from one nation traveling to a foreign destination for the purpose of attending that meeting.

Many of the areas covered throughout this book apply to foreign and international meetings as well, but there are some considerations that are unique to these meetings. The guidelines that follow address a number of those concerns, from local customs to site selection to overseas shipping.

An important element of a successful international meeting is building the culture of the host country into the event as much as possible. To overlook that unique resource is to waste one of the most pleasurable and unique opportunities an international meeting provides.

Guide 22

International And Foreign Meetings

Planning Considerations

- ✓ **International time differences**

- ✓ **Time allowances for international mail and shipping**

- ✓ **Selecting international suppliers, negotiations, contracting**

- ✓ **Language barriers and establishment of official language**

- ✓ **Translation and interpretation requirements**

- ✓ **Currency requirements and exchange procedures**

- ✓ **Document and health requirements**

- ✓ **Customs office procedures, requirements, limits, and restrictions**

- ✓ **Compatibility of equipment hardware with software; voltage**

- ✓ **Local travel assistance**

- ✓ **Budgetary additions and exchange-rate implications**

- ✓ **Local resources for legal, insurance-related and medical assistance**

Programming Considerations

- ✔ **Jet lag of attendees**

- ✔ **Expansion of free time and scheduling it to correspond to resort activities**

- ✔ **Emphasis on local culture:**
  - Themes
  - Entertainment
  - Activities

- ✔ **Language translations and interpretation requirements**

- ✔ **Speaker's fees and travel costs**

- ✔ **Compatibility of audiovisual and other media equipment**

- ✔ **Official language for program book**

Local Practices and Customs Considerations

- ✔ **Holidays:**
  - Local
  - National
  - Religious
  - Political

- ✔ **Dress codes:**
  - Daytime
  - Business
  - Dining
  - Touring

- ✔ **Gift giving:**
  - What
  - When
  - How to present

- ✔ **Religious practices:**
  - Days of worship and holidays
  - Restrictions on use of alcohol
  - Specific foods and preparation requirements
  - Appropriate invocations

✔ **Local laws:**
  • Curfews
  • Speed limits and other driving practices
  • Incidents requiring arrest-and-release procedures
  • Crime rate
  • General safety considerations

✔ **Labor laws:**
  • Hours of traditional workday
  • Regular and overtime rates
  • Unions and other labor practices
  • Reliability

✔ **Local political climate**
  • Attitude toward your country and nation of attendees
  • Internal political climate

✔ **Lifestyle and pace of life:**
  • Days and hours shops are open
  • Customary dining hours
  • Response time to service requests

✔ **Customs:**
  • Language
  • Tipping
  • Official introductions
  • Proper use of titles
  • Pronunciation of names
  • Seating order

Site Selection, Negotiation, Contractual Considerations

Key international considerations are listed below, but sites also should be evaluated according to the areas outlined in Chapter 4. You may place a greater emphasis on some criteria for international venues or locations; each country is governed and regulated according to different standards, values, and customs, particularly in areas that may affect the health and safety of your attendees. It's risky to assume that things are the same in foreign countries as what you are used to, and even in English-speaking countries, language differences can result in serious misunderstandings.

Country and City Selection

✔ **Accessibility of site and frequency of transportation service**

✔ **Ground and local transportation services**

✔ **Political environment**

✔ **Crime rate**

✔ **Customs procedures**

✔ **Climate and seasonal weather**

✔ **Availability of required resources**

✔ **Availability of quality services and suppliers**

✔ **Business and social interests of attendees**

✔ **Local holidays**

✔ **Size and type of facilities or hotels available**

✔ **Overall economy and level of costs**

✔ **Stability of currency and exchange rate**

Facility Selection

✔ **Multilingual capability of staff**

✔ **Availability of translation/Interpretation equipment and personnel:**
  - Type
  - Quality
  - Costs
  - Location of interpretation system

✔ **Electrical voltage**

✔ **Brands of audiovisual equipment available**

✔ **Systems of measurement for meeting-room size evaluation (metric or U.S.)**

✔ **Communication systems**
  - Telephones
  - Facsimile
  - Telex

✔ **Safety standards:**
  - Codes
  - Licenses
  - Certifications
  - Permits

✔ **Health standards and precautions:**
  - Water
  - Food preparation

✔ **Booking, scheduling, and contracting procedures**

Negotiation Considerations

✔ **Currency in which payments are to be made**

✔ **Exchange rate**

✔ **Method of payment:**
  - Bank transfer/draft
  - Cash
  - Travelers checks

✔ **Insurance coverage and acceptance of liabilities**

✔ **Language(s) in which contract will be prepared**

✔ **Extended service hours and expanded staffing level**

✔ **Special rate packages—may include:**
  - Air or ground transportation
  - Meals
  - Rate extensions for before or after the event
  - Waived or reduced fees for various activities
  - Any other special considerations for your attendees or meeting

Contractual Considerations

✔ **Contracts drawn in one country may not be legal or binding in another country.**

✔ **Contracts should state which country's laws will bind the parties.**

✔ **Contracts should be reviewed by legal counsel and an insurance agent familiar with the laws of both countries.**

✔ **All terms should be defined and interpretation should be mutually acceptable by both parties.**

✔ **Contracts should specify applicable local and national laws that may affect your meeting, such as taxes and collection procedures, energy regulations controlling the supply or hours of service, curfew, alcohol usage.**

Insurance Considerations

- ✓ **Advise your insurance agent of:**
  - Foreign destination
  - Staff members who will accompany you
  - Travel plans
  - Length of stay
  - Dollar value of each item to be shipped
  - Temporary foreign staff required; jobs they will do
  - Equipment to be taken
  - Equipment to be rented
  - Ground transportation excursions included in program
  - Local contractors you will use, their responsibilities and their subcontractors

- ✓ **Ask the agent to review your existing coverage and assess what additional insurance is required.**

- ✓ **Require hotel and all contractors to specify insurance coverages in their contracts.**

Attendee Services

Passport and Visa Requirements

- ✓ **In your first mailing, advise registered attendees to check their passports for validity during meeting and travel dates; inform them of need for visa(s).**

- ✓ **Request foreign consulate to send *you* visa applications or tourist cards (one for each registered attendee, spouse, child, if visa required, and guest) no later than six months prior to meeting.**

- ✓ **Mail applications to attendees for completion and submission to consulate.**

- ✓ **If using a visa expeditor (ask your travel agent about this service), are to be used, instruct attendees to return completed application to visa expediters.**

- ✓ **Remind attendees to record passport numbers and keep separate from passport.**

Immigration and Customs

Advise attendees:

✔ **What to expect at point of arrival**

✔ **Customs limitations and unacceptable items**

✔ **How to register or declare valuables, cameras, jewelry**

✔ **Currency in which duty must be paid**

✔ **Duty-free limits on quantity of certain items, such as:**
  • Liquor
  • Cigarettes
  • Overall cost limitations
  • Customs service policy (stringent or relaxed)

✔ **To take prescriptions in pharmacy-identified containers and pack in carry-on luggage**

Foreign Airports

(Flight attendants are a good source of information)
Before deplaning, advise attendees of:

✔ **Unusual or excessively stringent security measures**

✔ **Construction going on in areas involving them**

✔ **Location of in-transit area if this is an in-transit stop**

✔ **Length of layover**

✔ **Amount of departure tax and currency required for payment**

Currency Exchange Desk

✔ **Set up desk through local bank in city where meeting is being held.**

✔ **Identify currencies and exchange rates available.**

✔ **Provide multilingual staff.**

✔ **Provide information on hours open (especially important to know when banks are closed).**

✔ **State service charge.**

✔ **Be prepared to handle large dollar amounts in a variety of currencies**

✔ **Provide security for area**

Miscellaneous

Investigate the following:

✔ **Vacation options available before and after meeting:**
- Airfare layover cost differential, if any when requested at time of booking or after booking
- Worldwide medical insurance available for attendee to purchase if personal policies do not cover (give name, address, and phone number of company

✔ **Immunization shots required**

✔ **Procedure for medical emergencies. Attendees should carry with them at all times:**
- Names and phone numbers of family members to be contacted
- Name of attending physicians

✔ **VAT (value-added tax) of country**

Multilingual Requirements

✔ **Signs (official language and foreign languages):**
- Registration
- All other service desks
- Small group sessions
- Currency exchange
- Airport greeting (for all languages)

✔ **Printed materials:**
- Program books
- Handouts, other conference materials
- Registration materials

✔ **Multilingual staff:**
- Registration
- Other service desks

✔ **Attendee orientation (small groups—one for each language):**
- Local history and customs
- Key phrases in local language
- Fire safety procedures

- Medical emergencies:
  —House doctor or other local doctors
  —Whom to call
  —Room number of meeting manager or designated person
  —Location of embassy or consulate of home country
- Security inside and outside hotel
- Tourist attraction information, restaurants, entertainment
- Current currency-exchange rate
- Locations of nearby banks (hours and days open)

Currency

Depending on the arrangements you've made with your suppliers, you will most likely need access to large amounts of money for payments on-site. These include the hotel master bill, bills for local contractors, entertainment, and transportation, and all those expenses listed in Chapter 14. Suppliers will be less likely to bill you if you are not located in their country. In addition, you will need a small amount of local currency to pay customs fees, taxis, tips, and other out-of-pocket expenses. The fluctuations in currency rates make the task of handling large amounts of money very important. Careful planning can give your organization a financial advantage, and carelessness can cost you.

Sources of Currency

✔ **Local bank within your country:**
Large amounts must be ordered in advance. Specify denominations.

✔ **Local bank in the country where the meeting will be held:**
Rates may vary from bank to bank, but they are better than rates in the hotel.

✔ **Currency-exchange office:**
Office charges a fee, but usually has more currency available than do banks.

Method of Payment and Currency Rates

✔ **Check drawn in your currency:**
Rate is established at the time the check clears your bank.

✔ **Credit cards:**
Rate is established at the time the charge is credited to your account.

✔ **Wire transfer:**
Rate is established at the time payment is received.

✔ **Check or draft in foreign currency:**
Rate is established when the check is cashed or deposited to the holder's account.

✔ **Foreign bank account:**
Rate is established at time of deposit; if properly negotiated, money can earn interest until it is withdrawn.

Locking in a Good Rate

✔ **Identify a reliable source of currency to assist in decisions on how and when to buy or exchange the needed currency.**

✔ **Use a forwarding contract that locks in the rate at specified intervals when deposits are required by your organization.**

✔ **Use a bank draft, which transfers funds directly to a foreign account, allowing you to select the time to transfer based on the current rate.**

Printed Materials

Types of Materials Requiring Translation

✔ **Promotional materials, invitations**

✔ **Registration materials**

✔ **Confirmation materials and other information for attendees**

✔ **Handouts, abstracts, and other program materials**

✔ **Program book**

✔ **Proceedings**

✔ **International advertising copy**

✔ **International news releases**

Locating a Translator

Contact the International Association of Congress Interpreters or the American Association of Language Specialists (see Resources) for names and contact information for professional interpreters and translators if you do not already have qualified translators in the required languages.

Information the Translator Will Need

- ✔ **Technical nature of manuscript**

- ✔ **Language of original manuscript**

- ✔ **Translation language required**

- ✔ **Length of manuscript**

- ✔ **Time allowed for translation**

- ✔ **Literal or in-context translation or abstract**

- ✔ **Format of original and final translated manuscript:**
  - Typed
  - Double- or single-spaced
  - Language coded on each page
  - Pages numbered

- ✔ **Method for return of completed manuscript:**
  - Air
  - Registered
  - Overnight

- ✔ **Budget for translation services, payment procedures.**

Working With a Printer

- ✔ **Locate a printer who can set type and print in the required languages.**

- ✔ **Review samples of past printing in the language required, and have typesetting approved by translator for accuracy.**

- ✔ **Organize materials for easy identification by you and the printer.**

Promotional Mailings for International Meetings

- ✔ **Budget for increased costs of international mailings.**

- ✔ **Check postal regulations of countries processing the mailings.**

- ✔ **Match return address to country dispatching mailing.**

- ✔ **Allow additional time for receipt and response.**

- ✔ **Always send international mailings by air.**

Language Interpretation for Large Group Sessions

Interpreters work in teams of two and are permitted to work only a limited number of hours per day (in some instances, four hours per team per day). They work in fifteen- to thirty-minute shifts. A full day's session schedule (morning and afternoon) may require two teams per day for each language interpreted. The following types of multilingual translations may be used:

✔ **Simultaneous:**
Interpretation occurs as the speaker speaks. Interpreters broadcast translated information, usually from inside a soundproof booth.
   The preferred method is to use built-in systems. These are often available outside the United States and are often included in the cost of meeting room or at reasonable additional charge.

✔ **Consecutive:**
Follows at predetermined breaks or at conclusion of speaker's presentation. Interpreter gives translation from notes taken during speech.

✔ **Concurrent:**
Speaker pauses while interpreter translates. This method is not suitable for more than one language, but it works very well in small groups.

✔ **Whispered:**
Interpreter whispers to group members while speech is in progress.

Overseas Shipments

Documents Required

✔ **Commercial invoice:**
An inventory of each box specifying contents with descriptions, serial numbers (where applicable), quantity of each type of article, and listed value for each item. Prepared by company responsible for packing items in boxes.

✔ **Certificate of origin:**
A statement from the government indicating the country of origin of the shipment. Responsibility of the customs broker.

✔ **Carnet:**
A document that allows materials to enter, exist in and exit a country duty-free. Papers must be stamped at each foreign border the shipment crosses. Responsibility of the customs broker.

✔ **Consulor invoice:**

An acknowledgment by the local tourist office that the event is being held at a particular place. Responsibility of the customs broker.

✔ **Limited power of attorney:**

The document that authorizes the customs broker to complete necessary arrangements for your shipment during return to point of origin. Responsibility of the customs broker.

✔ **Export license:**

Applies only to export of military or highly sensitive materials.

Shipping Services and Service Providers

✔ **Customs brokers:**

These people obtain and prepare all necessary documents to get shipment through customs (foreign and domestic).

✔ **Freight forwarders and transportation coordinators:**
- Prepare bills of lading and other papers required for transporting shipment.
- Pick up packed containers at city of origin.
- Transport shipment to overseas carrier.
- Pick up containers from overseas carrier and return them to city of origin.
- Select and contact local movers at foreign arrival point.

✔ **Local shipping companies:**
- Pick up and pack items to be shipped in containers.
- Prepare commercial invoices.
- Contact freight forwarder.
- Receive goods from freight forwarder when returned.
- Notify shipper
- Deliver shipment to point of origin.

✔ **Professional Congress Organizers (PCOs):**

(International term for meeting management firms and meeting planners.)
- Charge a professional fee for acting as an "extension of your home office in managing administrative details
- Take care of meeting logistics.
- Handle nonpolicy or decisionmaking matters.
- Serve as liaison between meeting organization, outside suppliers, government agencies, hotel, and local tourist convention office.

✔ **Local agents:**

May be:
- Foreign-based corporate offices or affiliates
- International members, clients, or suppliers

✔ **National tourist offices or convention bureaus:**

(Usually based in one or more locations in most large countries, and many have international offices in key international cities such as New York.)

- Provide promotional materials:
  —National and local maps
  —Inexpensive promotional items
  —Posters
  —Postcards
  —Area maps
  —Tourist brochures
- Supply information on availability
- Liaison with destination management companies, hotels, PCOs, and other local suppliers
- Rarely provide recommendations for individual suppliers or companies
- Do not arrange for services

✔ **Destination Management Companies (DMCs)**

(Based in local host country. Fees charged to clients are based on services required.)

- Provide or subcontract services for:
  —Ground transportation to and from airport
  —Airport greeter(s)
  —Group tours in or outside city
  —Car rental
- Multilingual temporary help and interpreters
- Local or national information orientation for meeting staff and attendees
- Assistance with customs and local government agencies
- Coordination of local publicity and public relations
- Audiovisual equipment rental and support
- Local entertainment and theme events

GLOSSARY

account codes or code of accounts Numbers system given to specific categories of income or expense.

agenda Schedule giving time and sequence of topics and sessions at a meeting; often includes room or location and names of speakers, moderators and other program participants.

agent (1) Person who obtains engagements for entertainers. An agent is paid by the entertainers and has no contract for production responsibilities. (2) Person who acts, or causes acts to be performed, for another and who has no legal or financial responsibility other than for areas of professional liability resulting from those acts.

air space Space separating one meeting room from another

à la russe Method of food service in which waiter serves each guest a plate completely set up

amenities Services and special products (gifts) provided by a hotel or supplier beyond those normally included in the rate.

American plan Room plus three meals each day. This is also called *FAP* (full American plan).

antitrust laws Regulation of trade and commerce protecting against unfair business practices.

apron Part of a stage in front of the main curtain.

arrival pattern Anticipated dates and times of arrival of group members.

attendee Individual attending the meeting sessions.

audioconference *See* teleconference.

authorized signature Signature of person with authority to charge to facility's master account, guarantee payment, and contract for space, services, and supplies.

banquet checks Checks for various food-and-beverage events associated with a meeting.

banquet event order (BEO) Detailed instructions prepared by the hotel for an event; also called résumé, function sheet, event order (EO).

bar reading A detailed written record of liquor consumption during an event.

BEO *See* banquet event order.

Betamax SONY brand name.

bible *See* spec book.

bleed (printing term) An ink area that runs to edge of paper.

blueline (printing term) *See also* proof. Final proof of printed copy for client's approval before printing; also called brownline or silverprint.

block *See* room block.

book To commit meeting-room space, guest/sleeping rooms, entertainment, on a definite basis.

breakout sessions (breakouts) Small group sessions within the meeting, formed to discuss specific subjects that are often related to the topic of the previous general session.

breaks Periods between sessions; attendees often move from one session to another. Refreshments such as coffee or soda are often served. *See also* theme break.

brownline *See* blueline.

call brands Brands of liquor usually available based on preferences of attendees.

carnet Document permitting materials to cross a national border duty-free.

carousel projector 35mm slide projector using a carousel tray.

carousel tray Circular slide container used for projecting 35mm slides.

cartage Short-haul moving of exhibits; often incorrectly referred to as *drayage*.

cash bar Private bar at which guests pay for their own drinks individually. *See also* host bar.

cassette Self-enclosed two-reel tape module, such as an audio- or videocassette.

certificate of origin Statement from government stating origin of a foreign shipment.

CFO *See* chief financial officer.

check-in Procedure for guest arrivals and registration at hotels or at meeting registration areas.

check-out Procedure for guest departures from hotels; includes account settlement.

cherry picker (also known as a **highjacker**) Equipment used to lift a person to a given height.

chief financial officer (CFO) Individual in an organization responsible for the financial management of the company.

classroom setup Meeting-room setup with tables in front of chairs.

clinic A hands-on workshop type of educational experience where students can learn or improve skills by doing.

colloquium Informal group discussion on selected topics of mutual interest.

commercial invoice Document specifying content of a shipment of goods.

commissionable Type of sale in which a fee or a percentage of the amount of sale is to be paid to the agent or purchaser.

comp *See* complimentary.

complimentary (comp) Service, space, or item given at no charge.

concessions Sales of promotional items, such as albums, posters, T-shirts, by artists' representatives. Usually set up in conjunction with an artist's engagement.

conclave Gathering of a group with shared or special interests.

concurrent sessions Sessions on a variety of topics scheduled at the same time. Attendees choose which sessions they will attend.

conference Participatory meeting designed for discussion of subjects related to a specific topic or area. May include fact finding, problem solving, and consultation.

congress (1) Meeting of an association of delegates or representatives from constituent organizations. (2) European term for *convention*.

consular invoice Acknowledgment by local tourist office of meeting to be held in a stated city.

contingencies Promises made in agreements or contracts that can be affected by future uncertainties.

contract A legal and binding written agreement between two or more parties.

convention Assemblage of delegates, representatives, and members of an organization convened for a common purpose.

convention bureau Service organization that provides destination promotion, booking, and services, including convention personnel and housing.

convention services manager Employee of a facility or hotel who is responsible for the facility-related details of an event.

corkage fee Service charge placed on beer, liquor, and wine purchased elsewhere and brought into a facility. Glassware, ice, mixers, and service are sometimes provided.

corner booth Exhibit space with aisles on two sides; larger trade shows usually add an additional charge for such booths.

cover Table setting for one person. The term is often used in relation to number of waiters per cover or per person.

crew Stagehands, technicians, truck loaders responsible for the technical setup of a show.

customs (1) Local practices of a country or region. (2) System within a country that controls entry of people and products into that country.

customs broker Person or company that provides customs-clearing services to shippers of goods to and from another country.

cutoff date Designated day that facility will release to the general public a block of guest/sleeping rooms that had been reserved for a specific group.

dais *See* podium.

data base Collection of historical information to be used for current or future planning.

decorator General contractor or service contractor, usually hired to set up an exhibition.

delegate A voting representative at a meeting. The term is often incorrectly used to mean *attendee* or *participant*.

Destination management company (DMC) A company, based in the city, county, or state in which the meeting is being held. It handles local activities, including service contracts with contractors, tours, ground transportation, decorations, props, and theme events.

die-cutting (printing term) Process of cutting shapes into a sheet of paper. Used for cuts of paper not following a straight line.

dimmer (also known as **rheostat**) Device used to control light intensity.

discussion leader Person who introduces topic and controls discussion in the group.

dissolve In a slide or multimedia presentation, to change from one scene to another by blending visual images together. One image fades out as another fades in.

dissolve unit   Device that activates fade-out and fade-in of slides from one projector to another.
DMC   *See* destination management company.
double bed   Bed measuring 53 inches by 75 inches.
downstage   That part of a stage that is closest to the audience.
draping   Fabric used to create exhibit booths, finish or surround an area such as an audiovisual screen, or provide a backdrop for a stage or wall. *See also* pipe and drape.
drayage   Transfer of exhibit booths, equipment, materials, and properties from point of arrival (decorator storage) to exhibit site.
duotone   (printing term)   Photograph prepared for two-color reproduction.

early-bird rate   Special rate given to people who register early for a meeting.
easel   Three- or four-legged stand with rack used to hold cork/magnetic board, posters, flipcharts, signs.
elevated table   Counter-height table frequently used in registration area to provide a surface for writing.
elite (printing term)   A size of typewriter type that produces twelve typed characters or spaces per inch.
embossing (printing term)   Process of pressing paper into bas relief to produce a three-dimensional effect.
engineering   Department of facility or hotel responsible for keeping the building in working condition. Its responsibilities include electrical, lighting, temperature, and general repair.
event order (EO)   *See* banquet event order.
exhibit booth   Individual display area constructed to exhibit products or convey a message.
exhibit hall   Area within the facility where exhibits are located.
exhibit prospectus   Promotional materials and published specifications, rules, and regulations for prospective exhibitors. It is designed to encourage participation.
exhibition   An organized display of multi-company products and/or services. *See also* industrial show.
exhibition manager   *See* show manager.
exhibitor's kit (also called **service kit**)   Kit prepared and sent by decorator to all registered exhibitors. It contains information and supplier request forms (or names of local contractors) required by exhibitors.

FAP (full American plan)   *See* American plan.
flat rate   One price, based on average cost, for all guest/sleeping rooms in a hotel, exclusive of suites; may be flat-rate single or flat-rate double.
flipchart   Large pad of paper placed on an easel to be used by a speaker for illustrative purposes.
floor load   Maximum amount of weight per square foot a floor can support.
floppy disk   Diskette on which a program is created or stored for a computer.
foam core   Lightweight material with a styrofoam center used for signs, decorating, and exhibits.
foil-stamping (printing term)   Metallic or pigmented "foil leaf" used in stamping. Heat and pressure are used to create lettering or a design on a surface.
force majeure clause   Clause in an artist's contract that limits liability should a performance be prevented because of disruptive circumstances beyond the artist's control. Inclement weather usually does not apply.
foreign meeting   A meeting comprised of attendees from one nation traveling to a foreign destination for the purpose of attending that meeting. *See also* international meeting.
forum   An open discussion between audience, panel members, and moderator.
forward contract   A contract used to lock in a currency exchange rate.
four-color separation (printing term)   Process of printing full-color image utilizing four colored screened patterns from which printing plates can be engraved.
four-hour call   Usual minimum work period for which union labor must be paid.
freight forwarder   Company transporting goods from one site to another (interstate, international).
front desk   Area in a hotel where all guests check in and out when staying overnight, room assignments are made, and final guest bill is paid.
front-screen projection   Projection of an image onto the front surface of a light-reflecting screen from a projector placed within or behind the audience.
function bill   Check or bill prepared by the hotel stating the charges for each event or function.
function sheet   *See* banquet event order.
function space   Space in a facility where private functions, meetings, or events can be held.

gaffer's tape   Fabric tape used in anchoring cables to the floor; also known as duct, carpet, or electrical tape.
general session (also called **plenery session**)   A meeting of the full attendance.
graphics (printing term)   Illustrations, photographs, layout, combined with type style and copy.
gross square feet   The width multiplied by the length of the area.
group rate   Negotiated guest/sleeping room rate for a group.

GTD   *See* guaranteed number.

guaranteed number (GTD)   Those servings, meals, or rooms to be paid for regardless of whether they are actually consumed or occupied.

guest/sleeping room   Sleeping room for hotel guest (to be occupied for meeting attendee or participant).

half-round setup   A 60- or 72-inch round table with people seated only around the half of the table that faces the speaker or stage.

halftone (printing term)   Photograph that has been prepared for single-color reproduction.

handouts   Materials given to attendees at sessions, not in their registration packets.

hard disk   Disk that becomes the permanent memory in a computer.

hardware   Computer equipment.

header   Overhead illuminated display sign usually identifying areas for preregistration, on-site registration, information booth.

historical report   Report that gives history of a group.

history (also known as **past history, hotel history,** or **group history**)   Information about past meetings taken from data on hotels, organizations, corporations, program participants, or attendees.

honorarium   Voluntary payment made for services that legally require no fee.

hospitality suite   Room or suite used to entertain guests.

host bar (also called **open bar**)   Private bar at which drinks are paid for by a sponsor. *See also* cash bar.

house brand   Usually medium- or low-priced brand of liquor used by a facility instead of the more expensive or name brand.

house lights   Room lighting that operates separate from stage lighting.

housekeeping   Daily maid and cleaning service provided to guests occupying a guest/sleeping room in hotel. This department also usually provides irons, ironing boards, hair dryers, and other items requested by guests.

housing   The process of assigning hotel guest/sleeping rooms to attendees.

incidentals   All expenses, other than room and tax, billed to a guest's account, such as room service and telephone calls.

indemnification   Protection from liability under stated circumstances or exemption from incurred liabilities.

industrial show (also called **trade show, exhibition**)   An exhibit of numerous related or similar products by various companies for the purposes of introducing new products, sales promotion, and increased visibility to the general public.

in-house services   Those services (audiovisual, florist) available within a meeting facility.

institute   Instructional meeting providing intensive education on a given subject.

international meeting   A meeting comprised of attendees from two or more countries. It may be held outside the national borders of both countries or within the borders of one of the participant nations. *See also* foreign meeting.

king-size bed   Large bed usually measuring 76 inches by 80 inches. A *long* king-size bed measures 76 inches by 84 inches.

lapel microphone   *See* lavalier microphone.

lavalier microphone (also called **neck** or **lapel mike**)   Portable microphone that fastens around the speaker's neck or onto the speaker's clothing.

lead time   Time prior to meeting or other key event by which work is to be completed.

lectern   Slanted-top reading stand. This may be a small tabletop unit or a freestanding unit. It is often incorrectly called a podium, which is the riser or stage.

lectern microphone   Microphone attached to a lectern. It is often incorrectly called a podium mike.

lecture   Informative or instructional speech given by one person.

market   The potential consumer group likely to be interested in or to need a service or product.

marketing   Strategies designed to sell products or services.

master account   Account to which approved expenses incurred by the hotel can be charged.

master of ceremonies (all called, less formally, **moderator**)   Formal title for the person who presides over a program or dinner.

mixers (audiovisuals)   Recording devices by which sound from all microphones feeds into one system. These are usually required if three or more microphones are used in one room.

moderator   Person who presides over sessions, panels, and forums. *See also* master of ceremonies.

move-in   Date and time of installation of exhibit by decorator or exhibitors.

move-out   Date and time of dismantling of exhibits by exhibitors and decorator.

multi-image   Visual presentation using more than one projected image at a time.

multimedia   Use of two or more audiovisual media in one presentation. Usually audio material is synchronized with visual image presentation.

national tourist office (NTO)   Official government office of a country that provides services, such as promotion and customs information, to visitors coming into that country.

neck microphone   *See* lavalier microphone.

noncommissionable   Type of sale in which percentage of sale amount is not paid to the agent or purchaser.

no-show   Person who has made a reservation at the hotel or meeting and does not check in or arrive.

NTO   *See* national tourist office.

omnidirectional microphone   Microphone that picks up sound from all directions.

open bar   *See* host bar.

overflow   Hotel guest/sleeping rooms booked by planner for attendees after headquarters facilities are full.

overhead projector   Audiovisual equipment that projects an image on a screen by passing light through a transparency.

overset   Number of places set for a food event in addition to the guaranteed amount.

paid-out amount   Cash withdrawal requested by the planner to be charged to hotel's master account. It is often used for cash to set up registration cash boxes.

panel   Format for discussion by a moderator and two or more program participants (panelists).

participant (also known as **program participant**)   Person performing an assigned role in a program or meeting; frequently used incorrectly to mean attendee.

patch   (1) (*verb*) To temporarily join wires or slides by overlapping. (2) (*noun*) Plug-in connection between two lines.

PBX operator   Telephone switchboard operator.

PCO   *See* professional congress organizer.

performance bond   Guarantee that a facility will meet all contractual specifications.

pica (printing term)   Size of typewriter type that produces ten typed characters or spaces per inch.

pickup   Number of hotel guest/sleeping rooms actually used out of the room block.

pipe and drape   Tubing draped with fabric to create and separate exhibit booths.

planning schedule (also known as **timeline**)   Detailed outline of all activities and tasks required to produce a meeting, deadlines for each action, and assignments to the individual, department, or committee responsible for specific acts.

plenary session   *See* general session.

plus/plus (+/+)   Price plus taxes plus gratuities.

podium (also called **stage** or **dais**)   The platform on which a speaker stands; often a raised area (riser). It is often incorrectly called a *lectern*.

port   Location of telephone to be used during a teleconference (one phone equals 1 port).

post-convention briefing (post-con)   Meeting between the planner and key hotel staff after the main event is over to debrief and critique the meeting planning process and actual implementation details. May include suppliers.

poster session   Visual display of reports and papers, usually scientific, accompanied by authors or researchers.

pre-convention briefing (pre-con)   Meeting with planner, hotel department heads, and key suppliers to review purpose and details of upcoming event.

presenter   Person discussing and explaining a given topic in an informational session.

pre-set   Food, usually salad or dessert, placed on banquet tables prior to the seating of guests.

premium brands   Most expensive brands of liquor used by an establishment.

proceedings   Official transcript of the program content, usually written and bound.

professional congress organizer (PCO)   An international meeting planner whose services are primarily restricted to very large meetings. This term is used more often in Europe.

program book   Printed schedule of meeting events, function room locations, and other pertinent information; usually the official program for the meeting.

program design   Structure of meeting program elements to achieve meeting goals and objectives. Includes presentation method (format), topics, special events, free time, and breaks.

program participant   *See* participant.

projection distance   Required minimum and maximum distance between projector and screen for projecting a focused image.

proof   (1) (*noun*) Final copy of printed material for approval before printing. *See also* blueline. (2) (*verb*) To correct before final printing. (3) (*noun*) Standard measure of alcoholic strength (100 proof equals 50 percent alcohol content).

property   Lodging establishment such as a hotel, conference center, or meeting facility.

prospectus   Site selection data and meeting specifications submitted to prospective facilities. *See also* exhibit prospectus.

quad box   Box containing four electrical outlets.

queen-size bed   Bed usually measuring 60 inches by 80 inches.

rack rate   Hotel's standard guest/sleeping-room rate.

range rate   Price of guest/sleeping rooms based on a combination of minimum, middle, and maximum room rates. The number of rooms in each type varies.

rapporteur   Monitor who evaluates conference sessions.

rap sessions   Informal sessions with no specific agenda.

rear-screen projection   Image projected on the back surface of a screen placed between projector and audience.

registrant   Individual who has submitted a registration form, paid appropriate fees, and attends the meeting or event.

request for proposal (RFP)   A request from the buyer of a service or a product to the potential supplier outlining all the requirements of the buyer and necessary information for the supplier to prepare a bid.

résumé   *See* banquet event order.

reverse (printing term)   Effect produced by negative form of original type or art resulting in black or other color background with copy appearing in white or other color of paper on which it is printed.

rheostat   *See* dimmer.

RFP   *See* request for proposal.

room block (also called **block**)   (1) (*noun*) Number of rooms held for a group for a specified period of time. (2) (*verb*) To assign space.

room nights   Number of rooms blocked or occupied multiplied by number of nights each room is reserved or occupied.

rough layout   Sketchy or tentative rendering of approximate placement of art and type for printing or meeting-room setup.

round   Round banquet table, available in diameters of 60 inches or 72 inches.

round robin   Contest or tournament in which each participant is matched with every other participant.

sales meeting   Meeting to introduce new products and their applications and to motivate sales staff.

sans serif (printing term)   Typefaces without decorative cross strokes at top and bottom of letters.

screen left; screen right   Perspective from audience facing the screen.

security cages   Cages supplied to exhibitors to lock up materials.

seminar   Lecture or dialogue in which participants share experiences under the guidance of a discussion leader.

serif (printing term)   Type styles with decorative cross strokes at top and bottom of letters.

service kit   *See* exhibitor's kit.

service level   (1) Number of people one waiter is assigned to serve. (2) Types, coverage, and quality of services offered by a facility or contractor.

set   (1) (*noun*) Performance area including props, equipment, backdrops. (2) (*noun*) Length of time band or orchestra plays between breaks. (3) (*verb*) Make preparations for a predetermined number of attendees. (4) (*verb*) To arrange type for printed materials.

setup   (1) Way in which a function room is arranged. (2) Mixers, fruit, and glassware accompanying a liquor order.

show manager (also known as **exhibition manager**)   Person responsible for all aspects of an exhibition or trade show.

silverprint   *See* blueline.

simultaneous interpretation   Process of orally translating one language into another or signing for the deaf while the person is speaking.

software   Computer programs that cause equipment to "think"in a particular format. Generates programs and applications purchased or created for a computer.

sound board   Console with separate channels to control volume and sound quality produced by each microphone.

sound system   Audio speaker system used to amplify sound.

space rate   Cost per square foot for space.

speaker (sometimes referred to as a **program participant** if presentation is less formal than a speech)   Person who presents an address on a specific topic or topics.

spec book (also known as **staging guide** or **bible**)   Written specifications, requirements, and instructions for all functions, room setups, services, and purveyors. Includes names of key personnel and their areas of responsibility, special events, and any other related requirements.

special-rate package   A lowered, all-inclusive rate, frequently including one or more meals for two/three nights, that is offered to the general public. Often used to generate off-season or weekend business.

specifications   Complete description of meeting requirements, usually written. *See also* spec book.

sponsor   (1) *Limited sponsor*, one who assumes a specified financial responsibility. (2) *Meeting sponsor*, person(s) or organization assuming full responsibility for all costs and phases of producing a meeting.

sponsorship (often also called **sponsor**)　Offer by an outside organization to underwrite a specific event, such as a host bar.

spotlight　Strong movable light focusing upon a particular person or object, such as the light used on a stage.

stage　*See* podium.

stage left; stage right　Perspective of one who faces audience from the stage.

stage lighting　Lighting designated for stage area only.

staging guide　*See* spec book.

standing microphone　Microphone attached to a floor stand.

strike　(1) (*noun*) Union walkout. (2) (*verb*) To remove all scenery and props. (3) (*verb*) to dismantle and remove an exhibit.

stuffing　The act of placing assembled written materials in an envelope, folder, or other presentation packet.

supplier　Facility, company, agency, or person offering space, goods, or services.

symposium　Event at which experts discuss a particular subject and opinions are expressed.

table microphone　Microphone on a short stand placed on a table for seated speakers.

tabletop display　Portable display that can be set up on top of a table.

teleconference　Type of meeting that brings together three or more people in two or more locations through telecommunications. *Audioconference* refers to audio only, such as a telephone. *Videoconference* refers to a combined audio and visual link through satellite or other type of network.

teleprompter　Electronic device that allows display of script.

theater (or auditorium) setup　Chairs only, set up in rows facing head table, stage, or speaker. Variations are semicircular and V-shaped setups.

theme break　Break during formal program sessions (such as a coffee break) with special food and beverages pertaining to a theme and often including decorations, costumes, and entertainment.

throw　Projection distance.

time and materials　Method of charging for services and materials used on a cost-plus basis.

timeline　*See* planning schedule.

trade show　Exhibition of products and services that may or may not be open to the public. When associated with a meeting. This type of show is often only open to registered attendees. *See also* industrial show.

transparencies　A transparent plastic sheet or roll, clear or colored, that provides the image projected from an overhead projector to a screen.

turnover　Time required to break down and reset a meeting room.

twin bed　Bed measuring 38 inches by 75 inches.

two-by-two slide　Piece of 35mm photographic film usually in a 2-inch-by-2-inch cardboard, glass, or plastic mount.

upstage　Part of the stage farthest from the audience or camera.

velox (also known as **stats**) (printing term)　Photographic material used in preparing camera-ready art; a high-contrast black-and-white proof.

VHS　Videotape recorder and player utilizing the ½-inch VHS format. Not compatible with beta format.

videoconference　*See* teleconference.

VIP (very important person)　Organization officers, celebrity speakers, panel moderators, industry experts, or others who have distinguished themselves from the majority in attendance.

visa　Official document stamped inside a passport allowing a foreign visitor to enter and remain in a country for a specified period of time.

walk-in　Person requesting hotel accommodations who does not have a reservation, or prospective meeting attendee who did not register in advance.

wash light　Colored light that softly illuminates an area.

workshop　Training session in which participants, often through exercises and hands-on projects, develop skills and knowledge in a given field.

RESOURCES

Books

The following books are related to meeting management. For more information about adult learning, group communications, marketing, audiovisual equipment, culinary terms, graphics and printing and other aspects of meeting management, visit a book store or library.

Barrier Free Environments, Inc., and Harold Russell Associates, Inc. *The Planner's Guide to Barrier Free Meetings*. Raleigh, Va.: 1980.

The Convention Liaison Council Glossary. Washington, D.C.: The Convention Liaison Council, 1986.

The Convention Liaison Council Manual. 4th ed. Washington, D.C.: The Convention Liaison Council, 1985.

Nichols, Barbara C., ed. *Professional Meeting Management*. Birmingham, Ala.: Professional Convention Management Association, 1985.

A Special NAEM Report on the Applicability of State Sales Tax to Gratuities and Service Charges. Aurora, Ohio: National Association of Exposition Managers, Inc., 1988.

Successful Meetings Magazine Project Editor Regina M. McGee, in cooperation with the Convention Liaison Council Editorial Committee.

Trade and Professional Magazines

The following magazines contain information about meeting sites, resources for meeting managers, and information about meeting planning and the meetings industry.

Convene. Professional Convention Management Association, 100 Vestavia Office Park, Suite 220, Birmingham, Ala. 35216.

Convention World. Bayard Publications, Inc., 600 Summer St., Stamford, Conn. 06901.

Corporate & Incentive Travel. Coastal Communications Corporation, 488 Madison Ave., New York, N.Y. 10022.

Corporate Meetings & Incentives. Edgell Communications, Inc., 747 Third Ave., New York, N.Y. 10017.

Insurance Conference Planner. Bayard Publications, Inc., 600 Summer St., Stamford, Conn. 06901.

M&C Meetings & Conventions. News American Publishing, Inc., 500 Plaza Dr., Secaucus, N.J. 07096.

The Meeting Manager. Meeting Planners International, 1950 Stemmons Freeway, Dallas, Tex. 75207.

Meeting News. Gralla Publications, 1515 Broadway, New York, N.Y. 10036.

Special Events. Miramar Publishing Co., 2048 Cotner Ave., Los Angeles, Calif. 90025.

Successful Meetings. Bill Communications, 633 Third Ave., New York, N.Y. 10017.

Directories

Note: The trade magazines listed above also publish annual directories of meeting facilities and suppliers included in the subscription.

Audarena Stadium International Guide. Amusement Business, Box 24970, Nashville, Tenn. 37202.

Conventions & Meetings Canada. Conventions & Meetings Canada, 72 Wellington St., W., Suite 207, Markham, Ontario L3P 1A8.

International Association of Conference Centers Directory. International Association of Conference Centers, 45 Progress Parkway, Maryland Heights, Mo. 63043.

Meeting Planners International Buyers Guide. Meeting Planners International, 1950 Stemmons Freeway, Dallas, Tex. 75207.

Nationwide Directory of Corporate Meeting Planners. The Salesman's Guide, 1140 Broadway, Suite 1203, New York, N.Y. 10001.

OAG Travel Planner Hotel & Motel Redbook. Official Airlines Guides Inc., 2000 Clearwater Dr., Oak Brook, Ill. 60521.

Professional Associations

The following professional membership organizations are sources for educational programs and seminars, magazines and other publications, and networking opportunities.

American Society of Association Executives, 1575 Eye St., N.W., Washington, D.C. 20005.

American Society of Training and Development, 1630 Duke St., P.O. Box 1443, Alexandria, Va. 22313.

Insurance Conference Planners Association, c/o Bayard Publications, 600 Summer St., Stamford, Conn. 06901.

International Special Events Society, 3288 El Cajon Blvd., Suite 6, San Diego, Calif. 92104.

Meeting Planners International, 1950 Stemmons Freeway, Dallas, Tex. 75207.

National Association of Exposition Managers, 334 E. Garfield Rd., Aurora, Ohio 44202.

Professional Convention Management Association, 100 Vestavia Office Park, Suite 220, Birmingham, Ala. 35216.

Religious Conference Management Association, One Hoosier Dome, Suite 120, Indianapolis, Ind. 46225.

Society of Company Meeting Planners, 2600 Garden Rd., Suite 208, Monterey, Calif. 93940.

Society of Government Meeting Planners, 1213 Prince St., Alexandria, Va. 22314.

Trade Association

The Convention Liaison Council, 1575 Eye St., N.W., Washington, D.C. 20005.

INDEX

accessibility, in contract, 40–41
accidents, 107, 322
accountants, 74
account codes, 254–257
accounting, final, 125, 358
accounting system, by project, 181
addendums, to contracts, 43
administrative systems, of meeting
    management firms, 181
admonitions, 140
ad sales, in program book, 290–291
advertising
    camera-ready art for, 291
    contract for, 292
    in program book, 55–56
    timetable for, 290
agenda, 12, 76
agreements, 36–44, 260–273
    see also contracts
airlines
    fares for, 23
    official services of, 84
airports, foreign, 443
à la Russe (service), 339
alcohol
    allowances for, 340
    average per-person consumption of,
      123
    cost-saving ideas for, 341
    host vs. cash bar, 103
    liability and, 93, 95, 138–139
    math for, 130–131
    preventing excessive consumption, 95

American Association of Language
    Specialists, 446
American Society of Association
    Executives (ASAE), xii
annual meetings, 54
area, 365
art, insurance for, 140
art boards, 69
ASAE, *see* American Society of
    Association Executives
association meetings, vs. corporate
    meetings, xv
associations, 54, 117, 460–461
    volunteers in, 145
atmosphere, and program design, 13–14
attendance, 61
    goal for, 52
    monitoring on-site, 155–156
    report on, 48, 282
attendance summary form, 385
attendee needs
    chart of, 320–325
    determining, 80–82
    questionnaire, 318–320
attendees
    check-in by, 88
    directions for, 162
    emergency calls for, 89
    host committees and, 85
    information for, 86
    list of preregistered, 76
    participation levels of, 17–18
    profile on, 209, 282

attendees (*continued*)
  and registration, 71
  transportation for, 83–84
  see also disabled attendees
attendees' services, 80–89, 310–327
  at international meetings, 442–446
  on-site, 317–319
attention spans, 14
audience, 12
audioconference, 116
audiotapes
  of meetings, 86
  vs. brochure, 81
audiovisual companies, 115–116, 344–345
audiovisual equipment, 247, 270
  appearance of, 118–119
  for speaker, 220
  types of, 345–347
audiovisual presentations, 111–113, 212,
    344–352
  budgeting for, 123
  formulas for, 350
  measurements for, 132
  and retention, 14
audiovisual supplier request form, 115,
    351–352
automobile insurance, 366
average miles per hour, by bus, 314
averages, 134
awards, at special events, 97

badges, 73, 75, 306
  replacements for, 76
banquet checks, 154
banquet event order (BEO) number, 101,
    149
banquet setup, 32, 237
  diagram for, 243
bar graph, 135
bartending form, 103–104, 343
beds, standard sizes of, 236
beepers, 160
BEO, *see* banquet event order number
beverage, *see* alcohol; food and
    beverages
bids, 124
  deadline for, 29
  preparing, 420
  request for, 63
billable hours, 181–182, 422
billing
  from audiovisual companies, 115–116
  master account, 124–125
  percentage of gross, as fee, 423
  by phases, 424–425
  see also fees

binding, 67, 296
bleeds, 66
bluelines, 58, 64
board of directors
  registration of, 73
  special services for, 87
bonding, 139, 367
Bonneville, 116
book format, 67
bookings, multiple, in hotel, 33
booth assignment, 168–169
breach of contract, 368–369
break-even budgeting, 124, 127, 134–135,
    358–359
  math for, 361–364
breakout session, 212
breaks
  food at, 96
  importance of, 98
  and learning, 14
  time requirements for, 339
bribes, 185
brochures, 287
  audiotapes instead of, 81
  editing, 59
  error in, 68
  organization of, 81
  quantity printed, 68–69
  time requirement for, 58–59
budgets, 7, 12, 120–127, 210, 353–360
  break-even, *see* break-even budgeting
  and brochure, 60–61
  cost reductions in, 126
  deadlines for adding to, 123
  example of, 357
  executives' exceptions and, 125–126
  for exhibits, 164–165, 387–388
  final accounting for, 125
  and food and beverages, 99
  format for, 121–123
  formulas for, 123–124
  percentages and, 49
  and professional planner, 176–177
  for printing, 67–68
buffet, 339
  time requirement for, 339
  vs. seated meal, 110
bulk mail, 60, 65
bump loading, 315
business plan, 180, 415–416
business trips, xi
bus transportation, 314
  fees for, 316
  planning trip with, 316–317

camera-ready copy, 56
    for ads, 291
cancellation fee, and registration, 78
cancellation/interruption insurance, 138, 267
cancellation policy, in contract, 37, 42, 267
candles, 107
carnet, 448
cars, rental of, and insurance, 141
case study, 212
cash advances, 23
cash bar, 95
    vs. host, 103
cash flow, report on, 281
catering, 93
ceilings, and audiovisuals, 112
centerpieces, 107
certificate of insurance, 139
certificate of origin, 448
certification, for planners, 185
chain of command, 371
changes
    communicating, 149
    in planning, 10
    during printing process, 63–64, 65
charts, 135
checklists, 5, 8
checks, 154
    for meal function, 100
cheese, food allowances for, 340
cheshire labels, 66
child care, 321
    release form for, 326–327
children's programs, 87–88
classroom setup, 32, 237
    diagram for, 244
clerical personnel, 5
client expenses, 183–184
client expense summary form, 430
clients, 179
closed-circuit television, 118
clothing, 96, 323
CO (catering order) number, 101
cocktails
    food allowances for, 340
    time requirement for, 339
cocktail table, capacity of, 237
coffee, cost of, 109–110
coil binding, 296
color coding, 162
colors
    and budget, 67
    and printing costs, 63
    selecting, 66

commercial invoice, 448
commercial printers, 67
commissions, 28, 185, 421, 424
committees, 144, 373–375
communications, 7, 144, 310–311
    internal hotel system for, 160
    with suppliers, 376–377
companions' program, 93
competitive bids, 124
    see also bids
complimentary rooms, 39–40, 157, 235, 247
    in contract, 267
compound interest, 131, 362
comps, 71
compulsory meetings, 53
computers
    for badge printing, 75
    for data collection, 47–48
    planning software programs, 8
    and registration forms, 72
    scheduling on, 6, 7
    and ticket distribution, 76
    video graphics with, 347
concurrent session, 212
conference evaluation form, 278–279
conference setup, 32, 237
    diagram for, 242–243
confidentiality-of-information agreement, 183
confirmation
    of hotel registration, 39
    of registration, 73, 75
    to speakers, 228
conglomerate meetings, 53–54
construction, and contracts, 41
consulor invoice, 449
consultants, 10
    audiovisual, 112
contingencies, in contracts, 41–42
continuing-education transcripts, 47
contract employees, workers' compensation and, 139
contracts, 36–44, 260–273
    addendums to, 43
    breach of, 368–369
    cancellation in, 37, 42
    contingencies in, 41–42
    dates in, 39
    deadlines for signing, 33
    with decorator, 397–398
    deposits and, 126
    elements of, 38–39
    for exhibitors, 166, 395–396
    food and beverages in, 41

contracts (*continued*)
  function space in, 40
  guest/sleeping rooms in, 39–40
  hotel, 262–263, 265–273
  and information release, 28
  for international meetings, 441
  with meeting management firms, 175–176
  for meeting planner, 431–434
  negotiation of, 36–38, *see also* negotiation of contracts
  renovation and construction and, 41
  restrictions in, 42
  safety, security, and accessibility in, 40–41
  and site selection, 26
  with speakers, 221
convention bureaus, 30, 60, 83, 92, 261, 449
convention center, 40
Convention Liaison Council, 8, 185
convention rate, 235
convention services, 174
cool colors, 66
copying, *see* photocopying
copy preparation, 65, 293
corkage, 104–105
corporate attendees, services for, 313
corporate meetings, vs. association meetings, xv
corporate rate, 235
correspondence, 193
cost-of-living increases, for guest rooms, 39
costs
  of coffee, 109–110
  of decorator, 394–395
  defining, 353
  fixed vs. variable, 124, 358
  of food and beverages, 108, 341
  of graphic design, 63
  hotel contract and, 263
  of in-house meeting management, 173
  management of, 181
  per paid registrant, 72
  printing and, 300
  speakers and, 216
cover stock, 65
credit cards, 23, 57, 445
  for registration, 72
credit references, *see* reference checks
currency, need for, at international meetings, 445–446
currency exchange, 443–444
customs brokers, 449

cutoff date, 34–35, 236, 248
  for preregistration, 70, 79
daily checks, 154
daily rate, 423
dance floor, determining size of, 238
dances, 96
data
  analysis of, 46
  historical report of, 46–47, 274
  presentation of, 135
data collection, 45–51, 274–284
  benefit of, 45
  computerized, 47–48
  form for, 47, 276–277, 281–284
  observation and interviewing in, 48–49
  time for, 50–51
dates, in contract, 39
day rate, 235
deadlines, 5, 6, 144, 186–187
  for bids, 29
  for budget additions, 123
  for contract signing, 33
  problems with, 9
  for program book ads, 56
debate, 212
decimal numbers, translating fractions to, 364
decisionmakers, 3–4, 186
decorations, 107
decorators
  contract with, 397–398
  costs of, 394–395
  exhibitor's kit from, 393–394
  for exhibits, 169–170
delegation, 9
demonstrations, 212
deposits, 6, 126
destination management, 173
destination management companies, 405, 450
die-cutting, 66, 298
diet, 320
dinner, 106
  food allowances for, 340
  time requirement for, 339
direct mail, 285
directories, 460
disabled attendees, 33–34
  see also handicapped, the
disclaimers, for sporting events, 93
discrepancy, report on, 281
distribution services, 64
DMCs, *see* destination management companies

documentation, 10
donations, in-kind, 122
door monitors, 155, 156
dramatizations, and retention, 14
dress, 96, 323
drivers, 83

editing symbols, 65
education, 54, 210
electric pointers, 347
electronic writing boards, 118, 347
elevators, handicapped and, 239–240
embossing, 66, 298
emergencies, 107, 321
emergency calls, for attendees, 89
employees, *see* staff
enrichment program, 93
entertainment, 96, 332
    and exhibits, 168
entertainment committee, 374
envelopes, 65
EO, *see* event order
EP, *see* European plan
equipment, *see* audiovisual equipment
errors and omissions insurance, 366
escrow accounts, 126, 186
ethics, 185
European plan (EP), 340
evaluation, 155
    of conference, 278–279
    of exhibits, 398–399
    of program, 280
evaluation forms, 48, 50
event orders, 149
    number, 101
exhibit hall, contract for, 396–397
exhibitors, 76–77
    housing request form for, 404
    marketing to, 389–390
    registration form for, 402–403
exhibitor's kit, 393–394
exhibits, 163–171, 212, 247, 387–404
    administration of, 166–167
    booth assignment at, 168–169
    booth sizes for, 169, 389
    budgets for, 164–165, 387–388
    in contract, 270, 395–396
    decorator for, 169–170
    evaluation of, 398–399
    example schedule for, 400–401
    guide book to, 15
    increasing attendance at, 170–171
    marketing for, 165–166
    prospectus for, 390–392
    registration form for, 167

report on, 284
    rules and regulations for, 392–393
    sales at, 169
    site selection for, 163–164, 388–389
    sponsorships for, 170
    thefts at, 168
exhibits committee, 374
expenditures, 126–127, 254–257
    documenting, 47
    as percentages, 49
    report on, 281
expense reimbursement, for program
        participants, 23–24
experts, 8
export license, 449
exposition management companies, 173,
        405

facilitator, 215
facility contract, 262–263
facility personnel, form for, 383
familiarization exercise, 81
FAP, *see* full American plan
fax expenses, 183
fees
    for busing, 316
    of meeting management firms, 184–185
    and preregistration, 78
    for program participants, 23
    for registration, 71–72
    structures for, 421–425
    variables in, 420–421
film laminating, 298
final accounting, 125
    example of, 358
finance and budget committee, 373
financial agreement, with program
        participants, 23
financial management, 353–360
    see also budgets
financial reports, 281
    from computers, 48
finishing, of printed materials, 297–298
fire safety, 171, 240–242
first aid, 325
first-class mail, 60
fixed costs, 124, 358
fixed fee, 184, 421, 422
flat fees, 235, 421, 422
flip chart, 347
floor plans, 162
foil-stamping, 66
folds, of printed material, 67
food and beverages, 98–110, 336–343
    at breaks, 96

food and beverages (*continued*)
    buffet vs. seated meal, 110
    in contract, 41, 268–269
    cost of, 108, 341
    event types involving, 98–99
    formulas for, 339–341
    math for, 129–130
    new ideas for, 108–109
    record keeping for, 101–102
    seating for, 110
    and site selection, 32
    types of, 99
food-and-beverages meeting report, 101–
    102, 343
foreign airports, 443
foreign languages, 322, 444–445
foreign meetings, 435–450
    see also international meetings
formats, 15–16, 210
    selecting, 12, 212
forms, 5, 193
    attendance summary, 385
    audiovisual supplier request, 115, 351–
        352
    bar-tending, 103–104, 343
    child care release, 326–327
    client expense summary, 430
    data collection, 47, 281–284
    evaluation, 48, 50, 278–279
    exhibitor housing request, 404
    function attendance, 384
    hotel room registration, 288–289
    medical release and permission, 88
    negotiation, 264
    personnel, 383
    photocopying, 429
    postage usage, 428
    program evaluation, 280
    registration, 57, 72, 74–75, 288
    release and permission, 88
    room count, 155
    speakers, 22, 217–221
    timesheet, 427
fractions, 133
    translating to decimal, 364
freight forwarders, 449
French service, 339
front desk, 153
full American plan (FAP), 236, 340
full-time employees, *see* staff
function attendance
    form, 384
    report on, 282
    summary, 155
function data collection form, 276–277

function space, in contract, 40
furniture
    for registration, 77
    sizes and capacities of, 237

gala dinners, 90
gang printing, 67
general manager, of hotel, 29
government contracts, 121
government rate, 235
graphic design, 59, 62–69, 293–300
graphs, 135
gratuities, 133, 158–160
    for bartending, 104
    calculating, 362–363
    food and beverages and, 99, 106–107
    guidelines for, 382
    math for, 130
    and site selection, 30
gross billing, percentage of, as fee, 423
ground transportation, 83
group history, 46
group rate, 31, 39, 235
    from airlines, 84
guarantee policy, for holding rooms, 34
guarantees (meals), 100, 101, 130, 135,
    156–157
guest/sleeping rooms, 28, 82–83, 233
    comparative data summary of, 254
    in contract, 39–40
    evaluating, 31
    for exhibitors, 167
    fire safety in, 242
    guarantee of, 34
    for handicapped, 81, 240
    rate categories for, 235–236
    sharing, 35
guidelines, for program participants, 21

handicapped, the, 33–34, 323
    accessibility for, 239
    requirements of, 81, 239–240
    services for, 87
handouts, 15
hard profit, 181
Harold Russell Associates, *Planner's
    Guide to Barrier Free Meetings*, 33
health problems, 320
historical data report, 274
history
    analysis of, and registration, 71
    and budgeting, 120
    of group, 28, 46
hold harmless clause, 137
Holiday Inn, 117

holidays, and site selection, 30
honorariums, for participants, 23
hors d'oeuvres, 105–106
    allowances for, 340
hospitality center, 88, 105, 317
hospitality committee, 375
host bars
    math for, 130
    vs. cash bars, 103
host committees, 85
hotel
    general manager of, 29
    historical information from, 46
    in-house audiovisual services of, 112
    multiple bookings in, 33
    ownership of, 27
    profit of, 26, 27
    report on, 283
hotel bill, 100, 124–125
hotel contract, 262–263
    example of, 265–273
hotel market, 27
hotel pickup, 46, 131, 361–362
hotel pickup post-convention report,
    157–158, 386
hotel registration form, 57, 288–289
hotel reports, from computers, 48
hourly rate, 421, 423
hours for projects, management of, 181
housing, 82–83
    see also guest/sleeping rooms
housing bureau, 83

immigration and customs, 443
implementers, 4
incentive attendees, services for, 313
incentive houses, 173, 405
incentive meetings, 53
incentives
    in fees, 421
    for preregistration, 79
indemnification clauses, 137
industry experts, references on, 21
industry formulas, 129
informal time, and learning, 14
information booth, 317
information centers, 85
information sheets, for program
    participants, 24
in-kind donations, 122
inspection, for site selection, 29
insurance, 136–141, 366–367
    for art and jewelry, 140
    certificates of, 139
    in contract, 271

for international meetings, 442
for rental cars, 141
and sporting events, 93
types of, 137–138
see also liability
intellectual learning, 13
interconnect services, 349
interest calculation, 362
interest rates, 131
International Association of Congress
    Interpreters, 446
international holidays, and site selection,
    30
international meetings, 435–450
    attendee services at, 442–446
    contracts for, 441
    insurance for, 442
    local practices and, 438–439
    negotiation for, 441
    printing for, 446–447
    promotion of, 447
    site selection for, 439–441
interpreters, 446–448
interruption insurance, 138
interviews, 15
    for data collection, 48–49
invoices, 184
    commercial, 448
    consulor, 449
    see also billing

jewelry, insurance for, 140

keynote speaker, 215
kitchen, fire safety in, 241

labels, 66
labor, for exhibits, 170
labor unions, 31
labs, 212
lasers, 117–118, 347
late payments, 186
learning
    programming for, 211–212
    style of, 13–14
    visual presentations and, 111
lectern, 347
lectures, 15, 212
legal agreements, see contracts
lettering, size of, 86
letters of confirmation, to speakers, 228
liability
    in contract, 271
    liquor and, 93, 95, 138–139
    personal, 39

liability (*continued*)
  of professional planner, 138, 367–368, 425–426
  for sport injuries, 140–141
  see also insurance
liability insurance, 366
  and special events, 93
licenses, 139
  export, 449
limited power of attorney, 449
linens, 107
liquid measurements and yields, 340
liquor, *see* alcohol
location, *see* site selection
loose-leaf binding, 296
lost-and-found, 85, 322
lunch, 106
  food allowances for, 340
  learning during, 14
  time requirement for, 339

magazines, 459–460
mail, 60
mailing lists, 58, 59
mailings, 290
  report on, 284
  timetable for, 289
mailing services, 66
management
  on-site, 148–162
  of people, 142–147
  see also people management
MAP, *see* modified American plan
maps, 162
marketing, 52–61, 285–292
  see also promotions
marketing plan, 180, 416
marketing/public relations committee, 374
marketing strategy, 54–55
marrying the bottles, 104
master account, 100, 124–125, 270
master schedule, 9
materials, 15
math, 128–135, 361–365
mean, 134
median, 134
meeting cancellation insurance, 138, 267
meeting management, in-house vs. outside, 172–173, 406
meeting management firms, 172–178, 405
  administrative systems of, 181
  benefits of, 407
  business plan for, 180, 415–416
  choosing, 174

client expenses in, 183–184
  contract with, 175–176
  establishing, 179–187, 413–434
  fees of, 184–185
  in-house vs. outside, 176
  locating, 173–174
  marketing plan for, 180, 416
  negotiation with, 175, 412
  personnel changes in, 177
  procedures manuals of, 182–183
  selecting, 408–411
  selling project to, 174–175
  selling services of, 180–181
  services of, 406–407
  staff of, 181
  standards for, 185
  start-up costs of, 414–415
  types of, 173, 405–406
  see also planners
Meeting Planners International (MPI), xii, 117
  New England Chapter, 33
meeting purveyors, 151, 379
meeting rooms, 233, 247
  arrangement of, and participation levels, 17
  comfort of, 17
  in contracts, 40
  evaluating, 31–32
  fire safety in, 241
  measurements of, 131–132
  rental charges for, 131, 157
  setups for, 237
  square-footage allowances for, 237
meetings
  analysis of, 3
  association vs. corporate, xv
  detailed requirements of, 151
  international and foreign, 435–450
  pre-/post-convention, 152–155
  purpose of, 12
  taping of, 86, 114
  time allowances for, 213
  types of, 53–54
  see also special events
meeting schedule, 249–250
  in contract, 272–273
Megatrends (Naisbitt), xvi
memory, 14
message board, 89
message booth, 317
message centers, 85
metric conversions, 134, 364
microphones, 25, 31, 113–114, 346
miles per hour, average, by bus, 314

mirrored walls, and audiovisuals, 112
miscellaneous expenses, 127
mode, 134
moderators, 215
  selecting, 17
  worksheet for, 222–223
modified American plan (MAP), 236, 340
monitors, for video presentation, 114
motivation, 143, 148
movable walls, 17
MPI, *see* Meeting Planners International
multiassociation management firms, 173,
  405
multimedia presentations, 115
  see also audiovisual presentations
multiple mailings, of promotional
  material, 58

Naisbitt, John, *Megatrends*, xvi
National Association of Exposition
  Managers, xii, 107
negotiation of contracts, 36–38
  form for, 264
  guidelines for, 260–261
  for international meetings, 441
  with meeting management firms, 175,
    412
  and site selection, 29–30
networking, 76
New England Chapter of MPI, 33
newspapers, meeting listings in, 60
news releases, timetable for, 290
noise, and meeting room evaluation, 32
nonprofit organizations, public service
  announcements for, 60
no-shows, 157
numbers, reading, 134
nuts, food allowances for, 340

observation, in data collection, 48–49
office, for staff, 247
officers, special services for, 87
offset printing, vs. photocopying, 68
on-site management, 148–162, 378–386
on-site registration, 77–78
open space/aisles, layout allowances for,
  239
organization, in prospectus, 28
orientation sessions, 86
outside suppliers, management of, 145
overhead projection, 111, 119
overseas shipments, 448–449
overset policy, 100, 110, 156, 341
oversold rooms, 34, 39
ownership, of hotel, 27

package plans, room/food, 340
packaging, of promotional material, 57
page, 294
panel, 212
panel information worksheet, 223–225
panelist, 215
paper, 65
  cost of, 60
  for printing, 297
  standard sizes of, 65
participants, *see* program participants;
  speakers
participation levels, by attendees, 17–18
parties, private suite, 105
passports, 442
payment
  late, 186
  options for, 420
penalties, for cancellation, 42–43
penetration, in marketing strategy, 54
people management, 142–147, 371–377
  chain of command in, 371
  committees in, 144
  communication in, 144
  of outside suppliers, 145
  styles for, 143
  of volunteers, 145, 372–373
people movement, time allowances for,
  213
percentages, 49, 133, 135
  calculating, 363
perfect binding, 296
perimeter, 132, 365
permits, 139
per-person fee, 421, 423
personal liability, 39
personal values, and learning, 13
personnel, *see* staff
phase billing, 424–425
phone calls, billing for, 192
photocopying
  expenses for, 183
  form for, 429
  vs. offset printing, 68
photographer
  selecting, 333–334
  working with, 334–335
photography, 94–95
physical skills, learning, 13
pick-up, 46, 131, 361–362
  post-convention report on, 157–158,
    386
pie graph, 135
planners
  budget and, 176–177
  certification for, 185

planners (*continued*)
  contract for, 431–434
  control by, 177–178
  duties of, 4
  ethics of, 185
  locating, 407
  on-site role of, 152
  professional liability of, 138
  support services for, 175
  training for, xii
  see also meeting management firms
*Planner's Guide to Barrier Free
    Meetings* (Harold Russell
    Associates), 33
planning, 3–10, 191–208
  budget and, 120–121
  checklists for, 8
planning schedule, 6–7
  example of, 195–205
planning team, 3–5
plastic coating, 298
plenary session, 212
PMS number, 66
PMTs, 69
policies and procedures, 193–194
  establishing, 5–6
  exceptions to, 89
  manual of 182–183
  for registration, 70, 301–302
postage
  prepaid, 65
  expenses, 183
  requirements, 57
  usage, form for, 428
postal regulations, 65–66, 297
Postal Service, 60
post-convention meeting, 152–155
poster sessions, 212
power of attorney, limited, 449
pre-convention meeting, 152–155
prepaid postage, 65
preplanning questionnaire, 205–208
preregistration, 70, 78–79
press check, 64
press coverage, 60
press kits, 87
press releases, 60
pressure-sensitive labels, 66
price-fixing regulations, 124
prices, for food and beverages, 32
printed material, types of, 62
printer
  selecting, 63, 295
  types of, 67
printing, 62–69, 294–295
  agreement for, 298–299

budget for, 67–68
checking final product of, 64
copy preparation for, 65
cost-saving ideas for, 300
finishing, 67, 297–298
for international meetings, 446–447
paper for, 297
process for, 63–64
report on, 284
sequence schedule for, 295
special effects in, 66
private suite parties, 105
procedures, *see* policies and procedures
proceedings, 15
Professional Congress Organizers, 449
professional liability, 425–426
professional organizations, xii
professional taping service, 86
profits, 425
  of hotel, 26, 27
  from taping, 86
program, 207
  evaluation form for, 280
  at meals, service and, 108
  purpose of, 209
  report on, 283
  steps in planning, 209–211
  time allowances for, 213
program book, 15, 76, 401–402
  ads in, 55–56, 290–291
  "schedule-at-a-glance" in, 162
program committee, 374
program design, 11–18, 209–213
  atmosphere and, 13–14
  audience and, 12
  budget, 12
  formats in, 15–16
  handouts, 15
  meeting purpose and, 12
  time allotment, 12, 16
  topic, format, and speaker selection, 12
program moderator, *see* moderators
program participants, 19–25
  check-in for, 25
  content guidelines for, 21
  fees and honorariums for, 23
  locating, 20
  reference checks on, 21–22
  roles of, 20
  selection of, 12
  travel arrangements for, 24
  types of, 215
  voice quality of, 25
  worksheets for, 24
project-accounting system, 181

projectors, 345
projects, juggling simultaneous, 9
promotions, 52–61, 285–292
    to exhibitors, 165–166, 389–390
    of international meetings, 447
    multiple mailings of, 58
    packaging of, 57
    timetable for, 289–290
    types of, 55, 285
proofreading, 58, 68
proofs, black-and-white, *see* PMTs
property, 367
prospectus, 27–29, 233
    contents of, 234–235
    example of, 245–253
    for exhibits, 165, 390–392
psychological learning, 13
publications, promotion in, 285
publications centers, 85, 317
public meetings, 54
public relations firms, 173, 406
public service announcements, 60
purchase order, for registration, 73
purveyors, 151, 379

question-and-answer period, 16
questionnaire
    for attendees, 81
    preplanning, 205–208
quick-print companies, 67

rack rate, 31, 235
range rate, 235
"ready" room, 113
rear-screen projection, 119
receptions, 90, 341
    and learning, 14
    time requirement for, 339
reception setup, 237
record keeping, 192–193
    for food and beverages, 101–102
    systems for, 5
reference checks
    and deposit requirements, 126
    for hotels, 43
    on meeting management firms, 174,
        178
    on program participants, 21–22
    in site selection, 29
registration, 70–79, 301–309, 381
    categories for, 74, 301
    computer software for, 78
    confirmation of, 75
    daily check-out sheet, 307
    fees and policies for, 71–72

materials for, 76–77
on-site, 77–78
on-site supplies for, 305–306
policies and procedures for, 301–302
processing returns for, 73
reducing lines at, 78
site selection for, 302–303
timing for, 72
training for, 304
registration committee, 374
registration data collection form, 277
registration forms, 57, 72, 74–75, 288
    example of, 309
    for exhibitors, 167, 402–403
    hotel room, 288–289
registration workers, 74, 77, 303–304
    personal belongings of, 141
    time sheet for, 308
release and permission form, 88
releases, 140
    from speakers, for taping, 114
religious holidays, and site selection, 30
renovation, and contracts, 41
rental, of meeting rooms, 40
rental cars, insurance for, 141
repeat participation, at exhibits, 169
replacement badges, 76
reply cards, 297
reports, 49
request for proposal (RFP), 124, 174, 233
research, 21
    in budget preparation, 121
reservations, 154, 236
    in contract, 266
    guaranteeing, 34, 39
    for guest/sleeping rooms, 82–83
resources, 459–461
responsibility, 9
    waiver of, 35
restrictions, in contracts, 42
restrooms, for handicapped, 240
résumés, 22
retainers, 421, 424
retention levels, 14
    average, 211
revenues, 122, 126–127
    report on, 281
reverses, 66
reward, meeting as, 53
RFP, *see* request for proposal
risks
    assessing, 136–137
    reducing, 137, 369–370
    transfer of, 139
room block, 46, 236

room count form, 155
room/food package plans, 340
room measurements, 365
room rates, in contract, 266
rooms, *see* guest/sleeping rooms; meeting rooms
room setups, 154
round tables, 212
    capacity of, 237
rules and regulations, for exhibits, 392–393
run-of-the-house, 31, 236
rush jobs, for printers, 69
Russian/butler service, 339

saddle-wire binding, 296
safety, 140
    in contract, 40–41, 271
sales, at exhibits, 169
sales brochures, 15
sans serif type, 64
scavenger hunt, 89
"schedule-at-a-glance", in program, 162
schedules, 5, 249–250
    in contract, 272–273
    exhibits, 400–401
    maintaining, 16
    master, 9
    planning, 6–7, 195–205
    printing, 295
schoolroom setup, 32, 237
    diagram for, 244
scoring (creasing), 65
screens, 66, 113, 346
    height of, 132
    multiple, 119
    size and space requirements for, 349
seating, for dinners, 110
security, 74, 140, 154, 168
    in contract, 40–41
self-mailers, 65, 75
seminars, public, 54
serif type, 64
service levels, 43, 106
    in contract, 41, 269
setups, 161, 380
    in contract, 267
    diagrams for, 242–244
sewn binding, 296
shipping, 154, 158, 161–162
    overseas, 448–449
shuttle buses, time allowances for, 315
signs, 86, 162
    for registration, 77
simple interest, 362

site committee, 374
site selection, 26–35, 206, 230–259
    audiovisuals and, 112
    checklist for, 254–259
    convention bureaus and, 30
    decisions in, 231
    for exhibits, 163–164, 388–389
    food and beverages and, 32
    holidays and, 30
    inspections for, 29
    for international meetings, 439–441
    and liability, 367
    negotiation and, 29–30
    reference checks in, 29
    for registration, 302–303
    for special events, 92–93
slides, 115
    high-tech, 118
    screen for, 119
sliding fees, 423–424
smoking, 17
snacks, food allowances for, 340
soft profit, 181
software
    for data collection, 47
    for registration, 78
sound
    bleeds of, 17
    correcting problems of, 350
space requirements, in prospectus, 28
speaker information memo, 229
speaker requirement form, 22, 217–221
speakers, 19–25, 76
    audiovisual equipment for, 119
    back-up, 25
    confirmation letters to, 228
    financial agreement with, 221
    guidelines for, when taping, 114
    introductions of, 22–23
    locating, 214
    registration of, 73
    selection of, 12
    special services for, 87
    time allotment for, 14, 16
    types of, 215
    working with, 216
    see also program participants
speakers' bureau, 21
speakers' room, 113
special events, 90–97, 328–335
    photography for, 94–95
    selecting, 329–330
    site selection for, 92–93, 330–331
    theme development for, 91–92
    weather and, 95

special events committee, 375
specifications (spec) book, 100, 112, 149–
    152, 378–379
speeches, at special events, 97
spiral binding, 296
sponsor, 205
sponsorships, for exhibits, 170
sporting events, 90, 93–94, 321, 332–333
    and injury liability, 140–141
spotlights, 347
spotting, 83
spouse programs, 93, 321
spouses, as volunteers, 145
square-footage allowances,
    for meeting rooms, 237, 238
staff, 419
    billable hours of, 182
    form for, 383
    levels of, 154
    for meals, 106, 108, 339
    of meeting management firms, 181
    procedures manuals for, 182–183
    for registration, 74, 77, 303–304
    registration of, 73
    report on, 283
    support, 5
staff office, 247
staff turnover, in hotel, 27
staging, 83
staging guide (spec book), 100, 112, 149–
    152, 378–379
standards, for meeting management
    firms, 185
strikes, 31
suits, 36
suppliers, 375–377
    report on, 283
supplies
    for registration, 305–306
    shipping, 158
support personnel, 5

tables, capacity of, 237
talk show, 212
tape recorders, 346
taping, of session, 86, 114
target market, 416–417
tasks, in planning schedule, 6–7
taxes
    for food and beverages, 99, 106–107
    math for, 130
    and site selection, 30
team, for planning, 3–5
technical papers, 15
technical staff, 4

teleconferences, 116–117, 348–349
telephone
    as client expense, 183–184
    conference calls on, 116
telephone solicitations, timetable for, 290
television, 345
    closed-circuit, 118
television monitors, 162
temperature, of meeting rooms, 17
temporary workers, workers'
    compensation and, 139
text stock, 65
thank-you letters, 124
theater setup, 32, 237
    diagram for, 244
theft, 322
    at exhibits, 168
themes, 107, 210
    for exhibits, 167–168
    for parties, 90, 331–332
thoughtfulness, 24
ticket-exchanges, 76, 102–103
tickets, 76
tickler filing system, 9
time allowances, 12, 16, 213
time requirements
    for food, 339
    for meeting planning, 177
timesheets, 182
    form for, 427
timing
    and food choices, 99
    in marketing strategy, 55
tipping, 158–160
    see also gratuities
topic, selection of, 12
"to-scale" floor plans, 132
tourism, spending for, xi
tourist offices, 449
tournament, 93
tours, 90, 212, 321
trainer, 215
training, for registration, 304
translations, 446–448
transparencies, electronic, 347
transportation, 313–316, 321
    for attendees, 83–84
    comparative data summary for, 258
    and liability, 367
travel agencies, 173, 405
travel arrangements, for program
    participants, 24
trends, 129
triangle, square footage of, 132
type styles, 64

unions, 31
universities, 117
use rate, 235
U.S. measures, conversion to metric, 134, 364

values, personal, and learning, 13
variable costs, 124, 358
varnishing, 297–298
vegetarians, 109
veloxes, 69
video, 114
videoconferences, 116
video games, 88
video monitors, 345, 350
video projection, 346
video recorders, 346
VideoStar, 116
videotapes, of meetings, 86
VIPs
    registration of, 73
    reserved seating for, 102
visas, 442
visual presentations, and learning, 111
voice quality, of program participants, 25

volunteers, 85, 145, 161
    assigning, 146
    managing, 372–373
    reliability of, 146

waiters, 339
    average number of, 106
    and mealtime program, 108
waiver of responsibility, 35, 140
walkie-talkies, 160
walk-ins, 157
wall, movable, 17
warm colors, 66
weather, 100
    and special events, 95
windows, and audiovisuals, 112
wire transfer, 445
wives' program, 93, 321
workers' compensation, 139, 366
worksheets, for program participants, 24
workshop information worksheet, 225–227
workshop leader, 215
workshops, 212
writing boards, electronic, 118, 347

ZIP code, sorting mailing by, 66